Fighting the Forces

Fighting the Forces

What's at Stake in
Buffy the Vampire Slayer

Edited by
Rhonda V. Wilcox
and
David Lavery

ROWMAN & LITTLEFIELD PUBLISHERS, INC.
Lanham • Boulder • New York • Oxford

ROWMAN & LITTLEFIELD PUBLISHERS, INC.

Published in the United States of America
by Rowman & Littlefield Publishers, Inc.
4720 Boston Way, Lanham, Maryland 20706
www.rowmanlittlefield.com

12 Hid's Copse Road, Cumnor Hill, Oxford OX2 9JJ, England

British Library Cataloguing in Publication Information Available

Library of Congress Cataloging-in-Publication Data

Fighting the forces : what's at stake in Buffy the Vampire Slayer / edited by Rhonda V.
Wilcox and David Lavery.
     p. cm.
   Includes bibliographical references and index.
   ISBN 0-7425-1680-6 (alk. paper)—ISBN 0-7425-1681-4 (pbk. : alk. paper)
     1. Buffy, the vampire slayer (Television program) 2. Buffy the Vampire Slayer
(Fictitious character) I. Wilcox, Rhonda. II. Lavery, David, 1949–

PN1992.77.B84 F54 2001
791.45'72—dc21   2001041930

Printed in the United States of America

♾ ™ The paper used in this publication meets the minimum requirements of
American National Standard for Information Sciences—Permanence of Paper
for Printed Library Materials, ANSI/NISO Z39.48-1992.

Spike [intrigued]: Heard of me, have you? [He walks a little closer. The two male Watchers shift nervously and hold their weapons.]
Female Watcher [embarrassed smile]: I . . . wrote my thesis on you.

—"Checkpoint" (5012)

Contents

                            Contents

Foreword

The Color of the Dark in Buffy the Vampire Slayer

Camille Bacon-Smith

We cannot really begin talking about television images without first laying certain old-think presuppositions to rest. Outside of the rare "landmark" broadcast, cultural interpreters of television narratives have often imputed to the creators of television drama a raw avarice that results in technically slick production values supporting only the most basic content for the television screen. Art is seen to occur by accident, if at all, in the otherwise calculated search for mesmerizing images to hypnotize the audience between sales pitches. Meaning, in this formulation, is the outcome of cultural biases filling out a skeletal narrative structure that conforms to the generic expectations of a pleasure-seeking audience. The "false consciousness" shared by the viewer and the creator obscure the cultural biases and unconscious drives fueling the "true" message uncovered by the scholar in a display of superior sensibility.

Most critics locate the source of the essentialist message of film in the script. This is patently untrue in cinema, of course, as becomes evident when one contrasts the two defining statements of film production: Designers claim that their design is in support of the narrative of the script, and yet the scriptwriter is recognizably the least important member of a film (Tashiro). Even popular cinema belongs to the auteur director, such as Steven Spielberg, Tim Burton, or John Woo. Many popular action films targeted to an international audience provide minimal dialogue or plot and aspire only to top their last effort in pyrotechnic visual display. Only in the limited number of producer-director-writer talents, like M. Night Shyamalan, does one find the script taking even second place in film.

Ignoring the contradiction, however, scholars continue to ascribe intentional meaning to the visual image only as it serves the development of character within the plot. Critical analysis, including as a recent example C. S. Tashiro's *Pretty Pictures* (1998), decries the image's primacy of service to the narrative but continues to ascribe nonnarrative pleasure of the image to the unintentional. Tashiro, for instance, goes to great lengths to demonstrate how the nonnarrative image, occurring in the narrative film, serves to obstruct or damage the narrative intention.

Ironically, of course, what is not true for film—primacy of some writer, if not writing—is more true for television, where "producer" is the title for a senior writer and/or the creator and head writer of the television movie or series. The entire television production serves the intentions of the person in control of the television script, often in conflict with the network executive who may prefer a more homogenized product. That does not mean, however, that the script encompasses the meaning of the finished production. Rather, the writer of depth and authority can depend on a meshing of the visual and verbal to create both a narrative message and a metaphoric one, as well as metanarrative commentary.

Few scholars until now would credit television writers with the vision to understand the complexity of their own products. By imputing to television drama only a naively defined narrative intentionality focused on the lowest-common-denominator viewer, scholars have served their own agenda. If a scholar denies that a television producer has created meaning beyond the most simplistic level of mimesis, then he can also dismiss the objections of the creator who disagrees with the analysis. The claim of "false consciousness," as mentioned previously, strips the creator of his authority to speak on behalf of his own creation.

This interpretation is so pervasive in film and television criticism that some young writers, trained in the film schools where the criticism is taught, skitter schizophrenically between their own love of their medium and the cynical reminder that entertainment television is a "sausage factory," producing lowest-common-denominator material digestible by the largest number of potential viewers (Sloan; Kindler).

The model is most damaging, of course, because it is partly true. No one scorns their own audience more than some network executives. A newcomer to the industry who has been indoctrinated into the belief that her art is a matter of creating empty intellectual calories for the insatiable maw of a mindless consumer-audience may produce ground-network-product until she either becomes an executive or breaks out of the box the critics and accountants have put her in. She may spite the critics and struggle against an industry culture of cynicism and mediocrity to spin television gold from narrative straw.

In studying the scholarship at UCLA, New York University, or wherever they trained in their craft, however, the producers, directors, actors, designers, and cinematographers in the creative arts, including television, have learned how to apply theory to their work. While some television creators may justify their own lack of talent by adopting the cynicism of the critics, their more gifted (and usually more successful) competitors are perfectly able to construct polyvalent, laminated meanings *on purpose.* Nowhere is this more obvious than in the television gold Joss Whedon has spun out of vampire straw: *Buffy the Vampire Slayer.*

In choosing the extended form of narrative—arc television drama— Whedon has improved on his movie creation, *Buffy the Vampire Slayer,* as the vehicle for his message about the emotional and psychological morass of high school. In Sarah Michelle Gellar's Buffy, he created the positive heroic role model for girls lacking in network television. From light and dark to sound and silence to every aspect of the image, Whedon has layered and crossed meanings, deliberately constructing in design, *by design,* more questions than his narrative answers.

Buffy the Vampire Slayer therefore symbolically presents the struggle of good and evil, desire and duty, in the playing out of battles between the champion of light and the murky shadow self of the dark. When Buffy and her companions play out the struggle between the light and dark of human nature, the viewer grows to understand that neither side can ever completely win or lose, because each is a part of the whole they make between them.

NOTE

This foreword is the introduction to the article "The Color of the Dark," by Camille Bacon-Smith. The article, an examination of the use of color theory in the design of *Buffy,* can be found in its entirety at <http://www.voicenet.com/~camille>.

Acknowledgments

First of all, we both wish to thank all the wonderful contributors to this volume (and indeed all those who wanted to contribute)—without them we would have no book. In particular, we wish to thank Elyce Rae Helford, both for introducing us to the folks at Rowman & Littlefield and for agreeing to comment on parts of the manuscript, and Mary Alice Money, for help during e-mail difficulties (among many other reasons). Thanks also to Christine Gatliffe of Rowman & Littlefield for her encouragement of the project. We are indebted to Richard Gess for the cover photography (and to Rachel Pomberg for lending a hand). And, above all, we thank the creators of our primary source.

From David Lavery: Thanks to Rhonda Wilcox for her most excellent collaboration during a very difficult time in her professional life. Thanks to my family, who have endured my newfound obsession. And special thanks to my students Chris Peltier, Erin Gonzalez, Becky Short, and Brian Loggins—without their powers of persuasion (and videotapes), I would never have come over to *Buffy*.

From Rhonda Wilcox: Thanks first to David Lavery, for his energy, acuity, expertise, and generosity of mind. That my first time editing such a collection should be with David is a gift. Thanks to all my family and friends for their support and, even more important, their understanding of the significance of this work. Special thanks to my husband, Richard Gess ("That was 'Tales of Brave Ulysses'—it's Cream"), and my son, Jefferson Gess ("Look, Spike can bite her because she's already dead"): their enthusiastic attention and, ultimately, their patience were important contributions. I want to express appreciation, too, to Cindy Bowers, whose work as a list mistress years ago sparked early commentary about *Buffy* (on a list devoted to another series) by J. P. Williams, Catherine Siemann, and me, as well as Grace Lee, Cynthia Hoffman, and others I will wish I had named. Some who will read this book know that I have been in a very stressful situation over the course of the project: I am one of over a dozen people who have been involved in a particular fight for freedom of speech and against sexual discrimination. It has meant a great deal to be part of a supportive group during this time—as any *Buffy* watcher could tell you. I therefore want to add my thanks to Marlin Adams, Jeanne Beckwith, Don Butts, Brett Cox, Gary Cox, Tricia Daughrity, Bill Day, Deborah Johnston, Mary Alice Money, Rhonda Morgan, and Marvin Thomas and also to AAUP members Luanne Fowler, Jon House, and Hutch Johnson (not to mention the members of the Popular Culture Association in the South). You all have helped me to keep going.

Sooner or later, everyone has to decide whether or not to fight the forces.

Introduction

Rhonda V. Wilcox and David Lavery

In every generation there is a chosen one. She alone will stand against the vampires, the demons, the forces of darkness. She is the Slayer.

—Opening voice-over on *Buffy the Vampire Slayer*

The dead rose. We should've at least had an assembly.

—Xander Harris in "The Harvest" (1002)[1]

I have often said, "There will never be a 'Very Special Episode' of *Buffy*."

—Joss Whedon (qtd. in Rochlin 19)

For every television series, the original vision grows within a press of forces—both social and artistic expectations, conventions of the business and the art. Bad television—predictable, commercial, exploitative—simply yields to the forces. Good television, like the character of the Vampire Slayer Buffy, fights those forces—even while it partakes of them as part of its nature: again, like the Slayer, whose strength incorporates the Shadow.

Joss Whedon, creator of *Buffy the Vampire Slayer*, has often said that the original kernel of an idea for *Buffy* came with the reversal of an image from traditional horror: a fragile-looking young woman walks into a dark place, is attacked—and then turns and destroys her attacker. Thus the character of Buffy was born to fight the forces of darkness—vampires, demons, monsters of all varieties, as the first epigraph declares. But in that same kernel, and in the naming of the character, Whedon implies other forces to be fought: social forces that restrict and constrain us (not the least dangerous of which is humorlessness). The name "Buffy" suggests the lightest of lightweight *girls* of stereotypical limitation—thoughtless, materialistic, superficial. Yet this is the name of the heroine who will, over the years of the series, repeatedly risk (and finally give) her life and—perhaps even more frightening—her social status to do what is right.

The series thus challenges the forces of gender stereotyping. (There is, in fact, a Web site titled "Buffy the Patriarchy Slayer" [<http://daringivens. home.mindspring.com/btps.html>]). As article after article has noted, Buffy kicks butt—and viewers rejoice. At least many do. Many have also pointed out that Buffy often battles evil in skimpy attire (not to mention hair that has grown blonder and blonder)—admittedly good for the ratings, but does it undermine the attempt to present a strong female? Others ask if *Buffy* condones violence, or is it contextualized to emphasize the cost? And does the series's treatment of those who are different, monstrous, or Other, suggest an element of racism or, in some cases, a repudiation of it? What of the choice to introduce a lesbian relationship? The list could go on. Clearly, *Buffy* engages the social forces, and it deserves careful analysis from that perspective.

The second epigraph, from one of the Scooby Gang (Buffy's friends and helpers), indicates one of the rules of engagement. Heroic characters in this series view the world "with healthy irony," in the words of Buffy's best friend, Willow ("The Initiative," 4007). A full examination of the series demands not just structural analysis but also a recognition of the play and power of language. In the third-season opener, with Buffy missing, Willow points out, "The Slayer always says a pun or witty play on words, and I think it throws off the vampires," and Xander responds, "I've always been amazed with how Buffy fought, but in a way I feel like we took her punning for granted" ("Anne," 3001). Buffy is not alone in her facility with words: magazine articles and Web sites quote the witty sayings of *Buffy*'s characters. The grace and wit of the language embody one element of the heroism of the characters (Wilcox, "There"). The fact that the scripts for *Buffy* are now being published in book form in the popular press indicates the importance of language in the series. In fact, linguistic adeptness might be considered a prerequisite for heroic status in this series. It marks, for example, Forrest Gates, the African American buddy of Buffy's second steady boyfriend, Riley Finn: when Riley demands agreement that Buffy is "cool," the exasperated Forrest replies, "She's cool; she's hot; she's tepid; she's all-temperature Buffy" ("Doomed," 4011). (One is thus the more shocked when Forrest, several episodes later, is killed.) These ironic, highly self-conscious, and often culturally allusive comments not only validate the characters but also constantly spin the interpretation of the series, with lines like Buffy's "I need to go find something slutty to wear tonight" ("The Initiative," 4007) or the brave but nonaggressive Xander's "I laugh in the face of danger—then I hide until it goes away" ("The Witch," 1003).

"Buffy, I believe the subtext here is rapidly becoming text," says Buffy's mentor, the Watcher Rupert Giles, in the cemetery one evening ("Ted," 2011). Never underestimate the power of the subtext; certainly, Joss Whedon does not, as the third epigraph indicates. With that comment, Whedon takes aim at those television series that claim redeeming social value by focusing episodes on unmediated social topics such as AIDS or alcoholism. Whedon specifically mentions *Beverly Hills 90210*, but one could add the names of many series—*The Wonder Years, Party of Five, Seventh Heaven*— to those that, over the years, have advertised those "very special" episodes. In the world of *Buffy*, by contrast, the problems that teenagers face become literal monsters. A mother really can take over her daughter's life ("The Witch," 1003); a strict stepfather-to-be is indeed a heartless machine ("Ted," 2011); a young lesbian fears that her nature is demonic ("Goodbye Iowa," 4014; "Family," 5006); a girl who has sex with even the nicest-seeming guy may discover that he afterward becomes a monster ("Innocence," 2014).

And there are even further levels of meaning beyond the endemic use of metaphor in the story lines per se. For instance, the striking differentiation of teen versus adult language in *Buffy* has often been noted. This linguistic separateness emphasizes the lack of communication between the generations, as does the series's use of the symbolism of monsters to represent social problems. Parents' inability to deal with real-world horrors is suggested through Buffy's concerned but naive mother, who throughout two seasons never sees the monsters or knows that her daughter is the Slayer. The symbolism re-creates the need to bridge generational division, which is suggested by the language pattern: itself thus a larger symbol, a macro-symbol. Or one might note the visual elements—the semiotics of such a scene as the fight between Buffy and the rogue Slayer Faith, with the interplay of red and black in the clothing. The avenues to meaning in this series are many.

Of course, *Buffy*'s use of symbolism, while relatively uncommon in television, is hardly new in the world of narrative art. Whedon and company build on the traditions of many well-established patterns: the stories of vampires, the lore of witches, the phyla of fairy tales. In lesser hands the forces of these literary conventions would result in predictable, boring work. But Whedon and company follow Ezra Pound's dictum (and some of his allusive, "sampling" methods) to "make it new," resurrecting dead forms and avoiding the half-life of literary vampirism.

Whedon and company's choice to use symbolism (of various sorts and levels) invites the viewer to join in the construction of meaning for the series. Some viewers do so while watching; others do so, in fan relationships of varying intensity and form; more and more are doing so, as do the scholars in this volume. In some ways, like Buffy herself, the viewer must struggle to reach meaning. With its complexity and careful continuity, the series encourages active viewing. Thus, in a sense, the mediation is the message.

Activated viewers find themselves rooting for *Buffy*'s protagonists as they fight the forces of darkness and rooting too for Joss Whedon and company as they fight the forces of media and culture in order to keep *Buffy* not only true to its original vision but capable of the sort of regenerative imagination necessary to the multiseason life of a television series.

BUFFY THE VAMPIRE SLAYER AS QUALITY TELEVISION

> A quality series enlightens, enriches, challenges, involves, and confronts. It dares to take risks, it is honest and illuminating, it appeals to the intellect and touches the emotions. It requires concentration and attention, and it provokes thought.
>
> —Dorothy Swanson, founder of Viewers for Quality Television
> (qtd. in Robert Thompson 13)

In 2000 *Buffy the Vampire Slayer* won the Viewers for Quality Television "Founders Award," given annually to a series that "has made a significant contribution to quality television without receiving due recognition." Buffy defenders, whether frustrated television critics,[2] high school advocates facing skeptics,[3] or college professors inviting ostracism, know all about the neglect the award was meant to remedy. In "Demons, Aliens, Teens and Television," published in *Television Quarterly*, Richard Campbell (who wrote the essay with his daughter Caitlin) offers the following account, instantly recognizable to most academics who have been won over by the series, of his own *Buffy* conversion:

> I have my 16-year-old daughter, Caitlin, to blame for this. An honor student, soccer player, and avid reader, she introduced me to *Buffy* and the WB a couple of years ago. At the time, I just thought I would do my fatherly/media critic duty: watch a few episodes and point out the error of her TV ways. But something else happened. I got hooked. I liked *Buffy*. The improbable story of a teenage vampire slayer, set against the backdrop of life at Sunnydale High School (Buffy's now moved on to college), kept my interest with its sly humor, action adventure, and wide-ranging portraits of teens and teachers. To me, this was not only a skillfully written show but dead-on in capturing the conversational rhythms of teenagers and exploring issues that permeated their lives—friendship, jealousy, self-esteem, responsibility, rules, sex, good, and evil. Watching *Buffy*, I got insights about the occasional clumsy ways of adults in turning responsibility over to teens so they can make decisions, learn the consequences, and grow up.

The case for *Buffy* as quality television—and concomitantly the rationale for why it is worthy of serious critical investigation—is, we would suggest, a no-brainer. According to Robert J. Thompson, "quality television" exhibits a number of distinctive tendencies/characteristics, touchstones against which we may test *Buffy*.

1. "Quality TV usually has a quality pedigree." Although Joss Whedon is not David Lynch (the cocreator of *Twin Peaks* and Thompson's prime example, as a movie auteur, of a pedigree-quality television figure), *Buffy*'s creator does bring a certain cachet. A graduate of Wesleyan University with a degree in film studies, Joss Whedon admits that his original dream had long been to "head toward the movie world" (Interview with David Bianculli). Though it was in the movies that he made his first breakthrough, when Fran Rubel Kuzui directed his screenplay of *Buffy* in 1992;[4] though he has contributed, often as a highly paid—and sometimes uncredited—"script doctor" to a variety of films both before (*Speed* [1994], *Toy Story* [1995], *Waterworld* [1995], *Twister* [1996]) and after (*Alien Resurrection* [1997], *X-Men* [2000], *Titan A.E.* [2000]) the television series *Buffy* came on the air in 1997; and though Anthony Stewart Head has remarked that "it's only a matter of time before we lose him to the cinema" (Interview with BBC Online), Whedon himself confesses that "I have always felt my movie career was an abysmal failure" (qtd. in Tracy 44).

   Whedon can, however, claim a unique genealogy in the medium in which he has experienced his greatest success. He is a third-generation contributor to television; both Whedon's grandfather and father wrote for television: after a career in radio (writing for such shows as *The Great Gildersleeve*), his grandfather went on to contribute to *Donna Reed*, *Mayberry RFD*, *The Dick Van Dyke Show*, and *Room 222*. Whedon's father wrote for *Captain Kangaroo*, *The Dick Cavett Show*, *The Electric Company*, *Alice*, *Benson*, *Golden Girls*, and *It's a Living*. Joss Whedon himself contributed to both *Roseanne* and *Parenthood* prior to the making of the original *Buffy* film. If Whedon does stay in television, he could well become, along with the likes of David E. Kelley (*Picket Fences*, *The Practice*, *Ally McBeal*, *Boston Public*) and Aaron Sorkin (*Sports Night*, *West Wing*), a significant creative force in network television.

2. "Desirable demographics notwithstanding, quality shows must often undergo a noble struggle against profit-mongering networks and non-appreciative audiences." The path of *Buffy* to a secure home on the WB was, by all accounts, a long, strange trip. Born as a campy and largely unsuccessful feature film in 1992, written by Whedon but directed by Fran Rubel Kuzui, *Buffy* ended up on the WB as the result of the efforts of Gail Berman, the production executive of Sandollar. Whedon and company's relationship with the network has been until

recently anything but adversarial, however. In an interview on National Public Radio's *Fresh Air,* Whedon tells David Bianculli that the
WB never sought to make the show lighter and even encouraged exploration of "the dark side." Still, the series has never garnered high
Nielsen numbers (usually ranking in the bottom 25 percent among all
television series) and has been consistently overlooked for Emmy
nominations.[5] With the very recent news that *Buffy* will move to UPN
beginning with the sixth season, it remains to be seen if its demographics will change as its budget increases.

3. "Quality TV tends to have a large ensemble cast." The core of *Buffy*'s
excellent cast—Sarah Michelle Gellar as Buffy Summers, a high school
and, later, college student in Sunnydale, California, with the after-
school job of Vampire Slayer; Alyson Hannigan as Buffy's best bud,
Willow Rosenberg, brilliant student, computer genius, and aspiring
witch; Nicholas Brendon as Xander Harris, class clown, schlemiel,
and loyal friend; and Anthony Stewart Head as Rupert Giles, school
librarian, quintessential Englishman, and Buffy's Watcher—has, of
course, been with the show since its inception. But *Buffy*'s ensemble
has included many other important players as well, including Kristine
Sutherland as Buffy's mother, Joyce; David Boreanaz as Angel, an
over-two-centuries-old vampire, now cursed with a soul, who came to
Sunnydale to be Buffy's protector; Charisma Carpenter as Cordelia
Chase, rich, bitchy Buffy adversary who eventually becomes a Scooby;
Seth Green as Oz, sardonic musician (guitar player for Dingoes Ate
My Baby), boyfriend of Willow, and werewolf; James Marsters as
Spike, bleached-blond, punk British vampire, sired by Drusilla;
Kendra, the short-lived second Vampire Slayer to be seen in the series;
Eliza Dushku as Faith, another Vampire Slayer, who in the third sea-
son goes over to the dark side; Emma Caulfield as Anya, a former
vengeance demon (Anyanka) and Xander's lover; Marc Blucas as Riley Finn, UC Sunnydale graduate assistant who is secretly a leader of
The Initiative (the university's secret paramilitary antidemon force)
and Buffy's post-Angel lover; and many occasional/recurring perform-
ers: Amber Benson as Tara, an aspiring witch and Willow's new love;
Robia LaMorte as Jenny Calendar, techno-pagan, computer teacher,
and Giles's love; Juliet Landau as Drusilla, mad, visionary British
vampire sired by Angel; Harry Groener as Mayor Richard Wilkins III,
century-old demon who built Sunnydale and aspires to ascend to immortality; Alexis Denisof as Wesley Wyndam-Pryce, a second, more
priggish Watcher who replaces Giles when he is relieved of his duties;
and Armin Shimerman as Principal Snyder, Sunnydale High School's
chief administrator and nemesis of the Scooby Gang (eaten by Mayor
Wilkins).

4. "Quality TV has a memory." In his *Fresh Air* interview, Whedon has expressed his disappointment with the lack of memory exhibited by the characters on *The X-Files*, especially Scully's inability to accept the reality of the supernatural despite weekly proof. On *Buffy*, however, characters remember, and we remember with them. In season 4's all-dream-sequence finale "Restless," for example, Buffy strips Willow of her "costume," returning her to the same "softer side of Sears" unfashionable outfit she had worn seventy-eight episodes before in *Buffy*'s first episode, "Welcome to the Hellmouth." In season 5's "Forever" (5017), we see Giles listening to Cream's "Tales of Brave Ulysses" after attending the funeral of Buffy's mother; attentive viewers recall that he had played the same song for Joyce Summers during their drug-induced reversion to teenageness in "Band Candy" (3006)—a night he and Joyce had sex together. As Ken Tucker observes, in *Buffy* "people *change*: They quake with fear in one episode and muster up demon-defying courage in the next. They can begin as allies and end up as murderers [. . .] or begin as murderers and end up as noble heroes [. . .]" (23). Such changes can happen because the series has a real, a palpable, past.[6]

5. "Quality TV creates a new genre by mixing old ones." Joss Whedon has said on several occasions that he sees *Buffy* as "*My So Called Life* meets *The X-Files*," but *Buffy*, only the second multiseason vampire series ever to air on television,[7] would seem to be the result of the recombinant DNA of several other kinds of shows as well. As Joyce Millman has observed, *Buffy* is daring "because it defiantly and lovingly takes its tone and shape from oft-dismissed genres like daytime soaps, gothic romances, Grade-B horror flicks and supernatural fantasies, and it elevates—no, celebrates—these misunderstood and mistreated pop art forms."

6. "Quality TV tends to be literary and writer-based." Whedon has compared working on *Buffy* as a continuing story to the work of a novelist and invokes his own favorite writer, Charles Dickens, who published his novels in serialized form. Again and again, Whedon has spoken of writing as his constant first love[8] and praised writing for television over writing for the movies.[9] In five years of work on *Buffy*, he has assembled a group of writers—among them Marti Noxon, David Fury, Jane Espenson, and Douglas Petrie—who are able to think very much like he does.

7. "Quality TV is self-conscious." Official *Buffy* publications like the two volumes of *The Watcher's Guide*, not to mention numerous Web sites (e.g., Buffyguide.com) devote significant space both to series continuity and to popular culture references and allusions. As any newcomer to the series quickly realizes, *Buffy* constantly and pervasively

draws on its own past history, but it casts its nets widely beyond its own developing text. "Any text that has slept with another text," Robert Stam has noted, extending a central insight of STD prevention into the realm of film theory, "has necessarily slept with all the texts the other text has slept with" (202). Whether it is Xander about to have sex for the first time with Faith ("The Zeppo," 3013) admitting he's "never been up with people [. . .] before," Giles admitting to Olivia ("Hush," 4010) that he "wasn't actually one of the original members of Pink Floyd," Willow's questioning lament (in "Halloween," 2006) that Buffy "couldn't have dressed up like Xena?" or Buffy twice mangling the name of the demon Acathla as "Al Franken" and "Alfalfa" ("Becoming," part 1, 2021), the series offers us humor that only the textually promiscuous are likely to get.

8. "The subject matter of quality TV tends toward the controversial." As Whedon concedes in his *Fresh Air* interview, drawing comparison to *Star Trek* three decades ago,[10] the genre of *Buffy*, already marginalized, has probably enabled it to get away with things that would have seemed more controversial on mainstream shows. Willow's turn toward lesbianism in season 4, for example, caused very little buzz in the media. Nevertheless, three season 3 episodes "Earshot" and "Graduation Day," parts 1 and 2 (3021 and 3022), were not allowed to air as scheduled because their subject matter was seen as too controversial in the wake of the Columbine High School massacre.[11]

9. "Quality TV aspires toward 'realism.'" David Bianculli has called *Buffy* "a fantasy show that rings truer than most shows on TV," and Ken Tucker has said "for all the show's fantasy trappings, [Buffy's] more realistically drawn than any other teenager on TV" (22). "Emotional realism" is what Joss Whedon is interested in. Everything is grounded in the audience's identification with what they are going through. Whedon tells Bianculli about appearing in a chat room after "Innocence" (2014), an episode in which Angel breaks the curse that had given him a soul by having sex with Buffy, becoming again the fiendishly evil Angelus. When a young woman responded on-line by confessing to Whedon that "this exact same thing happened to me," Whedon explains, he knew he was accomplishing precisely what he had hoped for with the series.[12]

"The Body" (5016), a season 5 episode concerning the unexpected death of Buffy's mother and its difficult aftermath, perhaps exemplifies best this commitment to emotional realism. Written and directed by *Buffy*'s creator, "The Body" is almost without monsters (only the token appearance of a single vampire in the morgue in its closing scene reminds us that we are watching a show about the everyday battle against supernatural evil). In

"The Body," an episode acclaimed by many critics, the Scooby Gang must battle equally difficult enemies like grief, regret, loss, anger, and immaturity.

An article in *Entertainment Weekly* a few years back made the argument that television at the end of the century may well be better than the movies. The proposition at first glance seems preposterous—how could a medium that had produced so many masterpieces, so many great auteurs, from Chaplin to Scorsese, be thought inferior to a household appliance? *Entertainment Weekly*'s case was nevertheless compelling: the very best series television, the prime examples of what has come to be called "quality television," it insisted, takes more risks, tackles more relevant issues more provocatively, does more with character, gives women juicier roles, and goes deeper than the movies do, largely because of the generous amount of time available, thanks to twenty-two episodes a year and multiyear durations. *Buffy*, for example, by its fifth year on the air, had (at season's end) approximately 4,000 minutes, or sixty-seven hours, of narrative time in which to become itself, roughly equivalent to thirty-three feature films.

ABOUT THIS VOLUME

> I've been indexing the Watcher Diaries covering the last couple of centuries. You'd be amazed at how numbingly pompous and long-winded some of these Watchers were.
>
> —Giles, in "What's My Line?" part 1 (2009)

This volume began in the spring of 2000 when David Lavery, a newcomer to *Buffy*, introduced to the Buffyverse by his students at Middle Tennessee State University in the fall of 1999, approached Rhonda Wilcox, author of one of the first scholarly studies of the show (" 'There Will Never Be a "Very Special" *Buffy*': *Buffy* and the Monsters of Teen Life," *Journal of Popular Film and Television* 27.2 [1999]: 16–23),[13] about collaborating on a collection of critical essays on the series. Many e-mails and an internationally circulated call for papers resulted in almost a gross of proposals by scholars and fans from the United States, Canada, Scotland, England, and Australia hoping to contribute.

The wealth of material inspired the editors to launch an e-journal devoted to *Buffy* as well: *Slayage: The Online International Journal of Buffy Studies* (<http://www.slayage.tv>), which, in addition to publishing many valuable essays proposed for the present volume but unable to be included because of lack of space, will in the years ahead make available new critical essays on *Buffy*. *Slayage* will also provide a discussion forum for readers of this volume to address questions to its editors and authors and an opportunity for each of the volume's contributors to post on-line, in light of recent developments in the series, updates or addenda to his or her chapter. (The reader should bear in mind that the chapters in this volume were written at the end of the fourth season and reflect only in passing season 5 developments, which had not yet been completed as we went to press.)

The many meanings of *Buffy* are reflected in the various voices of the interpreters assembled in this volume. Scholars from English, communications, women's studies, sociology, religion, and other fields, all writing with at least the first four seasons of the series in mind, present their different perspectives, sometimes analyzing the same scenes and lines in radically different fashion, from cultural studies to Jungian analysis, from problematizing to praise. The editors have chosen such a various group with a purpose: their multiplicity reflects the polysemic variety of this rich text.

We have divided this volume into three parts. The first part, "Forces of Society and Culture: Gender, Generations, Violence, Class, Race, and Religion," contains many chapters that consider more than one of these categories. Rhonda V. Wilcox argues that the underlying narrative structures of death in the series successfully confront issues of gender and violence. Elyce Rae Helford discusses the containment of girls' anger as an indicator of cultural oppression and examines the implications of class and race in the representations of three Slayers: Buffy, Kendra, and Faith. Patricia Pender, surveying criticism of *Buffy*, contends that much of it takes an either/or view of the series's feminism, while instead *Buffy* avoids oversimplifying polarities and challenges viewers through feminist camp. Farah Mendlesohn suggests that a potential queer reading of the Buffy/Willow relationship is denied in erotic terms but is favored in political terms through the increasing strength of the quieter character, Willow. J. P. Williams analyzes the flawed mother-daughter relationships in the series and the problematic search for strong substitutes, from Gwendolyn Post to Maggie Walsh to Jenny Calendar. Karen Eileen Overbey and Lahney Preston-Matto celebrate the speech act as the most positive weapon in *Buffy*, exploring its spoken and textual expressions through Buffy, Xander, Willow, and Giles. Lynne Edwards investigates the Black Slayer Kendra as a modern version of the tragic mulatta myth, whose failed quest for legitimacy suggests that assimilation equals death for blacks. Mary Alice Money explores the metaphoric implications of the rehabilitation of characters (such as Spike) who represent cultural or racial Others—with *Buffy*'s own version of Huck Finn confronting the metaphoric racism. Denying the "otherness" of *Buffy* vampires, Gregory Erickson discusses the paradoxical epistemology of belief and disbelief in American culture in general and *Buffy* in particular: where is God, and how does *Buffy* inform our understanding of American spirituality? Catherine Siemann juxtaposes two archetypal California girls, pointing out the parallels between Gidget with the mid-Victorians and Buffy's darker world with the nineteenth-century fin de siècle, in particular three literary movements—the New Woman, Decadence, and the Gothic—all in the context of the increasing complexity of the teenager's moral universe. Several of these chapters might also fit under the second part, "Forces of Art and Imagination (Past): Vampires, Magic, and Monsters," which begins with *Buffy*'s version of *Frankenstein*. Anita Rose explains that, through its reimagining of Mary Shelley's work, *Buffy* employs Romantic ideology in contemporary contexts and terms, moving from the solitary Romantic hero to the community of the Scooby Gang. Diane DeKelb-Rittenhouse surveys the literary tradition of the vampire Lothario as it makes its way from the *dhampire* of folklore to the Byronic Lord Ruthven to *Buffy*'s modern variants, Angel and Spike. Elisabeth Krimmer and Shilpa Raval consider the relationship of Angel and Buffy in the context of Liebestod (love-death) stories such as *Romeo and Juliet* and *Tristan and Isolde*, comparing the thematic impossibility of love's fulfillment with the structural deferral of serial television. Donald G. Keller examines the sometimes supernatural dreams of Buffy and her shadow-self Faith through the lens of Jung and Freud (with a side view of imagery from Eliot's *The Waste Land*). Tanya Krzywinska investigates witchcraft, magic, and the Manichaean in popular culture in general and *Buffy* in particular, arguing that a self-conscious mixture of sitcom, fantasy, and horror allows the series to negotiate between absolute categories of good and evil and a more relativistic approach (especially through the witchcraft of Willow)—all based on a foundational myth recalling H. P. Lovecraft. Sarah E. Skwire moves beyond Bettelheim to point out that *Buffy*, as it does with nearly every other convention, turns the didactic nature of the fairy tale on its head, so that the instructors become the instructed and Buffy's own relationship to the category of "adult" or "child" can be gauged. In the third part, "Forces of Art and Imagination (Present): Fan Relationships, Metaphoric and Real," Kristina Busse discusses the Buffyverse fan fiction in terms of family dynamics and the contested role of women, as this fiction invokes the ambiguous emotional demands of motherhood, with its contradictory roles of mother/caregiver as well as partner/lover. S. Renee Dechert argues that *Buffy*'s music works to reinforce the communal identity between the program and its fans because the musicians are often relative outsiders, yet the fans must have "inside" knowledge (often Internet derived) to recognize them. Justine Larbalestier points out that some *Buffy* episodes acknowledge the fun that fans have playing with fan fiction by putting seemingly impossible scenarios ("What if Buffy and Spike were engaged?") on the screen while at the same time reasserting control by making those scenarios part of the official *Buffy* universe: one episode even serves as a metaphor for a fan-controlled alternate world. Finally, Amanda Zweerink and Sarah N. Gatson describe the fan world of The Bronze, named after the teen hangout on *Buffy*, as a changing Internet community that in some ways replicates (although imperfectly) the idea of community so important to the series, with its Posting Board Party illustrating problems of class structure that the series confronts.

An afterword examining Buffy's creator Joss Whedon, an episode guide, and a composite bibliography complete the volume.

NOTES

1. The episode numbering system we have used here and throughout indicates season and episode. Thus, 1002 = first season, second episode.

2. Joyce Millman, Salon.com's television critic, has given up trying to convince doubters: "To those of you who've never seen *Buffy the Vampire Slayer* and *Angel*," she writes, "well, I'm sorry, but you are beyond my help."

3. Both Hannah Tucker (daughter of *Entertainment Weekly* critic Ken Tucker) and Caitlin Campbell (daughter of media scholar Richard Campbell) have addressed in print the perils of the high school defender of *Buffy*. In "High School Confidential," Tucker notes, "I can never speak about *Buffy the Vampire Slayer* so passionately as when confronted with a skeptic. There are about four *Buffy* fans at my high school, so far as I can tell. So, by 'skeptic' I mean a large percentage of my peers. Typical response from a boy, eyes rolling: 'C'mon, she's a blond chick in a Wonderbra who fights vampires.'"

4. For an insightful discussion of the transformation of *Buffy* from movie into television series, see Moss.

5. A fan-based postcard campaign protested the series's lack of Emmy nominations in 2001 with the message "Grr, Argh," recalling Whedon's Mutant Enemy company's insignia.

6. In a wonderful essay on Salon.com, "Please Sir, May I Have a Mother?" Sarah Vowell observes that "series television, more than any other form, is perfect to explore family dynamics. Novels, even long ones, end. Movies are great moments—love at first sight, murder, that time Lassie came home. But family life unfolds over time. And the seeming monotony of TV is inherently equipped to deal with ongoing stories, not to mention ongoing quibbles—Frasier's campaign against his father's ugly chair, Lisa Simpson's doomed attempts to enlighten her anarchic brood. To get the true story of a family, it has to be done over the long haul." The extended family of *Buffy* is, admittedly a bit unorthodox, but Vowell's observation rings true for it as well. It is truly a "long haul" show.

7. The other, of course, was *Forever Knight* (1992–94) on CBS and in first-run syndication.

8. "It's easier to write an episode than direct it," Whedon has explained. "Well, not easier, but scheduling-wise, I usually direct an episode when there is something I desperately want to say—where there's a moment that I want to capture, an idea I want to try out. To create something, that means actually writing it. I may actually direct a couple of episodes that I don't write next year, just because of my time being as it is. By and large, the only time I've done it is when I've co-written with David Greenwalt. The bottom line is that I like to create. To me, the writing is the most important thing, and if I'm going to take the time to direct something and it

really pulls a lot out of my schedule, usually I want it to be something of my own. At the same time, it would certainly be interesting to direct somebody else's script" (<http://www.fanforum.com/buffy/news/786.shtml>).

9. "Being a writer in Hollywood is not all it's cracked up to be," Whedon has admitted. "People blow their noses on you. When I went on the set of *Alien* [*Resurrection*], people are nice enough but I am standing in a corner. On *Buffy*, I'm telling these stories. Not only am I telling them, I'm telling them every eight days. [. . .] The movies I write, if they ever get made, take several thousand years. But television is a writer's medium so there's a better chance things will come out the way you originally envisioned them" (qtd. in Tracy 24).

10. It is nothing new for the science fiction and fantasy category of television series to symbolically represent teen difficulties: Harvey Greenberg's essay "In Search of Spock" explains how in the 1960s *Star Trek* represented teens' alienation in the famous half-Vulcan character. *Buffy* is especially successful at that symbolic representation.

11. For an excellent (and highly critical) consideration of the issues involved in the WB decision, see Charles Taylor.

12. "I can't write a character if I don't at some level understand where they're coming from and how they feel about the world," Whedon has explained. "That even includes Principal Snyder, who is probably one of our most cardboard cutout villainous characters. In "Band Candy" we got a glimpse into what he was like in high school, and it became very clear that he was the kid that everybody was constantly trying to ditch. He was the nerd who was eager to be friends with everybody and was constantly snubbed. And that made it clear how he became the child-hating martinet that we had so much fun with. So I feel that if you don't love a character, then you have no business writing them. I hate stock villains, I hate people who are just there to be cannon fodder. And it's not like that never happens on the shows—it's not like I'm gonna go write the history of the second thug from the left—but when I read a script, I have to at least believe that the second thug from the left is acting as he sees fit, and as he would in the given situation" (Whedon, interview with ET Online).

13. This essay is republished in *Slayage* (<http://www.middleenglish.org/slayage/essays/slayage2/wilcox.htm>).

I

✳

FORCES OF SOCIETY AND CULTURE

GENDER, GENERATIONS, VIOLENCE, CLASS, RACE, AND RELIGION

1

"Who Died and Made Her the Boss?"

Patterns of Mortality in Buffy

Rhonda V. Wilcox

"Feminism has sort of a negative connotation. It makes you think of women that don't shave their legs. [. . .] I hate the word," says Sarah Michelle Gellar, star of *Buffy the Vampire Slayer* (Mendlesohn). Nonetheless, Buffy, like Xena the Warrior Princess, is widely cited as a role model for her daring heroism (Pozner). Magazines such as the *Nation* and *George* commend the series for "taking on the regular assortment of challenges that threaten to suck the lifeblood out of teenage girls" (Stoller, "The 20" 113). As Gellar says elsewhere, "We basically just take high school and use horror as the metaphor for it" ("Hot Summers" 30). In Buffy's world, the problems teenagers face become literal monsters. Internet predators are demons; drink-doctoring frat boys have sold their souls for success in the business world; a girl who has sex with even the nicest-seeming male discovers that he afterward may become a monster (Wilcox, "There"). Joan Gordon and Veronica Hollinger's *Blood Read: The Vampire as Metaphor in Contemporary Culture* provides precedent in literary history for the kind of symbolic operation to be found in *Buffy*. And in this symbolic world, Buffy confronts monsters and prevails. But the show's feminist elements do not stop there. Many of the underlying structures of the series also work against stereotypical depictions of male interactions, particularly in terms of patterns of mortality. Three such patterns that are broken are the patriarchal order of succession through death; the mortal vulnerability of love objects for television series protagonists, or what I call the Little Joe Phenomenon; and the demonizing of those whom the protagonist kills.

PATRIARCHAL SUCCESSION VERSUS COMMUNAL ACTION

The opening voice-over of the series intones, "In every generation there is a Chosen One. She *alone* will stand against the vampires, the demons, and the forces of darkness. She is the Slayer." Buffy is one of a long line of single champions, leaders of the fight against evil. Like the king in a patriarchal succession, each Slayer is born to the position and assumes it only on the death of the preceding Slayer. And like many a ruler, Buffy occasionally complains that she cannot avoid her responsibility—that she will be relieved of the burden only through death. As she says to her adviser, Watcher Rupert Giles, "If you don't like the way I'm doing my job, why don't you find someone else? Oh—that's right—there can be only one. Long as I'm alive, there is no one else. Well, there you go—I don't have to be the Slayer: I could be dead" ("What's My Line?" part 1, 2009).

But from the start, the series counterbalances the idea of the lonely hero with the presentation of a community of friends—a more typically female method of operation (as Carol Gilligan, among others, has pointed out). In the first episode, Buffy's classmate Xander Harris overhears her secret. He shares the information with his best friend, Willow Rosenberg (or "Will"), and they become the core of Buffy's support group. A different kind of support is provided by Angel, a dark, mysterious, handsome character who turns out to be a vampire with a heart of gold. In his introductory scene, he identifies himself to Buffy as "a friend," and he hopes to help the Slayer destroy other vampires. Buffy and her friends are advised by Giles, the librarian—who, though his title is "Watcher," sometimes actively participates in the fighting. They are eventually joined by cheerleader Cordelia Chase, who wants to fight demons even less than Buffy ever did; Oz, a rock guitarist and werewolf; and later the ex-demon Anya and the aspiring witch Tara (among others). Xander refers to these friends as "The Scooby Gang," in self-mocking reference to the perennially rerun cartoon series that features friends who are teen detectives. When a foreign visitor discovers Buffy's support group, she asks, "Did anyone explain to you what secret identity means?" and inquires whether Giles has given permission for Buffy to have friends ("What's My Line?" part 2, 2010).

To paraphrase Mae West, permission had nothing to do with it. There is a clear resistance to the hierarchical control of the patriarchal Watchers' Council which Giles at first represents. Though Giles once mentions that his grandmother was a watcher ("Never Kill a Boy on the First Date," 1005) and one other female watcher—a dead one—is mentioned in "Faith, Hope, and Trick" (3003), the dozen or so Watchers' Council members who are seen on screen are, for four seasons, all male—with the exception of evil renegade Watcher Gwendolyn Post, who is killed in "Revelations" (3007). Each of the members of the Scooby Gang becomes involved in the fight against dark forces through caring, basic decency, and an unwillingness to accept orders to stay out of it. And time and again, their intervention saves the day when Buffy could not have triumphed alone. Cordelia tears through a high school hall in her flashy car, or Willow tears through the Internet, or Xander stakes a vampire, or Angel uses his vampire strength, or Giles finds just the right book to solve the problem. In "Halloween" (2006), for example, Buffy is changed by a spell cast by the costume she wears: she believes herself to be a lady of the eighteenth century, unable to fight. Around the city similar transformations happen to those who bought their costumes at the same shop: little children become actual devils, Xander becomes a soldier, Willow becomes a ghost. In the midst of the chaos and the temporary amnesia of many of the characters, mild-mannered Willow takes charge: "You guys stay here while I get some help. If something tries to get in, just fight it off." And the amnesia-free Cordelia asks, "Who died and made *her* the boss?" No one has died, but in this episode Buffy is *not* the boss; her friends take over to protect her. Power is not limited to a single line, despite the series's voice-over opening.

Another such significant intervention occurs in the last episode of season 1, "Prophecy Girl" (1012). In this episode, Buffy is horrified to overhear Giles and Angel discussing her prophesied death: she is to be killed by the Master (her first-season vampire nemesis). At first she wants to refuse her fate, but at last she goes to face him—and is, indeed, killed, left face down in a muddy pool of water in her white prom dress. Xander and Angel, however, have pursued her to try to help; and when they find her, it is Xander who brings her back to life through mouth-to-mouth resuscitation. (As Angel points out, he being undead has no breath to offer.) Without her friends, Buffy would have simply stayed dead; but with them, she returns from the dead stronger than she has ever been before.

This incident also leads to another departure from the pattern of succession. For the Slayer there is never a problem with entailment; there is only one Slayer at any given time. Or at least that has been the case until Buffy. Because she has, however briefly, died, a new Slayer has been activated—Kendra the Vampire Slayer, a young foreign woman of high kicks and uncertain accent ("What's My Line?" parts 1 and 2, 2009 and 2010; on the accent, see Tracy 205). Xander's reaction is, "I knew this 'I'm the only one, I'm the only one' thing was just an attention-getter." Kendra points out that her unidentified culture takes the calling of Slayer very seriously: she has studied the texts for years (Buffy calls her a "She-Giles"), and she was sent to live with her Watcher, Sam Zabuto, before the age at which she could remember her parents. She not only has no friends; she notes that she does not have a last name; her entire identity is her calling. She apparently never even had toys, though in a later episode we learn that she has named her favorite stake "Mr. Pointy."

This series is certainly self-aware enough to be conscious of the humorous Freudian elements of this sad little bit of business with Kendra's stake, as the facial expressions of the actors indicate. In short, it is only too appropriate that Kendra's one marginally personal possession is a phallic symbol, given the forces she has been taught to serve. She has absorbed the view of the mainly masculine, hierarchical Watchers, and she advises Buffy against having friends or emotions. Buffy in turn teaches that her emotions can give her power. And once again, in the climactic scene of the two-part episode, all the friends—Xander, Willow, Giles, Cordelia, and this time Kendra too—fight to save Buffy, Angel, and the day. In many of its strongest moments, Buffy is a show of friendship, not of single combat. And it subverts the very pattern of patriarchal succession that it purports to highlight.

In fact, the failure of this traditional pattern is highlighted by two negative examples—one a multiepisode narrative sequence and the other a character. At the end of season 2, traumatized by a series of losses and problems (of which more later), Buffy runs away, leaving Sunnydale ("Becoming," parts 1 and 2, 2021 and 2022). Her spiral downward is witnessed by a helpful visiting demon called Whistler, who seems to have unusual knowledge of Buffy's circumstances and future (enabling him to achieve voice-over status). With Giles under torture and Xander and Cordelia attending a comatose Willow in the hospital, Whistler tells Buffy, "In the end you're always by yourself—you're all you've got." Even in these dire conditions, Buffy is not completely alone: she accepts help from her enemy the phallically named, punk vampire Spike (later a semi-Scooby). Spike and Buffy need to fight the same vampires, and, as he says, "I can't fight them alone and neither can you." "I hate you," she says. "And I'm all you've got," he replies. Once the fight is over, however, she is truly alone. Expelled from school and kicked out by her mother, she does not wait to reconnect with her friends but instead, in her misery, runs away from home. In one of the many poignant connections of this fantasy series to real life, Buffy on the bus leaving Sunnydale looks like any teen runaway.

Clearly, her loneliness is not a triumph, despite the fact that Whistler's words suggest a heroic test to be passed. And as in Campbell's monomyth, the hero Buffy will travel to a strange land (in this case, Los Angeles), fight monsters, and return home changed. But the pattern here is not celebrated. The third season opens with a repeat of Whistler's words, "You're all you've got" (3001). The name of the episode is "Anne"—a very unheroic name; it is Buffy Summers's middle name, and the name she chooses to go by as she tries to lose herself and her pain. She becomes a waitress and avoids conflict even to the extent of refraining from objection when a customer slaps her on the behind. She lives and works alone.

Even at her lowest, however, Buffy cannot refuse to help someone in need, and so she is led to reconnect with humanity. A young woman called

Lily identifies herself to Buffy as Chanterelle, who has been helped by Buffy in the past, in Sunnydale. When Lily/Chanterelle recognizes Buffy and asks for help, Buffy is drawn into a larger world of runaways and their problems. In *Buffy,* runaways literally go to hell. Time passes at a different rate there, so after they are used up in labor and suffering, they are returned to the normal world a few days later but many years older. Thus, Buffy encounters old people (actually, the young runaways) on the streets muttering, "I'm no one"—the phrase taught them by demons, and the goal Buffy seems to have been aiming for. But the demons make the mistake of carting Buffy off to their local branch of hell along with a batch of battered teens. Fighting to release them, she reclaims her identity, reclaims her name: "I'm Buffy—the Vampire Slayer. And you are?" After leading the runaways back, she gives her place—her job as a waitress, her tiny apartment, and even her name, Anne—to Lily/Chanterelle,[1] and Buffy returns to Sunnydale, to face reconnection with her friends and family.

One of the most uncomfortable episodes of the series is "Dead Man's Party," the episode in which Buffy must attempt to retrieve the connection with family and friends that she disrupted at the end of the second season (3002). (Her absence was emphasized by Whedon's correlating it with the series' summer hiatus.) It is a measure of the seriousness and depth of Buffy's original connection with her friends and her mother that all the characters involved have difficulty repairing the break. They attempt to welcome her back with a raucous party, but they can barely stand to converse with her and fear that she will leave again. In fact, Willow and Buffy's mother at one point find her in her room packing a small bag. She is undecided whether to stay or go, finding it difficult to deal with the unexpressed depth of their blame for her running away. To Xander, Buffy says, "I just had to deal with this on my own." "And you see how well that one worked out," he replies. The characters' failed attempts to bury their anger are represented by the zombies who appear to attack the party—zombies who are channeled by a mask from the art shop of Buffy's mom, perhaps the most wounded by the separation. As they fight the zombies together, the characters achieve a catharsis and are able to reunite, though it is clear the emotional wounds are not completely healed—there is not what Todd Gitlin has called "the click of a solution" ("Prime Time Ideology" 447). Overall, then, the narrative sequence in "Becoming" (parts 1 and 2), "Anne," and "Dead Man's Party" shows that when you go it alone, you go to hell; and if you return, you must grapple with the buried feelings that will rise. In effect, the choice to fight alone, while heroic, is also presented as wrong.

The next episode, "Faith, Hope, and Trick" (3003), introduces Faith, a character who provides a negative example for solo heroics. Spike's lover Drusilla having killed Kendra, yet another Slayer has been called. As with Kendra, Faith's very existence subverts the pattern of patriarchal succession.

And although she shows up unannounced, she seems at first willing to be part of a communal effort. After killing a vampire, she says, "Thanks, B [her nickname for Buffy]—couldn't have done it without you." Since Buffy's help has been minimal at best in this scene, Faith's comment in their first encounter is insouciant politeness, mere professional courtesy. She has some glimpses of what the Scooby Gang's friendship is like; near the beginning, she says, "If I'd had friends like you in high school—I probably still would have dropped out, but I might have been sad about it." But Faith has no deep understanding of the need for or the value of shared effort or community, and that is what in the end will make her dangerous.

Faith has unfortunately arrived at a difficult moment in the life of both Slayers. For Buffy's part, having recently returned from hell, she is exceptionally vulnerable. She is trying to reclaim her place in Sunnydale, and she is jealous of the ease with which fast-talking Faith fascinates them all: "She gets along with my friends, my Watcher, my mom [. . .]." For Faith's part, though she is genuinely friendly at first, she is increasingly defensive because she is hiding something: her Watcher has been killed by a demon, and Faith was powerless to stop the death. Faith has never had a group of supportive friends, and her mother was an alcoholic (both Buffy's and Faith's fathers are gone). Working alone, Faith has failed (and one should never overlook the significance of naming and language in *Buffy*). Having lost her Watcher, the only person truly connected to her, Faith feels guilty but represses that guilt under bravado. Unwelcomed by Buffy—who has yet to recover her own faith in herself and her loved ones—Faith invests herself fully in the masculinized role of solo hero.

In fact, Faith's situation clearly echoes Buffy's recent problems. When Buffy goes to visit Faith, she finds her in lodging comparable in its grim loneliness to Buffy's in "Anne." "So—what brings you to the poor side of town?" Faith asks. Now knowing Faith's most immediate problem—a dead Watcher and a pursuing demon—and having realized that Faith must have come to Sunnydale not just for fun but for help, Buffy tries to repair their faulty relationship: "Faith, you came here for a reason. I can help." "You can mind your own business. I'm the one who can handle this" is the answer. Though Faith's manner is much harsher than Buffy's, she clearly reiterates the choices Buffy has recently made—and highlights how wrong those choices are. The show even frames the comparison with a particular scene: just as Joyce Summers and Willow found Buffy in her room packing a small bag in the immediately preceding episode, so now Buffy finds Faith in her room packing a small bag. To Faith's claim that she will be able to deal with the problem alone, Buffy says, "Yeah—you're a real badass when it comes to packing." In the end, Buffy helps Faith, and they attempt a relationship. Faith thus continues the series' demonstration of the falseness of the idea expressed in its oft-recited motto "She *alone* will stand against [. . .] the forces of darkness." Solo heroics and patriarchal succession are both undercut by Faith.

Perhaps the most direct denial of the pattern, however, comes in the last two episodes of season 4. In "Primeval" (4021), Buffy is only able to defeat Adam—the Frankensteinian construction of that bastion of scientific rationality, The Initiative—a creature patched together with many demon parts—by a mystic combination with the core of the Scooby Gang. Having recently fallen out because of conflicts purposefully ripened by the psychologically perceptive Spike, the four central characters—Willow, Xander, Giles, and Buffy—must put aside their differences to join in fighting Adam. This monstrous creation who blasphemously bears the name the Bible gives to the first created human is defeated by the magically joined power of the four friends. But their ability to join after long-simmering conflict is surprisingly quick, under the stress of emergency; and the cost of that joining appears in the dream episode finale of the season, "Restless" (4022). Each of the four acts of the teleplay is constituted of the dream of one of the main characters: Willow, Xander, Giles, then Buffy. Each dream shows the psychic cost that the dreamer has paid. And most significantly for this discussion, each character is pursued, and the first three are dream-killed by a horror identified only at the end: the prehistorically first Slayer, who demands that Buffy slay alone: "No friends—just the kill. We are alone," she growls. But Buffy says, "I am not alone. [. . .] There's trees in the desert since you moved out. And I don't sleep on a bed of bones. Now give me back my friends!" And "You're not the source of me," she adds. Again, linear succession and lonely heroics are repudiated, here quite explicitly, in favor of friendship and communal action.

THE LITTLE JOE PHENOMENON

In spite of the importance of friends in the series, there is no doubt that Buffy is the hero: this is not *ER* or *Hill St. Blues*. And, important as he is, Angel is not Buffy's partner in the way that *The Avengers'* Steed and Mrs. Peel are partners, or *The X-Files'* Mulder and Scully, or even *The New Adventures of Superman's* Lois and Clark. One risk for the central heroic character is what I have earlier referred to as the Little Joe Phenomenon. This is essentially a variation on an element of the American monomyth pattern described by Robert Jewett and John Shelton Lawrence, which notes the tendency of the lonely hero to evade romantic commitment. The Little Joe Phenomenon is an extreme version. Anyone who has ever frequently watched *Bonanza* knows that it is a mortal risk for a woman to love or be loved by Little Joe: the beloved will be dead by the end of the episode. Similarly, when Richard Chamberlain's Dr. Kildare fell in love with Yvette

Mimieux's character in the "Tiger, Tiger" episode, we knew that she would choose to cast her free-spirited epileptic self upon a surfboard and so exit his life (not to mention her own). And the mutated Harlan Ellison piece that became *Star Trek*'s "City on the Edge of Forever" is one of the most famous exemplars of the pattern in which the hero must be left fatally free of romantic entanglements. Captain Kirk must purposefully allow his beloved Edith Keeler to die in order to save the world.

    Buffy sets about undermining this pattern as early as the fourth episode, "Never Kill a Boy on the First Date" (1005). Buffy is attracted to a high school boy named Owen, who, as Willow says, "can brood for forty minutes straight" and is therefore desired by many high school girls. He believes he recognizes a kindred spirit in Buffy, with whom he discusses his favorite reading: "The thing about Emily Dickinson I love is that she's just so incredibly morbid." (Buffy asserts that she, too, is fond of "Emily Dickens.") When Buffy has to race off from their date to attend to trouble at a cemetery, Owen follows and is almost immediately put in harm's way. "You killed my date," shouts Buffy at one point; but he has only been knocked unconscious. Nonetheless, Buffy comes to see that, despite her attraction to him, her secret life endangers him—and so, before he can tragically die, she simply gives him up. As she says, "Xander and Willow know the score," but the danger-loving Owen could easily end up dead. For an experienced television watcher, Buffy's choice to break up with Owen says more about loss than many a convenient television death.

    Less easy to eliminate than her relationship with Owen is the confusion that constitutes Buffy's relationship with Angel. As Giles says, "A vampire in love with a Slayer—it's rather poetic, really—in a maudlin sort of way" ("Out of Mind, Out of Sight," 1011). In terms of the Little Joe Phenomenon, it might be said that one of the conveniences (or inconveniences?) of this relationship is that Angel is, of course, already dead. He has been a vampire for over 200 years. The heroic Buffy does not have to worry about his safety as she would have had to do for Owen (or for that matter her other high school friends). On the contrary, as a vampire he is gifted with superhuman strength and stealth. Nonetheless, like any vampire, he can be destroyed by sun or stake. And in fact, in "Becoming," the closing episode of the second season, Buffy is forced to stab Angel herself in order to save the world (shades of "City on the Edge of Forever"). Earlier in the season, Angel had reverted to his evil vampire self, Angelus. In the *Buffy* version of vampire lore, a demon inhabits the body and memory of someone who becomes a vampire; the human soul disappears. The gypsy curse that restored Angel's soul had been placed on him so that he would experience pain from the knowledge of the evil he had done as a vampire. When he achieves one moment of pure happiness—through making love with Buffy—his soul is once again exiled. I have elsewhere described (and am not alone in noting) the symbolic implications of Buffy's first lovemaking: the idea that her more experienced, older lover would (in his Angelus persona) scorn her as "easy" certainly directly translates to a typical teen fear. The pattern suggests male power and female vulnerability.

Angelus battles Buffy for half a season; meanwhile Willow, who has begun to study witchcraft, discovers a way to restore his soul. She finally succeeds at the very moment that Buffy is about to dispatch the evil Angelus. Buffy's Angel returns, but in order to save the world, she must kill him. As Beth Braun notes, the scene in which Buffy stabs Angel is phallically charged. While poignant, it hardly seems to challenge stereotypically masculine patterns of heroic killing and vengeance.

Angel, however, will not stay dead. Like *Star Trek*'s Mr. Spock, he goes seriously elsewhere for quite a long time (see, e.g., the film *The Search for Spock*). And like Mr. Spock, Angel returns mentally impaired (a little death will do that to a person). He drops naked out of nowhere onto the stone floor on which Buffy has, in a gesture of renunciation, laid the friendship ring he gave her. After his return, she secretly nurses him back to health and sanity at the cost of her multiepisode third-season relationship with a nice, normal high school boy (who, like Owen, does not die when they break up—and whose last name indicates her sacrifice: he is Scott Hope of "Faith, Hope, and Trick"). Furthermore, Buffy and Angel can never make love again, or he will presumably once again lose his soul. In sum, she accepts more of a burden rather than having the quick fix of the tragic death of the love object. Buffy is no Little Joe. Indeed, odd though it may sound, the Buffy/Angel relationship may have more in common with the Kirk/Spock relationship: they come from two different worlds, they risk their lives for each other, and they cannot safely consummate their relationship in the world of series television. To put the parallels in another way, theirs is a relationship of both friendship and transcendent love that has more than the usual barriers to physical communion. As Patricia Frazer Lamb and Diana L. Veith have pointed out, this "truly 'bonded' relationship" (236) actually represents the kind appreciated by many female fans. It is in stark contrast to the fictional equivalent of the one-night stand that constitutes the Little Joe pattern.

The defection of Angel to his own series mutes but does not completely negate the Angel/Buffy relationship (the two characters occasionally visit). The fourth season also includes two other sexual relationships for Buffy. One—notable but minor—is with Parker Abrams, who beds and discards Buffy ("The Harsh Light of Day," 4003). Rather than being supernaturally perceptive, she foolishly involves herself with a manipulative phony; the series clearly displays her vulnerability, with the odious Parker appearing in several fourth-season episodes—that is, Buffy's first year in college. It is part of the strength of the characterization that Buffy's human frailty is shown, then surmounted. In terms of the Little Joe phenomenon, and from the point of view of many friends and fans, Parker's death might be quite satisfying. However, when Buffy and Parker are placed in a dangerous situation, she saves his life, even though she is mentally impaired at the time ("Beer Bad," 4005). Rather than getting dead, Parker simply gets knocked out—by Buffy herself, not some male protector.

The second, and major, sexual relationship is with Riley Finn, who seems on the surface to be the quintessentially normal guy—a psychology grad student from the Midwest (and a cowboy in Willow's dream in "Restless") who wants to take Buffy on picnics. Riley, however, also turns out to be a commander in the secret military force called The Initiative, which fights Sunnydale's monsters with science and guns—and without knowledge of the Slayer and her world. When Riley learns her nature, he is pleased by Buffy's heroism and comes to fight alongside her. His role is important enough that he becomes a regular in the credits. In the fifth season he and Buffy painfully part company, but he leaves alive.

Thus, Buffy has had two major romantic relationships without having her work or character displaced from center stage; and it has not been necessary to kill the characters in order to maintain her centrality. She can actually deal with relationships and go on being heroic.[2] Buffy's human strength is such that the series does not need to rely on the Little Joe Phenomenon.

THE EXPENSE OF KILLING

The third stereotypically masculine pattern to be undermined is the demonizing of those whom the hero kills. Perhaps the most clear-cut recent example of this pattern can be found in the film *Independence Day*. In that blockbuster, not only do the enemy invaders look like monsters, but the male president of the United States is given telepathic knowledge of the fact that they are monstrous to the core, and so can be killed absolutely without guilt. If ever there were Other, these are They. It might be argued that *Buffy* follows the same pattern. In episode after episode, Buffy kills without qualms those who oppose her: her enemies are monsters. There are, however, two elements of the text that work against this pattern. One has already been mentioned: as numerous articles have noted, the series makes clear that these monsters are symbolic representations of social problems (Stoller, "The 20"; Wilcox, "There"). Buffy attacks not people but problems. Nonetheless, the constant quick killing can be seen as desensitizing. Probably no television series has shown a sharper examination of a death in the family than *Buffy*'s fifth-season episode "The Body" (5016), which is comparable in emotional force to the discovery of the body of Laura Palmer in David Lynch and Mark Frost's 1990–91 series *Twin Peaks*. But what of the death of the enemy, the Other? It is to the series's credit that in the third season, this issue is directly confronted.

The source of the confrontation is the third Slayer, Faith. Faith is much rougher than ex-cheerleader Buffy ever was. As noted, she turns up in Sunnydale after her Watcher has been killed by one of the monsters. Her reaction is to embrace the violence of the task to which she is destined and to promiscuously enjoy sex afterward (she deflowers Xander in "The Zeppo," 3013). Though Buffy does see Faith first as a rival, she later sees her as a friend. And in fact, in season 3 Buffy is torn between two friends: the powerful, emotional Faith and the quiet, intelligent, controlled Willow—Faith and Will.

Buffy has in the past displayed some of the urges Faith acts on—most notably in the first episode of the second season, "When She Was Bad," in which Buffy sexually teases Xander, torments Angel, and endangers all and sundry. But Faith carries these urges to the extreme. In "Bad Girls," the third-season episode in which Buffy follows Faith rather than Willow, Faith kills a human being—a cardinal sin for a Slayer (3014). Though the killing is accidental, she tries to hide it and even to blame Buffy. As Whedon emphasizes, when vampires are staked on *Buffy,* they disappear in a cloud of dust: "It shows that they're monsters; I didn't really want to have a high school girl killing *people* every week" (Interview, "Angel"). But this man bleeds. The way the series deals with this event, in multiple episodes, highlights the seriousness and consequences of killing.[3]

And Buffy herself is involved in the judgment—not only because she is at first accused of the crime but also because Faith is Buffy's dark double. Faith herself says as much to Buffy in the course of the third-season episode "Consequences" (3015): "You know exactly what I'm about because you have it in you too. I've seen it, B. You've got the lust—and I'm not just talking about screwing vampires. [. . .] You know it could be you." In response, Buffy hits her, to which Faith smiles, "There's my girl." And in the succeeding episode, "Doppelgängland" (3016), the idea of the double is highlighted when we see a dark Willow, a vampire Willow from an alternate reality. "Some people just don't have that [evil] in them," asserts Willow near the beginning of the episode; but by the end we see that even she, and certainly Buffy, can contain that darkness.

Of Buffy's inner circle, Angel is the one who best knows the dangerous sense of power that killing can give—and the temptation it would pose for a Slayer. With Buffy's collaboration, he tries to help Faith and touches once again on the theme of connection: "You can't do this alone." Faith pretends to accept, but she does so in hopes of activating the evil Angelus ("Enemies," 3017). This she attempts under the guidance of the town's mayor—an interesting representative of patriarchal order. While most in Sunnydale refuse to see its dark side, there are nevertheless many in power who do so—including Mayor Richard Wilkins, who has sold his soul to the devil and therefore has few reelection worries. Having parted ways with Buffy over the issue of the accidental murder, Faith has secretly offered herself in employment to the forces in power—that is, the patriarchy—specifically, the mayor's office.

And the gosh-darn, germ-hating, *Reader's Digest*-reading mayor, the emblem of the all-American politician, is both head of the local patriarchal power structure and a father figure to Faith, whom he actually induces to consume milk and cookies. Working for him, Faith later reaches the point when she can simply tell a scientist murder victim, "Boss wants you dead," and when asked why, answer, "Never thought to ask" ("Graduation Day," part 1, 3021). She has become part of the worst version of unquestioning service of the power structure for the sake of the approval, comfort, and support of the father. The mayor feeds Faith, dresses her, and buys her toys (a PlayStation; an especially vicious knife). He clearly feels affection for his killer: after she kills the scientist, he says, "No father could be prouder." The series presents their comfort of each other's loneliness with sympathetic understanding, but their relationship is pathological. In contrast, Buffy, not long after, refuses to take orders any more from the patriarchal Watchers' Council, referring to her decision as "graduation."

Buffy and Angel force Faith to reveal her complicity with the mayor in "Enemies" (3017). Faith believes she has reactivated Angelus (though not, as Buffy later points out, by making love to Angel, who would not); she reveals the mayor's plans to become a full-fledged demon as part of Sunnydale High's graduation ceremony, at which a good time will not be had by all. Once she realizes Buffy and Angel have duped her, Faith turns to attack. The two slayers visually mirror each other: Faith dressed in bloodred and Buffy in black with touches of red, dark-haired Faith to blond Buffy, they hold knives at each other's throats. "What're you gonna do, B—— kill me? You become me. You're not ready for that [and she kisses Buffy on the forehead] yet." Faith herself is never simplistically demonized, but clearly she, in her promiscuity and violence, represents the shadow self that Buffy could become. And that self contains murder.

Eventually Faith's alliance with the mayor and his power structure means that she and Buffy will confront each other. Faith shoots Angel with a poison for which the only cure (though she does not know it) is the blood of a Slayer. Buffy decides to give him Faith's. Faith taunts her, "You gonna feed me to Angel? You know you're not gonna take me alive." "Not a problem," Buffy answers. "Well look at you—all dressed up in big sister's clothes," says Faith. "You told me I was just like you," responds Buffy. Buffy wins the fierce fight, and Faith, in Shakespearean style, announces, "You killed me" ("Graduation Day," part 1).

In fact, though Buffy has indeed stabbed Faith, she has not killed her. Faith, with superhuman Slayer effort, purposefully falls off the rooftop where they have fought, landing on a passing truck bed and ending up comatose in the local hospital. Then Buffy is brought in, hospitalized because she herself has later decided to give an almost fatal amount of blood to save Angel ("Graduation Day," part 2, 3022). With Faith on pink sheets and Buffy on blue, they lie in adjoining rooms, and the mayor rages, "Did you see what she did to my Faith?"—accentuating, as he often does, the Hawthornean double entendre of her name. (One of the most famous examples of symbolic nomenclature in literature is Hawthorne's "Faith" in "Young Goodman Brown," another narrative that contemplates the supernatural.) Given Faith's battered condition, it is easy to see why Angel must physically fight to restrain the mayor from killing the unconscious Buffy.

But while the two men struggle in conscious antagonism, the young women reach a reconciliation in dream. In one of the most beautifully shot and scored scenes of the series, Buffy and an apparently healed Faith meet in Faith's light-filled apartment. Suggestive images and remarks drift through the dream. A cat is in the apartment, and Buffy asks, "Who's gonna look after him?" Faith tells her, "It's a she. And aren't these things supposed to take care of themselves?" "A higher power guiding us," responds Buffy. "Pretty sure that's not what I meant," says Faith. Once again the different perspectives of independence (taking care of oneself) versus the sustaining help of community are obliquely touched on (not to mention a hint of a question of gender roles). There is a glimpse of Faith in her hospital bed, and then, back in the glowing light of the dream place, the emotionally and physically damaged young woman says to Buffy, "Scar tissue. It fades—it all fades. Want to know the deal? Human weakness. It never goes away. Even his." And Buffy asks, "Is this your mind or mine?" "Beats me," Faith says ("Graduation Day," part 2). In terms of the needs of the plot, this scene provides Buffy with a clue to better be able to defeat the demonic mayor. But in terms of theme, the scene has much larger significance. Human weakness can be both good and bad; the mayor's human weakness turns out to be his love of Faith, and in general in *Buffy*, characters' acknowledgment of their own and others' human weakness helps them keep from making Faith's mistakes, helps keep them from killing too easily. The tragic error is hubris, especially a Slayer's hubris—disregard for human weakness. The person you kill is as human as you. And the interweaving of Buffy and Faith as the dark and light is clear: "Is this your mind or mine?"

In fact, in the fourth season, the connection is made even clearer—through body instead of mind. Faith emerges from her coma and, using a device bequeathed her by the now-dead mayor, exchanges bodies with Buffy in order to elude capture ("This Year's Girl" and "Who Are You?" 4015 and 4016). She starts by privately mocking Buffy's life and friends—speaking, appropriately enough, to her Buffy face in the mirror. But as people continue to treat her as if she were Buffy—to treat her with love, affection, and support—she begins to genuinely *act* like Buffy, fulfilling Buffy's earlier comment, "different circumstances, that could be me" ("Doppelgängland"). About to leave town, she returns to free several hostages that vampires are holding in a church, saying, "I'm Buffy; I have to do this." And when one vampire asks if she's the Slayer, she answers, "The one and only"; Faith is still trying to fight alone (she knocks aside Riley, who is trying to help). When the real Buffy fights to reverse the spell, Faith, in Buffy's body, batters her own body, saying to it—herself—"You're nothing—disgusting, murderous bitch—you're nothing." She echoes the language of the lost teens of "Anne," the episode in which Buffy briefly follows—alone—the road to hell. Faith ends up leaving town (again like Buffy in "Anne") and eventually chooses to save lives (in the *Angel* series) by turning herself in to the police in order to atone. Thus, simple dualism is not allowed—virgin/whore, devil/angel, hero/villain. Buffy and Faith are both aspects of each other and complex characters in their own right. Either of them might be capable of killing; and the ones they might kill are not simply monsters. Killing is not cheap in this world.

Buffy often manages an impressive convergence of realism with heroic romance. It is a rich text, with a humane and believable mixture of attitudes. Such a mixture can be seen in the attitude of its star as well: Sarah Michelle Gellar, though she hates the term "feminism," says in the same interview that "feminism is just about not being weak" (Mendlesohn). Through the diffusion of the patriarchal succession, the denial of Little Joe love, and the expense and shame of killing, *Buffy* works against stereotypical male constructions of relationship and thus displays that strength.

POSTSCRIPT

As my thirteen-year-old son, Jeff Gess, has often pointed out, the words "who died" have always flashed by in the opening montage with *Buffy*'s theme song. We now know that it is Buffy who died. The patterns of mortality for this series again (as in the first season) include the hero—but now, rather than being briefly drowned and resuscitated, she has been dead and buried (in "The Gift"). Once more, however, note the underlying structures. In the episodes after her mother's death, Buffy has become a mother to her sister. Elisabeth Bronfen's *Over Her Dead Body* reminds us that in traditional mythic and psychological patterns, a woman, often a mother-figure, must be sacrificed to grant order to the world (27–35). Buffy's rebirth reverses that pattern. Furthermore, the key elements of Buffy's fatal conflict are all female—victim, villain, and hero—thus the series directs us away from possible implications of male superiority. The imperiled maiden is Buffy's little sister, Dawn; the villain is Glory, a female god—and in fact a parodic version of the overdressed blonde bimbo some have considered Buffy. As such, she is an appropriate foe for Buffy to defeat prior to her rebirth. With her friends, Buffy defeats Glory; but the conflict damages the world. Buffy is not conquered by any other being but voluntarily sacrifices her life to heal the wounds of the universe. And with the extratextual, Buffy's creator, Joss Whedon, delicately balances mythic power and postmodern self-consciousness: Buffy rises again on another network.

NOTES

An earlier version of this chapter was presented at the International Conference on the Fantastic in the Arts, Fort Lauderdale, FL, March 17–20, 1999.

1. Anne/Lily/Chanterelle reappears on *Angel* (season 2).

2. In the fifth season's "I Was Made to Love You" (5015), Buffy says, "I don't need a guy right now. I need me. I need to get comfortable being alone with Buffy." This mature assertion comes immediately before her mother's death, which thrusts her further into adulthood.

3. Compare Money on "The Wish" (3009) in chapter 8 of this volume.

2

"My Emotions Give Me Power"

The Containment of Girls' Anger in Buffy

Elyce Rae Helford

Anger is loaded with information and energy.

—Lorde 127

You feel it, right? How the anger gives you fire? A Slayer needs that.

—Buffy, to Kendra in "What's My Line?" part 2 (2010)[1]

FEMINIST ANGER AND U.S. MEDIA CULTURE

The case for displaying anger has been central to feminist struggles for justice and equality. Anger is a natural response to oppression, a necessary component of resistance, and an articulation of a compelling need for social change. To create change, direct confrontation is often necessary, which "cannot be conducted in the mode of nice girls, of managing the egos of and patiently teaching those who oppress [. . .]." (Lesage 426). To express feminist anger thus requires faith in aggressiveness, requires that women are "willing to offend and be offensive" (Rowe 8).

A willingness to offend—and pay the social consequences of offense—may be too high a price for many girls and women. Nonetheless, girls and women do feel and display anger. Numerous popular psychological and sociological volumes on the development of girls' emotions argue that "patriarchal norms" teach girls quickly to shun anger. For example, Lyn Mikel Brown, in *Raising Their Voices: The Politics of Girls' Anger,* posits that U.S. girls first become aware at adolescence of the "patriarchal

18

framework [. . .] and name its effects on their lives"; they learn that they must "narrow their feelings and modulate their voices [. . .] to make a smooth transition into the dominant culture" (x). In particular, Brown argues, these girls learn that strong feelings such as anger will push others away (x). Similarly, in her self-help book *The Dance of Anger: A Woman's Guide to Changing the Patterns of Intimate Relationships,* Harriet Goldhor Lerner states that taboos against women's anger make even knowing that one is angry difficult (2). She concludes that women "learn to fear our own anger, not only because it brings about the disapproval of others, but also because it signals the necessity for change" (3).

Such popular studies well articulate our culture's powerful antianger messages for women and explain the oppressiveness of such messages. Brown, for example, conducted the research for *Raising Their Voices* in order to challenge other feminist studies that conclude that contemporary white girls suffer from low self-esteem and low self-confidence because they do not actively resist dominant cultural notions of femininity (vii). She praises the "loud and indignant voices" of young women she calls "resisters," commending "the clarity of their vision, and their willingness to stay with what they knew and experienced in the face of pressure to conform" (viii). Along similar lines, Lerner does not advise against feeling or displaying anger as women. "It exists for a reason," she explains, "and always deserves our respect and attention. We all have a right to *everything* we feel—and certainly our anger is no exception" (4).

To interpret these messages beyond surface rhetoric, however, we must interrogate the assumptions that govern them. The work of Brown and Lerner, as examples of a larger discursive and cultural trend regarding girls' and women's anger, relies on a universalization of experience and an essentialism that draws conclusions (however "positive" and well intentioned) from within a preestablished framework of who and what girls and women are. To study girls' resistance, Brown begins with generalized white, middle-class assumptions about girls. She establishes unified standards and finds that some girls may sometimes resist them. However, if we begin with the assumption that standards for girls always already vary widely on the basis of class, race, ethnicity, region, religion, nationality, ability, and other determinants of identity and socialization, we see that both norms and resistance exist in more complex relations than any generalizations can account for. Similarly, Lerner gives advice based on a presumption that all women who pick up her book share similar life experiences. Thus, she can create from all of angry womankind two categories—the "nice lady" and the "bitch" (5)—and then reduce even this dualism, making anger into a solitary coping strategy: to "protect others, to blur our clarity of self and to ensure that change does not occur" (5). While she does not blame "angry women" for the oppressions that bind them, neither does she complicate an understanding of oppression by class, race, or other elements of women's identities. Therefore, she cannot conclude that anger serves important political ends and varies in form and usage depending on diverse factors of cultural identity.

Oversimplification in studies of girls' and women's anger means that certain articulations of anger and the benefits of anger may be ignored. If one begins with the presumption that a generic classification called "woman" is discouraged from displaying a generic classification of "anger," one may see resistance where there is socially sanctioned expression, or one may fail to see resistance where it exists. Taking issues such as race and class into consideration makes this problem plain. In the first documented research on anger and African American women, for example, Dr. Sandra Thomas concludes that whereas Caucasian women receive messages in youth that anger is "unfeminine and unladylike," African American women learn that anger "confers power and [can] be deliberately used to gain or maintain control of situations" (qtd. in Clark). While the category of "Caucasian women" still requires additional deconstruction, Thomas's study does begin to suggest the difficulties of making any pronouncements at all about "women" or "women's anger."

Popular media follow this tendency toward oversimplification and essentialism with even less attention to the dangers of doing so. Because prime-time television is based on economic imperatives that protect the status quo, it generally situates narratives within a fictional world normalized by white, middle-class standards. Thus, a series such as *Buffy the Vampire Slayer* emphasizes the problematic assumptions about who girls and women are and can be that I have just critiqued. Careful exploration of the assumptions and conclusions *Buffy* draws about girls' anger, in particular, must therefore begin with emphasis on the limited race and class differences the series does permit and the conclusions the series seems to draw about such differences.

On prime-time television, middle-class white female characters may be ostracized for expressing their anger, while white male characters may regularly be encouraged to vent their aggressive emotions. Representations of working-class white women, by contrast, may experience relatively greater freedom in expressing anger because their class status relegates them to limited spheres of power and influence; hence, their anger may not even be recognized socially. Of course, such characters generally do not evince economic difference from their middle-class sisters. Prime-time television rarely features central female characters whose economic status means they cannot wear Hollywood-style clothing and makeup, for example. These characters may reject certain stereotypical middle-class values (and even such values are often media created), but they normally have food on the table and highly coifed hair. Nonetheless, even within this limited portrayal of difference, what may appear to be freedom is also a means of control. In the world outside of television, expression of anger may be used as a reason to keep working-class women culturally disenfranchised; in television, this may be translated into the reduction of working-class women to objects of ridicule in sitcoms or objects of derision in drama.

From women and men of color, regardless of social class, the expression of anger is threatening. Anger expressed by those who are racially marginalized often appears on television as a threat to socially approved standards of appropriate conduct. "Civilized" society, which has evolved directly from an era of vast Western colonization, prizes decorum, prudence, and constrained public bodily comportment. So, while anger may tend to mark middle-class white women as "unladylike," it marks those identified as racially Other as asocial and "uncitizenlike." The result is that anger becomes a means through which television's characters of color may be disempowered, disregarded, or disposed of.

In the following pages, I examine this complex politics of representation through a study of the ways in which displays of girls' anger are rewarded, contained, and punished on *Buffy*. Because they offer some opportunity to investigate differences of class and race, I focus, in particular, on the three Slayer characters introduced in the present day of the series: Buffy, Kendra, and Faith.[2] I show how the display of anger in these three female characters determines their relative levels of empowerment within the cultural setting of the series. I argue that Buffy, the white, middle-class protagonist, carefully controls, redirects, and uses humor to diffuse her anger in order to maintain heroic power while upholding a "ladylike" identity. Kendra, the second Slayer, rarely expresses anger, and never through the humor deemed essential for girls by the series. With her dark skin and Jamaican accent, she exemplifies the ways in which the series denies people of color access to insider status or heroic power. Moreover, Kendra provides an essential lesson on how *not* to look, think, or act on *Buffy* because she faces the ultimate form of disempowerment: she is killed during her third appearance. The third Slayer, Faith, is a white girl depicted as lower in social class than Buffy. She is rebellious, sexual, and expresses her anger openly, often with relish. If Faith cannot ultimately achieve model heroism, she does attain antihero and then villain status. She thus challenges certain limits in representations of women's power. Nevertheless, Faith is ultimately condemned in the text to isolation and self-loathing, for what the series makes plain is excessive rage. By studying representations of anger in the three Slayers, I work to provide some tentative answers to questions surrounding girls' anger and issues of gender, race, and class in contemporary U.S. culture.[3]

BUFFY: CONTROLLING ANGER

I would like to suggest that those structures for expressing women's anger do exist—in the genres of laughter [. . .].

—Kathleen Rowe 8

A cranky Slayer is a careless Slayer.

—Buffy in "Never Kill a Boy on the First Date" (1005)

As the series's heroic protagonist, Buffy Summers provides *Buffy*'s primary perspectives on gender, race, class, and anger. Through Buffy we see what a Slayer is and should be, and because being a Slayer entails heroic behavior, through Buffy we see what it means to handle anger "properly" as a girl. Following the trend in research on girls' anger and popular celebrations of so-called girl power, *Buffy* rejects the message that anger is entirely inappropriate for nice, middle-class white girls. Of course, not just any display of anger will do. Over the course of the program's first four seasons, we learn that "proper" display means, above all, to enact anger in a contained manner through the employment of wit and humor and through an appearance of calm despite a necessary lack of control over life.

To help viewers identify with Buffy, *Buffy* works carefully and subtly to create standards of normalcy that seem to champion "difference." *Buffy* makes its strongest appeal to those who see themselves as never having been able to achieve popularity in high school. Keying in to a white, middle-class interpretation of adolescent angst, the series defines Buffy and her pals as "outsiders." Buffy must display strength and aggressiveness that leave most high school boys cold; Willow is the shy computer "geek"; and Xander is the nerd. Cordelia, at one time a highly popular snob, must yield her reputation with the "in crowd" when she falls for Xander. To be Buffy or to hang out with Buffy, one must accept the status of social outcast in the high school world of the first three seasons of the series.

Yet this form of "difference" actually masks a far more significant structure of marginalization. Buffy and her friends may be alienated from the most popular kids in school; however, their difference is actually the normalcy through which the series draws viewer identification. To produce its sympathetic "outsiders," *Buffy* neglects significant social differences, such as race and class. The series thus draws distinctions between heroic characters whose marginal position makes them heroes and disposable villains (vampires, demons, etc.) whose social difference justifies their violent expulsion from the show—the ultimate form of marginalization. *Buffy* denies the white, middle-class privilege of its heroes even though they are, in fact, the center around which various degrees of deviation in the series get measured (Ono 172). True Otherness on *Buffy* is about excessiveness. Relationship to white middle-class appearance and behavioral norms, not to popularity or supernatural powers, is what tells a hero from a wanna-be on *Buffy* and generally determines which villains will live and which will die.

Given this framework, Buffy perfectly fits the program's self-fashioned standards of normalcy. There is no danger of emotional excessiveness from Buffy, unless it is to portray normative (hetero)romantic anguish or to demonstrate the "normal" tendency to err in judgment from time to time as a teen. As far as anger is concerned, Buffy feels it, but her manner of display is almost always redirection, primarily in the form of sarcasm or biting humor.[4] And, as the protagonist, Buffy's wit is always paramount. For example, in the third-season episode "Becoming," she confronts the demon Whistler, who teases her with the possibility that he has information she needs. Buffy is frustrated and angry at his game playing, but she does not yell at him or attack him. Instead, she redirects her anger through a harsh sense of humor: "If you have information worth hearing then I am grateful for it. If you want to crack jokes then I will pull out your rib cage and wear it as a hat" ("Becoming," part 2, 2022). Her wit is bleak and graphic; it outdoes Whistler and allows Buffy to vent a very "unladylike" fury without losing her cool. Choosing to taunt or deride others in this manner rather than straightforwardly expressing anger means viewers witness a combination of anger, humor, and violence that simultaneously addresses and trivializes girls' anger. Trivialization occurs for two reasons. First, such mockery denies the importance of direct, assertive expressions of anger. Second, Buffy models behavior that girls and women in the world outside *Buffy* cannot emulate. Mocking threats to disembowel others simply do not earn respect outside the site of fantasy television.

That the series champions redirection in particular is made plain in numerous episodes throughout the first four seasons of *Buffy*, which often follow a similar structure. Many episodes begin with Buffy using humor to mask anger while she displays physical aggression that is rarely portrayed as problematic or out of control. Typical is the teaser from the first-season episode "Never Kill a Boy on the First Date," in which Buffy is patrolling in Sunnydale Cemetery and must kill a newly awakened vampire as it emerges from the grave. After a few well-placed kicks, Buffy reaches out to stake the vampire, quipping, "We haven't been properly introduced. I'm Buffy and you're . . . history." Humor lightens the violence of this and many other similar scenes in *Buffy*.

Given the premise of the series, aggression and violence are central and unavoidable. Buffy is the Slayer; she must kill. As long as she does not seem to enjoy committing acts of physical violence overmuch, she is not condemned within the framework of the series. Despite her emotional control, however, midway or later in the typical episode Buffy experiences a crisis that she cannot cope with through humor or calm deployment of physical power. She becomes momentarily excessive in her emotional response, snapping at a friend, harshly backtalking her well-meaning mentor Giles, or lashing out at an innocent bystander. For example, in "What's My Line?" part 1 (2009), Buffy and friends must participate in Sunnydale High's Career Week. Because she is destined to be the Slayer, Buffy is alienated by the experience. Willow pushes the issue, asking if she is not just a bit curious about what she might have been if she were not the Slayer. Buffy snaps, "Do the words 'sealed in fate' ring any bells for you, Will? Why go there?" Willow's hurt look encourages Xander to come to her defense. As is the norm for all sympathetic characters on *Buffy,* Xander expresses his frustration through wit. He quips, "You know, with that kind of attitude, you could have had a bright future as an employee of the DMV [Department of Motor Vehicles]." Buffy is quick to regain control of her emotions and turn from an inappropriate display of anger to a self-effacing sense of humor. Looking down, she tells Willow and Xander, "I'm sorry. It's just—unless hell freezes over and every vamp in Sunnydale puts in for early retirement, I'd say my future is pretty much a nonissue." Concluding her apology with her trademark pout clarifies that if Buffy is justified in her resentment of her lack of control over her life, self-pity will get her more sympathy than anger. There is generally only one scene, at most, per episode in which Buffy vents frustration in this manner. By the typical episode's climax, viewers learn the proper lesson concerning girls' displays of anger as Buffy returns to use of humor and accepts her fate as the Slayer.

It is important to acknowledge that Buffy is fully justified in feeling anger about the burdens that being a Slayer puts on her personal life, especially when she is rejected for "unfeminine" behavior or faces restrictions that keep her chained to a lifestyle over which she has little choice. Read metaphorically, Buffy stands in for various groups of girls who experience justified feminist anger at having their lives directed by circumstances or individuals beyond their control. From girls who face unpopularity because of their appearance (from acne to skin color to body size) to girls who reject heteronormativity to girls who must work from an early age and find there is no time for studying *or* socializing to girls with disabilities who lose dating opportunities because they seem either too helpless or too unfeminine in their independence, there is ample reason for diverse girls' frustration and anger at the injustices of living within a culture that objectifies women and encourages passivity and obedience to authority and social norms. Thus, as the heroine, Buffy's response to these injustices is instructive. Through her rates of success with various reactions and coping strategies, *Buffy* provides a lesson in how, when, and why to use or not use anger in life as a teen girl.

While it might be expected that Buffy feels anger when she kills villains, this is rarely the case. However, if girls' anger is most important as a catalyst for social change, anger at individual vampires or even rage at the Hellmouth that exists in Sunnydale is relatively pointless. The entire reason for a Slayer's coming into being is that evil can never be completely vanquished. So Buffy's anger is most often directed at the ways in which being a Slayer impacts her personal life. Numerous times Buffy expresses her desire for a "normal" life. Often, because he is an authority figure and also a confidant, Buffy vents her frustration at Giles. In "Never Kill a Boy on the First Date," Buffy wants to go out as "just a girl" with Owen, a popular high school classmate. Giles, however, insists that she spend the evening in the cemetery, waiting for a prophecy to manifest itself in the form of a Slayer-killing vampire. He attempts to express sympathy and lighten the mood as they sit together in the empty cemetery, stating, "Well, you know what they say: 90 percent of the vampire slaying game is waiting." Buffy responds, "You couldn't have told me that 90 percent ago?" Buffy *is* angry. She is losing her opportunity to pursue a romantic relationship with a boy she likes; she is bored sitting in the cemetery with Giles and no enemies in sight; she resents that being a Slayer means she cannot do what she wants to do.

In another scene from the same episode, Giles continues his attempt to dissuade Buffy from dating "normal" men, reminding her that she could put others at risk if her identity as the Slayer were to become known. Buffy responds, "Well, in that case, I won't wear my button that says, 'I'm a Slayer. Ask me how.'" Buffy here expresses anger at Giles's condescension and his attempt to control her behavior. However, she does not simply confront his paternalism or tell him she knows the risks and must make her own decisions; instead, she uses a witty joke to get her point across. Giles, for his part, does not and need not respond. He has not been confronted in a manner that requires change in his relationship to Buffy. Buffy appears as the bratty if witty ingrate, and Giles can and does dismiss her concerns. This strategy does not mean that Buffy is not angry, of course, or that she does not seek to change her situation. However, her indirectness means that other characters and viewers who could register her anger as valid and worthy of respect may not.

Such moments in *Buffy* exemplify well Buffy's tendency to shy away from direct expressions of anger. In political terms, however, these interactions mean more. Buffy's indirectness well exemplifies popular sentiment that white, middle-class girls tend to avoid directness in the face of others' judgment or rejection. Buffy rarely acts assertively with authority figures or boys she wants to date if indirectness will suffice, and the series allows her to succeed through indirection: Buffy does get boyfriends and does manage, over time, to have a reasonable social life while fulfilling her responsibilities as Slayer.

Now and then, Buffy does express her anger directly. In another scene from "Never Kill a Boy on the First Date," we see such an exceptional moment. Buffy sits on a table in the library while Giles demands that she obey him as her Watcher; he insists that she forgo her date with Owen. She matches his aggressive stance and asks him how he thinks he is going to force her to do anything. He immediately retreats to a more rational, assertive stance, stating that he will use mature reasoning to persuade her rather than authoritarian demands (that he cannot back up with physical force). Although she enacts the role of rebellious teen daring a father figure to lose his cool, she does challenge Giles directly and effectively. Such confrontation is rarely seen from Buffy because it risks her status as sympathetic protagonist. In other words, though Buffy need not always be the "lady" of the polar opposites Harriet Goldhor Lerner outlines in *The Dance of Anger,* she must also not become the "bitch."

At the end of "Never Kill a Boy on the First Date," Buffy returns to her normative humorous-angry behavior as the Slayer. When finally on her date with Owen, she ends up in a battle with a vampire. Owen tries to defend her, but he is knocked out by the vampire, and Buffy fears he may be dead. Without "excessive" emotion, she twice remarks, "You killed my date," as she beats the vampire. Her anger at never being able to have a "normal" date empowers her in her fight with the vampire, and her use of humor reassures viewers that this anger is contained. She is not a "cranky" Slayer or a hostile freak, but neither is she an assertive adult, directly expressing her anger to create empowering change in her life. She is once again *Buffy*'s normal, status quo heroine.

KENDRA: DENOUNCING ANGER

[I want to speak] to my sisters of Color who like me still tremble their rage under harness, or who sometimes question the expression of our rage as useless and disruptive [. . .].

—Lorde 127

Emotions are weakness, Buffy. You shouldn't entertain them.

—Kendra in "What's My Line?" part 2 (2010)

When Buffy is drowned in first-season finale "Prophecy Girl," she is briefly declared dead; her death brings another Slayer into being. Kendra is a teen with a Jamaican accent whose parents heeded a "calling" when she was an infant and turned her over to a Watcher who trained her in preparation for the role of Slayer, should it one day become necessary. Kendra provides a foil to Buffy, illustrating in heightened form the insider/outsider dichotomy based on race and culture that is central to the series. Kendra has faced an isolated, intensely serious life from an early age. She is forbidden from attending school, so she has never socialized or made friends. She has never known her parents, apart from seeing pictures of them. She may not even speak to boys. Such aspects of her life clearly render Buffy a privileged, well-socialized girl; they make Buffy's complaints about not being permitted to lead a normal life trivial.

However, the series is structured around the maintenance of Buffy's "difference." Therefore, during the two-part episode "What's My Line?" in which Kendra's character is developed, emphasis is placed on "choices" Kendra makes, such as strict obedience to her Watcher and devoted studiousness. Buffy calls her "She-Giles" and repeatedly implies that she is a nerdy teacher's pet. Thus, despite an upbringing and lifestyle that leave her far more truly an outsider than Buffy and pals, she is rendered an extreme insider.

That Kendra has a Jamaican accent means she also shares with Giles the status of foreigner. However, unlike Giles, Kendra is not white. Though we are never told exactly where Kendra comes from, when she describes the reason she never knew her parents, she makes reference to the fact that "the calling is taken [seriously] by my people." The term "people" suggests a tribal affiliation that is entirely alien to Californian Buffy and friends, even to postcolonial British Giles. Moreover, Kendra's dark skin, thick accent, sexy clothing, elaborate jewelry, and heavy makeup (especially lipstick accenting her full lips) actively signify her Otherness. Nonetheless, the series enables Buffy to retain her outsider status when we learn that there is an official Slayer's Handbook that Kendra has memorized and that Giles knows about but has decided not to share with the anti-intellectual Buffy.

To further marginalize Kendra while maintaining Buffy's rebellious outsider identity, Buffy ridicules Kendra in several scenes. Buffy makes fun of Kendra's ignorance of U.S. slang, invoking anti-immigrant racism. When Buffy tells Kendra she must not go "wiggy," Kendra does not understand. Buffy explains, "You know, no kicko, no fighto," deriding Kendra's language skills. Later, Buffy experiences frustration in trying to explain to Kendra that the vampire Angel is her "friend." Buffy impatiently tries "people you hang with?" then "amigo?" implying in a racist manner that Kendra's lack of understanding is about language skills rather than a valid query of Buffy's priorities as a Slayer. Buffy even goes further, rendering Kendra less than human when, during the scene in which she and Giles are laughing together, Buffy snaps, just out of earshot, "Down, girl," as though she is talking to a dog. Finally, Buffy calls Kendra "the Pink Ranger," a reference to the children's show *Mighty Morphin' Power Rangers,* rendering her an overeager and cartoonish superhero type, less "real" than Buffy.

Kendra's "unrealness" has additional implications: the scripting brands Kendra a more fictional character than Buffy. In the climactic fight scene, one of the villains slashes Kendra's shirtsleeve with a knife. "That's me favorite shirt!" Kendra shouts, then, "That's me only shirt." A clever reference to pulp superheroes who seem to own only one costume, this comment means more in the context of *Buffy*. Kendra is sent to Sunnydale by her Watcher; she arrives by sneaking aboard a cargo plane. That she would come with no provisions whatsoever, not even a change of clothes, seems suspicious. Also problematic is the paradox of Kendra's assertions that she is not permitted to talk to boys and never dates, combined with her glamorous and sexy appearance. In many ways, Kendra seems established to challenge racist and sexist cultural myths of the fiery, exotic islander. Instead, her construction as a character merely establishes the validity of such myths by invoking them through opposition. Such problems in her characterization can make us ask whether Kendra is truly a character in her own right or simply a one-dimensional plot device to further the development of Buffy, the "real" hero.

In order to reify Buffy's heroic status, much of Kendra's brief appearance in the series is devoted to Buffy's distinguishing herself as superior to this second(ary) Slayer. Differences between the two on the subject of anger are central to Buffy's efforts. In one scene, Kendra remarks that Buffy's life is very different from hers. Buffy, being competitive and condescending, replies, "You mean the part where I occasionally have one?" Again, Buffy does not yield her outsider status; she only "occasionally" has a life outside of Slayer work. However, Kendra is clearly alien to Buffy's worldview. Maintaining a polite, respectful stance, Kendra says, "Please—I don't feel sorry for myself. Why should you?" Turning from scorn to pity, Buffy tells Kendra her life sounds "very lonely." Kendra tells Buffy to shun emotions as a form of weakness, and the two begin a discussion about the issue:

> *Buffy:* Kendra, my emotions give me power. They're total assets.
> *Kendra:* Maybe, for you. But I prefer to keep an even mind.
> *Buffy:* I guess that explains it.
> *Kendra:* Explains what?
> *Buffy:* Oh, well, when we were fighting. You're amazing. Your technique, it's flawless; it's better than mine.
> *Kendra:* I know.
> *Buffy:* Still—I would have kicked your butt in the end. And you know why? No imagination.
> *Kendra:* Really? You think so?

The two continue their discussion, Buffy opining that Kendra has "potential" but lacks the real drive to win. Kendra becomes furious:

Kendra: Potential? I could wipe the floor with you right now.
Buffy [smiling]: That would be anger you're feeling.
Kendra: What?
Buffy: You feel it, right? How the anger gives you fire? A Slayer needs that.

Xander intrudes to break up the conversation, but Buffy has taught her lesson. Despite the fact that Kendra has greater dedication to her role as Slayer, that she is better educated in slaying than Buffy, that she fights vampires as effectively as Buffy, and that she endeavors not to show Buffy the disrespect Buffy shows her, Buffy is able to demonstrate her superiority.

Given Buffy's rudeness, condescension, competitiveness, and the ethnocentrism that drives these traits, it is not surprising that Kendra does display anger at her once or twice. Nonetheless, it is not in *Buffy*-sanctioned form. For example, when Buffy brattily remarks, "I don't take orders. I do things my way," Kendra replies, "No wonder you died." We may smile at this quip because it is so cutting and so apt: Buffy's rashness did cost her own life, at least momentarily. However, Kendra does not display awareness of this comment as wit. Throughout much of "What's My Line?" Kendra maintains a flat affect. She rarely smiles, she never rebels against her Slayer destiny, and, as she tells Buffy, she finds anger a weakness. Thus, when Buffy makes plain that saving her vampire boyfriend Angel is even more important to her than stopping the evil vampire Drusilla, Kendra calls her a fool and again wishes her dead, saying, "Good riddance, then." By the second jibe, not only Kendra but also viewers are unlikely to find humor in this condemnation. And such direct display of anger dooms Kendra. It is not Buffy who dies at a vampire's hands but Kendra. From this outcome, we learn that a girl should not be overconfident or disrespectful but that she is in far more danger if she is a girl of color with too much hostility and too little sense of humor.

Kendra's lack of warmth also condemns her. Buffy may fight for independence from others' rules and regulations, but she deeply values her emotional connection to her friends, her mother, and Giles. Thus, Buffy is independent while Kendra is isolated. We see this distinction and another lesson in proper behavior for girls when Kendra leaves town at the end of "What's My Line?" part 2. As the Slayers part, they acknowledge that they are both "freaks" and not alone anymore, yet Kendra will not hug Buffy. "I don't hug," Kendra states. "Right—no—good—hate hugs," Buffy replies, smiling. We know that this is again condescension and that Kendra is wrong not to embrace her sister Slayer. Kendra rejects Buffy's way of being, and this is lethal to would-be heroes on *Buffy*.

Ultimately, Kendra is proved to be a failed, unheroic Slayer in her short stint on the series. Echoing the fate of the demons and vampires who metaphorically represent true Otherness in the series,[5] Kendra is killed, mercilessly and quickly, and is as quickly forgotten by the other characters as are the legion of nameless vampire thugs that Buffy dispatches every week. Kendra's sole legacy to Buffy seems to be the pet name "Mr. Pointy" for her slaying stake. Buffy at first ridicules this small display of sentiment by Kendra, then she adopts it after Kendra's death. When she calls her stake "Mr. Pointy" in front of others, Buffy experiences a bit of the ridicule she heaped on Kendra. We may interpret this as residual guilt or another example of Buffy's efforts at self-marginalization. In either case, it neither brings Kendra back to life nor illustrates any significant impact of Kendra's existence on the lives of others. In life and death, Kendra merely encapsulates what can never be deemed heroic on *Buffy*.

FAITH: RELISHING ANGER

Women's anger is most commonly depicted through displacement onto images of female insanity or perversity [. . .].

—Lesage 422

Police Officer: This Faith chick is definitely dangerous.
Faith [in Buffy's body]: She truly is.

—"Who Are You?" (4016)

Faith, the third Slayer, achieves some of what a hero should be according to *Buffy*. Unlike Kendra but like Buffy, Faith is white, native to the United States, and into trendy slang, resistance to authority, and boys. Moreover, Faith is far more thoroughly developed as a character over the course of a season and more. That Faith will turn out to be a villain, however, is just as guaranteed as that she can survive more than two and a half episodes. Though Kendra and Faith share a tendency toward emotional distance, Kendra does so to uphold extreme standards of Slayer perfection learned in isolation from loved ones, while Faith reacts, at least in part, to the alienation of a dysfunctional family upbringing. Similarly, though Slayers 2 and 3 both wear heavy makeup and sexy attire, Kendra's appearance counters her persona, while Faith uses her look to attract and have frequent, casual sex with men. Most generally, it seems that because Faith is more like Buffy on the surface (primarily by virtue of race and nationality), *Buffy* is able to maintain and develop her character more fully and compellingly.

One primary method through which Faith and Buffy are distinguished is through a television version of social class. Buffy may be a child of divorce, but she lives quite comfortably with her mother in a nice home with a closet full of clothes and always enough money to pay the bills and for any little extras she might need. Faith, by contrast, escapes what she describes in the episode "Faith, Hope, and Trick" as a highly dysfunctional home and the control of her first Watcher to live in a run-down motel room in Sunnydale. Because she is an effective con artist and is willing to steal, she is never without essentials. However, because she never repents her thievery, never attends school or displays other evidence of seeking education, and never dresses in the kind of attire Buffy wears as part of "proper" Sunnydale teen girlhood, the series casts her as lower in class than Buffy and her friends.

At first, Buffy is drawn to Faith's rebelliousness. Unlike her distant relationship with Kendra, Faith and Buffy become friends. Faith even persuades Buffy to steal. However, soon after, Faith accidentally kills a human being, and their friendship degenerates. Rather than acknowledge her wrongdoing, which would be accepting middle-class standards of propriety, Faith pretends to feel nothing and begins to spiral out of control. While secretly exhibiting distress and guilt, Faith tells Buffy that they are better than the rest of humanity and can do whatever they want without penalty or remorse ("Consequences," 3015). But she has gone too far: once a playmate who helped Buffy to take risks and challenge boundaries, Faith becomes a renegade whose example now easily pushes Buffy back to middle-class normalcy.

Intense guilt and self-loathing that she cloaks as anger begin to dominate Faith's personality after she and Buffy grow apart. Faith first becomes a double agent, working on behalf of demonic forces controlled by Sunnydale's mayor; then, when discovered, she becomes the mayor's protégée. Buffy retains hope that Faith is redeemable, but this changes when Faith attempts to seduce and join forces with Angel, whom she wrongly thinks she has led to his evil Angelus state. Faith unleashes venomous anger at Buffy, attacking her for her many social advantages and threatening to torture her. Though Buffy escapes and Faith flees, Faith's rapidly escalating rage and sadistic behavior finally drive Buffy to stab her on their next encounter, nearly killing her. Faith ends the season in a coma from which she is assumed never to be able to recover.

Yet Faith does recover, rejoining the series in season 4, more full of hostility and vengeance than ever. Understandable frustration at the injustice of life that gives a loving mother, economic privilege, and friends to Buffy but not to her becomes an excessive rage against everyone and everything for Faith. Emerging from her coma, Faith is bent on revenge. To attain this, in the episode "This Year's Girl" (4015), Faith finds the magical means and opportunity to swap bodies with Buffy. The goal of taking over Buffy's privileged life begins the season's emphasis on Faith's self-loathing. Faith's anger shifts from externalized rage with underlying self-doubt to vicious and unrelenting self-hatred.

That Faith envies Buffy is made plain in the later episodes of season 3; however, the fourth-season episode "Who Are You?" drives this message home even more unambiguously. In Buffy's body, Faith must convince others—from Buffy's mother, Joyce, to Giles, Willow, Xander, and Spike—that she is indeed Buffy. Through her impersonation, we see Faith's resentments of Buffy's privileged life. She smiles demurely, pouts, mimics excessive politeness and selflessness, uses expressions such as "I'm a busy little beaver" to ridicule Buffy's good-girl work ethic, and mocks Buffy's morals with the phrase "You can't do that because it's wrong."

An encounter with Spike, who has been implanted with a chip that disables him from committing acts of violence against human beings, provides an opportunity for Faith to be even more direct, to unleash her incredible anger. In the dimly lit atmosphere of the barlike teen hangout The Bronze, she asks Spike if he knows why he hates her (Buffy) so much, then answers the question for him:

> 'Cause I'm a stuck-up, tight ass with no sense of fun. 'Cause I can do anything I want and instead I choose to pout and whine and feel the burden of Slayerness. I mean, I could be rich, I could be famous, I could have anything, even you, Spike: I could ride you at a gallop until your legs buckled and your eyes rolled up. [. . .] And you know why I don't? Because it's "wrong" [she laughs, loudly].

Next, Faith (as Buffy) goes to visit Riley, Buffy's new college boyfriend. First, she explains to Riley why he never would have been fond of Faith, continuing to expel her anger: "No, you wouldn't have liked Faith. She's not proper and joyless like a girl should be. She has a tendency to give in to her animal instincts." With this, Faith begins to seduce Riley. As with Angel, Faith's attempts to possess Buffy's lovers make obvious her desire to have Buffy's life, to be Buffy. However, she cannot. Catlike, she crawls onto Riley's bed, poses for him, and asks, "What nasty little desire have you been itching to try out? Am I a bad girl? Do you want to hurt me?" This statement significantly transforms our view of Faith: she has shifted her discourse from Buffy-hating to self-hating. In the guise of submissive language and the form of a question, she names herself: the "bad girl" who deserves to be "hurt."

Riley, however, rejects this behavior and turns s/m play into gentle lovemaking. This deeply unsettles Faith. Worse yet, Riley says "I love you" afterward. Faith pushes him away, then asks, "Who are you? What do you want from [. . .] her?" When Riley, looking confused, asks, "Should I not have . . . ?" Faith announces, "This is meaningless." Riley notes that she is shaking and asks, "What happened?," to which Faith flatly replies, "Nothing. [. . .] *Nothing*." But Faith has been affected.

In the climactic scene of the episode, Faith goes to kill vampires who have taken over a church and captured hostages. Faith is still a Vampire Slayer, but now she is Buffy the Vampire Slayer. She tells the vampires, "You're not going to kill anyone [. . .] because it's wrong," and identifies herself as the "one and only" Slayer. Yet, soon after, Buffy (in Faith's body) shows up to confront her nemesis. The two fight, and Faith becomes wild, thrashing out, until it is obvious she is beating herself. Faith pins Buffy down, but Buffy remarks, "You can't win this." From within Buffy's body, Faith bludgeons her own body beneath her, yelling, "You think I'm afraid of you? [. . .] You disgusting, murderous bitch! You're nothing!" With this, the two are flung back into their own bodies, and Faith quickly rises and runs away. As the episode ends, Riley remarks, "She's had her fun," to which Buffy knowingly replies, "Yeah [. . .] fun." Our final image is of Faith, riding in a cattle car, expressionless. Clearly, Faith is no longer having fun; she has made plain to herself, to Buffy, and to viewers that she hates herself far more than she hates Buffy. Despite what may seem an "uptight" and rigid life for Buffy, it is Faith who is truly joyless.

When we next see Faith, it is on a first-season episode of the spin-off series *Angel*. Here the character goes furthest in denouncing her own actions and attitudes and in revealing that a girl must do penance for excessive rage. Faith appears to seek out Angel in order to reap vengeance on someone else she feels did her wrong. She seems to want to kill Angel, largely for preferring Buffy to her; however, when the climactic fight scene happens, she cannot. Angel will not fight her. When confronted with Angel's sympathy (for in his past he too has been "disgusting" and "murderous," though he cannot be a "bitch"), Faith cannot even muster anger. She flails at Angel's chest, begging him to kill her, sobbing, "I'm bad, I'm bad," over and over.

It is significant that Angel can identify with Faith and that he simultaneously achieves a level of forgiveness (by others and of himself) that Faith cannot. As Faith reaches out to Angel, we see how central gender is to determining heroic status in the world of *Buffy* and *Angel*. Angel has committed far more and far greater atrocities than Faith in his hundreds of years on earth; yet, white men's anger can apparently be far more easily forgiven than white women's: Angel is a hero starring in his own series, while Faith ends up mentally ill and imprisoned. In the next episode of *Angel*, Faith decides to turn herself in to police custody for her crimes. She is quiet, penitent, desexualized, solemn. Yet, she tells Angel, she feels good about doing the "right" thing. She is no longer the girl who loved to ridicule Buffy's and white middle-class America's definitions of right and wrong. And she teaches, blatantly, that girls' anger, when allowed free reign, is not only harmful to others but entirely self-destructive.

CONCLUSION

While Faith inhabits Buffy's body in "Who Are You?" Buffy faces the treatment reserved for the renegade Faith. The Watchers' Council sends out a group of hired thugs to capture Faith. Not knowing Buffy is inside Faith's body, they dehumanize and hurl abuse at her, concluding, "You're trash. We should have killed you while you were asleep." Buffy is shocked at the depth of their abuse; she protests that she is not Faith, but they reply, "Doesn't make you any less crazy": Buffy had earlier rejected the Watchers' Council. Nonetheless, even in this crisis, Buffy retains her heroic sense of wit to defeat them. As she works to free herself and make her escape, she quips, "I don't have time for bondage fun."

According to *Buffy,* Faith's behavior does indeed mean she is "[white] trash," and perversity such as s/m sexuality is the kind of "fun" Buffy neither needs nor enjoys. Kendra, too, renounces the kind of perverse excess of Faith; however, Kendra does not substitute another kind of proper "fun" to enable her to achieve empowered heroism on the series or even to survive. We learn from comparing Buffy, Faith, and Kendra that while Faith is condemned by those around her and herself, her whiteness and ability to espouse white middle-class American values (especially as she agrees to serve prison time for her violent crimes) means there truly is always hope for Faith. Though it seems likely that Faith will again go "bad," her superficial similarities to Buffy in race and nationality allow her ongoing potential for recuperation.

The example of Faith illustrates that media versions of class difference can determine whether one is a hero or a villain, while the example of Kendra reveals that the "wrong" race can stop a woman from attaining any empowerment. Unless Kendra returns as one of the legion of evil undead (to which most of *Buffy*'s literal and metaphoric people of color belong), we will not see her return to claim power, even villainy. Instead, *Buffy* seems likely to continue as it has for its first four seasons, championing a female version of heroism that can be achieved only by indirection and humor from the mouth of a nice middle-class white girl.

NOTES

1. Some quotations from seasons 1 and 2 that appear in this chapter are taken from Golden and Holder's *Buffy the Vampire Slayer: The Watcher's Guide.*

2. As with all studies of ongoing television series, this examination must stop at an arbitrary point in its development. I study the three Slayers as portrayed in *Buffy*'s first four seasons and in two first-season episodes of the spin-off *Angel.*

3. I am grateful to Kent A. Ono for his contributions to this chapter. My discussion of Kendra, in particular, has been significantly influenced and strengthened by his analysis of the character in "To Be a Vampire on *Buffy the Vampire Slayer.*"

4. Editors' note: See also chapter 6 on Buffy's use of humor as weapon.

5. For development of this argument, see Ono.

3

"I'm Buffy and You're . . . History"
The Postmodern Politics of Buffy

Patricia Pender

In Buffy's world, any encounter with the unknown, be it person or demon, initially forces us to evaluate it according to simple criteria: is it friend, or is it foe? The starkly polarized moral universe of vampire slaying provides an uncanny, and unlikely, double for political debates that circulate in contemporary cultural studies. Feminist critiques of popular culture frequently mobilize a strategy similar to Buffy's slaying technique when they question if any given text is part of the solution, or part of the problem: is *Buffy the Vampire Slayer* a groundbreaking, empowering, and transgressive text, or is its political potential compromised, commodity driven, and contained? Put simply, is *Buffy* good or bad? In this chapter I interrogate the polarized positions in this debate by examining the ambivalent gender dynamics of *Buffy*. Paying particular attention to representations of seriousness and silliness, to the avowedly political and the shamelessly postmodern, I suggest that *Buffy* is a television series that delights in deliberately and self-consciously baffling the binary; the juxtaposition of mundane reality and surreal fantasy in the lives of the Slayer and her friends evokes a world in which the sententious morality of black-and-white distinctions is itself demonized as an unnatural threat from an ancient past.

> *Pike [Buffy's movie boyfriend]:* Buffy, you're not like other girls.
> *Buffy:* Yes, I am.

This quote, from the 1992 film version of *Buffy the Vampire Slayer,* predates the television series by five years, yet it highlights one of the central

thematics of both texts, namely, the ambivalent position Buffy occupies between authentic adolescent and supernatural Slayer. Not surprisingly, assessment of the transgressive political potential of *Buffy* frequently involves
examining the heroine's relationship to contemporary cultural stereotypes.
At issue in this debate is the extent of Buffy's resemblance to and difference
from "regular" teenage girls and her resulting efficacy as an empowering
feminist role model. On the one hand, Buffy is celebrated, in the words of
Alyssa Katz, as "a supremely confident kicker of evil butt" (35). On the
other hand, she might justifiably be accused of subscribing to, and therefore
reinscribing, commercial and patriarchal standards of feminine beauty: she
is young, blond, slim, and vigilantly fashion conscious. In what follows I examine the rhetorics of transgression and containment that riddle both the
academic and the popular media response to *Buffy*. In doing so I hope to illuminate the ways in which the unspoken assumptions that underwrite
much of this criticism work inadvertently to circumscribe—to contain, in
effect—the political and transgressive potential of the series.

   If one of the principle motivations of popular cultural studies is to decode
the political subtext of any given work, then of central concern for students
of the *Buffy* phenomenon is the question, Is Buffy feminist? Assessing the recent development of "Women in Action" represented by such figures as
Sigourney Weaver's Ellen Ripley, Michelle Yeoh's Wing Chun, Sarah
Michelle Gellar's Buffy the Vampire Slayer, and Lucy Lawless's Xena: Warrior Princess, authors Anamika Samanta and Erin Franzman pose the question this way: "No longer damsels in distress, women are kicking ass and
saving the world from doom—in Hollywood Technicolor. But is happiness
really a warm gun? [. . .] Is this a sign? Are we on our way to mass physical empowerment? Or are we just headed for a whole new pack of stereotypes to live down?" (28). Rachel Fudge poses the question slightly differently in the journal *Bitch: Feminist Response to Pop Culture*: "Is Buffy really
an exhilarating post-third-wave heroine, or is she merely a caricature of 90's
pseudo-girl power, a cleverly crafted marketing scheme to hook the ever-
important youth demographic?" (18). However the question is phrased, the
concerns are remarkably similar: does Buffy represent an empowering feminist role model or a return to, and reinscription of, repressive patriarchal
stereotypes? While critical responses to this central question vary markedly,
they are alike in affirming the either/or structure of the binary "Good
Buffy/Bad Buffy." Collectively, such criticism relies on a model of feminist
agency that itself has important political implications.

   In her article "Media Criticism: The Sad State of Teen Television"
printed in *New Moon Network: For Adults Who Care about Girls,* Lynette
Lamb canvasses a range of television serials targeted to teenage girls,
among them *Buffy the Vampire Slayer, Sabrina the Teenage Witch,* and *Felicity,* and concludes, "Women and girls are portrayed no more fully or

honestly than they were when I was a teenager 25 years ago. Indeed, in some regards the situation is worse." Lamb argues that "like so many teens on prime time TV, Sabrina's and Buffy's major preoccupations are their appearance and their boyfriends, in roughly that order" (14). Lamb is relatively singular in her outright condemnation of *Buffy* as "bad." Other critics express unqualified approval of the series. For example, Jennifer L. Pozner writes in "Thwack! Pow! Yikes! Not Your Mother's Heroines" that "profeminist options are springing up on almost every network." She identifies *Buffy*, along with *Xena* and *The Simpsons,* as "three of the most subversive and campy programs on TV" and writes that Buffy, "cornered by three snarling freaks, [. . .] does what most high school girls wish they could do—thanks them for dropping by, tells them she's not in the mood, and kicks them into another dimension, literally." Pozner applauds, "How's that for a role model?" (12). Despite their opposing judgments of the series, the model of feminist agency mobilized by these critiques is quite similar. Lamb upholds one end of the binary "Good Buffy/Bad Buffy," while Pozner maintains the other. In the majority of critical responses to the series, however, the binary distinctions "feminist/not feminist" and "transgressive/contained" operate and circulate in a more fluid fashion.

A third style of critique suspends initial judgment of the series's politics in order to explore its conflicting representations of femininity and feminism. Thus, Micol Ostow, in an article titled "Why I Love Buffy," confesses that "I've never known quite how to explain my penchant for the program, but the bottom line is that *Buffy* and *Buffy* alone is the reason that I bothered to learn to set the timer on my VCR." Ostow applauds the show's "sheer camp appeal" but at the same time maintains that "one can hardly consider Buffy a feminist icon." She suggests that "for every few positive messages that it sends girls, [. . .] it creates some problematic scenarios" (20). Rachel Fudge argues that "while she may not be your typical feminist activist," Buffy's "anti-authority stance, her refusal to be intimidated by more powerful figures (whether the school principal or an archdemon)," has "deeply feminist potential." Fudge suggests that "Buffy is an ongoing lesson in this sisters-doing-it-for-themselves ideology" and maintains, in an interesting aside, that "the impulse that propels Buffy out on patrols, night after night, forgoing any semblance of 'normal' teenage life, is identical to the one that compels us third-wavers to spend endless hours discussing the feminist potentials and pitfalls of primetime television" (18).

The metacritical gesture which compares the task of the vampire slayer and the task of the feminist critic is not elaborated by Fudge, despite its potential to illuminate the institutional and intergenerational dimensions of Buffy's appeal. Critiques like those proffered by Ostow and Fudge suspend black-and-white judgment of the series in the interests of examining the ambivalence of *Buffy*'s political content, yet they cannot defer that judgment indefinitely. Indeed, while celebrating Buffy's strength, commitment, and sassiness, such analyses are haunted by the dark specter of her patriarchal containment, embodied, ironically enough, in her popularity, her commercial success, in effect, her *Sassy*-ness. Fudge writes, "Buffy could be the poster girl for an entire decade of girl-oriented mass media/culture. For better and most certainly for worse, she's *Sassy* incarnate, an angsty alternateen with a penchant for Delia's-style slip dresses" (18). Ostow's "Why I Love Buffy" tribute suggests that "some might find her utter femininity problematic" (20); the authors of "Women in Action," who insist that critics have so far failed to appreciate "Buffy's potential as a post-feminist icon," nevertheless characterize the series' star, Sarah Michelle Gellar, as a "Barbie doll-doppelganger" (28); and the recurring animadversions cast on Buffy's tank tops, high heels, and, most repetitively and insidiously, her cleavage suggest that, Slayer aside, Buffy herself is something of a stumbling block for feminist criticism.[1] As Fudge states, "Yup, she's strong and sassy all right, but she's the ultimate femme, never disturbing the delicate definition of physical femininity [. . .] the Buffster, for all her bravado and physical strength, is a girly girl through and through" (18). In the final analysis, such critiques cleave to the either/or binary of "Good Buffy/Bad Buffy" as much as their second-wave feminist counterparts. They suggest that Buffy can be either a feminist or a femme; there is no middle ground.

Paradoxically then, the specter that haunts feminist critiques of *Buffy*'s political content is the specter of her gender, the representation of her girlishness. Rachel Fudge summarizes this position succinctly when she states that "Buffy's unreconstructed, over-the-top girliness in the end compromises her feminist potential. Though this excessive femininity veers toward the cartoonish, in the end it's too earnest—too necessary—to be self-parody" (18). Buffy's femininity is repeatedly reconfigured as a species of *femme-inanity*, and it is this facet of her character that is presented, time and again, as contradicting, and thus undermining, her transgressive political potential. Such analyses leave off their discussion of the gender dynamics of *Buffy* at precisely the point that they become most interesting to me. How, for instance, does the exaggerated or cartoonish representation of Buffy's femininity mediate its "earnestness"? Does Buffy's femininity in fact *require* amelioration? And how does an understanding of her "over-the-top girliness" as "necessary" to her makeup challenge the very political judgments that are frequently made about her character?

In what follows, I would like to rethink the terms of the debate staged around Buffy's femininity by questioning the logic of the transgression/containment model. The model of feminist agency usually employed to analyze *Buffy* dictates that Buffy is "good" if she transgresses dominant stereotypes, "bad" if she is contained in cultural cliché. Yet this binary logic itself works to restrict a range of possible viewing positions and to contain *Buffy*'s political potential. As Jonathan Dollimore has argued, "Containment theory often presupposes an agency of change too subjective and a criterion of success too total. Thus subversion or transgression are implicitly judged by impossible criteria: complete transformation of the social (i.e. revolution), or total personal liberation within, or escape from it (i.e. redemption)" (85). By examining *Buffy's* ambivalent constructions of authenticity and originality, I hope to illuminate the series' own self-consciously parodic references to gender role playing: "Sorry, I'm an old-fashioned girl. I was raised to believe that the men dig up the corpses and the women have the babies" ("Some Assembly Required," 2002). I suggest that a more productive reading of the politics of *Buffy* is one that examines the challenges it poses under a rubric of feminist camp—a reading strategy flexible enough to recognize not only the ambivalence of the show's political content but also the constitutive incoherence of the very models usually employed to describe it.

The Lite Ages: "I am the chosen one and I choose to be shopping!"

—*Buffy the Vampire Slayer* (1992)

In her 1964 essay "Notes on Camp," Susan Sontag defines camp as "a failed seriousness, a love of exaggeration and artifice, the privileging of style over content and a being alive to the double sense in which things can be taken" (277). In *Guilty Pleasures: Feminist Camp from Mae West to Madonna,* Pamela Robertson highlights the efficacy of camp for a feminist politics: "For feminists, camp's appeal lies in its potential to serve as a form of gender parody. Gender parody becomes a critical tool, a way of initiating change in sex and gender roles" (10). Robertson suggests that "camp's attention to the artifice of feminine images of excess helps undermine and challenge the presumed naturalness of gender roles and to displace essentialist versions of an authentic female identity" (6). Feminist camp thus operates in two potentially conflicting directions: it revels in an aesthetics of surface play and eschews the depth model of moral seriousness, and at the same time it foregrounds the inevitably performative nature of gender role playing.

Buffy provides ample illustration of the doubled operations of feminist camp. Xander Harris, Buffy's long-term admirer and sidekick, provides one focus for the show's camp comedy. An archetype of a new 1990s embattled masculinity, Xander struggles with the machismo stereotypes of classic narrative film as he negotiates his role as handmaiden to Buffy's Slayer: "Cavalry's here; cavalry's a frightened guy with a rock, but it's here" ("Becoming," part 2, 2022). In the episode "Bewitched, Bothered and Bewildered" (2016), a disgruntled Xander conjures a spell that will make him the focus of attention and desire, with unexpectedly dire results. As he endeavors to escape the rampaging hordes of women out to seduce him, Xander decides,

"That's it. This has got to stop. It's time for me to act like man. And hide."
The poignancy of such moments is underscored by Buffy's occasional assumption of the quintessentially macho stance of the action hero, as exemplified in the following challenge to the demon Whistler: I've had a really
bad day, okay? If you have information worth hearing then I'm grateful for
it. If you want to crack jokes then I will pull out your rib cage and wear it
as a hat" ("Becoming," part 1, 2021). Both the rejection of seriousness and
the subtext of gender masquerade that are central characteristics of feminist
camp are evident in these gender reversals.

A product of late 1990s popular culture, *Buffy*'s protagonists participate
in what Mark Dery, in a clever tribute to both Edvard Munch's 1893 paint-
ing and Wes Craven's film of the same name, calls "the *Scream* meme":

> The *Scream* meme suggests that we're so ironic that we can't even take our
> own apocalypse—our lurking sense, on the eve of the future, of social disinte-
> gration and simmering discontent—seriously. This is the moment Walter Ben-
> jamin warned us of, when humankind's "self-alienation" reaches "such a de-
> gree that it can experience its own destruction as an aesthetic pleasure of the
> first order." (57)

Consider Xander's gag in "The Harvest" (1002): "The dead rose! We
should've at least had an assembly"; Buffy's comment in "Never Kill a Boy
on the First Date" (1005): "If the apocalypse comes—beep me"; or the
Scooby Gang's response to Giles's belated diagnosis of an earthquake in season 4's "Doomed" (4011):

> *Giles:* It's the end of the world.
> *Willow/Xander:* AGAIN??!!

The bathos of such exchanges is one of the series's signature textual strategies. Dery states that "delight in the delivery from depth, from the dead
weight of content, is quintessentially postmodern." He associates "the
Scream meme" with Frederic Jameson's notion of the "camp sublime,"
which he describes in the following manner: "camp in the sense that camp
delights in depthlessness, celebrates surface; sublime in the sense that this
'peculiar euphoria' is the postmodern equivalent, for Jameson, of what Edmund Burke called 'the Sublime'—the vertiginous loss of self in the presence
of nature's awful grandeur" (55–56).

In the late twentieth century it is the media, rather than nature, that induces this "vertiginous loss of self." Writes Dery,

> Increasingly, the media form the connective tissue of our lives. In the past,
> says J. G. Ballard, we assumed that the external world represented reality and
> that our mental worlds were the realm of fantasy. Now, he argues, these roles
> have been reversed: "We live in a world ruled by fictions of every kind—mass

merchandising, advertising, [. . .] the increasing blurring and intermingling of identities within the realm of consumer goods, the preempting of any free or original response to experience by the television screen." (36)

Unarguably a product of mass media, merchandising, and advertising, *Buffy* also insistently comments on its own historical moment. Joyce Summers, Buffy's mother, voices a familiar concern in the following exchange with Buffy's mentor, Giles:

> *Joyce:* I know she's having trouble with history. Is it too difficult for her, or is she not applying herself?
> *Giles:* She lives very much in the now, and history of course, is very much about the then [. . .]. ("Angel," 1007)

Targeted toward a generation whose sense of generation has been fostered by the multiplex cinema, video games, and the Internet, *Buffy* enjoys, to borrow the words of Mark Dery, "playing slip 'n' slide on a slick of pure surface: self-conscious quotes, appropriated styles, glib asides" (56). Buffy's response to an uncharacteristically skeptical Giles, "I cannot believe that you of all people are trying to Scully me" ("The Pack," 1006), might stand as symptomatic of the series' casual pop cultural frame of reference. Yet the operations of metaphor at work in the series as a whole attest to its canny acknowledgment and manipulation of the tropes of the world as text, of reality as fiction. As Alyssa Katz provocatively suggests in her review of the series, "Only sociopaths experience their teenage lives just once. Everyone else relives them again and again, occasionally with professional assistance, and some of us actually find entertainment value in this process" (36). Giles's comment to his troublesome charge in the episode, "Ted"—"Buffy, I believe the subtext here is rapidly becoming text"—might be read as the overarching textual strategy for the series as a whole.

Much of the comic effect of the *Buffy* series stems from its engagement with the twin poles of the camp sublime and from its volatile shifts from the sublime to the ridiculous. Buffy, experimentally rebellious in the episode "Reptile Boy," is stymied by the rapidity of the transition:

> *Buffy:* I told one lie, I had one drink.
> *Giles:* Yes. And you were very nearly devoured by a giant demon-snake. I think the words "let that be a lesson" are a tad redundant at this juncture. ("Reptile Boy," 2005)

Xander's ironic lament in "Teacher's Pet," "It's funny how the earth never opens up and swallows you when you want it to," points to the endless applicability of the high school/Hellmouth analogy. The analogy enacts a dizzying dance between the literal and the metaphorical. On a formal level, high school and hell are linked through the rhetorical figure of chiasmus, a trope that is depicted, appropriately enough, by the sign of the cross and that relates each concept in a mutually reciprocal movement (thus, high school equals hell, and hell equals high school). This chiastic relation is exemplified by Buffy's response to Willow's apology that she cannot help her friend study for finals: "I'll wing it. Of course if we go to Hell by then, I won't have to take them. [sudden fear] Or maybe I'll have to take them forever [. . .]" ("Becoming," part 1, 2009). Giles's warning about the slippage between text and subtext points to the well-recognized and almost interminable interpenetrability of the two motifs. It points as well to a larger rhetorical pattern to the series that is less well recognized.

If the high school/Hellmouth analogy that structures the show has been widely celebrated in the popular response to the series, the similar chiastic relation that structures Buffy's character has been less generally acknowledged. While critics have paid lip service to the "joke" of the ex-cheerleader turned demon hunter, they have usually tried to separate these disparate elements of her character in their political analyses of the series. Hence, the Slayer is celebrated at the expense of the girl, and the composite character is found inexplicably wanting. Yet the very title of the text enacts, on a microcosmic scale, the shift from ridiculous to sublime that is a celebrated feature of the series, and it insists on the chiastic relationship between its twin components, "Buffy" and "Vampire Slayer": Buffy is the Vampire Slayer/the Vampire Slayer is Buffy. While such a reduction might seem to beg the unanswerable response "Duh!" I believe the point is worth making precisely because so many critical responses to the show seem to miss it. The "joke" of the cheerleading demon hunter is not a one-line throwaway gag but the foundational myth and ongoing premise of the entire series.

In "Vampires, Postmodernity, and Postfeminism: *Buffy the Vampire Slayer,*" A. Susan Owen produces a sophisticated distillation of the critiques this essay has endeavored to explore. She writes,

> Buffy's power is domesticated by her oft articulated longing to be "normal"— to have a steady boyfriend (with all that entails) and to consume life uninterrupted by the demands of civic obligation. The narrative opposes the costs of leadership and political potency, with intimacy, stable relationships, and material comfort. [. . .] Moreover, in spite of Buffy's narrative agency and physical potency, her body project remains consistent with the rescripted body signs of American commodity advertising. In other words, political potency is both imagined and reduced to matters of consumer style. (30)

In a provocative, but to my mind poorly substantiated, move, Owen characterizes Buffy as "postfeminist" and concludes, "The series plays at transgression: as such it is quintessential television. But it remains to be seen whether transgressive play can challenge institutional relations of power" (31).

While such critiques significantly extend the terms of political analysis relevant to *Buffy*, in doing so they can be seen to raise the familiar specter of the transgression/containment debate, this time in a slightly different guise: does *Buffy* comment on twentieth-century popular culture or simply revel in it? And again, I would argue that this binary formulation is itself part of the bogey—a bogey that the series's own structure and rhetoric militate against. Buffy is strong, sexy, and subversive, not despite her immersion in popular culture but because of it. Alternatively vacuous and vengeful, she is a composite character; her politics cannot be extruded from her postmodernity. Cultural critique that juxtaposes style and substance in an hierarchical and mutually exclusive relation will always end up stuck with an outmoded and impossible model of feminist agency. If Buffy's form and Buffy's content are upheld as distinct and incompatible categories, then the inexorable logic of the binary will dictate, with awful irony, that Buffy cannot be a feminist because she has a cleavage.

That the alternative to the archaic "either/or" is an anarchic "neither and both" has become something of a critical truism in contemporary cultural studies. In Rachel Fudge's words, "Buffy constantly treads the fine line between girl-power schlock and feminist wish-fulfillment, never giving satisfaction to either one" (20). That *Buffy* nevertheless refuses the black-and-white moral distinctions of a more self-evident and sanctimonious style of politics is perhaps testament to the complexity of its cultural moment. It is certainly testament to the fact that the postmodern sublime, that "vertiginous loss of self," is virtually indistinguishable from the "peculiar euphoria" of the ridiculous. Instead of considering *Buffy* as a political blueprint for either feminist transgression or patriarchal containment (in the terms of Dollimore's "impossible criteria," "complete transformation of the social, [. . .] or total personal liberation within, or escape from it"), we might more usefully identify *Buffy* as a site of intense cultural negotiation in which competing definitions of the central terms in the debate—revolution/apocalypse, feminist/misogynist, transgression and containment—can be tested and refined. A criticism that insists on the necessity of either/or distinctions will be doomed to conclude with the unsatisfactory suggestion that you can take the Slayer out of the girl because you *cannot* take the girl out the Slayer. Buffy's response to the demon in "Never Kill a Boy on the First Date" (1005) might double for her response to the cultural critic that asks her to choose between her ostensibly split selves: "I don't think we've been properly introduced. I'm Buffy and you're . . . History."

NOTE

1. See especially Rachel Fudge, who says of Buffy that "she's no scarred, deep-in-shit Tank Girl—this slayer's tank tops are pastel and pristine, revealing plenty of

creamy, unmarred cleavage" and, on another occasion, that "her ever present tank tops showcase her rack quite efficiently" (20). See also Anamika Samanta and Erin Franzman, who maintain, somewhat confusingly, that "no one notices that Buffy is the smartest, strongest (literally and figuratively) teen role model television has seen in ages. Instead the show gets attention for its Lolita-esque star's abundant cleavage. If more cleavage means more advertising dollars (which in turn means the show stays on the air), then hopefully more young women and girls will be able to see the show and appreciate the finer points of Buffy, such as they are. You have to take what you can get these days" (28).

4

Surpassing the Love of Vampires

Or, Why (and How) a Queer Reading of the Buffy/Willow Relationship Is Denied

Farah Mendlesohn

The concept of a "queer reading" of a text is drawn from an experience of reader oppression and exclusion. A queer reading is constructed by a reader who, denied the obvious manifestation of homosexual desire, in a context in which heterosexual desire is normalized, seeks to identify the codes by which authors have indicated passionate relationships between same-sex members of their texts or have created available metaphors through cross-species relationships. Such readings may be imposed on a heterosexual author with no such intentions, or they may be experienced interpretations of known (but closeted) gay authors and actors. The requirements for such a reading, however, are relatively simple: that two characters labeled as inaccessible to each other for cultural reasons be seen acting in a manner that may be interpreted as flirtatious, loving, passionate (in the platonic sense), or tense, and in the final analysis, it is the tension between the two characters that is most productive of queer readings. Such tension provides the widest range of encoded behavior to interpret, but, significantly, it also provides the tension, opposition, and antagonism that conventional romance plots demand: only where there is tension can there be real love. However, should attraction become overt, should the homosexual interest become blatant, a queer reading as such is no longer possible, as it depends for its structure on hidden and coded messages.

We can see this best in *Xena: Warrior Princess*. Although it was initially intended as Superwoman-style adventures for young girls combined with eye candy for the adolescent male, it quickly acquired a huge following among feminists and lesbians. Although some of this was simply the delight in two strong female characters, the rapid emergence of slash fiction on the

Internet pointed to other reasons for its popularity. Slash fiction is fan fiction that posits a (usually gay) sexual relationship between the leading characters and is usually extremely explicit. The best known, and the oldest, is Kirk/Spock slash fiction. However, slash fiction is not, in and of itself, a queer reading. Kirk/Spock fiction is dominated by heterosexual women writers (Penley 479–500). Xena/Gabrielle slash is written by women who, in their bylines, suggest that they themselves are gay or bisexual. However, slash fiction relies on what cannot be shown on the screen. Xena/Gabrielle slash picked up on the self-chosen marginalization of the main characters, of their closeness, the opposition of their physical coding—tall, dark, and handsome; small, delicate strawberry blond—and spun it into conventional romance (Helford 135–62). But, in addition, the series editors took the decision to play on the rumor, choosing to emphasize the coding, introducing more flirtatious looks, witticisms, and references to mutual love. What they did not do, in part because of their early evening broadcast position, was to make the relationship overt. This choice allowed them both to encourage the queer reading and to protect it by maintaining the hidden agenda on which it rests.

However, the test of a theory, whether in science or in the humanities, is whether we can imagine circumstances in which, all the obvious ingredients being present, the theory does not apply. If a queer reading is something genuine that responds to specific structures, then there must be circumstances in which it does not work and reasons why this is the case. *Buffy*, a show that depends heavily on the interrelationship between the characters and that has succeeded in maintaining high levels of emotional tension throughout its first several seasons, is one of the more obvious candidates for a queer reading. The primary characters are marginalized because of their occupation, the secondary characters (the vampires) as a consequence of their intrinsic natures. The extent to which the vampire hunters come to identify with the vampires by the end of season 4 and throughout season 5 provides an avenue for the queer theorist to explore. The relationships between characters such as Angel and Spike, Angel and Xander, Buffy and Faith, and, most recently, Spike and Riley all sustain the tension that provokes queer reading, and evidence of this can be found on numerous slash sites. However, most queer readings (although not all) focus on the main protagonists in a show. It therefore seems sensible to examine the primary friendship that is presented: that between Buffy and Willow. What I intend to demonstrate in this chapter is how and where a queer reading is facilitated in the political relationship between Willow and Buffy but is deflected when we attempt a queer erotic reading of their partnership: I hope to prove the validity of the concept of the queer reading by demonstrating the circumstances in which it does not operate.

In her most recent book, *To Believe in Women,* Lillian Faderman asserts that for many nineteenth- and early-twentieth-century feminists, heterosexuality threatened to imperil their autonomy, their personal career growth, and their ability to pursue the goal of enfranchisement. Needing to create supportive and stable emotional lives, and in many cases to achieve erotic fulfillment, these women found their primary relationships with other women, usually with other women dedicated to, if not always as active in, the same cause. Many of these relationships were monogamous, others were not, but their shared attribute was a belief that their quality surpassed and outlasted the heterosexual romances that they witnessed elsewhere. In addition, these connections bound these women into a supportive network that created the women's movement as an ensemble campaign rather than the work of one lone hero(ine). This pattern operates within *Buffy,* structuring the relationships within the ensemble as an ensemble that is held together by the relationship between Buffy and Willow.

The ensemble as it exists at the end of season 4 is not the same structure as that created at the start of the series. The basic ensemble consists of Buffy, Giles her Watcher, and two equally weighted sidekicks, Willow and Xander. The relationship between Buffy and sidekicks is fairly straightforward: she fights vampires, and they provide friendship and people with whom Buffy is allowed to be truthful. While they may also assist in the actual slaying, and Willow's computer skills and later her witchcraft are invaluable, it is their emotional support that is crucial to their permanent status. In narrative terms, they also serve as recipients for the explanatory exposition, but with their role-playing gamelike characteristics, the additional characters in *Buffy* are crucial to the plot in ways which the majority of the assistants (known colloquially as screamers) on the long-running British series *Dr. Who* were not. As Rhonda Wilcox pointed out in chapter 1 of this volume, the necessary activities of the sidekicks on Buffy's behalf continually undercut the idea of the lone hero that the voice-over establishes in the show's opening credits.

The remaining member of the initial ensemble is Giles. For all his archetypal English bumbling, Giles offers Buffy a father substitute, whose role seems to be to lay down the rules that Buffy, the average adolescent, will seek to test. Buffy's struggles against Giles's authority are both a resistance to patriarchy and a simple depiction of teenage rebellion: their importance in the formation of Buffy as an adult are crucial, and it is consequently significant that Buffy does not simply "mature" into an acceptance of Giles's right-reasoning in contrast, for example, to the Angels in the 1970s series *Charlie's Angels,* required to defer to Charlie's judgment. Instead, by the end of season 3, Buffy has come to the conclusion that actually she does know better than either the Watchers' Council or Giles, and by season 5 Giles's role is much more advisory.

The remainder of the ensemble as it forms and dissolves over the seasons includes Angel, Oz, Cordelia, Jenny, Kendra (briefly), Spike, Faith, Anya, Riley, and Tara. Of these, Angel, Spike, Faith, and Riley are linked primarily to Buffy. Three of them (the men) have sexual/emotional relationships with Buffy, and the relationships between Xander and Willow and Spike and Willow also generate sexual tension. Faith's relationship with Buffy is also sexualized, but, in ways that I will discuss later, this possibility is left unstated. In contrast, Willow's relationship with Buffy is specifically desexualized.

The structure of the basic ensemble is designed to place Buffy at center stage; all attention within the ensemble is on her. However, Buffy's place at the center is not synonymous with autonomy and independence. Instead, the writers have constructed a matrix of interdependence and control that rests on relationships rather than rules.

As mere sidekicks, Xander and Willow, acting wholly within the usual paradigm of heroic fantasy, would be expected to reinforce the structures within which the hero is intended to develop. Instead, Xander's and Willow's roles are to subvert the structure within which Buffy operates. As Kendra (the first of the parallel slayers) points out, Buffy is supposed to have a secret identity: slayers are not supposed to have friends, and they are most certainly not supposed to have confessional buddies. Spike will demonstrate in season 4's "The Yoko Factor" (4020) that there are good reasons for this, but equally he asserts that it has been the reason for Buffy's longevity. The supportive roles also offer variety and complexity that ensure that Buffy's sidekicks do not act simply to enhance Buffy's autonomy. Instead, they place constraints on her behavior and demands on her emotions.

Because it is apparently unsexual, Willow's support is often presented as unconditional, an appearance enhanced by Willow's little-girl presentation until midway through the fourth season. But explicit statements are misleading, and Willow, even in the earliest episodes, clearly gains self-esteem from her contribution to matters of real import on the basis of talents that usually have little value in the teenage world. What Buffy does for Willow is give her a validation that, as an intellectual, she would normally anticipate only in adulthood. This continuously places a demand on Buffy that she operate within a team for their psychological benefit as well as hers, even where teamwork may be inappropriate or dangerous, and that she operate in ways that make use of her comrade's skills. While it is clear that in the long term this enhances Buffy's efficiency, we must not lose sight of the fact that it is at the expense of her emotional and professional autonomy. Buffy's affection for Willow means that at times she may choose to protect Willow (and others) rather than do her duty. This, of course, all adds tension to the scripts.

In seasons 1 and 2, Xander Harris's motives are explicitly, if confusedly, sexual: he wishes a romantic or physical relationship with Buffy. However, given his status as teenager and his frequently unpleasant sexual experiences ("Teacher's Pet," 1004; "Inca Mummy Girl," 2004), it is also possible to view Xander's continued interest in Buffy long after she has become clearly unavailable as stemming from his desire for validation, as both a man and a person. (It is thus ironic that it will be Xander who tries to teach Anya in season 4 that masculinity is not only about sex ["Fear, Itself," 4004].) In the context in which we are discussing Xander here, however, this relationship works to provide Buffy with an antilove interest that places her within a heterosocial matrix that later contributes to the denial of either a feminist political reading of the text or a queer reading of its relationships.

We can see this better if we consider the role of Giles. That he and not her mother is in control of Buffy's behavior undercuts the potentially powerful prime-time message that here is a successful single-mother/daughter relationship and contributes to a message that only cross-sex networks are stable. At the end of season 3 and in season 4, Giles's changed status offers opportunities for the series's writers to explore a cross-generational friendship. Up to a point, they have achieved this, but there is still a strong sense of Giles as scout master, with the Scooby Gang congregating in his house/hut. Undercutting this, however, is a growing sexual tension between Giles and Buffy, triggered by Giles's brief involvement with her mother, Joyce, in "Band Candy" early in season 3. Buffy's reaction to Giles's involvement with her mother is a complex mixture of adolescent disgust that adults actually have sex and betrayal that he has had a relationship behind her back. This is reinforced by the comparative unimportance of Giles's second girlfriend, Olivia, coupled with Buffy's reaction to discovering them together, and Buffy's continued tendency to take problems to him and not to Riley. While any development of this relationship is probably precluded by Giles's previous involvement with Joyce, it is significant in the network of men with which Buffy surrounds herself and to the sense that despite the importance of Willow to the show's emotional structure, Buffy's emotional well-being is usually (although not always) depicted as resting on male approval. We need to consider why this is the case.

Central to this chapter is my belief that Buffy's relationship matrix is primarily constructed on a heterosocial model that, whatever her relationship with Willow, is expected to take precedence. Heterosociality is the assumption that one's primary affiliations and loyalties cross the sex divide (and I specifically mean sex: genitals are the signifiers here) and that socialization and friendship should take place predominantly in mixed-sex groups. Although heterosociality need not have consequences for ideologies of gender and sex, the historical experience has been that it does. In a heterosocial model it becomes more important, not less, to maintain the gender divide: single-sexed groups may come under suspicion of sexual or political deviancy, and heterosociality may be fostered as a means to undercut other types of behavior. For example, the American temperance movement promoted heterosociality as a means to control men's drinking, while psychologists in the 1920s and 1930s promoted coeducation and family membership in country clubs because they believed single-sexed congregation encouraged lesbian (and political) activity in women. Ritualized dating patterns at a young age become signifiers of social normality and acceptance. However, heterosociality as practiced in any culture in which one sex is still more powerful than the other is unlikely to operate in any evenhanded manner, and deviation from it is specifically politicized: thus, men congregating as men, in football clubs or in boardrooms, is framed as natural, while women congregating as women to gain access to said football clubs or boardrooms is considered political. While women congregating with men may gain status from their affiliation with the more powerful group, a man who spends much of his time with women in social rather than sexual situations, as Xander does, may actually sacrifice status. Cordelia's disregard of first Xander and then Doyle (*Angel*, season 1) , both men who wish to be friends with women, seems to reinforce the point: their association with women whom they are not dating reduces their manhood rather than enhancing it.

At first sight this may seem peripheral to the discussion in this chapter, but it is easy for American audiences to remain oblivious to the extreme heterosocial nature of U.S. teen programming and to teen socialization in general. Britain, which on the surface strongly resembles the United States, has a much stronger pattern of homosocial behavior, reinforced by the continued prevalence of single-sex education (many school catchment areas have one boys', one girls', and one coed high school). Some coed schools in the United Kingdom still retain separate playgrounds. The heterosocial social structure and dating patterns that are depicted in *Buffy* are the norm only within this cultural setting, and it is their existence as "the norm" that allows our attention to be deflected from the degree to which they create a matrix that operates to deny Buffy the full potential of her relationship with Willow that a superficial analysis of the situation might expect.

Lillian Faderman's main argument is that, for the active woman, heterosexuality is a trap and a lure, that no matter how supportive the man, heterosexual relationships take a woman's attention away from her business. Even given that Buffy is unlikely to face compulsory maternity, Faderman's thesis appears to have substance. On the surface, Buffy's relationship with Willow perfectly matches Faderman's outline of the active, public campaigner with her female partner in the background providing material and emotional support. The history of female friendship in television is often rather less positive, and it is this context that makes the Buffy/Willow friendship feel unusual. The female friend in sitcoms has continually maintained an edge of ambiguity. Only when both friends are safely married (and in a predivorce television world such as in *I Love Lucy*) is a female television friendship made up of consistent loyalty and positive reinforcement; otherwise, female friendships on television have traditionally been full of rivalries and spitefulness (see Wilcox, "Lois's Locks" 106–11). Even Kate and Allie, on the show of the same name, frequently competed for male attention (despite a memorable episode in which they posed as a lesbian couple to classify as a "family" under the terms of their rent agreement), while *Cagney and Lacey* rested in part on both characters' envying the other's lifestyle from the safe vantage point of the outside. And *Friends* relies in part for its humor on the amused contempt of the characters for Phoebe, the "kooky" character who never gets a lasting romance. What Sharon Thompson (228–29) calls girl fearing and girl hating, depicted usually as competition for men or for status, has all too frequently structured the homosocial relationships depicted in programs such as *Beverly Hills 90210* and the films *Heathers* (1989) and *Clueless* (1995).

It is relatively easy to see the ways in which the writers could have chosen this route. Alyson Hannigan, with her winsome charm and, as Willow, her nerdish manner, could have been preselected to play the loveless but funny best friend against whom Buffy's status is measured. Instead, she is core to the friendship structure, her "weirdness" is deliberately displayed in attractive ways, and she experiences successful romance twice. But this is not to say that she is allowed to take the central role in the support team. While Willow may be operating on a homosocial model that may be subject to a queer reading (something to which I will return later), Buffy is not. One consequence is that while to the outsider Willow may seem central, the one character on whom Buffy absolutely depends, Buffy is less clear on this.

The relationship between Buffy and Willow begins with a very clear sense that Buffy is the dependent component. As the new girl in town, she needs both the friendship and the access route into high school society that Willow provides. Under normal circumstances, however, Buffy might have abandoned Willow. Buffy is cheerleader material, meant to hang out with the likes of Cordelia. That she does not is because her other activities mark her out as "weird," and the rumors about her previous school life rapidly reach the ears of the in-crowd. Buffy might yet have been reincorporated into the high school clique ("Reptile Boy," 2005), except that she refuses to conform to their requirements and chooses Willow and Xander instead. However, before we take this as a complete change of heart, we should be clear that had Buffy reentered the clique, it would probably have been as Cordelia's competitor, not follower. Buffy's choices, as Faith is aware, are in part about retaining the focus of attention ("Consequences," 3015; "Enemies," 3017; "The Prom," 3020; "Who Are You?" 4016); Buffy the clique leader becomes Buffy the gang leader—the shift is only marginal. Thus Buffy's friendship with Willow is structured from the beginning around the model of leader and acolyte, and in all such structures the viability of the friendship rests on the more dominant partner. Willow continually reflects her awareness of this in her hesitancy within the relationship, which, despite her own resistance against this ("I am not your sidekick," she says in "Fear, Itself," 4004), is never fully resolved, even after the balance of power begins to shift in season 4. That Willow structures the friendship around Buffy's "need" for her and for her skills remains a weak point that Spike is able to exploit at the end of season 4. Only in season 5, bolstered by her relationship with Tara and with Dawn, Buffy's virtual sister, does she accept her wider value to the ensemble.

According to Faderman's thesis, Buffy ought to gain more from Willow's support than from Angel's, and with only a few exceptions this seems to be true. Although Buffy, on a number of occasions, must redirect her activities in order to rescue Willow ("I Robot, You Jane," 1008; "Phases," 2015; "Lovers Walk," 3008), this carries with it less of the emotional confusion that rescue of Angel or Riley does. In part this is because Buffy is not dating Willow, but it is also because when rescuing Willow, Buffy fulfills the role of shining knight without conflict, constantly reinforcing both the importance of her work and her sense of competence. When she attempts this role with her male lovers, the thrill of rescue is too often diminished by their sulky attempts to resist the realization that they have been rescued by a woman (Xander, too, fits this mold until season 4). With Riley and the Initiative, there is the further sense that she might be superfluous, at least until Adam comes on the scene.

However, it is Willow to whom Buffy confesses and explores her loves, and although Willow expresses her doubts over the wisdom of dating a vampire, her characteristic hesitancy over proffering advice is more supportive of the development of emotional autonomy than are Giles's words. Why then am I suggesting that this friendship is flawed? The potential for Buffy to use Willow as her primary support is undermined by her relationship with the men in her life: Giles, Angel, and Riley. Each of these supplants Willow for a period of time, reasserting the old canard that female friends are those whom a woman sees between boyfriends. And this alteration in friendship is entirely Buffy's choice. Interestingly, we can best see this if we examine the parallels between Buffy and Cordelia.

Roz Kaveney points out that Cordelia is what Buffy was. In "Out of Mind, Out of Sight" (1011), Buffy's acceptance and forgiveness of her earlier self rests in part on an accounting of Cordelia's behavior: Cordelia is spiteful, Buffy left it behind when she first became the Slayer; Cordelia is obsessed with clothes, while Buffy, although still very much a clothes junkie ("The Freshman," 4001), has discovered that leather armor goes with anything. Cordelia organizes cliques; Buffy's gang is inclusive and protective. However, shaping and underpinning all of Cordelia's behavior is that thread of female misogyny that Sharon Thompson identifies in girl fearers/girl haters: for one reason or another, these are young women who have had very little positive experience of friendship with women and whose friendships with women are constructed around status seeking and competition in a game in which points are scored through the attraction of the male gaze: in a paradigm in which women are competitors, men, ironically, are more to be trusted. The girl fearer/girl hater, on discovering her man's infidelity, is much more likely to attack the new girlfriend than her man. Betrayed by yet another woman, she is also more likely to turn to another man for support than to a woman. Cordelia fits the picture perfectly: competitive and bitchy to other women, she is a self-declared daddy's girl, dating men for status (and drawing Buffy into her social circle only because she needs her for a high-status double date ["Reptile Boy," 2005]), despising herself for her genuine attraction to the low-status Xander, but willing to tell him, when she has told no one else, of her father's bankruptcy. In L.A. (*Angel*), she turns to Doyle and then to Wesley and Angel for support in a milieu in which again her female friends (whom we mainly see at parties) are competitors, not supporters. In Thompson's construct, girl fearers/girl haters do not simply dislike the women around them; they dislike and distrust all women as a class and prefer to seek security from men. Thus, despite Willow's occasional cattiness toward Cordelia, Willow's dislike of most of her immediate female peers, and her reliance on Giles and Xander, Willow does not fit this category. When Willow searches for validation, her mentors include Jenny Calendar, the computer teacher, and Buffy herself. Later she will be both mentor to and mentored by Tara, in addition to the support she offers Dawn. We might expect that Buffy, having shucked off much of the most obvious of Cordelia's behaviors, would also have rejected the girl-hater paradigm that Thompson outlines; instead, despite the support and nurturing that Willow offers, Buffy remains fixated on receiving validation from men.

Buffy's behavior in heterosexual relationships is constructed from a complex mix of deference and assertion but begins with her liking for very large men. This "choice" is in part television convention: modern heroes are large and spend their lives working out. Sarah Michelle Gellar's petite build means it is quite probable that both the character and the writers are enjoying several moments of visual irony, enjoying the image of small weak female that belies the fact that she could easily kill her lovers. Its effect, however, is to create a physical dynamic in which Buffy's physical responses to her lovers can seem quite childlike. That this is a visual affect, and that the writers are fully aware of it, is made clear and exploited in "Who Are You?" when it is Faith, inside Buffy's body, who beds Riley, in the process replicating some of the same moves with an aggressive mockery of Buffy's childlikeness. With Faith's body language but Buffy's physical presence, the writers were able to create the image of a child out of control, eliciting sympathy for a problematic character. With Buffy, however, once the irony is accepted, we are still left with a convention in which strong women seek out stronger men and are then disappointed when this strength proves, as it does in very physical ways with Riley, to be illusory. Further, Buffy's very childlikeness is eroticized, in marked contrast to the continued deeroticization of Willow even after she becomes sexually active. Although Willow is always presented as sexually attractive, and as Vamp Willow Alyson Hannigan is also very sexy, Willow, rather than Hannigan, is the pure child, even while that description is usually reserved for Buffy. While Willow's sexuality is muted by its cuddliness, signified by her choice of pink, of cuddly sweaters and dungarees, Buffy's childlikeness is displayed by her choice of low-cut tops as school wear.

Buffy's emotional dependence on men exists independently of issues of Slayerdom: she plans and executes most of the missions regardless of whether Angel or Riley is in tow. But Buffy appears wholly willing to abdicate control of her emotional life, first to Giles, who wishes she did not have one; then to Angel, who insists that for her sake he leave; and finally to Riley, who is the one to decide (admittedly with the help of Jonathan ["Superstar," 4017]) when they make up and how, after the breach over Faith, later concluding their relationship with an ultimatum. Apparent attempts at asserting autonomy, the break from Giles and the patriarchal Watchers' Council (there are at least three women watchers, but we meet only one), actually play out as a mere exchange of one male for another, and the end of her relationship with Riley is framed as *her* failure of maturity, rather than his insistence that she remains immature and dependent.

By season 4, Willow is both a hacker and a witch, a powerful combination, and is in a relationship with Oz that she and he have shaped to provide her with considerably more emotional autonomy than Buffy experiences. While Angel displaces Willow as Buffy's best buddy, in that it is Angel who receives her emotional confidences, Oz does not displace Buffy from Willow's affections, and her resulting confidence changes the manner in which Willow relates to Buffy. While still keen to please, Willow is less eager for approval from her heroine. Willow has greater ease with the university experience: not simply the academic side, which might be expected, but also the social and fashion environments. Willow has the confidence to withdraw from a Wicca group she regards as inane and to experiment with an original approach to dress, while Buffy looks as high school as ever and appears to have made no new friend by the end of season 4. In comparison to Willow, Buffy has little emotional support and is poorly equipped to accept the full value of the support that Willow offers. Combined with Buffy's tendency to rely on authority figures despite her repeated experiences of betrayal by the Watchers' Council, Giles, and even her mother, her need for male validation leads her straight into the arms of the exploitative Parker. It is not Willow's superior intelligence, therefore, that allows her to see through Parker but the fact that Willow has no need of this type of validation and that Willow's emotional intelligence is rather better established. When Oz leaves, Willow finds herself a new life. When Buffy loses Angel, she turns to Parker, and when she loses him, she is not truly consoled until she becomes involved with Riley. This pattern of dependence on masculine authority and emotional support also explains why Buffy is so smitten with both the Initiative and Maggie Walsh (possibly, but not necessarily, a comment on Joss Whedon's residence in the United Kingdom in the 1980s, when Margaret "Maggie" Thatcher reigned supreme, surrounded by her bevy of adoring males), all of whom replay her experience of authority figures, of apparent emotional need, and of betrayal. Yet it is clear that the writers have, to some degree, recognized these behaviors as cultural constructs: in the final analysis, Cave-Buffy shucks off sociocultural behavioral patterns and hits Parker firmly over the head with a stick ("Beer Bad," 4005).

The parental element to heterosexual relationships is not exclusive to Buffy: given differences of class and personal experience for which Thompson allows, Faith acts within a comparable, girl-hater/girl-fearer paradigm, something that helps explain why Faith is incapable of trusting Buffy but created her own "Watcher" father figure in the person of the Mayor and was later willing to turn to Angel for help. Elsewhere, even given that Oz leaves after killing Veruca, his decision to disappear denies Willow agency. When Oz returns, we see the same pattern. He decides that the best thing he can do for Willow is to leave. That her emotional life is not a hostage to fortune rests entirely on Tara's willingness for Willow to make the best decision for herself, although this too is problematic. While it could be argued that Oz simply anticipates the decision he thinks Willow will make, the authors fail to make clear that Tara is not second best. The blowing out of the candle (in "New Moon Rising," 4019) may indicate a happy ending, but that is not the same as allowing Willow full choice. If anything, it replicates the ambiguity and male control of the similarly "happy" ending of *Casablanca*.

The continual roll call of Buffy's male supporters and her need for their validation undermines the potential for a queer reading of Buffy's relationship with Willow. This, however, is the case only if we ignore Willow's experience of the situation. If we focus on Willow instead of Buffy, it is clear that although Buffy refuses the reinforcement that Willow can offer, Willow gains enormously from her relationship with Buffy.

The course of Willow's relationship with Buffy, as discussed earlier, is outlined in part by the development of skills that she can offer to the team. That the first of these skills, the ability to manipulate computer data and networks, is one she already has is crucial to her empowerment. Willow's involvement with Buffy allows her to relate an essentially "nerdish" skill to a "real"-world scenario. And instead of being isolating, Willow becomes Buffy's connection to the world of ordinariness. Willow, previously a school freak, becomes a route to normality. This growth in Willow's physical confidence is displayed not through a normalization of her attire but through an extension of Willow's taste beyond the margins of fashion.

Willow's development is the side of the homosocial partnership that Faderman either dismisses or does not necessarily understand. Faderman focuses almost entirely on the public half of the feminist partnerships she observes. That it might well be the supportive member of the same-sex partnership who stands most to gain does not occur to her. This becomes clearer if we stop assuming that less public is equivalent to fewer opportunities. Much of what Willow does is essentially gendered "male": this may in fact be why the writers introduced the witchcraft, as a way to regender Willow and to pick up on the association of witchcraft with female sexuality, with power, and with lesbianism. Given a relationship with a man with equivalent interests, it is hard to imagine the hesitant, unconfident Willow sustaining her edge. When we first meet Oz, he too is technically oriented, but his attempts to assist her are quickly rebuffed as they threaten Willow's status within the gang. Very quickly, this side of his character is hidden by the writers and subsumed into his musicianship. The threat that Oz represents, however, highlights the degree to which Willow has gained from her association with Buffy. What Willow's situation suggests is that a same-sex bonding can open opportunities for and empower the "domestic" partner as much as it empowers the "public" partner.

However, while Willow gains enormously from her association with Buffy, it is at a price. Kate Fillion (2–5) points out in her analysis of the development of the talents within the girl friendships that the weaker party often develops skills that the stronger feels she should have or that benefit the stronger of the two. In these terms we can see Willow's development as directed toward areas that benefit Buffy. Further, Willow's attempt to dress and act differently at various points in the show (including her decision to sleep with Oz) are all in part an effort to make her a worthy companion to the Slayer and thus "deserve" her love. In order to maintain her support of Buffy, she follows her to a university far inferior to the more obvious choices for one of her abilities: greater love hath no woman than that she give up MIT (season 2) or Oxford (season 3) for her friend. That this is framed in terms of "exploring opportunities for witchcraft" is problematic. If this is a world in which magic works, then presumably Oxford would have been just as suitable a venue (particularly given the inadequacy of UC Sunnydale's Wicca group). And both the episode "Anne" and the entire *Angel* series make it clear that demonic threats are not limited to Sunnydale.

That Willow's choice of UC Sunnydale does not completely undermine her is due entirely to her greater social success at the university relative to Buffy. What made Willow weird in high school establishes her as interesting in the new setting. In contrast, Buffy's relative emotional immaturity and relentlessly high school profile (both Spike and Faith are absolutely right about this) set her up for a number of problems. Again tracking Fillion's paradigm, until Spike intervenes, it is Buffy as much as Willow who feels the distance growing in the friendship. When Buffy is suffering the effects of Parker, her largest problem is that Willow is no longer waiting patiently at home.

By the end of season 3, if a queer reading of the text is possible, the scenario is set for a Buffy/Willow romance. Buffy's experience with Parker in the first episodes might make her open for something new, and Oz is dispatched in such a way that Willow's attention is drawn not just to the extent to which he shaped her life and made choices for her but also to how little she actually learned from him, either intellectually or emotionally. Oz leaves an emotional hole, but there is no sense that what Willow actually does with her time is changed, in the way it would be if she broke with Buffy. However, the writers do not choose the Buffy/Willow route. Instead, Buffy becomes involved with the most assertively "normal" male they can think up (see the cowboy scene in "Restless," 4022), and Willow stays single until she meets Tara. In the meantime the opportunity for a lesbian romance is deflected, and Buffy once again pulls away from Willow, looking first to Riley and then to the Initiative for physical backup, and is comprehensively betrayed, this time by a strong female role model, Maggie Walsh. Buffy recapitulates the lesson: support from men and from women with power comes at a price, that is, her physical and emotional subservience. Only with Willow can Buffy maintain anything like equality.

In the relationship between Willow and Buffy, we are offered a potentially subversive take on the romance genre, not simply because a lesbian attachment may be considered but because the friendship as it develops cuts across the contemporary romantic fiction trope, rejecting the tension that characterizes both conventional romance and queer readings. This helps explain why there are relatively few examples of Buffy/Willow slash fiction (relative to the number relating to Angel/Xander or Willow/Cordelia, for example). A main romantic fiction trope requires the lovers to begin as antagonists. The trope is reinforced by the tendency of protagonists to have little or nothing in common: attraction is the only common bond. The writers of the show, however, have chosen to employ three principal routes to romance: antagonism, lack of common interest, and compatibility of interest. The antagonist attraction is Xander's principal route into relationships with Cordelia, Faith (briefly), and Anya. That the writers chose Xander for this role suggests that this is the type of relationship they believe to be most immature. The "little in common" describes Willow's relationship with Oz because, despite a general nonmaterialist worldview, Oz's initial advertised interest in computers is allowed to slide. But it does not describe her relationship with Tara. The final arrangement, in which the protagonists share common interests, is depicted in Giles and Jenny, Willow and Tara, and Buffy with Angel and Riley. The indication is that these are more mature relationships, although Buffy's behavior, as I outlined previously, leads to some doubt, and this seems deliberate. Complementarity, rather than sizzling attraction, is the core of the mature relationship. However, if the writers were to follow this wholly, this should lead Buffy to Willow (the Xander relationship is excluded by his relative intellectual inferiority[1]). The slow-growth relationship we are shown as a sign of maturity is strongest between these two.

The potential for a Buffy/Willow relationship is neutralized in part by the desexualization of Willow in both appearance and behavior. Willow's dress continuously codes her as young, cuddly, and innocent. The preference for pinks and reds seems to infantilize her (only as Vampire Willow is the red placed against black). While such fashion "rules" are no longer as respected as they once were, it remains the case that for four seasons we never see Willow in the greens, blacks, or purples that one might associate with the "sexy" redhead.[2] Much of Willow's attractiveness to Spike ("Lovers Walk," 3008; "The Initiative," 4007) seems to be based on this induced innocence. Further, both Willow and Tara have so far been coded neutrally. This is clearly not to be a butch-femme relationship, and for that mercy we must be heartily grateful: apart from its sheer mundanity, it would have allowed the script writers to have depicted Willow as either seduced or experimenter—"Not a proper lesbian" in other words—although so far no one has actually said the "L" word.[3] The deeroticization is extended by the casting of Amber Benson as Tara, who is superficially very like Willow. While there is an argument for both common interests and mirroring here, it deprives the scenes of the antagonistic tension usually regarded as essential to conventional romance and eroticism and that do frame at least the early days of all Buffy's, Xander's, and Giles's romantic entanglements. This, therefore, is the lesbian as narcissist, reminiscent of fin de siècle paintings in which two women, posed to suggest a mirror image, gaze lovingly into each other's eyes (Creed 99). On the one hand, this is lesbianism for the male gaze; on the other hand, there is a clear sense that the producers were attempting to avoid this route, but its very openness and innocence desexualizes and removes the erotic tension crucial to a queer reading of the text.

If Willow's clothing downplays her sexuality, so too does her behavior. Although we are given a nice hint of future change in the overt sexualization and queering of Vamp Willow in "Doppelgängland" (3016), the sexualized behavior she exhibits does not become a feature of Willow's relationship with Tara. While Buffy exhibits overtly sexual behavior, Willow's romances are almost always depicted in terms of cuddles (until season 5, when she is allowed a little more petting). Her lovemaking with Oz is depicted off screen, and with Tara magic and rituals become substitute for romance and sexual tension. The blowing out of the candle at the end of "New Moon Rising" (4019), while rather touching, is horribly familiar to those of us who remember the classic lines at the end of chapter 21 of Radclyffe Hall's *The Well of Loneliness:* "And that night, they were not parted." The only exception, and a notable one, to this deeroticization is the scene in which Willow paints Sappho's poem "Ode to Aphrodite" on Tara's back, and it may well be that as the series becomes more consistently aimed at the adult market, this eroticization will develop. But at the moment, Willow's relationship with Tara, in addition to undercutting a queer reading of the Buffy/Willow relationship, actually undercuts a queer reading of Willow at all, first by neutralizing her sexuality and then by rechanneling thoughts of lesbian relationships in a safe direction.

As Willow matures, Buffy stays essentially the same person; Buffy continues to look to male figures for emotional support when they are available but uses Willow to "fill in" when her relationships become difficult. Willow, however, takes the gained confidence and employs it in the attraction of the painfully shy Tara, in which she repeats, in reverse, the primary dynamic of her relationship with Buffy. As Willow became more assertive in Buffy's presence, and with Buffy's support, so Tara stutters less either when with Willow or when acting in ways that support Willow. By the middle of the season, the relationship between Willow and Buffy appears much more equal, despite Willow's characteristically hesitant mode of speech. Unfortunately, all the evidence suggests that Buffy does not prize equality in emotional relationships.

The real winner in this situation is Willow, and to this degree the relationship between Buffy and Willow supports a queer reading within the paradigm that Faderman outlines. Buffy fails to exploit the supportive possibilities of this relationship, but it becomes the foundation of an empowered Willow and is eventually displaced onto her relationship with Tara at the same time as this relationship undercuts any attempt to read an erotic relationship into the Buffy/Willow dynamic.

It is not possible, in the end, to sustain a queer reading of the Buffy/Willow relationship, but this does not obviate the possibilities of a queer reading of the overall text. This reading, I suspect, is to be found instead in the Buffy/Faith dynamic, which clearly fits the model of antagonistic romance much more closely than the Willow/Buffy structure ever could. That Faith does not have a sexual relationship with Buffy is due primarily to the target audience, but it fails to obscure what Roz Kaveney has described as the mirroring relationship in which Faith, at least, is deeply involved in attempting to comprehend, while fiercely resenting, the way in which Buffy's mind and emotions operate. Faith is Buffy without restraint and inhibitions. The romance structure is reinforced by the physical mirroring of Buffy and Faith. Faith is the dark, boyish, and richly sexual figure juxtaposed against Buffy's fair, feminine, and oddly pure sexuality. In contrast, while she may resent it bitterly, Willow can only ever be a foil: both her looks and her skills operate as Buffy's backdrop rather than as her match. If Willow wishes to reject her sidekick status, she must move out of Buffy's shadow in other directions, which, in season 5, she is doing very successfully. Willow's development as a character acts within the political paradigm that Faderman has described, but as the quieter and more private member of the partnership, she is the one who gains most because she is the one who recognizes the value of the relationship. What Faderman did not understand was the possibility of the private partner becoming the public one in other contexts and applying the confidence thus gained. But despite the possibility of this political queer reading, the dynamics of the romance trope, the structure of heterosociality in which Buffy is embroiled, the writers' construction of a heterosocial ensemble, and Buffy's need for male validation coalesce to reduce the possibilities for a romantic/erotic queer reading of the Buffy/Willow relationship.

NOTES

1. Editors' note: For a contrasting view of Xander, see chapter 6 in this volume.

2. Editors' note: Near the end of season 5, Willow appears in such colors, for example, in "Intervention" (5018) and "Tough Love" (5019).

3. Editors' note: The word "lesbian" is used in season 5 when Willow, interrogated by the Watchers' Council, speaks the word while describing her relationship with Tara in "Checkpoint" (5012):

> *Nigel:* I need to know a little bit more about the Slayer, and about the both of you. Your relationship, whatever you can tell me.
> *Tara:* O-o-our relationship?
> *Willow:* We're friends.
> *Tara:* Good friends.
> *Willow:* Girlfriends, actually.
> *Tara:* Yes, we're girlfriends.
> *Willow:* We're in love. We're [. . .] lovers. [puts hand on Tara's knee] We're lesbian, gay-type lovers.
> *Nigel:* I meant your relationship with the Slayer.

5

Choosing Your Own Mother
Mother-Daughter Conflicts in Buffy

J. P. Williams

The scene is Joyce Summers's kitchen. Her teenage daughter announces that she is something called a "vampire slayer" and that she has to save the world from destruction. Joyce has trouble grasping all this. The characters talk at cross-purposes until Joyce issues an ultimatum: "You walk out of this house, don't even think about coming back." Buffy, of course, leaves anyway ("Becoming," part 2, 2022).

Joyce and Buffy's relationship raises issues about mothering that run throughout *Buffy the Vampire Slayer*. Even as it proclaims allegiance to ideals of female power, *Buffy* presents few positive female models for its teenage protagonists. A. Susan Owen claims that "social and mystical powers (on the side of good) are matrilineal in the series: only females can be vampire slayers, only females can have supernatural powers, and only females can discern who the predators are" (24). However, female power in *Buffy* is complicated. Buffy's power is directed by her Watcher, Rupert Giles, and the largely male Watchers' Council. Being part of a female slayer tradition does not help Buffy since Giles controls what she knows about slaying.

Buffy is overfathered and undermothered. Joyce is presented as well meaning but ineffectual. Other mother-daughter relationships on the series are downright deadly. The only hope the series provides is finding a motherlike figure to provide the inspiration and guidance biological relationships lack. Yet even this sort of relationship is perilous if a young woman seeks guidance from the wrong woman.

CHOSEN AND DISPOSABLE: SLAYING AS FEMALE TRADITION

A Slayer hunts vampires; Buffy is the Slayer; don't tell anyone. I think
that's all the vampire information you need.

—Giles in "The Harvest" (1002)

When Buffy overhears Giles discussing a prophecy that predicts her death,
she asks some pertinent questions: "So that's it, huh? I remember the drill.
One Slayer dies, next one's called. Wonder who she is. Will you train her,
or will they send someone else? Does it say how he's going to kill me? Think
it'll hurt?" ("Prophecy Girl," 1012). Giles has no answers for Buffy, who
has hit on the crux of the problem: although she is part of a line of female
warriors dating back thousands of years, that tradition is unavailable to her.
Her knowledge of Slayers and slaying is filtered through her father figure
Giles, who, in his dual roles of Watcher and librarian, controls Buffy's access to knowledge and parcels out information on a "need-to-know" basis.
The scene continues with Buffy expressing her anger that Giles has withheld
information. She turns her rage on the Watcher, throwing his books at him.
She yells, "Read me the signs! Tell me my fortune! You're so useful, sitting
here with all of your books. You're really a lot of help!" Giles's refusal to
discuss Buffy's Slayer heritage is presented as stemming from his fatherly affection for her. Various moments reinforce the father-daughter parallel, as
when Giles hands Buffy her high school diploma ("Graduation Day," part
2, 3022). Such father-daughter moments reinforce the notion that Giles
withholds information in order to protect Buffy.

No such feelings temper the workings of the heavily paternal Watchers'
Council. Although Giles alludes to the Council several times, the series reveals little about its workings.[1] From what is shown, however, the Council
appears to be largely male and British.[2] The Council's traditions are rigidly
adhered to (as in the ritual Buffy undergoes on her eighteenth birthday);
Watchers can be replaced, as Giles is, by order of the Council ("Helpless,"
3012). In "This Year's Girl" (4015) and "Who Are You?" (4016), as well
as in the *Angel* episode "Redemption," Council representatives appear as
thugs attempting to punish "renegade" Slayers such as Faith. The Council's
insistence that the Chosen One conform to their standards labels the Slayer
a disposable and replaceable commodity. The Council represents a male-
dominated hierarchy caring less about any particular girl who happens to
be the Slayer than about exercising control over the power she represents.

The problematic nature of Buffy's relationship to the Slayer tradition sur-
faces in her encounters with Kendra and the "spirit of the first Slayer" that
Buffy confronts in a dream. Both these Slayers are black and therefore coded
as Other in the overwhelmingly white world of Sunnydale.[3] Both are representatives of a gender and social order the Watchers' Council wishes to re-

strain. The first Slayer is Buffy's power uncontrolled; Kendra is that same power overdisciplined and overtrained. When Kendra reveals that she has studied the Slayer's handbook, Buffy asks, "Handbook? What handbook? How come I don't have a handbook?" (Giles replies that he believes the handbook "would be of no use in your case." ["What's My Line?" part 2, 2010]).

Kendra is, from the Council's point of view, the practically perfect Slayer: solemn, respectful, and efficient. She possesses more information about slaying than Buffy, but Kendra employs that knowledge exactly as her superiors instruct. By contrast, the Spirit is uncontrolled fury. Buffy recognizes the Spirit but rejects her. Rather than learning from this manifestation of the original Slayer, Buffy defeats the Spirit through mockery: "Are you quite finished? It's over, okay? I'm going to ignore you, and you're going to go away. You're really going to have to get over the whole primal power thing. You're not the source of me. Also, in terms of hair care, you really want to say, 'What kind of impression am I making in the workplace?' 'cause ——" ("Restless," 4022).

Buffy's use of language as a weapon is crucial. Belensky et al. group women's experiences into five epistemological categories, the first being silence. In this stage, "words were perceived as weapons. Words were used to separate and diminish people, not to connect and empower them. The silent women worried that they would be punished just for using words—any words" (24). The Spirit, who has no language of her own, is indeed vanquished by Buffy's pointed language—language specifically mocking the Spirit's appearance.[4]

Kendra, relying on her Watcher and her handbook, represents the second stage: received knowledge. "The ideas and ideals that these women hear in the words of others are concrete and dualistic. Things are right or wrong, true or false, good or bad, black and white. They assume that there is only one right answer to each question, and that all other answers and all contrary views are automatically wrong" (Belensky et al. 37).

The inference from Buffy's encounters with Kendra and the Spirit is that she has little to learn from other Slayers. They are as disposable to Buffy as they are to the Council. She can rely on Giles for any background information she needs concerning the demons she fights; the rest of slaying she makes up as she goes along. She has moved past silence and received knowledge to subjective knowledge, "disregard[ing] the knowledge and advice of remote experts" (Belensky et al. 68) in favor of an experiential perspective. Thus, Buffy cannot rely on the "matrilineal tradition" of slaying to guide her. Most of what she knows about that tradition is male dominated, and what she learns firsthand makes her view herself as unique. Without access to this tradition, it might be natural for Buffy to turn to her mother for guidance. However, mother-daughter relationships on *Buffy* are fraught with peril.

MOTHER DOESN'T KNOW BEST: JOYCE SUMMERS, SHEILA ROSENBERG, AND CATHERINE MADISON

Since when does it matter what I want? I wanted a normal, happy daughter. Instead, I got a Slayer.

—Joyce Summers in "Gingerbread" (3011)

Buffy the Vampire Slayer has been discussed as a female coming-of-age tale in which the hero faces monsters symbolizing real-life horrors that teenage girls encounter (see Wilcox, "There"). Series creator Joss Whedon acknowledges this aspect of the program: "What makes the show popular is the central myth of high school as horrific—the humiliation, the alienation, you know, the confusion of high school is taken to such great proportions that it becomes demonic" (Interview, "Welcome to the Hellmouth"). Given that the series foregrounds the parallels between adolescence as hell and life on the Hellmouth, it is unsurprising that conflicts between mother and daughters appear frequently on *Buffy.*

Nancy Chodorow's theories provide a framework for my discussion of mothers and daughters in *Buffy.* Chodorow's work describes how female personality development occurs in the traditional patriarchal family. Chodorow maintains that, while mother-infant interactions provide the earliest example of self-in-relation for both genders, men and women internalize this experience differently. For girls, being mothered is an intense symbiotic union with a parent essentially like themselves, resulting in an internalized image of the self existing primarily in relation to others.

The relationship between Joyce and Buffy Summers illustrates these issues. During the first two seasons, the plot requires that Joyce remain unaware of her daughter's other life. She is *Buffy's* Lois Lane, her intelligence and love for the hero called into question by her inability to perceive the hero's superpowers.[5] If anything, Joyce's failure to perceive Buffy's dual identity as Slayer and student is a greater failing than Lois Lane's traditional inability to envision Clark Kent without his glasses. Joyce carries the burden of society's expectation that mothers should instinctively understand their children. Her failure to comprehend her daughter's special abilities makes Joyce seem foolish and negligent.

To counter the charge of neglectfulness, the series has Joyce continually stating just how much she loves Buffy. These conversations usually take place in the Summers's house, reinforcing Joyce's relegation to the private space of the home. The most notable of these conversations occurs in "Passion" (2017), when Joyce states, "Buffy, you can shut me out of your life; I'm pretty much used to that. But don't expect me to stop caring about you 'cause it's never going to happen. I love you more than anything in the world." Joyce's declarations of love contain an undercurrent of desperation based on the fact that she cannot understand Buffy's world. The split between Joyce and Buffy is also indicated by the manner in which their scenes are filmed: they rarely inhabit the same frame, they are often separated by objects such as the dinner table, and they are placed at different ends of the same room. Joyce's attempts to discipline Buffy fail as well because she cannot comprehend what Buffy is talking about. In "Welcome to the Hellmouth," for example, Joyce attempts to reassure both herself and Buffy that they can make a fresh start in Sunnydale:

> *Joyce:* You're a good girl, Buffy. You just fell in with the wrong crowd. But that is all behind us now.
> *Buffy:* It is. From now on, I'm only going to hang out with the living. I mean, lively. People.
> *Joyce:* Okay. You have fun.

This conversation is an example of how *Buffy* uses language to emphasize the difference between the teen and adult worlds. As Wilcox observes, "Adults in general and Buffy's mom in particular consistently misinterpret what is happening in the teens' world. [. . .] This need for translation is emphasized throughout the series by the linguistic patterns of the different groups" ("There" 21).

Joyce does manage to physically protect Buffy in "School Hard" (2003) and takes her daughter's side against Principal Snyder after Buffy is expelled ("Dead Man's Party," 3002). Overall, however, her attempts to protect Buffy are ineffectual. It is Giles who succeeds in getting Buffy reinstated in school. Joyce's attempts to shield Buffy from harm demonstrate her misunderstanding regarding the details of Buffy's life. Joyce is at her most ineffectual in "Prophecy Girl" (1012), when she attributes Buffy's loss of appetite and sudden desire for a "mother-daughter vacation" to the fact that "the wrong somebody" asked her to a school dance. She tries to cheer Buffy up with the present of an expensive prom gown and an anecdote about how she met Buffy's father at a college dance. When Buffy maintains that she cannot go to the dance without a date, Joyce's reply is singularly inappropriate: "Is it written somewhere? You should do what you want." However, as Giles has informed Buffy, it is indeed written somewhere, and Buffy's destiny as the Slayer means that she cannot do what she wants.

Joyce's mothering also suffers through her stated reliance on expert discourse regarding child rearing. Attempting to keep Buffy from going out in "The Harvest" (1002), Joyce says, "The tapes all say I should get used to saying it. No." Wanting Buffy to confide in her, Joyce tries to reassure her daughter by saying, "You can tell me anything. I've read all the parenting books. You cannot surprise me" ("Passion"). Like Kendra, Joyce relies on received knowledge that proves inadequate. This contrasts directly with Giles, who understands that handbooks will not help him teach Buffy. Here the series reproduces the discourse Nina Leibman discusses in 1950s family sitcoms such as *Father Knows Best*. These series mocked the world of experts Joyce relies on, valorizing the father's commonsense approach to parenting.[6]

In "Becoming," part 2, Buffy confronts her mother, chiding Joyce for not seeing the truth: "Open your eyes, Mom. What do you think has been going on for the past two years—the fights, the weird occurrences? How many times have you washed blood out of my clothing, and you still haven't figured it out?" Buffy here confines her mother to the domestic realm; despite Joyce's job at "the gallery," it is her caretaker role that matters. She is the one who washes blood out of clothes. Thus, when Buffy dreams of Joyce in a wall, it is not just the wall separating them that matters. Buffy's dream reveals that she sees her mother as enclosed in a small space, a small life where "I made some lemonade, and I'm learning to play mah jongg" ("Restless," 4022). Buffy, by contrast, inhabits vast, open spaces. Identifying with her mother means entering this smaller domestic space, leaving her freedom behind. This image reflects Chodorow's description of how a girl attempts to disassociate herself from her mother during adolescence: "she tries to solve her ambivalent dependence and sense of oneness by projection and by splitting the good and bad aspects of objects; her mother and home represent bad, the extrafamilial world, good" (137).

The mother/daughter roles frequently get reversed between Joyce and Buffy. "Gingerbread" begins with a sort of "take-your-mother-to-work" day in which Joyce attempts to bond with her daughter by bringing Buffy a snack during patrol. When Joyce discovers the bodies of two murdered children, the mother-daughter dynamic is reversed. Joyce becomes the child traumatized on discovering that the world is a dangerous place; Buffy becomes the adult trying to offer explanation and comfort:

> *Buffy:* I'm so sorry that you had to see this, but I promise everything's going to be okay.
> *Joyce:* How?
> *Buffy:* Because I'm going to find whatever did it.
> *Joyce:* I guess. It's just you can't. You can't make it right.
> *Buffy:* I know. I'm sorry, but I'll take care of everything, I promise. Just try and calm down.

The accompanying action, in which Joyce begins sobbing and Buffy embraces her, visually reinforces the mother's infantilization. That image is immediately contrasted with a scene in which Buffy is upset and Giles is the calm one. Buffy is filmed here from Giles's point of view; he is at the top of the stairs looking down at Buffy, making her look smaller and childlike. Even though Buffy is the more experienced and mature than Joyce, she is still the child in Giles's eyes.

The murdered children are an illusion, created by a demon with a history of setting community members against one another. In this case, the split is largely along generational lines. Both Joyce Summers and Sheila Rosenberg turn against their daughters. This is an exaggeration of a dynamic that already exists, illustrated by Joyce's longtime inability to understand Buffy's double life and Sheila's neglect of Willow. Directly contrasted to Sheila's and Joyce's reactions toward their daughters is Buffy's unwavering belief in Willow and her attempt to protect her friend when Willow's locker is searched for proof of occult activity.

Both Sheila and the demon who directs Joyce's actions are presented as manifestations of the experts Joyce puts so much stock in. Sheila is an academic who pontificates about "the rise of mysticism among adolescents" and "the patriarchal bias in the *Mister Rogers* show." As a parent, however, Sheila is even less effective than Joyce. As Willow notes, her mother is "not interested in my extracurricular activities. Or my curricular activities." Sheila fails to notice her daughter's new haircut for almost a year, she has no idea who Willow is dating, and she thinks Willow's best friend is named Bunny Summers. When Willow attempts to connect with her mother, her revelations are treated as delusions. "Identification with mythical icons," Sheila tells Willow, "is perfectly typical of your age-group. It's a classic adolescent response to the pressure of incipient adulthood." As the expert who fails at relating to her own daughter, Sheila provides another indictment of the tenets Joyce relies on.

"Gingerbread" depicts the fear of losing the mother's love that threatens during adolescence. As Chodorow notes, during the female Oedipal conflict, mothers and daughters fear that their disconnection will result in tragedy:

> [Mothers] desire both to keep their daughters close and to push them into adulthood. This ambivalence in turn creates more anxiety in their daughters and provokes attempts by these daughters to break away [. . .]. This spiral, laden as it is with ambivalence, leaves mother and daughter convinced that any separation between them will bring disaster to both. (135)

The horror in the episode, therefore, is not the demon disguising itself as two angelic children; it is the moment Sheila turns on Willow. Raising her voice, calling Willow "witch," and then reminding her to take a coat because it is cold out, Sheila personifies the disaster that women fear will result from mother and daughter's psychological separation. However, there are also perils in an overidentification between mother and daughter. That dynamic can be observed in the relationship between Catherine and Amy Madison in "The Witch" (1003).

"The Witch" illustrates the inherent dangers in not allowing the mother-daughter separation to take place. When Buffy and Amy meet at cheerleading tryouts, Amy praises her mother, former Sunnydale High cheerleading sensation "Catherine the Great." Like Joyce, Catherine is a single parent, her high school sweetheart husband having "run off with Miss Trailer Trash" when Amy was twelve. Catherine, as Amy describes her, appears intensely devoted to her daughter; she coaches Amy through six hours of cheerleading practice each day and has bought her daughter "everything I ever wanted." Small wonder, then, that Amy gazes lovingly at the cheerleading photo and trophy Sunnydale High still displays as a symbol of her mother's glory days.

Buffy initially envies Amy and Catherine's relationship. She contrasts Catherine's attitude to that of Joyce, who is too busy with her gallery business to even notice what activity her daughter is pursuing. However, for once Joyce has summed up the situation accurately when she notes, "Sounds like her mom doesn't have a lot to do." Indeed, Catherine has nothing except cheerleading in her life. She has, in fact, appropriated her daughter's life and body through witchcraft. The pre-Oedipal mother-daughter bond here is prolonged unnaturally and at the cost of the daughter's psyche, which must reside in her mother's body. While Catherine relives her cheerleading days, Amy is relegated to her mother's place in the home. Thus, "The Witch" suggests that the mother wishes to prolong the bond for selfish reasons long past the time when the daughter wishes to switch her identification to the father.

Significantly, it is Buffy who recognizes that Amy and Catherine have changed places. As a teenager faced with her own mother-daughter issues, she is better placed than Giles to see the traumatized teenager hidden in the adult woman's body (not to mention the telltale batch of brownies the figure-conscious Catherine would never eat). Catherine must be cast out in order to put Amy back on the Oedipal track. Appropriately, the series' all-purpose father figure Giles casts the spell against Catherine; the feverish Buffy watches helplessly until mother and daughter revert to their proper bodies.

Catherine ultimately defeats herself. Her moment of glory as a cheerleader is undercut by the fact that, no matter how hard she trains, she cannot force Amy's body to perform as her own youthful body once did. Catherine's failure reinforces Buffy's response when Joyce suggests that her daughter pursue the extracurricular activity Joyce once enjoyed: "Well, this just in. I'm not you. I'm into my own thing." Finally, Catherine is defeated when her own spell turns against her.[7] Catherine's consciousness is imprisoned in the cheerleading trophy she had gazed at so lovingly, a symbol of the damage that can happen when the pre-Oedipal stage lasts too long.[8]

Released from her mother's influence, Amy moves to the Oedipal stage and life with father. She changes from Catherine's cheerleading garb into a loose-fitting T-shirt and pants; she happily tells Buffy about staying in on Saturday night to bake brownies with her father. And yet, Amy remains her mother's daughter in some respects. She casts spells to pass exams and performs a love spell for Xander with disastrous consequences ("Bewitched, Bothered and Bewildered," 2016). In "Gingerbread" (3011), she changes herself into a rat to avoid burning at the stake. Like her mother, however, Amy remains (as of the end of season 4) trapped by her own spell, a pet rat in Buffy and Willow's dorm room. That Amy cannot properly channel the power she inherits from her mother raises an important question for the young women of *Buffy*: if your mother is an inadequate model, is there another woman who can lead you through adolescence safely?

FINDING THE RIGHT MOTHER: GWENDOLYN POST, MAGGIE WALSH, AND JENNY CALENDAR

This isn't a fad, Rupert. We are creating a new society here.

—Jenny Calendar in "I Robot, You Jane" (1008)

Faith, Buffy, and Willow all seek substitute mothers, but the results illustrate the perils that can result from following the wrong mother figure. Faith (whose biological mother was an alcoholic) arguably has the worst luck. Her first female Watcher is murdered ("Faith, Hope and Trick," 3003). Then she encounters Watcher Gwendolyn Post. At first, the relationship with Mrs. Post seems promising; she compliments Faith on her "Spartan" lifestyle and assures the younger woman that they will enter into a long-term training program. For Faith, who has been abandoned by all the authority figures in her life, such a relationship could be crucial. However, Gwendolyn Post actually is in Sunnydale to obtain something called the Glove of Myhnegon. When she wears the glove, her real feelings emerge: "Faith, a word of advice—you're an idiot" ("Revelations," 3007). No wonder that the next parental figure Faith turns to is male.

For Buffy, the potential mother figure is college professor Maggie Walsh. Buffy's enthusiasm for Walsh, first as a psychology instructor and then as head of The Initiative, is so great that Giles seems threatened by it ("A New Man," 4012). Maggie Walsh, however, perceives Buffy as a threat. Walsh is, in fact, coded as the mother of sons—the monstrous Adam and Buffy's boyfriend Riley Finn. Walsh sends Buffy out to fight alone with a defective weapon, plotting the Slayer's death ("The I in Team," 4013). Thus, Walsh, like Gwendolyn Post and Catherine Madison, turns into a murderous mother figure, leaving Buffy with the ineffectual Joyce.

Willow has better luck in her relationship with Jenny Calendar.[9] Jenny first appears as Sunnydale High's computer science teacher in the episode "I Robot, You Jane." From the beginning, she talks about the patriarchal control of knowledge and how computers can be used to create a new society.

Her expertise in computers, therefore, is employed for political ends. Significantly, her remarks are addressed to Giles, who represents traditional sources of information. "You think," she tells Giles, "that knowledge should be kept in these carefully guarded repositories where only a handful of white guys can get at it." Jenny is part of a worldwide community of what she calls "techno-pagans." She demonstrates an impressive knowledge of the occult and a commitment to using technology for mystical ends. "You think the realm of the mystical is limited to ancient texts and relics?" she asks Giles "Has bad old science made the magic go away? The divine exists in cyberspace same as out here" ("I Robot, You Jane"). Jenny seems an appropriate mentor for Willow, combining as she does the computer expertise Willow has shown an aptitude for and Sheila Rosenberg's politically charged discourse. Thus, it is logical that Jenny appoints Willow as her successor, asking Willow to substitute teach shortly before her death ("Passion").

Jenny is revealed to be a member of the gypsy tribe that cursed Angel; she has been sent to Sunnydale to ensure that the curse remains unbroken. She is, in effect, Angel's Watcher, but with one important difference from Giles: she has not been given all the relevant information about the curse. Her uncle, who reminds Jenny of her responsibility to the tribe, does not tell her that Angel will lose his soul again if he experiences a moment of perfect happiness. This lack of knowledge prevents Jenny from warning Angel and Buffy about the danger if they make love; by extension, it is this lack of knowledge that leads to Jenny's death at Angelus's hands.

With Jenny's death, Willow takes over as computer teacher. But Jenny's death does not end her mentoring of Willow. In "I Only Have Eyes for You" (2019), Willow tells Giles that "I found a bunch of files and Internet sites on paganism and magic and stuff" on Jenny's computer. In the same episode, she tells Buffy that "I've been browsing on some of Ms. Calendar's pagan sites." Willow translates the computer data Jenny left behind, performing the ritual Jenny discovered to restore Angel's soul ("Becoming," part 2). As she develops along the path she discovered through Jenny's guidance, Willow continues studying witchcraft; she takes this study so seriously that she complains to Buffy when UC-Sunnydale's Wicca group turns out to be "a bunch of wanna-blessed-be's" ("Hush," 4010). Willow, devoted to the serious study of witchcraft she adopted from Jenny, complains about the group's faux-Wiccan pose: "You know, nowadays every girl with a henna tattoo and a spice rack thinks she's a sister to the dark ones" ("Hush"). Although Jenny herself never claims to be a witch ("I don't have that kind of power," she tells Giles in "I Robot, You Jane"), her study of the subject inspires Willow.

In many television series, characters who leave are simply stricken from the memories of those who remain. Jenny, however, continues to be a presence in the Slayerettes' lives. She occasionally appears in fantasy and/or dream sequences (e.g., "Amends," 3010), and characters often mention her (see, e.g., "I Only Have Eyes for You," 2019, and "Revelations," 3007). These references lead the viewer to conclude that Jenny remains an influence on *Buffy*'s characters. Her influence can also be seen in Willow's evolving fashion sense. Fashion and style are frequently indicators of character in *Buffy*, and Willow's fashion sense evolves in a manner reminiscent of Jenny's. Jenny alternates between leather jackets and long, flowing skirts—clothes visually at odds with the suits and conservative dresses of the more conventional teachers at Sunnydale High. When Buffy first comes to Sunnydale, Willow dresses in conservative jumpers her mother chooses for her. Willow moves from that schoolgirl look to more individualistic skirts and T-shirts, some of which recall Jenny's tastes. Jenny, moreover, is comfortable with her sexuality. Her banter with Giles (see especially the corkscrew comment in "I Robot, You Jane") suggests that she does not confine herself to patriarchal standards of sexuality. Willow, too, follows an unconventional path, her affections moving from Xander to Oz to Tara.

Yet there is a limit to Jenny's influence, and that limit suggests why it is ultimately difficult to label *Buffy* a feminist text. Jenny herself, after all, is a victim of the patriarchy she criticized. Trained to think in terms of the vengeance her tribe wants to exact on Angel, she is unable to transcend her early conditioning. As she explains to Giles shortly before her death, "I was raised by the people that Angel hurt the most. My duty to them was the first thing I was ever taught" ("Passion"). Jenny, the actively sexual woman who could debate Giles as an equal, is reduced to the position of obedient child in her dealings with her uncle. Her powerless position relative to her tribe is demonstrated by a scene with her uncle in "Innocence" (2014). As he finally explains the implications of the curse to Jenny, she is seated. The camera is positioned at a high angle, making Jenny appear small and powerless relative to her uncle.

Although Jenny inspires Willow, her death leaves no strong older woman for the younger characters to consult and demonstrates the limitations of *Buffy*'s feminist vision. Not even Jenny, a woman who speaks against patriarchy and envisions a new society that marries magic and technology, can escape the influence of the patriarchal order. Ultimately, she cannot defy her own fathers and survive without their aid. One of the images frequently highlighted in *Buffy*'s opening credits is the terrifying moment Angelus casually snaps Jenny's neck. The ultimate woman-in-jeopardy scene, it signals the limits of *Buffy*'s vision. Buffy may run down the halls of Sunnydale High confidently; for the mature woman, however, that path is a maze with death at its center. Jenny, the adult woman best equipped to survive *Buffy*'s world, cannot triumph. The Chosen One and her friends, therefore, will have to invent their own ideal of womanhood with few positive models to guide them. Whether *Buffy* will eventually provide an alternative model of womanhood is perhaps the series's most intriguing cliffhanger.

NOTES

1. Editors' note: In season 5, in "Checkpoint," we do learn quite a bit more about the Council when its leader, Travers (previously seen in "Helpless," 3012), and several of his assistants show up in Sunnydale with information about Glory.

2. Three female Watchers are mentioned: Giles's grandmother, Faith's original Watcher, and Gwendolyn Post.

3. The third Slayer Buffy encounters, Faith, is white; but her accent, lifestyle, and clothing code Faith as working class and therefore different from the average Sunnydale High student. (Editors' note: See chapter 2 in this volume.)

4. Buffy's comments about the Spirit's appearance are especially disturbing in light of the first Slayer's ethnic identity. WASP Buffy mocking the dreadlocked African woman has uncomfortable racial overtones. (Thanks to Danielle Dupre for calling my attention to this aspect of the episode.) (Editors' note: On language, see also chapter 6 in this volume.)

5. For a discussion of the gender politics of the secret identity convention in comics, see J. P. Williams.

6. This connection is doubly interesting because one of the sitcom writers whom Leibman interviewed was John Whedon, grandfather of *Buffy*'s creator.

7. This is in keeping with the Wiccan principle that "What is done will be returned to the doer. [. . .] It's an automatic response, like a ricochet" (Cunningham 136).

8. In a later episode ("Phases," 2015), Oz points out to Willow that the cheerleading trophy is unusual: its eyes seem to follow you. Presumably, Catherine and the trophy are destroyed along with the high school in "Graduation Day," part 2.

9. The surname "Calendar" is singularly appropriate since Jenny's days are numbered.

6

Staking in Tongues

Speech Act as Weapon in Buffy

Karen Eileen Overbey
and Lahney Preston-Matto

Once again, something is not quite right in Sunnydale: Jonathan has cast a spell of Augmentation, making him best-selling author, star athlete, chart-topping pop star, and master of arcana. In search of a counterspell, Giles, Xander, and Willow turn to their favorite method of research—consulting dusty books in Giles's study. Riley, a newcomer to the group, flips a page and wonders, "These spells—they really work?" Willow answers, "They work, Riley [. . .] but they take concentration, being attuned with the forces of the universe." "Right," adds Xander, reading from another tome. "You can't just go '*Librum Incendere*' and expect . . ." His book bursts into flames. Startled, he slams it shut, as a weary Giles reprimands him: "Xander, don't speak Latin in front of the books" ("Superstar," 4017).

This incident demonstrates—apart from the frail flammability of Giles's manuscript collection—the materiality of language in *Buffy the Vampire Slayer.* Words and utterances have palpable power, and their rules must be respected if they are to be wielded as weapons in the fight against evil. "*Librum Incendere*" is only one example of the potent and almost physical presence of language in the series. In "The Wish" (3009), Cordelia's wistful "I wish Buffy Summers had never come to Sunnydale" is taken literally through Anya's supernatural intervention; and in "Hush" (4010), language (or, at least, speech) is literally taken—stolen by The Gentlemen, the funereal, floating demons who terrorize Sunnydale.

"Hush" is rich with language play and makes communication a subject: Giles and Olivia stumble through small talk; Willow complains that the Wiccan "wanna-blessed-be's" are all talk ("Gaia, blah blah moon, menstrual lifeforce power [. . .]"); Anya shocks Xander with her inability to distinguish between private and public conversations; and Buffy babbles at Riley, bluffing her way around her identity. These localized disruptions in speech are a prelude to the global disruption caused by The Gentlemen, who steal the voices of Sunnydale in order to soundlessly cut out the hearts of seven people. The absence of language in "Hush" is a helpless horror: unable to speak to each other, the Slayer Squad cannot fight the forces of evil. What is it about language that is so crucial to combat in *Buffy*? Are speech acts truly weapons, as vital as crossbows and spinning roundhouse kicks?

The linguist John R. Searle insists on the importance of "speech acts" in daily life. He defines a speech act as language that both describes an action and *is* an action. His theory turns on the idea of language as rule-governed behavior; speech acts are instances of that behavior at work in the world, the linguistic performances of meaning (*Speech Acts* 16–18). Speakers who understand the rules of engagement can also manipulate them: if a language is not "adequate to the task" of expressing meaning, a radical speaker can "enrich the language by introducing new terms or other devices into it" (19–20). Searle identifies and characterizes different types of speech acts—making statements, giving commands, asking questions, and making promises (22–23)—and various modes of reference and expression used to particularize meaning. He also defines metaphors as speech acts: the dissimilarity between speech and meaning in metaphors forces performative gestures by both speaker and listener. "Dead metaphors," however, have lost any secondary meaning and thus require no performative gesture on the part of speaker or audience. Searle says dead metaphors are created from living ones: "an expression becomes a dead metaphor, and then finally becomes an idiom or acquires a new meaning different from the original meaning" (*Expression and Meaning* 86). So dead metaphors are not so much dead as undead. They die and are then reborn with a different purpose.

They die and are reborn, much like vampires. We should not be surprised, then, that Buffy and Company rarely, if ever, employ dead metaphors; they are on the cutting edge of language, creating new expressions, constantly manipulating older expressions in order to update them ("it's a turvy-topsy world," Willow says in "Pangs," 4008) or completely circumventing the expected use of language. So, is the language of *Buffy* rule governed? We suggest that it is: some rules are instructive and easily mastered—surely Xander will not twice "speak Latin in front of the books." Others are embedded in the structure of the show's reality and require a broader understanding of "language." Jonathan's Augmentation spell in "Superstar" proves him to be not a "radical speaker" but a cheater. His spell is an attempt, more than anything, to make him fluent in tongues with which he is neither familiar nor proficient. The Scooby Gang, however, knows the rules of language and languages and uses them to speak radically, enriching language with new terms and "other devices." The gang's language capabilities are integral to their ability to fight evil, and these skills involve much more than just spoken English. Xander and Buffy are not comfortable unless cracking wise, while Giles and Willow are more at ease with the written word. More important, each character has a specific relationship with language. If indeed there is a theory of language in *Buffy*, it is one that requires four specialized voices, in combination, to fight the forces of evil.

✖ ✖ ✖

Are we gonna fight, or is there just gonna be a monster sarcasm rally?

—"Stoner" Vampire, to Buffy, in "The Freshman" (4001)

Buffy is punny—even the undead know it. In ho-hum, day-to-day, hand-to-claw combat, her leaps and lunges are liberally peppered with spicy retorts. She taunts them: "You're a vampire. Oh, I'm sorry, was that an offensive term? Should I say 'undead American?'" ("When She Was Bad," 2001). She teases them: "Wow, that was really funny looking! Could you do it again?" Vampire: "I'll kill you for that." Buffy: "For that? What were you trying to kill me for before?" ("Helpless," 3012). She makes them play straight man: "Wanna see my impression of Gandhi? [The demon looks up, and Buffy thwacks his head with a lumpy club.] Well, you know . . . if he was really pissed off" ("Anne," 3001). And she is comically wounded when her humor falls flat:

> You know very well, you eat this late . . . [she stakes the vamp] you're gonna get heartburn. Get it? Heartburn? [He turns to dust.] That's it? That's all I get? One lame-ass vamp with no appreciation for my painstakingly thought-out puns. I don't think the forces of darkness are even trying. ("Wild at Heart," 4006)

Buffy is easily able to play with language in this way—it is tied to Slayage. But it is not a role that just anyone can fill, as Willow discovers when she substitutes for the AWOL Buffy in "Anne." "That's right, big boy," she entices the vamp, with Slayeresque attitude, "come and get it." The ensuing struggle is a messy sprawl of limbs, and the prey escapes unstaked. A breathless Xander queries Willow, "Come and get it big boy?!" Willow stutters,

> Well, well, the *Slayer* always says a pun or a witty play on words and I think it throws vampires off and makes them frightened that I'm wisecracking and okay, I didn't really have time to work on that one but *you* try it every time!

Humbled, Xander muses on the Slayer's skills: "I've always been amazed with how Buffy fought, but in a way I feel like we took her punning for granted."

Indeed. Buffy herself is flummoxed when, in the Jonathan-induced alternate reality of "Superstar," her tongue trips on what should be an easy return of Spike's "back off, Betty": "It's Buffy, you big . . . bleached . . . stupid guy!" Her heroic role, as well as her linguistic role, has been diminished by Jonathan's spell, and this is one of the niggling clues that leads to restoration.

But is Buffy's quipping just a display of intellectual cleavage? Or is there really something at stake? Joking at the moment of combat places Buffy in a long tradition of sardonic heroes: from Hamlet to Sherlock Holmes, from James Bond to Jackie Chan. Not only does it "throw vampires off" and make them "frightened," the joke disarms, making the foe witless. And in this witlessness, they are vulnerable. As Freud argued, an enemy ridiculed is made "small, inferior, despicable, or comic [. . . and] we achieve in a roundabout way the enjoyment of overcoming him" (*Jokes* 64). This kind of witty displacement depends on the dynamic between joke teller, listener, and butt of the joke. The joke creates a bond between joker (Buffy) and audience but requires active participation from both parties. The "butt" (vampire) is the outsider and the object of the joke.[1] Simultaneous physical and verbal combat gives Buffy twice the power for her punch.[2]

While Buffy's romping vernacular suffices for run-of-the-mill vampires, the old quip-and-stake is not the only kind of combative language in *Buffy*. More formalized and often esoteric languages must be employed for increasingly specialized categories of demon, and this requires linguistic skills beyond Buffy's ken. Buffy's companions—Xander, Willow, and Giles—have fluencies that complement and extend Buffy's own and allow her speech acts to have martial and material force. She is neither a solitary Speaker nor a solitary Slayer, and this (as we will see) is what makes Buffy-combat, and Buffy-speak, efficacious.

※ ※ ※

But Ho-Hos are a vital part of my cognitive process!

—Xander in "What's My Line?" part 1 (2009)

Xander—the typical American teenager who subsists almost solely on junk food. But this quote is perhaps more revealing. If we consider that old adage "You are what you eat," we realize that Xander is indeed a big Ho-Ho, not because he is chocolate covered with a rich and creamy filling[3] but because he is the one at whom his friends and we, as audience, laugh. An insecure class clown, Xander is clever with language, which is both belied and supported by his diet. There are not too many teenagers, we think, who would be able to construct such a sentence on the fly, wrapping yummy SAT-words in chocolaty self-deprecation.

Because his contributions to the group sometimes (or often) appear less valid, Xander sometimes (or often) finds himself wondering what his role is. Cordelia, in a spiteful moment, explains it perfectly: "It must be hard when all your friends have, like, superpowers. Slayers and werewolves and witches and vampires and you're this little nothing. You must feel like . . . like Jimmy Olsen." Wounded, Xander responds, "I happen to be an integral part of the group and I happen to have a lot to offer." But Cordelia stops him cold: "Integral part of the group. Xander. You're the useless part of the group. You're the Zeppo" ("The Zeppo," 3013).

As opposed to Buffy, who is always on the offensive in her language strikes, Xander is more comfortable on the (self-)defensive. In "The Zeppo," Xander has a series of run-ins with the school bully, Jack O'Toole. After hitting Jack's parked car, Xander apologizes profusely: "Okay, I can cover the damages. I don't have insurance in the strictest sense of the word, but I have a little money. . . . The important thing is that we're okay, and we can work this out like two reasonable—[Xander stumbles verbally, as Jack pulls a huge bowie knife out of the back of his pants]—frontiersmen." Xander cannot stop himself from parrying Jack's intended thrust. Xander is able to escape only by assuring the police officer who arrives that he and Jack were "just rasslin'. But not in a gay way." Xander cannot defuse everything through his joke-making, however; often, he delays the inevitable. But this gives the gang time to think up other plans of action. His language creates a safe space, a vocabularic shield, that provides room for him, his friends, and the audience to maneuver.

Xander's humor is not usually directed at anyone outside his circle, but, then, his circle includes vampires and demons. The inclusive nature of his humor increases the sense of safe space that Xander creates; when he makes fun of himself or one of the other members of Buffy and Company, he is being "ingratiating rather than aggressive" (Walker 123). As the only contemporary male consistently in the gang, Xander cannot be aggressive. For one thing, the others will know it is all male posturing, and for another, Buffy will kick his ass.[4] But as an integral part of the group, he can make fun of them and himself. This "allows [him] to participate in the process without alienating the members of the majority" (Walker 123). The group is what it is all about for Xander; it is what he lives for. He lacks Buffy's staking skills, and he is not as well versed in book learning as Willow and Giles, so he "participates" in the group dynamic by making them laugh and relieving their psychic burden.

But Xander is not simply self-deprecating. He relishes the English language, inventing unexpected references and altering parts of speech. In "Earshot" (3018), when the lunch lady has poisoned a vat of mulligan stew, Xander screams at his classmates, "Drop the spoons! Step away from the spoons!" as if he fancies himself in an episode of *Cops*. When Riley, mopey and jealous over Buffy's visit to Angel, notes that she has gone "running to L.A. to bone up on her history," Xander suggestively offers, "I'm sure it's boneless" ("The

Yoko Factor," 4020). It is Xander's love of language and fearlessness in the face of its challenges that really turn him on. He tells Cordelia to "go act bait-y" ("Anne," 3001), turning a noun into an adjective, and remarks to Willow that she looks like she has "just been diagnosed with cancer of the puppy" ("The Freshman," 4001), conflating two incongruous images to convey her utter dejection.[5] Cancer of the puppy is bad indeed.

Xander dominates when the conversation turns to matters sexual, however. He thinks about nothing but sex, ensuring his expertise in double entendres and innuendos. In "Earshot," when Buffy can read others' thoughts, Xander thinks, "What am I going to do? I think about sex all the time. Sex. Help. Four times five is thirty. Five times six is thirty-two. . . . Naked girls. Naked woman. Naked Buffy. Oh, stop me." Buffy asks Xander if that is "*all* he ever think[s] about," and Xander replies, "Actually . . . ? Bye!" and flees in terror. But Xander's sex talk is generative. He has not yet physically procreated, so his creative energy is channeled into language, creating new idioms and expressions— "Xander-speak," as Giles terms it in "I Only Have Eyes for You" (2019). In "Where the Wild Things Are" (4018), the crew battles a poltergeist created from the repressed erotic emotions of adolescents; Xander remarks, "So, with Buffy and Riley having . . . you know, acts of nakedness around the clock lately, maybe they set something free . . . like a big, bursting poltergasm." In reference to Buffy's sexual relations with Angel, Xander observes "[You're waiting] for Angel to go psycho again the next time you give him a happy?" and "Well, as long as [Buffy] and Angel don't get pelvic, we'll be okay, I guess" ("Revelations," 3007). "Poltergasm," "pelvic," and "happy," the last of which Xander has commuted from an adjective into a noun, are evidence of Xander's creative ability with language, formulating new words from a blend of two radically different sources or forcing words to become different parts of speech.

※ ※ ※

Willow: You think I'm boring.
Oz: I'd call that a radical interpretation of the text.

—"Doppelgängland" (3016)

Willow really geeks out on data. Book toting, laptop lugging, and always carrying (and sometimes dropping) knowledge, Willow is turned on by text:

> The energy, the collective intelligence, it's like this force, this penetrating force, and I can just feel my mind opening up, you know? And letting this place just thrust in and, and spurt knowledge into . . . That sentence ended up in a different place than it started out. ("The Freshman," 4001)

The words sometimes get away from her; unlike Xander, she is awkward in talk, blushing, stammering, and "very seldom naughty" ("Restless," 4022).

Her partners, too, seem uncomfortable in speech and body—monosyllabic Oz, tentative Tara. But with text, Willow is, well, a wunderkind.

Willow is a wiz with books, raider of the lost arcana. "Willow, look through the chronicles/for some reference to a warrior beast," croons Giles as the gang is pursued through their nightmares by a shadowy foe in "Restless." It is Will who discovers the source of Jonathan's omnipotence in "Superstar," finding the Augmentation spell among Giles's tomes. And it is Willow who is fluent in two languages crucial to the linguistic logic of *Buffy:* computer technology and the technology of magic.

Despite her insecurity about spell casting, Willow is widely recognized as a witch. Spike knows it when he demands that she cast a love spell for him in "Lovers Walk" (3008); MOO (Mothers Opposed to the Occult) know it when they put the torch to her, stakebound, in "Gingerbread" (3011), and Tara knows it from their first meeting, in "Hush." Willow's spells of protection and detection, discovery and subjugation, allow Team Buff to operate effectively on the Forces of Darkness. But Willow has another expertise: computers. As often as her face is shadowed in the pages of a spell book, it is illuminated by the glow of a monitor. She pulls up building schematics, accesses FBI records, and decrypts coded programs—all with quiet confidence and only partial (if any) explanations. Cyber is so much *her* space that it is sometimes uncooperative in her absence, as in "Gingerbread," when an exasperated Giles flails at the beeping keyboard: "Session interrupted? Who said you could interrupt?! Stupid, useless fad!" When Buffy arrives, she can only point to the computer and note, "We need to get some information." Oz offers to look around on the Web, but "Willow really knows the sites we'll need." She knows, and she finds—but no one quite knows how. Some secret, hacker-y thing, no doubt; it's almost magic:

> *Willow [excited]:* I think I'm onto something. I've been assuming the ciphertext was encrypted with an asymmetric algorithm. Then it hit me: a hexagonic key pattern. It's—[realizing Tara is staring] I'm scaring you now, huh?
> *Tara [smiling]:* A little. In a good way. It's like a different kind of magic. ("Primeval," 4021)

Willow's skills depend and center on text: not necessarily books but on sites of collected knowledge that must be accessed. Both magic and technology work this way in *Buffy;* both are textual archives that yield information when "read" correctly. Proficiency with the language of magic allows Willow to situate a current problem within its supernatural context—the spell, the alternate reality, the demonic power—while proficiency with the language of computers allows her to locate the mundane context—the engineering diagrams, the newspaper articles, the police files. Her "readings" of both magic and computers are active; she must analyze and apply these stored knowledges, activating the texts to make them effective in the context of the series.

As Searle suggests, language is often powerful in unexpected ways. But for Searle, language is more than just words; its power resides equally in syntax, grammar, and usage. Language, in this holistic sense, provides the context in which words have meaning. And in *Buffy*, magic is the syntax—it is magic that provides the rules that govern the language, magic that allows words to have such power because magic informs the reality of the series. From "*Librum Incendere*" to Jonathan's Augmentation spell, there is magic in linguistic force. And Willow, with her command of text and of magic, functions as a kind of linguist herself, exploring and exposing the systems of magical logic that give *Buffy* rhetorical potency.

So, while Xander's language skills are largely creative and Buffy's performative, we might call Willow's foundational; she builds a base of operations for the crew, establishing context from text, providing a sort of local landscape for the group's actions. But even with the terrain established in this way, there are still obstacles, and it requires another, specialized skill to negotiate them: the skill of the analyst, that bemused Englishman, Rupert Giles.

⚒ ⚒ ⚒

Yes, always behind on terms. I'm still trying not to refer to you lot as "bloody colonials."

—Giles, "Pangs" (4008)

Giles is the nominal head of Buffy and Company. He is Buffy's Watcher, he is an academic, and he is older ("very, very old," as Buffy reminds him in "The Freshman," 4001), so we may expect that he has more experience and knowledge than the rest of the gang. But Giles also has an ability that the others do not. He does not merely collect information (although his impressive store of "old" books and manuscripts seems to point in this direction); instead, he serves as the interpreter, the one who puts all the pieces of the puzzle together. He tells the gang what they are facing and how they must confront the vampire, demon, or other denizen of the dark. Buffy, Willow, and Xander, although they make fun of Giles, still deeply respect him. When the group is deciding where they should go to college (in "Choices"), Buffy begins by saying to Willow,

You, I can't believe you got into Oxford.
Willow: It's pretty exciting.
Oz: That's some deep academia there.
Buffy: There's where they make Gileses.
Willow: I know. I can learn and have scones.

But for a person with so much responsibility and knowledge, Giles is oddly uncomfortable with spoken language, particularly around Buffy. Perhaps this is because he moves more slowly than she does; Buffy often impatiently interrupts his explanations because he is not cutting to the chase fast enough for her. This makes Giles seem incomplete and interruptive in his speech patterns. When describing a life-endangering test Buffy must pass on her eighteenth birthday, Giles stutters throughout the entire speech: "It's a test, Buffy. It's given to the Slayer once she . . . uh, well, *if* she reaches her eighteenth birthday. The vampire you were to face . . . has escaped" ("Helpless"). On another occasion, Giles is upset about a prophecy that foretells Buffy's death: "Some prophecies are, are a bit dodgy. They're, they're mutable. Buffy herself has, has thwarted them time and time again, but this is the Codex . . ." ("Prophecy Girl"). These trailings off, these repetitions, force us to realize that Giles is not the suave and glib man he is supposed to be.

In "A New Man" (4012), Giles is transformed (via a mickey slipped into his drink) into a Fyarl demon. Giles still believes that he is himself, still talks to himself in his brand of British English, but everyone hears Fyarl. This unnerves Giles and gives Spike (who happens to speak Fyarl) ample opportunity for mocking. Giles becomes stammery again:

> *Spike:* And I'm supposed to just help you out of the evilness of my heart?
> *Giles:* You, you help me, and I don't, don't kill you.
> *Spike:* Oh, tremendously convincing. Try it again without the stutter.

Spike agrees to help if paid, and the two climb into Giles's Citroën—which Spike immediately insults. Giles insists that his car is "perfectly serviceable." Spike retorts, "Funny. Hearing a Fyarl demon say 'serviceable.' Had a couple of 'em working for me once. They're more like 'Like to crush. Crush now?'" Giles growls in response. Importantly, though, this is the first time that Giles has not been able to communicate with the group. He first sought out Xander, but hearing Giles's pleas for help as unintelligible roars of Fyarl ("Rrr. Grrbch fffahar lagggh!" for "Listen. Can't you understand me?"), Xander attacked demon-Giles with a saucepan. The disruption of normal communication here is as didactic as when Buffy cannot pun or Willow cannot compute: the interpreter is unintelligible.

Giles is the translator—he converts the old world into the new, makes comprehensible dark and demony things from the past that have not reared their ugly heads in hundreds of years but that have somehow now adapted to modern living. Trouble is, they are noted only in extremely old texts or even fairy tales. Giles is the one who bridges that gap. In "Hush," Giles's task is made more difficult by the fact that their normal mode of communication, speaking, has been wrested from them. Giles resorts to transparencies and an overhead projector—certainly an outmoded form of technology—to tell the tale of the "Gentlemen" in incongruously sweet pictures, his drawings almost childish. His representation of what they are after, hearts, look like cartoons or candies. Yet he is able to get across what must be done in order to fight these fairy tale monsters and restore Sunnydale to its state of almost normality.

Giles's role as translator and occasionally incomplete speaker reveals itself as potentially hazardous in "Fear, Itself" (4004). Giles is quite concerned when he realizes that Gachnar the Fear Demon is about to manifest. He frantically flips through books looking for a way to prevent its appearance. "I have it: 'The summoning spell for Gachnar can be shut down in one of two ways. Destroying the Mark of Gachnar . . .'" Buffy drops to one knee and punches through the floor, destroying Gachnar's icon. While Buffy looks smug, Giles continues reading: "'is not one of them and will, in fact, immediately bring forth the Fear Demon, itself.'" Buffy is too impatient to wait for wiser heads to prevail or even to let Giles finish his translation of the sentence. But Giles has made a mistake here too. The illustration of Gachnar is formidable, but when Gachnar manifests, he is only six inches high, and Buffy promptly stomps him with an impeccably well heeled boot. The final scene of the episode reveals Giles saying, "Oh, bloody Hell! The inscription!" When Buffy asks what is wrong, he acknowledges, "I should have translated the Gaelic inscription under the illustration of Gachnar." It says, he is forced to tell Buffy, "actual size."

The rules of language must be obeyed. Giles must be allowed to finish his sentences, but he is also obliged to complete the translation of all relevant material before passing it on to the gang. If he does not, there may very well be "dire consequences" ("Restless").

※ ※ ※

A Slayer with family and friends. That sure as hell wasn't in the brochure.

—Spike, "School Hard" (2003)

Spike is right; Buffy is not like other Slayers. She has "amigos" who assist her; Willow and Xander watch Buffy's back (Xander more closely than Willow, according to Cordelia in "Killed by Death," 2018), as do a host of other characters: Angel, Riley, Cordelia, Oz, Anya, and Tara. No other Slayer has ever had friends, let alone "civilian" assistants. All Slayers have Watchers, but Giles is unique in allowing Buffy her entourage. Kendra, a Slayer who is called when Buffy drowns ("I was only gone for a minute," Buffy says defensively in "What's My Line?" part 2, 2010), does not understand how Giles can allow others to know Buffy's identity. But both the personal relationships and the specialized language skills of the posse increase Buffy's ability to destroy demons. She trusts her friends, and relies on them for things she cannot do herself: referencing ancient manuscripts, incanting spells, speaking in tongues, hacking databases, coining phrases, and, when barred from familiar avenues, as in "Hush," inventing alternative communications.

No episode demonstrates the efficacy of the group dynamic more than "Primeval" (4021). Faced with their most enigmatic foe yet—the Frankensteinian Adam—Buffy and Company are temporarily at a loss. They must find a way to disable Adam's power source, a uranium core "embedded somewhere inside his chest." Willow weakly suggests some kind of extracting spell; Giles realizes that a paralyzing spell might do the trick but that he (the only one who speaks the required Sumerian) does not have the magical experience to incant it—and that the spell must be performed during combat. Frustrated, Xander moans, "So . . . no problem. All we need is a combo Buffy with Slayer strength, Giles's multilingual know-how and Willow's witchy power." Giles looks up at Xander, but Xander cuts him off, anticipating the usual reprimand, "Yeah, don't tell me, I'm just full of helpful suggestions." "As a matter of fact, Xander," Giles nods thoughtfully, "you are."

The spell itself requires and highlights the strengths of each of the four main characters. Willow, Xander, and Giles sit cross-legged on the floor of a room adjacent to the one in which Buffy confronts Adam. Willow places occult cards before herself, Xander, and Giles. As each card is revealed, the trio speak the names of the figures displayed in front of them: Willow is *Spiritus,* "Spirit"; Xander is *Animus,* "Heart"; and Giles is *Sophus,* "Mind." Willow places the final card, *Manus,* "The Hand," in the center of the triangle and begins an incantation: "We enjoin that we may inhabit the vessel—the hand . . . ," thus joining them with Buffy. A room away, Buffy faces Adam, and as the collective energies collide, she becomes *Über*-Buffy: charged, glowing, all-powerful. She speaks, and we hear four voices: "We are forever." She begins to chant in Sumerian, which only Giles is capable of understanding. She remains steadfast in facing Adam and successfully deflects his attacks—a shield that Xander's heart provides. Adam's ammunition transforms, as she raises a hand, into clouds and doves, an effect of Willow's magical, technological matrix. Finally, with her own hand, she divests Adam of his uranium core, saying (in English this time and reverting to her punning), "You could never hope to grasp the source of our power. But yours is right here."

Buffy *is* the speech act. She is the utterance that communicates meaning, drawing on the linguistic capabilities of her companions: invention, playfulness, contextualization, archival knowledge, compilation, and translation. Other Slayers have never confronted such a powerful foe or managed such harmonic power; they are solitary and silent. Kendra rarely speaks, and when she does, she is deferential, formal, and clearly uncomfortable. The "First Slayer" is unable to speak and must use Tara as her voice; solitary warriors do not need language—they need only to kill. But Buffy is able to survive longer than the other Slayers because she is embedded in language and because she embodies language. It is a very particular language, with its own vernacular, but it behaves like all languages in that it creates, it compiles, it translates, it follows well-defined rules, it draws on shared knowledge, and it must be wielded with precision in order to be effective. Of course, Buffy is able to access this language only with the help of her friends; without their assistance, she would have gone the way of the other Slayers long ago, and she would be merely a word.[6] Any Slayer can brandish a weapon, but for Buffy the Vampire Slayer, the tongue is as pointed as the stake.

NOTES

1. For more on this tripartite structure of joking, see Freud's chapter "Jokes as a Social Process" in *Jokes*.

2. Buffy is not exactly Freud's typical joke teller; his analytical model was gendered, with a male joke teller, just as Buffy's heroic predecessors are exclusively male. Her slaying is subversive—a threat to the Dark Order—and her humor is subversive in an aggressively "masculine" way. For a further social critique of Freud's joke theory, see Hill.

3. Despite his telling Spike in "Hush" that he is "very biteable [. . .] moist and delicious."

4. Their respective uses of humor make Xander Buffy's gendered opposite. Xander is self-deprecating, a type of humor traditionally associated with women (Barreca 23–24). In Walker's quote "ingratiating rather than aggressive," ingratiation is implicitly equated with femininity and aggression with masculinity. So neither Buffy, with her "masculine" joke telling/staking, nor Xander, with his "feminine" self-directed mocking, fulfills traditional gender roles (see note 2).

5. Xander is not the only one who does this. As Rhonda Wilcox ("There") points out, the creation and manipulation of language illustrates the difference between the teens and the threatening adult world they are preparing to enter.

6. And without the help of our friends, we would never have been able to complete this chapter. We would like to thank the following people for their playful language: Michael Matto, Collin McKinney, Eileen Reilly, Aaron Rosenfeld, and Rhonda V. Wilcox.

7

Slaying in Black and White
Kendra as Tragic Mulatta in Buffy

Lynne Edwards

In a February 2000 interview with *TV Guide,* Sarah Michelle Gellar explained *Buffy the Vampire Slayer*'s appeal to female fans this way: "They respond to Buffy because for years we didn't have a character young girls could look up to. [. . .] Buffy is not the smartest or the most beautiful. She's kind of awkward, but she is OK with who she is. The most important lesson we need to learn in our formative years is that it's OK to be an individual. It's OK to be you" ("Sarah Smiles" 19–22). Whedon attributes Buffy's emotional and physical complexity to Gellar, whose ability to display a full range of emotions, from giddy schoolgirl laughter to soul-wrenching sobs, has influenced the direction of the program; she takes the audience to the "dark place" (Golden and Holder 241). Whedon's use of myth to create a female hero who can go to a "dark place" is the program's greatest strength; it enables viewers to identify with Buffy and with the demons she battles. During the series's second season, however, Whedon took viewers to a new "dark place" when he introduced Kendra, the slayer sent to replace Buffy after her (temporary) demise in the "Prophecy Girl" episode at the end of the first season. As a replacement slayer, Kendra signifies the dynamic nature of the slayer identity; as a black slayer, she signifies the dynamic nature of race and race relations.

MYTH AND THE SLAYER

Kent Ono argues that *Buffy* conveys "debilitating images and ideas about people of color," particularly the character Kendra, a black vampire slayer (163). Ono further argues that these images function to affirm contemporary racial and gender hierarchies (167). Kenneth Burke suggests that because we are symbol-using actors, the language we use to respond to our environment reveals our true persuasive motive: identification (*Language* 20–21). We seek to understand and to be understood by others, and it is through identification that this understanding occurs. Through the use of symbolic acts (language) to create a sense of identification with one another, we are also able to create and maintain the hierarchies that serve as the foundation of our society.[1] Just as the use of commonly shared and understood symbols allows us to overcome individual uniqueness and to communicate with one another, the use of these symbols can also help us overcome differences in attitudes and beliefs to create a sense of identification with one another (Rybacki and Rybacki 74).

Myth is a commonly used device to achieve identification. Myth is a dynamic beast, steeped in formulaic tradition, yet ever changing within an evolving historical context; it is the "universal soul of the human race itself" (Leeming 5). Structurally, Campbell argues that there is one myth in many cultures, a "monomyth" with a hero on a quest to fulfill a preordained destiny. The quest, the essence of the monomyth, filled with fierce battles and brave deeds, is a rite of passage through which the hero proves him- or herself worthy (*Hero* 11). Functionally, myths illustrate historical "truths" with which we can identify and from which we learn how to transcend our ordinary existence (*Hero* 10). We achieve transcendence through myth because the common and familiar elements of myth ring true with us, regardless of the myth's factuality (Hart 242).

Myth is not simply a story, however, but also a type of speech, defined not by its goal but rather by its form. It is a "metalanguage" in which a sign become a signifier, given new meaning by the historical context in which it exists (Barthes, "Myth" 99). As Barthes explains, "Meaning in myth is based on understanding the culturally shared 'definition' of the characters and symbols in the myth; the 'truth' or meaning of the myth lies in the arrangement of these characters and symbols" (99–100). In his most well known analysis of mythic text, Barthes argues that a photograph of a black soldier saluting a French flag is an example of myth as metalanguage. On one level, the signs in the picture (a man in a uniform, a salute, and a flag) may represent nationalism, loyalty, or militarism. On the metalanguage level, the picture may represent a comment on race since the black soldier is himself a sign of colonialism and repression by the French, as symbolized by the flag sign (101–2).

In *Buffy*, Joss Whedon uses myth not only to capture the angst of high school but also to present alternative ways of seeing its "monsters":

> We're doing these sort of mythic-hero journeys in our minds. A lot of times, the story doesn't make sense until we figure out who's suffering and why.

Including the bad guy. If the bad guy's not hurting, not relating to her (Buffy), then it's just a cardboard guy to knock down. And the same thing goes for the audience. If they're not feeling it [. . .] it's not going to resonate. (Golden and Holder 241)

One reason that *Buffy* resonates with audiences is the familiarity of the mythic devices that Whedon employs. He skillfully weaves popular myth like Robert Louis Stevenson's *Dr. Jekyll and Mr. Hyde* and Mary Shelley's *Frankenstein*[2] into Buffy's weekly quest to fulfill her destiny as this generation's Slayer. Similar to these mythic creatures and their creators, monsters in *Buffy* are not just demons or witches. In Whedon's world, monsters are often the shy boy next door or the homecoming queen, and the hero who slays them is a girl. By making the hero of his myth a young white woman from California, Whedon creates Buffy as a sign imbued with cultural meanings about race, class, age, and gender in today's historical context. Similarly, by casting Bianca Lawson, a black actress, in the role of Kendra, the second slayer, he makes character a sign imbued with cultural meanings about gender, race, and race relations.

Similar to Barthes's black soldier, the Kendra character suggests a variety of readings. As our first introduction to other slayers, a black slayer suggests a liberal racial attitude on the part of the program's producers and the expectation that we, the audience, share these attitudes. As a black slayer, Kendra also signifies a truly "Other" slayer, a radical (and racial) departure from Buffy, with whom fans fiercely identify. However, when these two women are situated in a narrative in which the black slayer is initially rejected and then accepted by the white slayer, only to sacrificially die, the black slayer becomes a new sign; the hero-quest myth becomes an updated version of the "tragic mulatta" myth. As a replacement slayer, Kendra signifies the dynamic nature of the slayer identity; as a black slayer, she signifies the dynamic nature of race and race relations. The story of Kendra is a myth about a failed quest for legitimacy and acceptance.

THE TRAGIC MULATTA MYTH

While gender plays a significant role in our patriarchal society in terms of the "place" of women, race is another factor that cannot be ignored. Gender and racial discrimination are common experiences for many black women; in Burke's societal hierarchy, they are at the bottom of the "oppression chain" (hooks 19). Black women in the United States lag behind black men and whites in almost all economic indicators (Jaynes and Williams 267), a condition originated by two centuries of slavery and exacerbated by decades of legal discrimination. These conditions, unique to

black women in the United States, explain why the cultural images we have
of black women are so different than the images we have of white women
and other women of color (Jewell 35).

In his book *Toms, Coons, Mulattoes, Mammies and Bucks,* Donald
Bogle charges that media images of black women are narrow, stereo-
typic, and unflattering. These images are more than simple stereotypes;
they function as cultural myths. Each image represents a familiar historical narrative with mythic elements that we recognize when we see these
characters in television and film. Two of the oldest stereotypes are the
"mammy" and the "tragic mulatta." The "mammy" figure is "big, fat,
and cantankerous," a comedic figure who usually bosses her "good-for-
nothing" husband and others around (9). The "mammy" is a residual of
the southern plantation house slave who was charged with overseeing
domestic duties and rearing the slave owner's children. The "tragic mulatta" figure, in sharp contrast, is an attractive young woman with fair
skin who is sexually objectified in both the white and the black communities, although she is accepted in neither. The tragic mulatta's narrative
also originated on southern plantations where, as the illegitimate offspring of a slave owner and one of his slaves, she enjoyed special treatment from the slave owner while enduring derision and resentment from
the slave owner's wife and his other slaves.

The tragic mulatta myth[3] is about a fair-skinned black woman, usually of
mixed racial heritage, whose hair and facial features allow her to "pass" for
white. Her tragedy lies in her thwarted potential, in her marginalization;
she is the ultimate "other" who does not belong in either the black community from which she comes or the white society to which she aspires.
Darker-skinned black women resent her exotic attractiveness and her ability to pass for white, and black men who desire unattainable white women
sexually exploit her. White lovers abandon her when her true race is revealed, and white women resent the threat she poses to their racial and reproductive legitimacy. As a symbol of miscegenation by white fathers and
hypersexuality for white lovers,[4] her existence threatens both ancestral and
descendent purity for white women. The mulatta's ultimate threat to white
women is her claim to legitimacy through their shared bloodline and appearance, a claim that must be denied for the white woman to be the true,
legitimate bearer of reproductive meaning for her people.

The tragic mulatta story is a paradoxical myth in which success means
failure and failure means success for the heroine. If the tragic mulatta (the
heroine) successfully passes for white (the quest), she fails the black community by her denial of it, and she threatens the balance of power between
whites and blacks by gaining legitimacy through acceptance by the white
community. When her ruse fails, as it must, she returns home and succeeds
in maintaining her racial identity for the good of her community and for

racial relations with whites (her destiny). Her quest for legitimacy is doomed to fail; her destiny is to remain in her place.

This failed-quest theme of the tragic mulatta myth first appears on film in the character "Lydia" in D. W. Griffith's *Birth of a Nation*[5] and in later films about the subject. In the 1934 film *Imitation of Life,* based on the book by Fannie Hurst, Peola, the light-skinned daughter of a dark-skinned woman, attempts to pass as a white woman. Peola rejects her mother in order to completely "cross the color line"; however, she humbly returns to her roots when her mother dies. This plot is revisited in the 1949 film *Pinky,* a story about a light-skinned black girl who passes for white while studying to be a nurse in Boston. She is abandoned by her fiancé (a white doctor) when he discovers that she is black. Pinky, too, humbly returns to her roots (Bogle, *Blacks* 164).

According to Bogle, however, the true quest of the tragic mulatta is not to be white; rather, it is to have access to the same opportunities and privileges that whites enjoy (60). Literary critics Hazel Carby and Barbara Christian agree. When the tragic mulatta myth is told by black female novelists, the quest is not for acceptance by whites or to pass for white but rather for acceptance by the black community and justice from whites. In Zora Neale Hurston's 1937 novel *Their Eyes Were Watching God,* the mulatta heroine, Janie Starks, struggles for and ultimately gains acceptance from her community, if not from the men who marry her for her beauty. Ida Long, the mulatta figure in Bebe Moore Campbell's 1992 novel *Your Blues Ain't Like Mine,* fights to learn the identity of her white father and to obtain her rightful share of his estate. The tragic mulattas of black women's novels are not symbols of racial envy. Instead, as Carby argues, they are a "vehicle for an exploration of the relationship between the races and, at the same time [. . .] a narrative device of mediation" (89). The tragic mulatta represents the desires of blacks and the fears of whites within an historical context.

As historical contexts evolve, so too does the tragic mulatta myth. In this post–civil rights era of affirmative action and racial tolerance, the relationship between blacks and whites has improved to an uneasy peace, but at a price for those blacks who wish to maintain a sense of racial identity. Those blacks who are most readily accepted by whites are those who are most assimilated into white culture through shared language, cultural values, and aspirations. The tragic mulatta myth has evolved accordingly.[6] In this new tragic mulatta myth, we see a solitary or "token" black character in a predominantly white cast of a television program. Instead of a fair-skinned black woman attempting to deny her racial identity in order to pass for white, today's "tragic mulatta" appears to be fully accepted by and integrated into her white peer group. Unfortunately, she is merely window dressing, incorporated into story lines only for comedic or shock value or to infuse the program with a sense of cultural currency.

Often referred to as a token black character, today's "tragic mulatta" characters may not appear particularly tragic, but the narrative elements surrounding them look familiar. She is not necessarily racially mixed (however, she is not dark-skinned) or actively trying to pass for white, but she is still on a quest for legitimacy. Unlike with the classic tragic mulatta, her white peers accept her claim of legitimacy. This acceptance, however, is contingent on her assimilation into the dominant culture. From hair and clothing styles to Anglo names and values, these tragic mulattas are no different from their white peers, except for their race. Their tragedy lies in the fear that should their racial "otherness" becomes too obvious, they will be rejected by their white peers. The threat to white peers lies not in the mulatta's sexuality but in her claim of legitimacy. For the new mulatta, there is no denial by whites. Instead, this threat is diffused by the appearance of acceptance by whites, an acceptance that is, in reality, a denial of her race by whites. By denying her race as an issue, whites can deny her "otherness."

In the television series *Boy Meets World* and *Saved by the Bell,* the sole black female characters, Angela and Lisa, respectively, are racially and culturally marooned without other black supporting characters to provide substantive plotlines. There is no indication of racial or cultural difference between these solitary characters and the rest of the cast; they are fully assimilated and acculturated. Whereas the classic tragic mulatta is denied legitimacy by the white community and is forced to return home for fulfillment, today's tragic mulatta finds legitimacy and acceptance but no fulfillment. Unfortunately, she cannot return home to find it—she already *is* home.

JOURNEY OF THE "OTHER": KENDRA THE VAMPIRE SLAYER

Like the classic tragic mulatta figure's, Kendra's quest for legitimacy, to be accepted as this generation's slayer, is denied because of the threat she poses to Buffy's identity as *the* slayer and to Buffy's relationships with her lover (Angel) and her father figure (Giles). As an updated version of the tragic mulatta figure, however, Kendra's threat lies not in her sexuality[7] but rather in the legitimacy of her claim. Kendra is also a Slayer-hero in Whedon's mythic world. In "What's My Line?" part 1 (2009), Kendra journeys to Sunnydale to assume the role of the Slayer, called to duty by Buffy's temporary death at the hands of the Master in the "Prophecy Girl" episode. Since Buffy is alive, however, she and Kendra join forces to defeat a trio of demon assassins and (against Kendra's better judgment) to save Angel from Spike and Drusilla. When Kendra returns in the season finale to help Buffy defeat Angelus, Drusilla, and Spike in "Becoming," part 1 (2021), Kendra's Slayer-quest comes to a brutal end when Drusilla kills her. Ironically, Buffy's

Slayer-quest is ultimately fulfilled when she is finally able to slay Angelus. Unlike Buffy, however, Kendra, as a tragic mulatta figure, fulfills her destiny in death. She leaves home on a quest to fulfill what she believes to be her destiny, only to be rejected as an unwelcome "other." Although she is ultimately accepted by Buffy, the acceptance is on Buffy's terms; Kendra is assimilated. When she returns to Sunnydale to help Buffy again, Kendra pays for her assimilation with her life.

Kendra's representation of the tragic mulatta myth begins with her physical appearance. We are first introduced to Kendra in the baggage section of an airplane, where, as the script describes her, "we stop on an ethnic young woman (seventeen), her feline, feral eyes getting used to the sudden light. She's a predator, a hunter, and her name is Kendra" ("What's My Line?" part 1). Kendra, played by actress Bianca Lawson, is exotically attractive and bears some resemblance to tragic mulattas of old with her fair skin, green eyes, and long, flowing hair coupled with features that resemble those of an African American.

In addition to her physical appearance, the name "Kendra" carries ethnic connotations, too. Inasmuch as the name "Buffy" suggests certain racial, gender, and class characteristics (middle- to upper-class white female), the name "Kendra" reinforces the character's racial identity. Kendra's clothing and speech further distinguish her as ethnic "other." She wears hoop earrings and other large, clunky jewelry and speaks in a Jamaican patois.[8] Her Jamaican accent further serves as evidence of her ethnic otherness. She not only looks different but also sounds different, so different, in fact, that she does not understand "Buffy-speak," forcing her to ask what "chick fight thing" ("What's My Line?" part 1) and "wiggy" ("What's My Line?" part 2, 2010) mean. As Barthes's first sign in myth metalanguage, we see Kendra as an "ethnic" female, a sign that carries multiple meanings with it, similar to Barthes's French soldier. Although there is no direct identification or discussion of Kendra's racial identity, viewers are assured through character and discursive signs that Kendra is definitely not white; she is Other.

Once her physical image as "other" is firmly established, Kendra's tragic mulatta narrative begins to unfold. Although Kendra does not escape from her home (we never learn where) for a better life in Sunnydale in the classic tragic mulatta sense, she begins to question her upbringing when she meets Buffy. Unlike Buffy, Kendra does not live with her parents; she was "given" to her Watcher at such a young age that she no longer remembers her parents. Kendra is also not allowed to have friends, to have contact with boys, or to attend school. While Giles is a father figure for Buffy, we do not get the impression that Kendra has a similar relationship with her Watcher, whom she refers to as "Mr. Zabuto." When Buffy questions her satisfaction with her life, Kendra claims not to be bothered while at the same time avoiding eye contact with Buffy. When she is introduced to Buffy's lifestyle—friends, school, boyfriend—she appears to be wistful. Like the tragic mulatta, Kendra becomes dissatisfied with her life when introduced to Buffy's world; however, Kendra is not readily accepted into it. Her presence is a threat to everything that Buffy has and to everything that Buffy is. Buffy rejects Kendra in an effort to eliminate this threat.

The catalyst for Kendra's rejection is her claim of legitimacy, that she too is a vampire slayer. A central theme of the tragic mulatta myth is that identity revelation is the catalyst for rejection, whereupon legitimacy and acceptance are denied, and the same is true for the Kendra narrative. After rejecting Kendra by denying her slayer identity, Buffy continues her rejection of Kendra by attacking her slaying skills. Buffy calls Kendra a "rookie" when Kendra mistakes her for a vampire. She mocks Kendra's "John Wayne" style of dealing with the unknown, for asking questions with her fists instead of her brain, asking Kendra if she plans to "attack people until you find a bad one" ("What's My Line?" part 2). Buffy insists that Kendra should be sent home—that Kendra is unwelcome and unwanted.

What Buffy's rejection of Kendra reveals, however, is the other side of the mulatta's tragedy—the perceived threat she poses to the white woman's way of life. Buffy is threatened by Kendra's presence because it challenges her position as *the* slayer. Kendra represents Buffy's mortality and fallibility. It is, after all, Buffy's fault that Kendra is in Sunnydale. Buffy's death "activated" Kendra, and it was Buffy's fallibility that led to her death. Buffy does not acknowledge that she frequently makes similar errors in judgment. She too mistook Kendra for a demon, and she too fights without thinking, which Kendra alludes to when she sarcastically comments to Buffy, "No wonder you died." Buffy also does not confess to Kendra that she has a desire to escape her slayer destiny, that being replaced might not be such a bad thing. In fact, she even muses to Willow that it would be nice to walk away from being a slayer and to let Kendra take over. However, none of her qualms prevent Buffy from belittling and challenging Kendra's skills as a slayer. Buffy, ironically, chafes under the noose of her destiny until it is, symbolically, taken away from her by Kendra's presence.

Kendra is also a perceived threat to Buffy's relationship with Giles. As mentioned earlier, Kendra does not appear to share a familial relationship with her Watcher, Mr. Zabuto. His insistence that Kendra train in isolation and focus solely on her studies is a sharp contrast to Giles's more paternal relationship with Buffy. In Buffy's opinion, Kendra, whom she refers to as "she-Giles," is the model slayer for a staid Watcher like Giles. Buffy notes, peevishly, how much Kendra and Giles have in common and then laments that Giles would probably prefer a slayer like Kendra. It is clear too that despite the fact that Mr. Zabuto is the only "family" she has, Kendra does not enjoy as close a relationship with her Watcher as Buffy has with Giles, as evidenced by her use of the formal title "mister" when speaking of him. Buffy simply calls Giles by his surname with no title (his full name is Rupert Giles). However, Giles is a surrogate father for Buffy, so much so that the Watchers' Council eventually removes him from his position as her Watcher because of his emotional attachment to her. While Kendra seems to be the answer to Buffy's desire to escape her destiny, Buffy treats her as a threat to her relationship with Giles. Ultimately, however, it is her threat to Buffy's relationship with Angel that fuels Buffy's rejection of Kendra.

Kendra proves to be a threat to Buffy's relationship with Angel when, on her arrival to Sunnydale, Kendra attempts to slay Angel. In fact, Buffy is so threatened by Kendra's desire to slay Angel that she warns Kendra that she will kill her if Angel dies. Kendra beseeches Buffy to come to her senses about Angel, that he clouds her judgment, and that it is her duty as a slayer to kill him, but to no avail. Buffy's feelings for Angel prevent her from doing her job, fulfilling her destiny. By pointing this out to Buffy and by demonstrating her willingness to destroy Angel, Kendra becomes more legitimate and thereby a greater threat to Buffy's slayer identity. Slayers are supposed to kill vampires, not fall in love with them.

Despite Kendra's threat to Buffy's legitimacy as *the* slayer and to her relationships with Giles and Angel, Buffy does come to accept Kendra. The road to acceptance begins when Buffy, in front of Giles and the Scooby Gang, thanks Kendra for saving her life during an assassin's attack at school. Her acknowledgment of Kendra's fighting skills is the first step in their tenuous collaboration to save Angel. Buffy begins to include Kendra in her plans to rescue Angel, even following up on a lead that Kendra established. Their relationship progresses to the point where Buffy is comfortable enough with Kendra to jokingly mock her patois. The true sign of her acceptance of Kendra as an equal, however, comes during their battle with Spike to save Angel. As the two women take turns punching him, Buffy and Kendra share a one-liner. "This is your lucky day, Spike," Buffy tells him. "Two slayers," Kendra continues. "No waiting," Buffy finishes ("What's My Line?" part 2). This shared joke is Buffy's first acknowledgment of Kendra as a vampire slayer and as her equal.

Kendra begins to accept Buffy's style of slaying, too. While she disagrees with Buffy's plan to follow Willie the Snitch into an underground tunnel, Kendra does take advantage of Buffy's circle of friends by fetching them as reinforcements to help save Buffy. Kendra puts aside years of training to save Buffy from the vampires' trap; she begins to slay on Buffy's terms. Unfortunately, the acceptance comes only when Kendra begins to accept Buffy's way of slaying, when Kendra is assimilated. From acting without instructions from the Watcher to enlisting the aid of others and saving a vampire, Kendra becomes more and more like Buffy, albeit begrudgingly. The more Kendra becomes like Buffy, the more willing Buffy is to accept her.

This acceptance, however, accentuates Kendra's otherness. As they battle demons together, for example, Kendra laments that she has only one shirt when a demon slices into it; when Kendra is ready to leave Sunnydale (wearing a shirt borrowed from Buffy), Buffy has to explain to her how to properly ride in an airplane. These interactions suggest a social inadequacy on Kendra's part, a sense of lacking that serves to remind us, and Buffy, that Kendra is different. Despite their differences, however, Buffy finally appears ready to accept Kendra as she is. When Kendra rebuffs a farewell hug from Buffy, Buffy does not attempt to change Kendra's mind, nor does she mock Kendra for maintaining her distance. Instead, Buffy responds, "No. Good. Hate hugs" ("What's My Line?" part 2).

Ultimately, Kendra, like other tragic mulattas, returns home in defeat. Although she has helped Buffy defeat the assassins and save Angel, she is not *the* slayer; her legitimacy is denied. When Kendra returns at the end of the season to help Buffy defeat Angelus, however, she faces the ultimate defeat—Drusilla kills her while Buffy continues to fulfill her destiny as the Slayer. Kendra's death is symbolic of the new mulatta tragedy, the ultimate loss of identity and self in order to gain acceptance. The Kendra who returns to Sunnydale is a far cry from the rigid and socially challenged slayer that we knew before. She is warmer and far more outgoing; she jokingly jumps out from behind dark bushes to scare Buffy when she arrives: "I just wanted to test your reflexes. Sorry, I couldn't help myself" ("Becoming," part 1). This time, Kendra is a welcomed sight and is immediately included in Buffy's plans to kill Angelus. Unlike the old Kendra, this new, assimilated Kendra does not object to Buffy's plans to work alone, nor does she chastise Buffy for her decision to continue her relationship with Angel; she appears sympathetic to her friend's pain. Kendra remains behind to protect Buffy's friends and offers to Buffy "Mr. Pointy," her favorite stake, to slay Angelus.

Unfortunately, the new Kendra's participation in Buffy's flawed plan to challenge Angelus leads to her death at Drusilla's hands. Symbolically, this suggests that assimilation equals death for blacks. As in the tales of tragic mulattas everywhere, by attempting to be something she is not, Kendra suffers the ultimate punishment.

CONCLUSION

From slayers to lovers, black women have held a few high-visibility, high-impact roles on *Buffy*. In recent episodes, viewers have been introduced to Olivia, Giles's new love interest ("The Freshman," 4001), and to Sineya, the first Slayer ("Restless," 4022). Viewers also learned that one of the two slayers that Spike killed was a black woman and that it is her black duster he wears as his signature cloak ("Fool for Love," 5007). While their presence suggests an appreciation of the "other" on Whedon's part, the actual portrayals of these black women suggest that some stereotypes about black women are still at work in our culture. While Sineya is the "mother" of all slayers, the Slayer Eve as it were, she is also a primitive creature who is unable to speak for herself and who, Giles claims, can be defeated through his intellect ("Restless").[9] Although Giles is ultimately proven wrong when Sineya "kills" him in his sleep, the primitive nature of the first Slayer continues to haunt Buffy as she becomes more and more aggressive—a hunter like Sineya. Olivia, despite her obvious affection for Giles and her "mother" role in Giles's dreams about the first Slayer, abandons Giles, Buffy, and the Scooby Gang in fear of The Gentlemen from the "Hush" episode (4010). The absence of a supporting narrative like Jenny Calendar's reduces Olivia to a mere sexual object whose race adds additional connotation to her relationship with Giles; he is imbued with an aura of sexual prowess for being able to "satisfy" a black lover (Collins 79).

In each instance, the use of black actresses for these characters is both significant and suggestive. That the "mother" of all slayers is African is not only a powerful addition to the slayer mythology but also a larger statement regarding the African origins of humankind and the battle against evil. However, the fact that Tara, a white female character, had to "speak" for Sineya is troubling, given the psychic link that Buffy has shared with other female characters, particularly Faith in "Graduation Day," parts 1 and 2 (3021 and 3022), and Drusilla in "Surprise" (2013). Equally suggestive is the fact that the only two slayers known to be killed by a vampire (Spike) are both women of color, one black and the other Chinese ("Fool for Love"). Giles's black girlfriend's presentation has several implications, too. On one hand, their relationship suggests that Whedon holds some very liberal attitudes concerning interracial dating; however, a black girlfriend in the season premiere may serve only a shock value for viewers. She could also signify change in Giles; he is more hip, more loose than previously thought.

Finally, Kendra the tragic mulatta offers the most complex development of a black female character in *Buffy* thus far. She is both intelligent and shy like Willow, attractive and aggressive like Buffy, sharp-tongued and sexy like Cordelia. However, her subtle similarity to other, white female characters is undercut by her overt differences, her blatant "otherness." Unlike Willow, she passively accepts information from her Watcher and her studies; she does not seek it out. Similarly, she passively accepts guidance and direction from her Watcher; Buffy is an independent thinker and maverick. Cordelia trades on her sexuality and sharp tongue for status among her peers; Kendra awkwardly denies her sexuality and uses her barbs to keep others at a distance. Even Faith, who comes from a radically different lifestyle than the others and who eventually tries to kill Buffy, is at first more readily accepted than Kendra. Like the classic tragic mulatta figure, Kendra cannot overcome her "otherness" to gain the full acceptance of her white peers. Like the new tragic mulatta figure, it is only in the figurative "death" of her identity and in her literal death that Kendra finally gains acceptance and legitimacy.

In the book *Mammies No More*, Lisa Anderson claims that "the 'problem of the mulatto' remains with American culture to the present. However, perhaps it is more appropriate to say the problem of race remains with the culture, for it is certainly not the person of mixed race who is problematic but the way in which racial categories have functioned as class symbols" (80). As long as race and race relations continue to be relevant topics, it is fair to assume that *Buffy* will continue to include black characters, in one form or another, to explore these issues. It is also fair to assume that the program's reliance on cultural myth will continually lead to marginalized representations of these black characters, like Forrest, Riley's Initiative sidekick, and the revelation (in flashback) that one of Spike's two slayer victims was black. However, it would be a mistake to dismiss these representations as perpetuating cultural stereotypes of people of color. Since blacks have historically been and continue to be marginalized in society, their depiction as such in Whedon's mythic world may serve, as Joseph Campbell suggests, to illustrate and to illuminate historical "truths" from which black and white viewers can learn how to transcend their ordinary existence (*Hero* 10).

NOTES

1. For a fuller discussion of these concepts, see also Burke's *Language as Symbolic Action* and *Rhetoric of Motives*.

2. In "Beauty and the Beasts" (3004), a male student creates a potion to make himself more "manly" for his girlfriend, only to turn into a monster who kills perceived rivals in fits of jealous rage. In "Some Assembly Required" (2002), a student brings his brother back from the dead and seeks to create a mate for him by harvesting body parts from dead female students.

3. Lisa Anderson identifies three basic tragic mulatta myths: the sexually promiscuous mulatta, the mulatta who desires a white husband or lover, and the "passing" mulatta (53). Since all three myths heavily borrow elements from one another, they are being treated as a single myth in this chapter.

4. For further discussion on the sexual promiscuity myth attributed to black women in general, see Collins.

5. Lydia is a mulatta character and the mistress of Senator Stoneman, a white abolitionist.

6. For further discussion of the evolution of the tragic mulatta/o in theater, film, and television, see Lisa Anderson. For the use of the device in television science fiction, see Wilcox ("Dating").

7. Kendra lacks the overt sexuality and aggressiveness of the traditional mulatta character. She is tongue-tied when interacting with Xander and deferential with Giles, in contrast to her aggressive attacks against male vampires and other predators. Kendra is also well read, at least where her slayer training is concerned; however, she is passive in accepting direction from her Watcher compared to Buffy's aggressive independence from Giles.

8. According to an interview with Bianca Lawson, the actress who played Kendra, the directors asked her to use an accent (Golden and Holder 232).

9. Editors' note: Although in "Intervention" (5018) Sineya appears to speak, her image is only a "form" taken by a Spirit Guide for Buffy's quest.

8

The Undemonization of Supporting Characters in *Buffy*

Mary Alice Money

Buffy the Vampire Slayer continually illuminates the lives of young people as they are initiated into high school, college, and reality. Naturally, any series that is, on the surface, about vampires must be about transformation. Often the plots turn on that old standby, the harsh recognition of the evil in people who first appear to be good—or "cool"—from on-line friends who are really demons ("I Robot, You Jane," 1008) to prospective stepfathers who are depraved predators ("Ted," 2011). It would be difficult to enumerate the assorted teachers, counselors, mayors, Watchers, and other authority figures who have been revealed as corrupt or evil. Such transformations or disjunctions between appearance and reality are expected on television as in life, and they do provide opportunities for lead characters to reveal that necessary quality of a hero, the ability to perceive, to *know* the inner nature of a person. But in the third, fourth, and fifth seasons of *Buffy,* the series integrates a more original and complex theme: the undemonization and rehabilitation of supporting characters who had first become known to the audience as annoyingly obnoxious or thoroughly evil creations or simply as different. On a deeper level, in these rehabilitated humans and demons the main characters and the audience confront the Other: the marginalized figures who are worthy of inclusion, the nonhumans who are people after all, the strangers who become us. In *Buffy,* these figures stand in for race in American society; the characters' successful and unsuccessful attempts to deal with the Other often illuminate the ways in which society may come to terms with differences in race, culture, and lifestyle.

The rehabilitation theme is introduced in the transformations of Angel, soulful vampire extraordinaire, when he loses his soul and reverts to Angelus, evil *Über*-vampire ("Surprise," 2013). Several episodes and many ghastly murders later, Angel's soul is restored by Willow's spell just in time for him to be killed and sent to hell by Buffy—something about this being the only way to save the world on the second season finale ("Becoming," parts 1 and 2, 2021 and 2022). Angelus's sins have been so dreadful that Angel can regain the viewers' good graces only through suffering a century in hell (time runs differently there) and returning to Sunnydale helpless and totally vulnerable until Buffy helps him recover to fight the forces of evil again. While Angel provides the paradigm, other characters undergo less horrific traumas on their way to rehabilitation. Spike and Cordelia, as well as Anya, Wesley, and other less significant characters, reveal a previously unsuspected vulnerability that nullifies some of their less attractive traits. These traits may vary from superficiality to a predilection for mass murder, but the technique is the same. Viewers begin to see them as somewhat sympathetic or less two-dimensional individuals; then each character is rehabilitated to become a more acceptable, even likable character. The thematic turning point occurs in the third season in two consecutive episodes, "Lovers Walk" (3008) and "The Wish" (3009), and is further developed in the fourth and fifth seasons as Riley learns the differences between Hostiles and creatures on our side, Anya joins the Scooby Gang, and even Spike loses his bite.

A vampire and a demon, in different episodes, set the rehabilitation theme in motion. In "Lovers Walk," the evil vampire Spike returns to Sunnydale a lovelorn wreck, crying on various characters' shoulders rather than nibbling on necks. (Granted, he does drain one woman, but she is the magic store clerk who has only a few lines; walk-ons hardly count.) Drusilla, the love of his undead life, has dumped him because he had allied himself with the Slayer ("Becoming," parts 1 and 2). Although his motive was to rescue Dru, she was so repulsed that she humiliated him by letting him catch her making out with a chaos demon (Spike: "Have you ever seen a chaos demon? All slime and antlers.") and left without even caring enough to cut off Spike's head. The plot of "Lovers Walk" deals with Spike's kidnapping Willow and Xander to force Willow to cast a love spell that will ensure Dru's devotion; at least that is the pretext for the plot. In reality, the episode sets out to define the rocky course and transformations of each couple's love and, in essence, some basic attitudes of the series. Most obviously, the episode shows a transformed Spike. In *The Watcher's Guide*, Golden and Holder explain the differences between demons and humans:

> What makes them human is their *capacity* for feeling emotion; what makes them demons is their inability to change; their emotions don't grow or lead to good as human emotions can. [. . .] In Whedon's universe, at least, there seems to be a continuum running between the opposite poles of human and demon;

in other words, some demons are more human than others, and some humans behave like demons. Or, to put it another way, what makes us human is our capacity to change, to feel emotions, to choose good over evil. (138–39)

As early as the second season, the Judge had recognized "the stink of humanity—love and jealousy" on Spike and Drusilla ("Innocence," 2014). Spike is becoming somewhat less demonized, more human because he does love and can change—true, only temporarily, but he changes. However, "Lovers Walk" shifts the character of Spike not by making him a sweet, heartbroken, humanized lover but rather by showing his vulnerability in making him a rejected, drunken lover who will even descend to compromising his depravity and dealing with humans in order to regain Dru. Any self-respecting vampire is totally amoral and ruthless, as evidenced by Spike's earlier cruelties, not to mention Angelus's acts of both gratuitous and calculated viciousness. But when Spike becomes an object of ridicule and a source of amusement, he loses some of his terror. Somehow it is difficult to maintain fear when the fearful creature turns sweetly nostalgic and weeps over the good times with Dru: "I used to bring her rats. With the morning paper." Halfway through the episode, he agrees to release his hostages if Angel and Buffy help him find the ingredients for Willow's love spell. Yet he does not regain his soul or transform into a good vampire. In a moment of epiphany, he realizes that each person—Buffy, Angel, or he himself—can achieve fulfillment only by remaining true to his/her/its own nature. (Shades of Polonius! *Hamlet*'s nobleman advised, "To thine own self be true," a few years before Spike discovered the precept.) Amidst the carnage of helping Buffy and Angel defeat an attacking vampire gang in the magic shop, Spike is invigorated by the violence and determines a new course of action:

Now, that was fun. [. . .] It's been so long since I had a decent spot of violence. Really puts things in perspective. [. . .] Oh, sod the spell. Your friends are in the factory. [. . .] I'll find [Drusilla], wherever she is, tie her up, torture her 'til she likes me again. [. . .] Love's a funny thing. ("Lovers Walk")

The old Spike is back, at least until he drives off into the sunrise in his window-blackened, tail-finned DeSoto, radio blaring Gary Oldman mimicking Sid Vicious's version of "I Did It My Way."

Ironically, the episode ends with everyone except Spike made acutely miserable by love. Cordelia and Oz are brokenhearted after seeing captives Willow and Xander kissing, and Willow and Xander are brokenhearted from their brief betrayal of their sweethearts; acknowledging the attraction between Willow and Xander changes all the relationships. Neither do Buffy and Angel escape the misery of love. Before the momentous battle of the magic shop, Spike becomes annoyed with Buffy's and Angel's transparent self-deception that they are now just friends. In a moment of cruel clarity, he informs them that they will *never* be "just friends"; though they will love and battle and perhaps even kill each other, they can never be mere friends. Now that epiphany is forced upon them, Buffy and Angel face the reality that they can neither eradicate nor consummate their grand passion. (There will be that one day of wild abandon in an alternate-time-line episode on *Angel,* but that is far in the future.) The rehabilitated characters repeatedly manifest this trait of insensitively revealing painful truths, often in counterpoint to the sophisticated, metaphorical slang and wordplay that the major characters use to distance themselves from and cope with brutal reality. In an interview for *The Watcher's Guide 2,* James Marsters points out that before "Lovers Walk," he, in his portrayal of Spike,

> functioned solely as a villain, which is not sustainable. At some point either the villain kills whoever he's wanting to kill or he gets killed and he hopes he has a good death. If neither of those two things happen, then the character gets bleached out and becomes a bumbling fool, and so I never had any thought that was a possibility. I was just looking for a good body count and a good death. But Joss [Whedon] told me that he wanted me to be the new Cordelia. I would be the person who would be telling everybody that they're idiots. (qtd. in Holder 267)

Not even peroxide could "bleach out" Spike as he continues to state the facts with brutal honesty even in the fourth and fifth seasons, when his vampiric impotence forces him to ally with—shudder—the Good Guys.

In "The Wish," the episode following "Lovers Walk," vengeance demon Anyanka (disguised as Anya, a new Sunnydale High student) grants selfish Cordelia an alternate reality of a Buffyless Sunnydale and ritually effects the transformation by presenting Cordelia with her ancient amulet of power. Immediately, Sunnydale becomes a horrific dystopia controlled by the Master's legions; only Giles, Oz, and a few "White Hats" try to rescue what humans they can. The Bronze becomes a vampire hangout complete with caged (human) snacks. Even more horrifically, vampires Xander and Willow murder Cordelia and drain her blood, and Willow plays with the Master's puppy: a captive Angel whom she tortures for Xander's voyeuristic pleasure. Giles, acting on Cordelia's earlier pleas to find Buffy, manages to bring the Slayer from Cleveland. (Cleveland? An untold story lurks here.) This alternate-reality Buffy is almost as frightening as the alternate Xander and Willow. Without her friends, she is as cold and dispassionate, as emotionally dead, as the real world's Slayer Faith. Buffy condescendingly dismisses Giles's frantic research for the key to the dead Cordelia's mysterious necklace and, with no preparation or knowledge, simply stalks into the factory for a showdown with the Master. Buffy is almost killed by an arrow from Xander—our formerly sweet, dopey Xander—but Angel steps in front of Buffy, takes the arrow, and turns to dust. Buffy hardly notices. Angel dies for Buffy, and *she hardly notices*. In the melee, Buffy and Oz meet and stake the vampire Willow and Xander, then Buffy is caught by the Master and her neck snapped. An instant later, Giles destroys Anyanka's amulet, thus destroying the entire alternate reality and, incidentally, Anyanka's demonic powers.

In earlier episodes, viewers might occasionally have spared a thought for the vampires being objectified and killed so remorselessly, but seeing Buffy efficiently turn her real-world closest friends into puffs of dust is a harrowing experience. Viewers are forced, consciously or subconsciously, to consider the possibility that other disposable or dangerous representatives of the Other just might be capable of humanity also. The demon races stand in for society's ethnic groups or cultures or genders that the majority fears, hates, and "demonizes." While Kent Ono cites these "killable" characters as evidence of *Buffy*'s racism (170), their undemonization demarginalizes them. Meanwhile, viewers are led to an inescapable conclusion about the hero: without the love of friends and the knowledge of the forces of evil, a Slayer is just an imperfect killing machine, almost as soulless and dead as the vampires she stakes. Yes, love *is* a funny thing.

Back to the definition: how could a demon/vampire become undemonized? By loving, by changing, by choosing—by becoming vulnerable to the dangers of being human. How does a human become less human? By disregarding love, by becoming inflexible, by operating as a machine without choice, knowledge, or wisdom. The patterns are established; the remainder of the third, fourth, and fifth seasons develop those patterns. As less admirable but important characters (whether obnoxious or noxious) are developed into humans/demons/vampires of complexity and vulnerability, they are rehabilitated. Not all the "Good" characters are ready to buy the demon world a Coke, but they do become more complex and admirable heroes as they recognize the complexities and individuality of those from the "Other" side.

In the *Buffy* pilot ("Welcome to the Hellmouth," 1001), Cordelia Chase is, in one critic's words, "a sly parody of the bitch-cheerleader stereotype, the consummate high school 'insider'" (Owen 26). Yet even in the first season, Cordelia reveals herself to be more than the stereotype. Golden and Holder astutely point out the beginnings of her "rehabilitation" in *The Watcher's Guide* as she acknowledges the emptiness of her popularity in "Out of Mind, Out of Sight" (1011), rescues Willow and Jenny Calendar in "Prophecy Girl" (1012), and advises Buffy in "When She Was Bad" (2001) (64). But it is after she is made vulnerable by losing Xander to Willow in "Lovers Walk" and by "dying" in "The Wish" that she gradually becomes much more sympathetic. Even Xander's repeated, abject apologies for betraying her fail to restore her broken heart—or her broken pride; after all, this is Cordelia. When she returns to school in "The Wish," even her Cordettes ridicule her for being rejected by a boy with no score on the popularity scale. Crushed, she is ready for revenge when Anya offers to grant her wishes. Of course, in the alternate, Buffyless Sunnydale, she quickly realizes her foolishness in blaming Buffy for all her problems and begs Giles to find the Slayer. More significant is her behavior when, at episode's end, the original wishing ritual with Anyanka replays without Anya's now destroyed amulet. Cordelia, even with no memory of her alternate reality, discards the wish for Buffy to disappear and makes all sorts of increasingly whimsical wishes, obviously treating her first wish as a moment of weakness. Then she confidently walks away, Cordelia again, her power restored even as the stunned Anya realizes that her power is gone. Cordelia clearly is a better, stronger person than her original image implied.

As the third season progresses, Cordelia becomes more vulnerable when her tax-dodging father loses the Chase family fortune. Rich, snobbish, nothing-but-designer-clothes Cordelia is reduced to secretly working in a dress shop in order to buy her senior prom dress off the rack. How far the mighty have fallen! It is Xander who discovers her plight and secretly buys the dress for her ("The Prom," 3020). She also becomes more sympathetic as she fights alongside Buffy—when she really, really has to. Even her formerly insensitive remarks begin to sound more like insight and truth. Just as Spike often cuts through romantic fluff to state the brutal truth, so does Cordelia. In "Earshot" (3018), Buffy contracts a telepathic demon's power, and immediately all her friends begin to censor their thoughts around her or avoid her entirely. Even her mentor, Giles, and her mother, Joyce, avoid her. (Especially do Giles and Joyce avoid her; they fear giving away their tryst atop a police cruiser in "Band Candy," 3006.) Only Cordelia is unaffected. She is so forthright—or self-centered—that her words express exactly what she thinks no matter whom she might offend or hurt. Perhaps her name is an intentional allusion to that other Cordelia, in Shakespeare's *King Lear,* who is also known for speaking blunt truths.[1] By the time the character leaves *Buffy* at the end of the third season, she is ready to be developed into a strong costar in the spin-off series *Angel.* Her characteristic frankness (insensitivity?) is exactly the tart antidote that the WB's reigning Byronic hero needs. (Romantics will be pleased that the Byronic hero is not dead. Just undead.) After all, who else would dare tell Angel to stop moping around and wear brighter colors? So what if he is the only extant vampire with a soul and can never again make love to the only woman in the world he yearns for with all his unbeating heart? Some other people have terrible problems, too—like being down to one's last pair of designer pumps.

Wesley Wyndam-Pryce, also much improved in *Angel,* first appears in *Buffy* as Buffy's new Watcher ("Bad Girls," 3014), embodying the concept of Watcher-as-jerk, at best. He is responsible for arranging the Council's kidnapping of Faith that, perhaps, pushes her over the line into conscious evil. Yet even he is partially rehabilitated as early as "The Prom" and other episodes by his silly crush on Cordelia. Giles finally tells the wimpy Brit to go ahead and ask Cordelia to dance—she is old enough. As in the case of Spike, looking ridiculous can help make a formerly unlikable character a bit less annoying. (And this is clearly the only comparison, tenuous though it may be, between Spike and Wesley Wyndam-Pryce.) Certainly he has redeemed himself in *Angel*. After a pretentious and ignominious introduction as "rogue demon hunter" (his own description), his character has revealed vulnerability through hints of childhood abuse, and heroism through increasingly effective work with Angel, Cordelia, and Gunn.

The fourth and fifth seasons of *Buffy* continue to reinforce and reinvent the patterns. The most serious attempt at rehabilitation is that of Faith. For all her toughness and amoral brutality, she has always been fragile in her unadmitted neediness for love and her denial of her own worth. When she forces a body exchange with Buffy in "This Year's Girl" (4015) and "Who Are You?" (4016), she is so affected (infected?) by Buffy's altruism that she begins to seek redemption in *Angel*. Yet Whedon could change the pattern completely with Faith; people in the Buffyverse are never quite predictable. In the final first-season episodes of *Angel*, viewers expect another redemption and rehabilitation when Lindsey MacDonald, star attorney for Wolfram & Hart, reveals inside information to Angel and saves some lives. But in the next episode, Lindsey recants and returns to villainy. As Angel comments, "He made his choice." Even a series about a noble vampire still has some grasp on reality; demons might be rehabilitated—but lawyers? Highly improbable. In the second season, Angel eventually allows Darla and Drusilla to have their way with seventeen captive attorneys of Wolfram & Hart. However, even the depraved Darla spares Lindsey (and Lilah) to fight the forces of Good in the coming war.

At times during *Buffy*'s fourth and fifth seasons, the patterns of rehabilitation are played as jokes. Thus, Giles is transformed (by his old friend Ethan Rayne) into an apparent demon in "A New Man" (4012) and is nearly killed before Buffy recognizes the true Giles within. In "Something Blue"(4009), one of the most outrageously comic episodes so far, Willow's spell goes awry and causes Buffy and Spike to fall instantly in love and plan their wedding. This is carrying rehabilitation a bit far, much to the delight of the viewers. Then the joke takes an even more unexpected turn in season 5 as Spike develops a dangerously real crush on Buffy. Another character who was introduced in season 3 as a villain, Anyanka the vengeance demon, also becomes a source of comedy as a new member of the Scooby Gang. After losing her powers in "The Wish" when Giles destroyed her amulet, she becomes vulnerable to all the pains that eighteen-year-old flesh is heir to. Her basic modes of rehabilitation are her vulnerability through lust, then love for Xander and her embarrassingly frank comments arising from naïveté about all human interaction. In *The Monster Book*, Marti Noxon, writer of "The Wish," explains that "this disgruntled ex-demon" is quite useful because "we [. . .] needed a Cordelialike character around who would tell it like it is, who doesn't suffer fools gladly and is very opinionated" (qtd. in Golden, Bissette, and Sniegoski 34). In the superb episode "The Body" (5016), Whedon gives Anya one of *Buffy*'s finest speeches when she haltingly states the inscrutability of death that every human feels but fears to express:

> [crying]: I don't understand how this all happens. How we go through this. I mean, I knew her, and then she's [sniffling], there's just a body, and I don't understand why she just can't get back in it and not be dead anymore. It's stupid. It's mortal and stupid. [still teary] And, and Xander's crying and not talking, and, and I was having fruit punch, and I thought, well, Joyce will never have any more fruit punch ever, and she'll never have eggs, or yawn or brush her hair, not ever, and no one will explain to me why.

Riley Finn of The Initiative is a focus of the patterns in the fourth season. His charm, integrity, courage, and skill make him worthy of Buffy. He is another outsider who is brought into the Slayer's circle. But he is an outsider not because he does not believe in demons, vampires, and other things that go bump in the night; indeed, Riley believes in them all and reduces them to a single dichotomy: Human Good, Demon Bad. He, as a young leader of The Initiative, further reduces all that Bad to little mechanized patterns: microchips can control all Bad. All Bumping Things are things that must be killed—but it is okay to experiment on them first. After all, demons are an inferior, entirely different race; they are Other personified. His view of the universe is sometimes almost as simplistic (in different ways) as that of Faith, the most mechanized of Slayers. But when he is admitted to Buffy's heart and bed and to the Scooby Gang's inner circle, he learns otherwise. The escaped Hostile 17 is an individual being—Spike—who has a history with Buffy. And one vampire—Angel—is not demonic at all. And not all demons are automatically evil and deserving of instant death. The concept that some demons could be neutral or even good had been introduced as early as the appearance of Whistler, Angel's mentor, in "Becoming," parts 1 and 2. It is worth noting that in *Angel,* many more demons are individualized and undemonized: in early episodes the half-demon Doyle is cohero, and gladiator demons enslaved by Wolfram & Hart are freed by Angel, Wesley, and Cordelia. When Angel and Doyle rescue a shipload of persecuted bracken demons from jackbooted racist demons, the parallel with Nazis is inescapable: any viewer with knowledge of World War II shudders at the sight of the neo-Aryan bund of black-leather demons crashing through doors to slaughter innocents, all in the name of racial purity. The second season features the empathic demon Host of a demon karaoke club, a divinely decadent individual out of Whedon's vivid imagination by way of *Cabaret*.

In the fourth season of *Buffy*, Spike is the instrument of much of Riley Finn's instruction. When The Initiative's implanted microchip renders him incapable of harming any human, he literally, physically, becomes vulnerable to all humans. For protection and, perhaps, a degree of friendship, he joins the Scooby Gang.[2] Of course, he lives (in a manner of speaking) only for the day that he can once again wreak havoc among the humans, beginning with the despised Buffy, for whom he, William the Bloody himself, harbors some hidden tenderness. For the nonce he is impotently good, like Milton's Satan nearly beguiled by Eve. Fortunately for his sanity, he discovers in "Doomed" (4011) that he *can* fight demons without being disabled by pain from the microchip; then he is ready to "kick demon ass" with the best of the Scooby Gang. Nevertheless, he remains true to himself as much as possible, having learned his lesson in "Lovers Walk." Whenever he has a chance to avoid endangering himself to help the good guys, he does so. He even aids the cyborg Adam's plot to separate the friends in "The Yoko Factor" (4020) and fights on the right side in the fourth-season finale only to save himself ("Primeval," 4021). Spike does, at least, help educate Riley in the shades of gray between black, white, and blood red.

Just when Riley has begun to deal humanely with the undemonized characters of *Buffy*, he must face the psychological and physical demons within himself. From Riley's first appearance ("The Freshman," 4001), he is presented as a *normal* prospective boyfriend with a bit of the aw-shucks charm of a young Jimmy Stewart or of his own namesake, Huck Finn. Granted, this graduate student is a paragon of intelligence and good looks; but even after his commando secret identity is revealed in "Hush" (4010), he still seems the sunny antithesis of Buffy's first great love, the always shadowed Angel. Indeed, when in "Restless" (4022) Buffy dreams her worst fear of Riley, she imagines him not as a ruthless killer bent on the genocide of all supernatural creatures but as a sophisticated company man in a three-piece suit, coldly planning the business of taking over the world. Yet that warped dream reveals something else in Buffy's worst fears: beside Riley is Adam, the Frankenstein-like monster now a handsome human but still intent on monstrous domination. Buffy is reflecting Riley's own worst fear, that he himself is a monster, a demonic creature as unnatural as those Hostiles he once hunted. Riley has discovered that Professor Maggie Walsh had given him dangerous biological enhancements and microchips of his own; to some degree he *is* Adam's brother, an unnatural thing, a controllable cyborg. Above all, he fears to embrace and defeat the demon, the Other within himself. He overlooks his own inherent decency and integrity, his ability to learn and grow, and his worthiness of Buffy. In "Into the Woods" (5010), his identity crisis causes him to doubt Buffy's love and leads him first to a vampire brothel and then back to his old military cadre on a secret mission where even Buffy will not find him: like Huck, Riley Finn lights out for the territory. He surrenders. By ceasing to risk the hazards of seeking love and identity, he escapes to clear-cut physical danger in some faraway covert action where he can once more separate himself from another group of Hostiles. As his black helicopter lifts off into the night sky, he neither sees nor hears the frantic Buffy calling him back. Ironically, in hiding his insecurity and heartbreak, he appears to be more of an unfeeling automaton than Adam ever was.

Throughout *Buffy*, the formerly unheroic characters take on characteristics of the archetypal heroes, and thus does *Buffy* add a few more transformations to the complex mix of heroism, humor, and wit at world's end. As Michael Ventura explains in *Psychology Today*, *Buffy* postulates that "the heart of society is demonic. Society is Hell. [. . .] And to be human is to constantly fight demons" (58). Sometimes even a noble character like Riley Finn can no longer bear to cope with his own fear of becoming a demonic thing. However, just as real humans can become demonic, so can obnoxious and noxious beings become human and even heroic. Increasingly, the heroes begin to recognize the Other figure as an individual person instead of reacting to the figure as merely an unchanging member of a certain race, gender, or culture. And as soon as viewers recognize the patterns of undemonization, Joss Whedon brings about another metamorphosis of character patterns within *Buffy the Vampire Slayer*.

NOTES

1. I am indebted to Rhonda Wilcox for pointing out this allusion.

2. Editors' note: In "The Gift" (5022), Spike cheerfully mauls Shakespeare's *Henry V* by referring to the Scooby Gang as "we band of buggered," after trading quips with Giles about the St. Crispin's Day Speech.

9

"Sometimes You Need a Story"
American Christianity, Vampires, and Buffy

Gregory Erickson

Ah, it is the fault of our science that it wants to explain all; and if it ex-plain not, then it says there is nothing to explain. But yet we see around us every day the growth of new beliefs, which think themselves new, and which are yet but the old, which pretend to be young.

—Abraham Van Helsing, M.D., Ph.D. (qtd. in Stoker 210)

[Americans] have revised the traditional religion into a faith that better fits our national temperament, aspirations, and anxieties.

—Bloom 45

As Christians, we need to understand the realm of the satanic supernatu-ral because it does exist and we are participants of the battle.

—Larson 17

People have a tendency to rationalize what they can and forget what they can't.

—Rupert Giles in "Welcome to the Hellmouth" (1001)

POPULAR CULTURE, RELIGION, AND VAMPIRES

A special television news flash announces that several "frightfully disfig-
ured, almost inhuman" terrorists have barricaded themselves in a church
with the congregation. In reality, it is three vampires that hold the group of
hostages, and Buffy and her friends race across town to stop them. The
parishioners fearfully sit awaiting what seems to be certain death, or worse,
as the vampires stride among the wooden pews inside the small, traditional
stone church. With the cross prominently in the background, one of the
vampires looks around, admires the stained glass, approaches the altar, and
shouts arrogantly, "I've been avoiding this place for so many years, and it's
nothing. [. . .] Where is the thing I was so afraid of? You know, the Lord?"
("Who Are You?" 4016).

The question, although phrased by a vampire, is one that is important to
an understanding of *Buffy the Vampire Slayer.* Where is the Lord? Where
indeed? Is there any God for these vampires to fear? But the question is
much bigger than this. What God do Americans, a "religion mad" popula-
tion (Bloom 37), bring to and get from our other obsession: popular culture? Where does a cultural phenomenon like *Buffy* fit into our spiritual
epistemology?

BUFFY THE VAMPIRE SLAYER

I began this chapter with the idea that religion can be found anywhere and
often most usefully where we do not expect it. I wanted to look, as Lévi-
Strauss would say, not for "how men think in myths but how myths operate in men's minds without their being aware of it" (12). My choice of *Buffy*
as a focal point is partly random, partly because it has some implicit relationship to folklore and religion, and because it seems characteristically
American. One could do the same kind of interpretation with *The X-Files*,
the Super Bowl, or, as Mark Taylor does, with Las Vegas. I am not offering
a reading of religion or of a television series, and the danger in a writing like
this is that it is easy to relate *anything* to religion in ways that do not really
accomplish much. To be successful, I must offer some insight about culture,
not just television, and in a way that goes deeper than surface parallels. As
anthropologist Clifford Geertz says, "We must descend into detail, past the
misleading tags, past the metaphysical types, past the empty similarities to
grasp firmly the essential character of [. . .] the various sorts of individuals
within each culture" (53). For Geertz, religion and religious symbols are
both models *for* and models *of* culture (90–91). A cultural phenomenon like
vampires is both produced by and part of a society inextricably tied up in

its religion. We can see in the American treatment of vampires, and in *Buffy*, the same complexities and paradoxes as in American Christianity.

In exploring this issue, I will come from several different directions. First I will discuss how the show portrays the world of demons and vampires, drawing comparisons with the development of the vampire in American popular culture and with the development of the American Christ. Then I will look at the implied religion of both *Buffy* and American culture. I will conclude with sections on the extremes of belief and disbelief in American culture and show how *Buffy* is a product and a part of this paradoxical epistemology.

Buffy Summers, the chosen Slayer, and her friends live in the town of Sunnydale, a fictional southern California town situated on a "Hellmouth," or a "mystical center of convergence." This allows all sorts of demons and vampires to pass through and also serves as a constant reminder that adolescence is literally hell. Buffy constantly struggles with fulfilling her appointed role and living a normal life. She must live up to her responsibilities as the Slayer, pass a math test, and try to get a date for Saturday night: "If the apocalypse comes, beep me" ("Never Kill a Boy on the First Date," 1005). She can viciously snap the neck of a hellhound, pull a formal dress out of her weapons bag, and calmly walk into the senior prom, where her date is an over-200-year-old vampire ("The Prom," 3020). As Buffy and her friends have grown older and entered college or the workforce, they continue to face the typical traumas of youth with a twist. Buffy's annoying dormitory roommate turns out to be a demon, her boyfriend works for a secret military operation, and the gang's first return to the old high school is to close the mouth of hell and save the world ("Doomed," 4011).

As critics have noted, *Buffy* both questions and fulfills traditional modes of cultural thought,[1] and the space it allocates to religion likewise pulls in both directions. In the opening of one episode, Buffy, wearing a crucifix given to her by Angel—a crucifix that has saved her life in the past—answers the question "Have you accepted Jesus Christ as your personal savior?" with "You know, I meant to and then I just got really busy" ("The Freshman," 4001). Like many quotes from *Buffy*, this is both humorous and meaningful. We laugh, but we also sense the cultural "in-betweenness" that the show embodies. Watching the show is a more complex experience than we might think: "Viewers must understand both the language and the symbolism to see the reality. Life and language are not so simple as problem-of-the-week television would suggest, and *Buffy* acknowledges that fact" (Wilcox, "There" 16). Behind the witty dialogue and the engaging characters, behind the metaphors of monsters and demons, the show occupies a space between belief and disbelief, between an absolute morality and nihilism.

VAMPIRE LEGEND: FROM FOLKLORE TO FILM TO *BUFFY*

Both vampires and Christianity had murky beginnings, matured in medieval Europe, went through extreme manifestations throughout the Renaissance, survived the Enlightenment, and were brought to and changed by America. Alan Dundes writes that vampires are an example of a topic or subject that is found on all three levels of culture: elite culture, popular culture, and folklore (160), and, like any figure that inhabits legend, lore, psychology, and literature (and we must include God in this category), the vampire has a complex history that cannot be reduced to any simple pattern of historic development. Yet, as Auerbach says, "every age embraces the vampire it needs" (145), and ultimately they "matter because, when properly understood, they make us see that our lives are implicated in theirs and our times are inescapable" (9).

Early vampires in Eastern European folklore were peasants who came out of the grave to kill their relatives and townspeople. Their reason for becoming vampires could be that they died poorly (drunk, unbaptized, or from suicide) or simply that they were seeking revenge (on a young wife's lover, for example). By the time of Bram Stoker's *Dracula*, the vampire had become an aristocrat. He lives a solitary life in a mansion or a castle, has a title, and embodies pure Christian evil. The Victorian vampire is undead, unhuman, and very literally an Antichrist, risen from the dead, offering the possibility of eternal life. As Jules Zanger says, "The solitary Dracula could, like the Old Testament God, only relate to humans and only within a very narrow range of interlocking emotions" (22). In contrast, contemporary American Hollywood vampires are in many ways indistinguishable from surrounding beings. They look and evidently smell human. Often they eat and drink and smoke, fall in love, get angry, and feel compassion. In movies like *Near Dark* and *The Lost Boys,* they are vampires for the same social reasons that people become criminals or that kids go wrong.

Criticism has often focused on the domestication of the vampire in America or, as Zanger puts it, a movement from "Count Dracula to Ted Bundy."[2] This "new" vampire, Zanger continues, commits evil acts as "expressions of individual personality" rather than any "cosmic conflict between God and Satan" (18–19). While American films of the 1970s and 1980s may have reduced vampires to "anti-family" (Nixon 124) or "sadistic psychopaths" (Zanger 21), *Buffy* complicates things by creating a sense of randomness. On *Buffy,* vampires have the memories and personalities of humans but the souls of demons, and anyone—good, bad, rich, poor, handsome, ugly, old, or young—can become or be a vampire at any time. What had become a morality tale is instantly deconstructed by a world where rational (read adult or Great Tradition) systems are ineffective. In unexpected but characteristically American ways, *Buffy* restores some of the metaphysical concerns abandoned by Hollywood and serves as a window through which to view the complicated world of both popular culture and popular religion.

BUFFY AND AMERICAN CHRISTIANITY

In looking at the history of the vampire, we can find in the relationship of the European vampire to the American vampire a parallel to the relationship between the Christ of Europe, whom Augustine saw as "an enigma and as through a glass" (160), and the American Christ, who "walks and talks with you" and is a "friend." (*Jesus Christ: Who Is He?* a Jehovah's Witness tract asks and offers a picture of a kindly good-looking man smiling and reaching out his hand in a greeting.) Indeed, the American Jesus is "not a first century Jew, but a 19th or 20th century American, whose principal difference is that he already has risen from the dead" (Bloom 65). American culture, like all culture, creates its own supernatural, and in this context, vampires in movies like *Near Dark* and *The Lost Boys* are just troublemaking kids who happen to be undead. The established "otherness" of vampires is completely dissolved by the time we get to Buffy, who even has conventional human sex with a vampire, or, as fellow slayer Faith says to her in admiration, "you've boinked the undead" ("Revelations," 3007).

Both American Christianity and American vampires exhibit similar traces of, and shifts away from, their European roots. Peter Williams says, "Almost from their collective beginnings, Americans have been reluctant to accept the established religions of the Old World without questions or dissent" (2). Or, as Anne Rice's Louis says, "I had met the European vampire, the creature of the old World. He was dead" (*Interview with the Vampire* 192). The American vampire, like the American Christ, is a new creature created by a new culture.

In summing up his book *American Originals: Homemade Varieties of Christianity*, Paul Conkin characterizes indigenous American Christianity by its lack of stress on the issue of a trinity, by a lack of commitment to great creeds, and by the creation by American prophets of new and different gods (316–18). In looking at the recent American vampire, and specifically at the vampires on *Buffy*, we see reflections of these ways of thinking; this American originality manifests itself in the creation of new ways of creating and killing vampires as much as in the creation of new scriptures.

In folklore, the most important thing is to cut off the head and burn the vampire's body. The staking was intended to keep the creature in the grave rather than to kill it. In Stoker, you drive a stake through the heart, fill the mouth with garlic, and cut off the head; blood spurts everywhere, the creature shrieks and moans, the soul is saved. In recent movies, vampires are killed by exploding trucks and slashed by chain saws. On *Buffy*, it is different—more ambiguous and ironic. In the first of many battles at the teen club The Bronze, we see vampires killed in ways that reflect traditional methods but also parody them. Buffy beheads a vampire by flinging a cymbal from a drum set Frisbee-style across the room, the Jewish Willow shyly throws a jar of holy water on a vampire; Xander impales one with a wooden stake, but only by accident when he is bumped from behind. The climactic kill comes when Buffy fools the head vampire into thinking that a lamp is really daylight and then stabs him from behind ("The Harvest," 1002). While traditional methods are used, each is given a twist and a new attitude. Vampires killed on *Buffy* explode neatly into powder, leaving no corpse, no unpleasant trace of death. The hateful revenge of most recent films, like *From Dusk till Dawn*, is gone. Also missing is the horror, spurting blood, and Christian angst in Stoker's *Dracula*, as Lucy Westenra's lover drives the stake home to give her soul eternal life. In a similar incident, with a characteristically ironic reversal, Buffy must kill Angel after he has reverted to being an evil vampire. But far from putting his soul at rest, she kills him just after his soul has been restored and sends him to suffer in hell ("Becoming," part 2, 2022). In this scene, revenge and salvation are subverted, and good and evil are not so clearly defined.

Killing the undead mathematically results in a double negative and therefore life and brings us to the ideas of resurrection and salvation. A thought attributed to Alfred Jarry is provocative here: if Christ had been impaled rather than crucified, he asks, what gesture would we make going into church? When it comes to vampires, if we ward off with a crucifix and kill with a stake, would we ward off with a stake and kill with a cross (Epstein)? The relationship between the killing of a vampire and the crucifixion is complex. Throughout much of vampire history, the killing of a vampire has been associated with saving its eternal soul. In *Dracula*, Van Helsing urges them to "strike in God's name, that all may be well with the dead that we love, and the Un-dead pass away" (Stoker 230). And after the deed is finished, "no longer she is the Devil's Un-dead. She is God's true dead whose soul is with him" (238).

While this is an idea that has waned in American vampire lore, we can look at how ideas about vampire killing and salvation have developed and changed and make a parallel here with changes in ideas of Christian conversion. American Christianity has always emphasized conversion and favors the instantaneous: one is "born again," and no education is necessary. In *Buffy*, a vampire is produced easily, and the characteristic vampire face emerges and disappears instantly. In contrast, the transformation (itself an eighteenth-century concept of vampirism) in Stoker, we recall, is excruciatingly slow. We see both Lucy and Mina get sicker and paler; their gums draw back, and their teeth slowly extend over days and weeks as characters endlessly record and re-record the process. We are never allowed to forget the constant battle between Christ and Satan.

THEOLOGY: WEAPONS, SYMBOLS, AND CROSSES

In *Buffy*, we see no heaven, no God, no Christ. There are no functioning churches, and there is no serious prayer. In isolated episodes, Cordelia prays and Riley goes to church, but both incidents are presented in humorous ways that are more about characterization than religion. There are occasional references to the sacred/pagan nature of humans versus demons and vampires, but the creatures of the night are usually the only ones who get to quote the Bible. The Christian symbolism of holy water and crosses is left unstated. The presence and effectiveness of both have lessened throughout the run of the series, and by the third year a vampire looks at a cross and a vial of holy water, sneers "whatever," and walks away ("Doppelgängland," 3016).

As Nietzsche says, however, it was Christianity that established the Devil in the world, and *Buffy* has a fully developed world of hell, evil, and the devil. What does this "mean"? Montague Summers, a vampire-believing scholar, states, "For the haunting of a vampire three things are necessary: the Vampire, the Devil, and the permission of Almighty God" (qtd. in Dundes 162). Does a demonic presence require at least an implied Christian one? Can we have an evil without a sacred? Buffy's cross is never related to Christ, but a vampire says, "This is the most fun I've had since the crucifixion" ("School Hard," 2003), and a church is used by Spike in a mock crucifixion ritual to restore the evil, mad Drusilla to health: "From the blood of this site she will rise again [. . .]" ("What's My Line?" part 2, 2010). As Quincy, the Winchester-toting American member of the male posse in Stoker's *Dracula* might say, "Just what in Hell is going on here?"

To begin, what does the cross signify on the show? It appears to be neither Christian nor non-Christian.[3] It is constantly present—in the opening credits, around Buffy's neck, and in her bag of weapons along with holy water, a crossbow, and a collection of wooden stakes, knives, and axes—but it has no privileged status. The cross is no more a weapon than a crossbow, a broken pool cue, or a well-placed karate kick. The ambiguity of the cross is emphasized by Buffy's first great nemesis, the Master, who defiantly calls it "two pieces of wood," even as he sizzles from touching it. By contrast, in Stoker's *Dracula*, we have the same combination of physical and Christian weapons, but the Christianity is always emphasized. A prayer always accompanies the stake. The truest cross, in any traditional sense, in the whole of *Buffy* is the burned image of the cross pressed into Angel's skin from when he embraces Buffy. Here, in Angel, and only here, in the negative image of a symbol burned into the skin of a tormented vampire, does the cross stand for anything remotely Christian. Angel, the eternal soul, has given the gift, and the cross represents his suffering and sacrifice.

In current American culture as well, as present as the cross is, what it signifies is ambiguous. No longer the space of Christ's suffering, or a sign of religious opulence, the American cross, as Harold Bloom says, is the empty cross from which "Jesus has already risen." "Resurrection," he says, "is the entire concern of the American Religion" (40). As Bloom interprets it, American religion quests for the forty days when the disciples were with Christ. The Bible says little about this period: there is no text, just company. No theology, just power. No dogma, just friendship. Buffy's cross, as well, is a simulacrum—a copy with no original—a sacred and powerful sign, signifying nothing.

This American distrust of theology is seen in the emphasis on the clergy being "called" and not on their education. Faith and experience are all; intellectual knowledge is always suspect. In recent American vampire stories, we see this reflected in the metamorphosis of Stoker's intellectual Dr. Van Helsing. In American films his role is often eliminated, reduced, or made fun of. In *The Lost Boys,* for example, we have the Frog brothers, a ridiculous pair of teenagers running a comic book shop who seem to be the only people in town who have any sense of the vampires surrounding them. In *Buffy,* the role of Van Helsing is shared by Giles, the friendly British librarian with all the occult books—"you bought the Time-Life series?" Buffy teases him ("Welcome to the Hellmouth," 1001)—who is wrong as often as he is right, and the bookish Willow, who gets her information from the Internet. Buffy herself is not required to read the "Slayer's handbook" and is repeatedly rewarded for trusting her instincts over knowledge.

DEMONS AND REALITY

As Willow says, "The dark can get pretty dark. Sometimes you need a story" ("Lie to Me," 2007), and the creative role of fear is clearly a connecting thread between vampires and Christianity. Theories of vampire folktales point to the fear of death, the fear of what happens to a body rotting in the grave, and fear of disease as related to a belief in vampires. According to Laurence Rickels in *The Vampire Lectures,* the crosses on grave sites were originally put there not to commemorate but to keep the dead person in the grave. In Stoker's *Dracula,* there is obviously a fear of sexuality and, as has been pointed to by many critics, a fear of strong sexual women. In *Buffy,* vampires and demons stand for, among other things, fears faced by young people: fear of sex, fear of becoming adult, fear of not fitting in. Obviously, fear plays a role in the history of Christianity, but in looking specifically at American popular religion, Bloom asks, "When people frighten themselves into faith as millions of Americans do, what ought religious criticism to do with that fright?" (257).

The presence of fear in religion and in vampire stories is essentially irrational, and I now want to address this irrationality, to point to some slippage and some marginalized aspects that I cannot reconcile in any logical way. What makes American religion so interesting is the ways in which it cannot be interpreted, captured, or written down in a short chapter. Its antistructure is always working; we never know when we are cast into the role of the adults on *Buffy*, existing in what seems a sensible rational world yet not seeing the reality all around us. To conclude, I want to juxtapose *Buffy* with two seemingly opposite sides of belief: the belief in literal biblical demons and an American spirituality that acknowledges the absence of God. The paradoxical American religion contains both these sides, and *Buffy* resides in and around the contradictions.

At the same time that the American vampire has moved from *Near Dark* and *The Lost Boys* to *Buffy*, there has been another and perhaps related movement in the American imagination. A growing number of Christian evangelicals have been engaging in what they call "spiritual warfare," by which they mean active battle with evil demons. In his book *Warfare Prayer*, C. Peter Wagner explains that since "Satan can be in only one place at one time," he must "delegate the responsibility" by maintaining a "hierarchy of demonic forces to carry out his purpose" (63). Outside of some pretty blatant racism, there is much in Wagner's book that would work in a *Buffy* episode. He describes in detail the physical characteristics of demons, and he even writes of a rift in a town that allowed demons to come in and take control of a city. He calls it the "Devil's Corner," and Buffy calls it the "Hellmouth," but it is essentially the same thing. These beliefs are not as marginal as we might want to think. Wagner's books sell in the millions, and articles on demons have appeared in mainstream southern Baptist publications.[4]

How "real" are these beliefs in demons? What does it mean to call them "real"? To call them "beliefs"? Does a practicing Catholic "believe" he is drinking blood? Do I "believe" that my hand is made out of atoms and is therefore mostly empty space? As shows like *Buffy* seem to take the literal role of vampires and demons less seriously, at the same time we have books like Wagner's, proclaiming a real demon presence that most of us are supposedly unaware of. Is there a connection? Do all these gods and demons come from similar imaginative spaces? These questions lie at the heart of the American consciousness, popular and spiritual. As any good postmodernist knows, absence and presence are not, and have never been, opposites, and the experience of American Christianity involves both.

POSTMODERNISM: FRAGMENTS AND MARGINS

If we were to use one word or concept to define American Christianity, ⟩ would be *experience*. From Jonathan Edwards to Ralph Waldo Emerson to William James to Jimmy Swaggart, experience, not doctrine, has been the preferred mode of spiritual contact. For an American, God is known to exist because he is *felt*. God is felt in dreams, visions, and body movements. Only something experienced is real; a conversion must be felt to be true. The unique American God is "an experiential God, radical within our own being" (Bloom 45). This God stems from an American originality that can produce a Sunnydale or a *Book of Mormon*.

So finally, after all this, I want to think about how *Buffy* is truly a postmodern American religious experience, not in the familiar sense of a religious experience, but as one that connects the ideas I have been exploring in this chapter. Can we see a *Buffy* episode, for example, in a way that acknowledges that "everything eternal and true is *not*" and yet that "God maintains himself in this process" (Hegel 323)? Can we do this in a way that takes into account its characteristically American religious aspects? Mark Taylor, for example, sees this Hegelian God rising out of negation in the music videos of Madonna or the architecture of Las Vegas; he sees the modern image as a "constructive subject that creates the world in its own image" ("Betting" 103). Could we say that popular culture and vampire tales create a subjective or absent God that reveals the American soul?

This absence is the imaginative space for our art, our religion, and our vampires. Our fear, belief, disbelief, conservatism, and innovation exist both at the center and in the margin and fragments of this imaginative space. Vampires "may look marginal, feeding on human history from some limbo of their own, but they have always been central: what vampires are in any given generation is a part of what I am and what my times have become" (Auerbach 1).

As represented on *Buffy*, none of this feels rebuilt from old scraps of stories, but, in the spirit of American Christianity, it is an experienced conversion; Dracula is born again as Angel, the good-hearted avenger with a cross seared into his skin, one sexual encounter away from becoming evil again, and as Spike, a trash-talking punk rocker, somehow both likable and purely evil. And, as we have seen, *Buffy* implies a divine presence and seeks a transcendent G(o)od at the same time that it denies this existence. What is Buffy's cross for? Where does Buffy get her powers from? Why is Angel allowed to return from hell? Why is there a hell? Questions like these are suggested but are left generally unasked and always unanswered. At the beginning of the fifth season, Buffy becomes more aware of some of these issues, asking Giles to become her Watcher again to help her work out answers. But as she experiences her most powerful opponent yet, the loss of another

117

h of her mother, any sense of a divine presence or a
 ꞁdes her.[5]

 episode, we experience evil that refuses to be evil,
 remain secular; each episode as a fragment of a non-
 gaps in language between worlds; the familiar as apocalyp-
 ꞁe apocalyptic as familiar. The gaps and uncertainties are filled by
 vampires themselves. In a sense, a viewer can exist only as a vampire—
neither Sunnydale student nor naive adult, but an ambiguous and change-
able creature. *Buffy* creates a world of absence/presence, immortality/
mortality, sacred/secular, where the experience is always on the edge or in
the gaps of perception. It is an ironic world just this side of literal belief in
demons but one that is also close to the spiritual experience—praised by
medieval Christian mystics and contemporary theologians—of gazing on a
space where God is not.

In examining aspects of popular culture not generally thought to be religious, Taylor's question "How *not* to think God?" comes to mind (*Nots*
11). Since the Enlightenment, intellectuals have tried to provide some sort
of closure to religion. But as postmodernism stresses fragmented and marginalized texts, we have returned to the idea of God because it cannot be
framed or totalized. While America has often been characterized as simpli-
fying God (and vampires), there is another side that is constantly slipping.
The characteristically American phrase "I know that God exists" can be
read to say just the opposite. (If we can *know,* then God becomes of this reality, an empirical object that we can possess, and therefore is not God.)
Somewhere in all these images of demons, the death and life of vampires becomes hopelessly (or hopefully) reversed. The postmodern God is desired
but not found. The American Christ both is and is not. Negation and affir-
mation can never be separated, and in this world of hypertext Bibles and
Buffy chat rooms, of spiritual warfare and vampire Web sites, the virtual
becomes real and the real virtual.

We create, in our monsters, in our gods, and in our theories, reflections of who we are. As Max Weber says, "Man is an animal suspended
in webs of significance he himself has spun" (qtd. in Geertz 5). Yet, like
vampires, we cannot always see ourselves in the mirror. As Auerbach
says, "There is no such creature as 'the vampire.' There are only vampires" (5). And although it is perhaps our historical insistence on a
monotheistic theology that has created the need to be one autonomous
individual, in looking at American religion we see that there are many
Gods and many Christs, just as each of us is endlessly fragmented. If one
of the purposes of monsters has been to help us define who we are, a
show like *Buffy,* where the categories and boundaries are constantly
blurred, can help us further understand the confusing and complicated
stories we continue to tell ourselves.

NOTES

Thanks to Jennifer Lemberg, who read and commented on many drafts of this chapter and listened to me talk endlessly about my ideas on religion and *Buffy the Vampire Slayer.*

1. For example, see Owen.

2. See Gordon and Hollinger, eds., *Blood Read,* especially the chapter by Zanger and Nixon, "When Hollywood Sucks, or Hungry Girls, Lost Boys, and Vampirism in the Age of Reagan," and Gordon and Hollinger, "Introduction."

3. Although the Christian significance of the cross is usually ignored, it is referred to humorously in an episode where Willow (who is Jewish) spreads crosses around her house to protect her from the evil Angelus during the night but must take care to hide them from her father ("Passion," 2017).

4. For example, *The Commission,* February–March 1991, and *Christian Single,* October 1999.

5. An interesting contrast is provided by *Angel,* the spin-off series to *Buffy.* On *Angel,* more serious attention is given to sacred texts and prophecies, characters ask advice from oracles, Angel is guided by the mysterious "Powers That Be," and references are made to a plan amidst the chaos. All in all, it is a world that implies a divine presence.

10

Darkness Falls on the Endless Summer
Buffy as Gidget for the Fin de Siècle

Catherine Siemann

Buffy: Mom, I've accepted that you've had sex. I am not ready to know
   that you had Farrah hair.
Joyce: This is Gidget hair. Don't they teach you anything in history?

—"The Witch" (1003)

Ah, to be young in Southern California. The cultural myth of the Endless
Summer, propagated in songs by the Beach Boys and movies featuring
Frankie Avalon and Annette Funicello, or a surfer girl named Gidget, took
hold in the public consciousness in the 1950s and 1960s and never really let
go. It is less about a place than it is about a time of life; the sunshine, palm
trees, and endless perfect waves merely provide the backdrop for an idyllic
version of the teenage experience. But while the iconography of the Endless
Summer remains, other images regarding both the geographic space and the
time of life have overlaid it: images of urban decay in Los Angeles, images
of the complexity and pain of teenage life. As the twentieth century has
made way for the twenty-first, the archetypal Southern California teenager
is no longer Gidget the surfer girl but Buffy the Vampire Slayer.

Gidget Lawrence, played by Sally Field in the 1965–66 television series
Gidget, which in turn derived from a popular series of movies, represented
for audiences the typical, if idealized, California teenager. Gidget was lively,
pretty, and popular, and her favorite pastimes involved the pleasures of the
beach, primarily surfing and flirting with boys. Buffy Summers, played by
Sarah Michelle Gellar in television's *Buffy the Vampire Slayer,* itself derived
from a 1992 box-office failure, represents a reworking of the same archetype from a very different cultural perspective. Like Gidget, Buffy is lively

and pretty, petite and flirtatious, and is dressed in the latest fashions. Even her surname, Summers, echoes the California myth. Buffy, however, is anything but popular. She is an ex-cheerleader who fell from grace when she learned of her destiny as the Slayer, the one girl in all the world who can stand against the forces of darkness. For her, the Endless Summer has become irrelevant; despite her Southern California location, she is seen at the beach only three times in the entire series, once in a dream sequence ("Anne," 3001) and once at a swim-team pep rally that quickly turns sinister ("Go Fish," 2020). Not until the fifth-season premiere, "Buffy vs. Dracula" (5001), is she actually seen having fun with her friends at a beach picnic. So while Gidget spent her high school years catching waves and sunshine, approved of by her peers and her teachers, her late-century counterpart spends much of her time in the darkness, misunderstood by all but a few, patrolling against the forces of evil. The supernatural forces that Buffy must face parallel a similar resurgence of Gothic imagery in the popular culture of the turn of the previous century and make Buffy the California Girl for the fin de siècle.

There is something symbolic about a century's closing decade that suggests a winding down, even an apocalypse. Elaine Showalter, in *Sexual Anarchy,* explains that "the crises of the *fin de siècle* [. . .] are more intensely experienced, more emotionally fraught, more weighted with symbolic and historical meaning, because we invest them with the metaphors of death and rebirth that we project onto the final decade and years of a century" (2). Showalter draws a clear parallel between the closes of the nineteenth and twentieth centuries: "From urban homelessness to imperial decline, from sexual revolution to sexual epidemics, the last decades of the twentieth century seem to be repeating the problems, themes and metaphors of the *fin de siècle*" (1).

Apocalyptic notions abound: the end of society, the end of culture, the end of morality and the family, the end, in fact, of the world as we know it. While at the millennial close of the twentieth century few actually expected an End of Days, widespread hysteria about the possible Y2K shutdown of all computerized functions had even the most optimistic stocking bottled water for the foreseen apocalyptic end of Western civilization, or at least a minor inconvenience.

Fin de siècle periods tend to be marked by artistic movements that reflect their particular anxieties as well. The 1790s marked the height of popularity of the Gothic, with its emphasis on the macabre and supernatural, reflecting the political upheaval of the time and the resultant fears of loss of control. Three literary movements associated with the close of the nineteenth century both reflect the issues of their own time and are useful in examining cultural productions of the late twentieth century: the New Woman novel, the Decadent, and the resurgence of the Gothic. We will return to these in this chapter.

In stark contrast to the fin de siècle anxieties of *Buffy*, the mid-twentieth-century world of *Gidget* can be readily paralleled to the world of the mid-Victorians. The middle period of the nineteenth century was one of growth and hope. The expansion of empire, the rising standard of living for the growing middle class, and the optimistic outlook of midcentury was reflected in the novels of Dickens, with their inevitably happy endings and the strong value placed on hearth and home. In the fiction of the period, sexuality was kept under wraps, and the prevailing standards were rarely questioned. So, too, the mid-twentieth-century world of *Gidget*. Gidget was adventurous enough that plots could be centered around her mishaps in exploring the world around her. But away from her surfboard and the local malt shop, she was centered in a loving home where father knew best and frequently provided the answers. In her sunny world, the biggest crises were about why she did not have a date for the luau, whether she ought to go to boarding school in Paris, or whether the local hamburger joint might close down. Everything was comfortably resolved at the end of the thirty minutes.[1] In the shadowed fin de siècle world of *Buffy*, however, teenage pleasures are compromised by the ever-present fear of death. When Buffy's group of friends gets together on a Saturday night, they may be going to The Bronze to dance, but odds are slightly more than even that they are going to save the world from the forces of darkness and destruction, again.

It must be emphasized that looking at *Gidget* and *Buffy* together is not a random comparison between, say, *The Patty Duke Show* and *My So-Called Life*. Nor should *Gidget*, a half-hour situation comedy, be measured and found wanting by *Buffy*'s yardstick. It is a different type of program as well as from a different era, and shows of its genre exist still on the airwaves. But unlikely as it sounds, Gidget and Buffy are not so very different in their essentials as characters, as archetypal California Girls; rather, it is the world that shapes them that is different. On the most obvious level, both girls are high school students, both are athletic and flirtatious, both place a high value on enjoying themselves, but both have a strong sense of responsibility. Both even have cute names that, at first, make it hard to take them seriously, although Gidget's is a nickname and a mark of her acceptance by the surfer subculture, while Buffy's is a given name.[2] The essential similarities between the two characters can be demonstrated by a plot summary of the movies that gave rise to them. In the following I describe both *Gidget*, the 1959 movie starring Sandra Dee, and *Buffy the Vampire Slayer*, the 1992 movie starring Kristy Swanson:

> A teenage girl is growing up in Los Angeles. She's blond, pretty, and popular, but she's different from the other girls, and an event occurs that separates her from the pack. She becomes alienated from her social circle but initiated into a strange new world filled with new challenges, which make unexpected de-

mands on her. An older man mentors her and helps her adapt to situations where her athletic skill and quick wits lead to her proving herself by successfully overcoming some significant obstacles. She faces her greatest challenge at the big social event that marks the end of a season, which she attends dressed pretty in pink. After a major confrontation that provides her greatest challenge yet, she ends up conquering romantically, too, securing the romantic attentions of the young man whom the audience has seen she is destined for all along.

In *Gidget,* the strange new world was that of the surfers' community, while in *Buffy,* it is the fight against vampires, but in both the heroine's journey is essentially the same. The two television series differ more in their episodic format—certainly none of the series' episodes parallel each other as the two movies do. Buffy and her mother have left Los Angeles for the small town of Sunnydale in the wake of trouble resulting from her vampire slaying activities. Yet the characters have acquired additional qualities in common. While the Gidget of the television series was no longer the stereotypical California blonde, the Buffy of the television series is no longer statuesque Kristy Swanson but petite Sarah Michelle Gellar, whose stature is more comparable to Sally Field's. The image of Buffy kickboxing large vampires and demons is now as incongruous as that of Gidget, whose nickname was an amalgam of "girl midget," riding the big waves. The two-parent households of the movies have been replaced by single-parent households in both series. Gidget lived with her (presumably widowed) father, while Buffy lives with her divorced mother. Each of the girls also acquires a less socially successful best friend, presumably to establish that despite her own attractive appearance and behavior, she is far from shallow and appreciates qualities that lie beneath the surface. Gidget's was LaRue, a frankly unattractive girl whose sun allergies set her apart in the midst of Southern California sun and fun. Buffy's closest female friend, Willow, begins the series as a shy computer nerd, although she blossoms, in part as a result of her connection with Buffy.

Perhaps most significantly, Buffy wants to *be* Gidget. This is played up in the first season with her refusal of her calling in "Welcome to the Hellmouth," her attempts at cheerleading ("The Witch," 1003) and dating ("Never Kill a Boy on the First Date," 1005), and her reminiscences of popularity ("Out of Mind, Out of Sight," 1011). With her acceptance of the responsibilities of her role as the Chosen One and her growing romantic attachment to Angel, the vampire with a soul, her priorities begin to shift. By the third season, it is Buffy who is hesitant to get involved with ordinary high school student Scott Hope ("Faith, Hope and Trick," 3003), and, when her Slayer powers are weakened in "Helpless" (3012), she is forced to admit to herself just how much of her identity has become bound up in fighting the forces of darkness. In the fourth season, with Angel sent off to his own spin-off series set in a much more *noir* Los Angeles than Gidget's, Buffy begins a romance with wholesome midwestern grad student Riley Finn, but their relationship only deepens when she learns of his secret identity as a military demon hunter. Buffy has reached the point where, despite a superficially normal dormitory life at UC-Sunnydale, she can truly connect only with those who share her secret world. And despite what she might wish, Buffy is *not* Gidget. The situations she faces are more complex and morally ambiguous than Gidget's. The fantasy-horror elements of *Buffy,* as we will see, actually enable the show to give a more truthful representation of the difficulties of growing up. The distance between Buffy's world and Gidget's can be represented by elements present in three characteristic fin de siècle literary movements: the New Woman, Decadence, and the Gothic.

The New Woman novel parallels feminist issues and empowerment in the twentieth century. While the feminist movement had sought to win public support for the "woman question" throughout the nineteenth century, and women had organized politically around specific causes, the New Woman was a late-century manifestation. Her personal autonomy, economic independence, and sexual self-determination led the New Woman to be seen as a threat, undermining the social order. New Woman novels, like George Gissing's *The Odd Women* and Grant Allen's *The Woman Who Did,* are ambivalent about their subjects, admiring and judgmental at once, not unlike many twentieth-century commentators on feminism.

Is Buffy a feminist heroine? Tom Carson, writing in the *Village Voice,* thinks so: he calls *Buffy* "a female empowerment saga" (51). Micol Ostow, while praising Buffy as a model of "feminine" strength, says, "One can hardly consider Buffy a feminist icon" (20). While the answer to this complex question is beyond the scope of this chapter, the answer depends on one's definition of feminism. Buffy is not a feminist icon if, to so qualify, she must be free from the need for male approval; she is vulnerable and often shallow about her appearance. She *is* a feminist icon, however, because she is an empowered yet ordinary woman with ordinary problems who nonetheless has accepted the responsibility that comes with her strength and who consistently achieves the extraordinary because she must.

The physical prowess of Gidget at surfing and Buffy in fighting vampires and demons gives concrete manifestation to the competence and independence that marks both of them as empowered. As stated previously, both women are small and delicate-looking, so this athleticism is unexpected. While Gidget's surfing was a centerpiece in the original movie, television budgets confined her board mostly to a prop on the series. Nevertheless, her affinity for the sport was an established character trait. Buffy, as the Slayer, possesses supernatural strength. She is strong enough that when, in "The Yoko Factor" (4020), she breaks up a fight between current and former boyfriends Riley and Angel with a threat, both take her entirely seriously: "I see one more display of testosterone poisoning, and I will personally put you both in the hospital. Anybody think I'm exaggerating?" The two men, both much larger than she and in excellent shape, defer to her because they know from experience that she is not.

However, it is the way that power is expressed that sets them apart. The New Woman is independent. But Gidget had to resort to subterfuge in order to get her way. As Susan Douglas describes it, "Gidget liked to take charge, set up new situations, and control events, but [she] also wanted to be appealing to boys, who were sometimes put off by girls who were too spunky and aggressive." Thus, one of Gidget's least appealing qualities—to a late-century eye—was actually a carefully thought-out tactic. "It was usually 'perkiness'—assertiveness masquerading as cuteness—that provided the middle ground [she] needed to get [her] way and get male approval, two goals that were often mutually exclusive. By donning this disguise, Gidget [. . .] got to be thought of as [a] girl while assuming the prerogatives of boys. [She] disdained the passivity and helplessness of overly feminized girls" (108). Gidget achieved her goals, but only at the cost of disguising her strong will.

Buffy, on the other hand, has no need to mask her assertiveness. In "Primeval" (4021), she says, "Sorry, I don't jump through hoops on command. I've never really been one to toe the line." While her open defiance sets her at odds in school—for example, in "School Hard" (2003), where the principal has categorized her as one of Sunnydale High's two worst troublemakers—it serves her well in her calling. Nor, unlike Gidget, does she worry about losing boys through outright assertiveness. In "A New Man" (4012), after she defeats Riley in a fight, he comments on her strength and on the way she is in charge: "You're, like, make the plan, execute the plan. No one giving you orders." She simply acknowledges, "I'm the Slayer," and he says, "I like it," before declaring his intent to train harder and "take you down." Masculine admiration wars with masculine difficulty at conceding superior strength to a woman, but for the time Riley stays.

Shifting gender roles, particularly with regard to sexuality, are also a factor of Decadence. The Decadent has two faces: the *Fleurs du Mal* celebration of decay, disease, and dis-ease, the jaded pursuit of the artificial and of extreme sensations, as well as the outsider's moralistic view of the same as social decline. Decadence represents a new set of social circumstances, one in which personal and sexual freedom prevail and where a loss of innocence is at once mourned and celebrated. In the terms of the representatives of so-called family values who elevate midcentury norms of family and morality to a point of near idolatry, the sunny innocence of *Gidget* can be seen as the Edenic precursor to the decadent falling off, the decaying morality of late in the century.

Gidget and Buffy both come from single-parent households. But Gidget, according to Susan Douglas, had "a great Electra fantasy: Mom gone and a kind, handsome, well-to-do and indulgent Dad all to yourself" (110). In fact, while Gidget and her widowed father had an almost symbiotic relationship, the only misunderstandings and disruptions came from within Gidget's own generation, caused by her married sister and psychologist brother-in-law. These characters were custom-made to provide family conflict, something that the almost too-understanding Russell Lawrence experienced only in odd moments with his darling daughter. Although Gidget's peer group was important to her, *Gidget* demonstrated again and again that it was hearth and home that provided her ultimate refuge and standard of values.

Buffy, on the other hand, comes from a more characteristic late-century single-parent household, one on which the breakdown of the nuclear family has made its mark. Her divorced mother, Joyce Summers, means well but simply cannot understand her teenage daughter. While she hopefully reads parenting books, thinking they will give her useful advice in dealing with Buffy, there is no self-help book for the parents of a vampire slayer. Buffy's absentee father, Hank, essentially disappears from the series after "When She Was Bad" (2001), the second-season premiere. Her true father figure is her Watcher, Rupert Giles, sent from England to guide and train her. While their relationship is at first antagonistic, Buffy's desire to lead the most normal life possible in conflict with his need to prepare her as thoroughly as possible for what she must face, the relationship deepens over the course of the series.

Joyce Summers acknowledges it first, in the third season's premiere episode, "Anne" (3001), when she tells Giles that she blames not herself but him for the crisis that has led Buffy to run away from home: "You've been this huge influence on her, guiding her. You had this whole relationship with her behind my back. I feel like you've taken her away from me." *Buffy* resists the typical television outcome: under the influence of a magic spell, Giles and Joyce have a fling ("Band Candy," 3006), but it is never repeated because pairing them romantically would neatly re-create the nuclear family in Buffy's life. When the nature of Giles's fatherly feelings toward Buffy is acknowledged, however, he loses his power. At the end of third season's "Helpless," he is relieved of his duties as Watcher because he has developed "a father's love" for his charge and can no longer exercise the necessary objectivity. In the fourth season we see him suffering from empty nest syndrome as Buffy's freshman year of college leaves her increasingly independent of him; he experiences something of a midlife crisis that has him performing acoustic rock at a local coffeehouse.

Witty *Buffy*, at first glance, has nothing in common with the fever dreams of the Decadent poets and artists. And yet, like them, it has a surreal quality, one haunted by vampires and strangely seductive evil. As the Decadents saw the end of the century as a winding down, so Buffy is faced with the literal end of the world on a not-infrequent basis. Here the Decadent spills over into the Gothic.

Critics writing on the Gothic have carefully developed the equations between the underlying cultural anxieties and their Gothic manifestations. The fin de siècle period saw a new flowering of the Gothic with works like Stevenson's *Dr. Jekyll and Mr. Hyde,* Stoker's *Dracula,* and Wilde's Decadent-Gothic *The Picture of Dorian Gray.* These and other late Victorian Gothic works used the supernatural to explore contemporary anxieties about sexuality, religion and morals, science and psychology, imperialism, and the Other. But *Buffy* wears its metaphoric conceit on its sleeve. Its vision of high school as hell enables the series' creator, Joss Whedon, to represent the pains and pleasures of growing up as horrific in a very literal manner. As he has said, "Sunnydale High is based on every high school in America. So many kids feel like their school is built on a Hellmouth. What makes the show popular is the central myth of high school as horrific. The humiliation, the alienation, you know, the confusion of high school is taken to such great proportions that it becomes demonic" (Interview, "Welcome to the Hellmouth/The Harvest").

Late Victorian Gothic works dealt with anxieties of "class, race, and nationality," writes Judith Halberstam, while in the twentieth century, Gothic centers primarily around sexuality and gender (24). Sexuality is only one portion of Buffy's Gothic anxiety, but it is an important one. While Gidget's greatest sexual threat was the unwelcome advances of a "makeout king," whose attempts to kiss her were foiled by her own quick wits ("Love and the Single Gidget"), Buffy's loss of virginity reflects a teenager's ultimate fears about sexuality. On the night of her seventeenth birthday, when she chooses to sleep with her boyfriend, the good vampire Angel, the Decadent and Gothic imagery goes haywire ("Surprise," 2013, and "Innocence," 2014). Buffy's virginity is not the only thing lost that night; Angel's soul, restored to him by a gypsy curse for the purpose of making him suffer with the knowledge of his vampiric misdeeds, is taken from him when he knows "one moment of true happiness" ("Innocence"). For this, read orgasm with the woman he loves. Angel transforms from a tormented Byronic hero to the preening figure of Byron himself, dressing in fetish-oriented leather pants and engaging in a strongly implied sadomasochistic relationship with the insane vampire Drusilla (and with the hint of a ménage à trois with her jealous paramour, the punk rock vampire Spike). The evil Angelus goes on a killing spree that includes Giles's beloved, Jenny Calendar, and attempts to suck the world into hell. This would be quite a fin de siècle—a *fin de tout,* in fact. "We're about to make history . . . end," Angelus says ("Becoming," part 2, 2022).

Micol Ostow declares this scenario highly problematic: "Buffy made a carefully-thought-out decision to have sex (for her first time) with her steady boyfriend, within the context of their loving relationship. Shortly after the act he reverts back into his evil vampire self, and for the duration of the season he slowly and cruelly stalks her. I guess we're not supposed to control our own sexuality, after all" (20). But this denies the psychology of the Gothic. It is not about our choices; it is mostly about our fears. *Buffy* does not make a statement about whether Buffy's sexual behavior was correct; it examines common fears and apprehensions about what *might happen* when we explore our sexuality by taking the worst-case scenario and using the supernatural to magnify it.[3] To refuse to face our fears keeps us from empowerment.

The nature of the late twentieth-century Gothic is in many ways less clear-cut than its predecessor. Judith Halberstam explains that "postmodern Gothic warns us to be suspicious of monster hunters, monster makers, and above all, discourses invested in purity and innocence. The monster always represents the disruption of categories, the destruction of boundaries, and the presence of impurities and so we need monsters and we need to recognize and celebrate our own monstrosities" (27).

For the first several seasons, *Buffy* seemed to have a clear take on its monsters: vampires and demons were evil and had to be destroyed. The only exception was Angel, the vampire with a soul, and Buffy learned to her cost that even he was high risk. The discourses of innocence matched anything *Gidget* might have to offer—the solid midcentury values of right and wrong. However, as Buffy grows up, her moral universe becomes more complex. Her friends begin to make choices or have misfortunes: Willow begins to practice witchcraft, and Oz becomes a werewolf. The beneficent demon Whistler makes his appearance in the second-season finale, while the vampire Spike temporarily allies himself with Buffy against Angelus's plan to suck the world into hell. The third season compounds the complexity when Angel returns, soul restored. The slayer Faith goes bad, and Buffy and Giles are morally implicated in her fall. By the fourth season, when Buffy has entered college, demon hunters like The Initiative are not necessarily allies, while some demons are; the fifth season ambiguously explores the possibility of redemption for a soulless but now Buffy-smitten Spike.

This new complexity is highlighted in the episode "New Moon Rising" (4019). Buffy has adapted a degree of moral relativism. When Riley is horrified to learn that Oz is a werewolf, Buffy explodes: "Oz is not dangerous. Something happened to him; it wasn't his fault. God, I never knew you were such a bigot." Thinking of her own past with Angel, she tries to explain to him that "it's just different with different demons. There are creatures, vampires for instance, that aren't evil at all." Later on, when Riley has sacrificed his military career to rescue Oz from the laboratories of The Initiative, he says, "I was in a totally black and white space, people versus monsters, and it isn't like that [. . .]."

This complexity, this willingness to face the intensified fears of the turn of the century head on, is what makes *Buffy* successful on its own terms. Young and pretty, empowered and responsible, flawed but willing to face difficult choices, Buffy Summers is the archetypal California Girl—that is to say, an icon of teenage possibilities—for the fin de siècle.

NOTES

1. *Gidget,* produced in 1965–66, existed on a cusp. By 1967, the "Summer of Love," anti–Vietnam War protests and the counterculture had achieved a critical mass, and the innocence of *Gidget* would no longer be tenable. Only once did the series face the things that are to come, in the episode "All the Best Diseases Are Taken," when Gidget convinced Bob Dylan–like folk-protest singer Billy Roy Soames to participate in her protest rally. But the rally was to protest increased movie ticket prices, and the ever-understanding Russell Lawrence reliably bridged the generation gap by approving of his daughter's stand on principle.

2. While Buffy's name seems to have been chosen for maximum incongruity, it is rarely commented on in the series. In the third-season episode "The Wish" (3009), the viewer finally gets the long-awaited payoff. Alternate-universe versions of Buffy's friends Willow and Xander, here vampires, comment on hearing that the Slayer is coming to town, "Buffy, oooh. Scary," says Vamp Willow, while Xander, sardonically witty even when undead, agrees, "Someone has to talk to her people. That name is striking fear in nobody's hearts." In response to a question concerning the title, Joss Whedon responded, "I believe that anyone who isn't open to a show with this title isn't invited to the party. I made the title very specifically to say, 'This is what it is.' It wears itself on its sleeve. It's sophomoric, it's silly, it's comedy-horror-action; it's all there in the title. Having the metaphor to work with makes the show better, and having the silly title makes the show cooler. At least to me."

3. Editors' note: On the ultimate implications of the Buffy/Angel consummation, see also chapter 13 in this volume.

II

✣

Forces of Art
and Imagination (Past)
Vampires, Magic, and Monsters

11

Of Creatures and Creators
Buffy *Does* Frankenstein

Anita Rose

To many fans of the Joss Whedon's *Buffy the Vampire Slayer* and Mary Shelley's nineteenth-century Gothic novel *Frankenstein, or, the Modern Prometheus,* the two would appear to share little beyond an affection for the macabre and the unexplainable. Yet the popular show about a California teenager who battles the forces of darkness confronts many of the issues that Shelley—herself only nineteen when she began the novel—addressed; like Shelley, the creators of *Buffy* use a popular imaginative genre to address complex philosophical and ethical questions.[1] Mary Shelley wrote *Frankenstein* within the context of British literary Romanticism and liberal responses to industrialization, democratic ideals, and the constructions of gender.[2] Feminist literary critics have noted the ways in which Shelley responds to and subverts the ideology and the conventions of Romanticism (see Gilbert and Gubar; Mellor, *Romanticism and Gender* and *Romanticism and Feminism*). That *Buffy* adopts and adapts many Romantic Gothic conventions is addressed elsewhere in this volume. With the 1999–2000 season's narrative arc concerning The Initiative and the creature Adam, Buffy and the Scooby Gang embody a modern reimagining of Romantic ideology that Mary Shelley herself would likely have appreciated. Far from anti- or ironically Romantic, *Buffy* employs Romantic ideology in contemporary contexts and terms and suggests alternatives within that framework.

First written in 1818 and extensively revised in 1831, *Frankenstein* continues to reach deep into the subconscious of the modern reader to provide a powerful mythic construct. The enduring popularity of this story of a noble, well-intentioned, but ultimately destructive scientist suggests something that cuts close to the psyche. The students at the small liberal arts college where I teach British literature are often familiar with Victor Frankenstein's creature only as a staple of campy, old-style horror movies. However, as we begin the novel, they connect immediately with Shelley's tale. These students, too often accustomed to thinking of nineteenth-century literature as antiquated and irrelevant to their lives, come to see that many important modern issues are anticipated brilliantly in Shelley's compelling and tragic story. The novel examines questions no less profound (and no less timely) than the relationship of a creation to its creator, the impact of love and acceptance on the formation of character, the harm that disinterested science can do, and the arrogance inherent in an obsessive quest for knowledge. In the twenty-first century, these questions are relevant as we contemplate the role and purpose of religion in modern society, the fragmentation of community, and the potential of science and technology to profoundly change our lives. Simply put, the novel still speaks to us. In the nearly two centuries since Shelley's novel was first conceived, the manifestations and permutations of these questions have changed—sometimes dramatically—but their relevance remains. Indeed, the omnipresence of technology and mechanization in every aspect of early twenty-first-century life makes the Creature's implicit questioning of "Who am I; what am I; why am I?" more urgent and poignant than ever.

One measure of an idea's currency is how well it holds up for succeeding generations but also, more importantly, how well the basic questions it posits bear up to the evolution of human thought and experience and the change that is inevitable. The 1999–2000 season Adam story line on *Buffy* has obvious connections to the Frankenstein story. The narrative arc concerning Adam is punctuated with sly references to his creator Maggie Walsh as a "mad scientist" ("Goodbye Iowa," 4014) and Adam as "all Frankenstein-looking" ("The Yoko Factor," 4020). In Adam's "coming out" episode, "Goodbye Iowa," the writers of *Buffy* pay homage to the Frankenstein story in many ways. Among Adam's first victims is a small boy, just as the Creature's first victim is the young brother of Victor Frankenstein. Just as Victor's brother tells the Creature he is hideous, so this young resident of Sunnydale answers Adam's question of "What am I?" with "You're a monster." Later, when Adam is describing this encounter to Buffy, he says, "Killing the boy just made me feel. Why do I feel?" Like Frankenstein's creature, Walsh's creation wants to know himself, know his purpose. The scene that immediately precedes this murder also pays tribute to the famous scene in James Whale's film version of *Frankenstein* (1931), in which Boris Karloff as the creature approaches, befriends, and then murders a little girl playing by the water. In the *Buffy* version, the camera follows Adam as he comes on a young boy playing alone in the woods. However, the similarities between the two run deeper and are more complex than simply the "creature feature" aspect of the narrative line, and *Buffy*'s refashioning is no mere modernization of a classic tale.

Beyond the striking and obvious parallels between Shelley's novel and the *Buffy* story line are some important reworkings of Shelley's narrative. *Frankenstein* anticipated modern anxieties and fears about industrialization and science and their effects on morality and humanity; in *Buffy*, those effects have, in a sense, arrived. The characters, story line, and outcome both acknowledge the issues raised in Shelley's novel and suggest antipatriarchal and postfeminist solutions to the problems Shelley saw in Romantic ideology. In so doing, the show also affirms the possibility of retaining our humanity in an increasingly mechanized and impersonal world and posits ways in which we may do this. *Buffy*, working from modern strengths as well as weaknesses, powerfully announces the arrival of evils that Mary Shelley foresaw. Far from simply imitative, the narrative arc in *Buffy* offers an alternative response to the ethical and philosophical questions the modern world presents as we consider the ways that technology and that which is often seen as progress can alter nature.

In *Frankenstein*, Shelley asks vital questions about our relationship to our creator and about the morality of science. Traditional literary Romanticism expresses admiration for a male Romantic hero who struggles with the opposing forces within his psyche. The conflicting pulls of social/antisocial impulses, emotion/intellect, and, perhaps most important for this examination, nature and technology often manifest these opposing forces. The Romantic hero relies on a sympathetic connection with the "Other" to look back on the complexities and dualities within the human psyche. *Buffy*, with a female hero at its center, constitutes a feminine narrative, but in this refashioning of Shelley's tale for the twenty-first century, the presence of a force to be reckoned with like Buffy Summers extends the reassessment of the solitary, noble, and misunderstood Romantic male hero begun in Shelley's novel.

Shelley's novel tells the story of Victor Frankenstein, a young man from an aristocratic and loving (if somewhat passive) Genevese family. Victor's family includes his father, several brothers, and an adopted, much-loved "cousin/sister" Elizabeth; the reader quickly learns that it was the "fondest hope" of Victor's late mother that Victor and Elizabeth eventually marry. However, when Victor goes to the University at Ingolstadt, he indulges his interest in alchemy and medieval science, feverishly, furtively attempting to create life. When his experiment comes to successful fruition, he is repulsed by the "demonical corpse to which [he] had so miserably given life" (59). He immediately runs in terror from the laboratory. The now-living Creature, horrifically made from materials gained from the "dissecting room and the slaughter-house" (56), is left to negotiate an unfamiliar and unfriendly world without the guidance of his creator.

Victor's creature wanders the countryside, dimly aware that he is outcast, until he finds protection from a harsh winter in a secret hovel attached to the home of the De Lacey family. The De Laceys are political exiles—a blind patriarch, daughter, son, and daughter-in-law. The Creature learns to speak and read by secretly observing the family as they interact. More important, though, the Creature learns of warm, loving human relationships between father and child, sister and brother, and husband and wife. At winter's end, the now-articulate Creature shows himself to the De Laceys in an attempt at friendship and companionship and is violently rejected by the De Laceys because of his fearsome appearance. The Creature then approaches Victor to ask for a mate to ease his loneliness. He laments, "I am alone and miserable," and demands that Victor "create a female [. . .] with whom I can live in the interchange of those sympathies necessary for my being. [. . .] I demand it of you as a right which you must not refuse" (124). Victor at first agrees and later reneges out of fear and revulsion.

Keenly feeling his isolation, the Creature seeks revenge on the creator who made him hideous and then abandoned him. From this point on, the Creature pursues Victor and all those close to him. Victor never admits his deed or his connection to this murderous being, and he watches helplessly as everyone he loves is destroyed. Eventually, Victor is as isolated and friendless as the Creature himself. The tale ends with Victor's death in the Arctic, where he has gone to seek out and destroy his creation. The Creature laments the death of his creator and father to Walton, the ship's captain who has borne witness to this final scene, and disappears into the icy wilderness.

Shelley's novel is a complicated, concentric narrative, with three first-person narrators. The story opens through letters from Walton to his sister, then, when Victor appears alongside Walton's ice-bound ship, Victor tells Walton his story. The Creature speaks in the center of the narrative, and the story is again taken up by Victor and concluded with the remainder of Walton's letters. Initially, Victor seems a tragic Romantic hero, guilty of overreaching pride and ambition but full of good and noble intentions, yet it is Shelley's depiction of the Creature that makes this story remarkable. With the Creature's narrative, Shelley invites the reader to understand the Creature, this awful "Other" that we are initially repelled by. The Creature, though destructive and horrible, is nonetheless a deeply sympathetic character. His tragedy is that he was brought into a hostile world and abandoned by the one being who could—and should—love and teach him: his maker. Denied love and guidance, the Creature becomes malevolent and bitter. The reader comes to understand the pain of the Creature's rejection as well as his resentment of Victor. By novel's end, Victor, though still the protagonist of the tale, seems guilty of something much more profound than hubris.

From this disturbing narrative come questions that anticipate many modern philosophical and ethical dilemmas. Just because technology makes a thing possible, is it right to do it? Is science really a rational suspension of subjective moral judgment, or does that presumed amorality mask a deeper immorality? Is the pursuit of empirical knowledge always noble? What are the consequences of tampering with the natural order? To what extent are we responsible for the actions of others? Is evil innate or learned? Are we ruled by reason or emotion? Are we essentially good or evil? Mary Shelley spoke to the fears of a rapidly changing, increasingly industrialized and urban nineteenth-century world; a careful look at modern-day culture reveals that these fears have not yet abated, and there is reason to argue that these questions are even more apt today than in Shelley's time.

In *Buffy*, the hubris and arrogance of science is taken for granted, and a thoroughly modern fear is added: that of the "military industrial complex" and its potentially unholy alliance with the academy. In Shelley's novel, the university is a breeding ground for the amoral pursuit of knowledge; in *Buffy*, the site for experimentation is a secret military operation. Indeed, the academy and the military are conflated in the person of Professor Maggie Walsh, psychology professor by day, covert government operative by night. The story unfolds as Buffy becomes more and more involved with good-guy Riley Finn, a handsome teaching assistant to her psych professor, Walsh. The viewer learns that UC-Sunnydale is home to a shadowy paramilitary demon-fighting organization called The Initiative that has ties to the U.S. government. The Initiative seems unaware of—or unconcerned about—the Slayer and her abilities; her existence is regarded as a mythic bit of "demon superstition" ("A New Man," 4012). Even after Maggie Walsh gets a sense of what Buffy is capable of, she skeptically refers to Buffy's technique as "pok[ing] them [demons] with a sharp stick" ("The I in Team," 4013). Buffy and The Initiative commandos are increasingly at odds. We know, although it is some time before Buffy does, that Riley Finn is an important person within The Initiative. For a time, neither Buffy nor Riley knows of the other's "secret life."

Eventually, word filters down to the street that a secret, sinister project called "314" is afoot in The Initiative, promising to upset the balance in nature that has existed for ages between the human world and the demon one, a balance of which the Slayer is a part. The Initiative, it would seem, is meddling with fundamental forces it does not understand, much as Victor Frankenstein meddled with the creation process as he reanimated dead matter to create life. The final scene of "A New Man" shows Walsh passing into a top-secret area of Initiative headquarters; the room she enters is number 314. The viewer soon learns that Walsh has created a cyber-demon fighter made of human, demon, and mechanical parts. This creature is named, perhaps hopefully, Adam. Walsh's project goes terribly awry when Adam awakes, and his first act is to kill "Mommy"—Professor Walsh ("The I in Team"). Adam leaves the confines of The Initiative and enters the unsuspecting world of Sunnydale. What was for Frankenstein's creature deadly compensation for lack of parental love and guidance becomes in Adam a murderous "design flaw." Adam's quest to understand a reason and purpose for his existence leads to an attempt to eradicate both humans and demons and create a new race of "cyber-demonoids." One important way *Buffy* reconfigures Shelley's story centers on the access to technology that Adam has. Frankenstein's creature still must depend on his creator to make another creature. Adam's first act is to kill his creator because he does not "need" her for anything since he has access to all The Initiative's high-tech tools. It is worse than Shelley could have imagined, in a way, and it is up to Buffy's often low-tech blend of magic, intuition, and raw emotion to save the day. Ultimately, Buffy and the Scooby Gang (Willow, Xander, and ex-Watcher Rupert Giles) find a way to defeat Adam and restore order.

Buffy's refashioning of Shelley's story also entails a reimagining of the Romantic hero. Male Romantic poets like Wordsworth, Byron, and Mary Shelley's husband, Percy, persisted in a view of the Romantic hero as a lonely, sensitive, often misunderstood crusader against the injustices of the fates and the cruelty of man. However, women, such as Mary Shelley, writing in the Romantic tradition offer a different perspective on this male Romantic hero, who emerged as a response to a growing interest in "natural" man and the antiaristocratic sentiments that fueled both the American and the French Revolutions. In addition, Romantic ideology suggested that answers were found within, and the individual took on primary importance. Introspective and independent, the Romantic hero is the prototype for the brooding loner.[3] Victor Frankenstein as hero represents the solitary scientific, masculine mind in his quest to create life and disregard natural forces, while the creature reflects the human desire to belong, to be a part of a community. Moreover, his malice is a direct result of the human community's rejection of him as the product of a grotesquely unnatural process.

All this suggests that Shelley took an unsentimental view of the consequences of the actions of the solitary, driven Romantic hero. Frankenstein ultimately fails and, in his failure, takes along everyone and everything he loves or values. Shelley's protagonist is full of noble intentions, wishing only to benefit humankind in his endeavor to create life. In Victor's mind, he is guilty primarily of the sin of rash action in his haste to do good. It is through the Creature's narrative that the full destructive impact of Victor's actions becomes apparent and Shelley is thus able to illustrate brilliantly the deadly ripple effect of Victor's "experiment." Romantic heroes frequently must suffer for their art—or, in Victor's case, his work. What is too often left unexamined is the devastating impact of this self-indulgent suffering on others. Shelley, in *Frankenstein,* takes careful note of the complexities and paradoxes inherent in this worldview. These paradoxes are even more problematic in *Buffy's* refashioning.

The creature Adam appears as either a central or peripheral presence in a number of episodes in the fourth season: "A New Man," "The I in Team," "Goodbye Iowa," "The Yoko Factor" (4020), and finally "Primeval" (4021). In these episodes, initial mention is made of 314; Adam comes to life, kills his creator, and escapes The Initiative to explore this new world on his own. The final two episodes reveal Adam's master plan for humans and demons and the roles that Buffy, Riley, and the Scooby Gang will play in this plan. This narrative presents a postfeminist alternative in which gender expectations are deflected. Walsh, though female and Adam's creator, is far from the nurturing mother figure, even though Adam calls her "Mother" and "Mommy." Buffy herself presents a postfeminist version of the Romantic hero—she is a tough, powerful demon fighter who acts alone when she must but retains strong and important ties to the community.

A critical moment in the reimagining of Shelley's story comes when Adam's first act is to kill Walsh. Frankenstein's creature, though full of potential danger and violence, still wants his creator's acceptance and, further, needs Victor to provide him with a mate and a purpose in an otherwise wretched life. By severing ties with his creator so definitively, Adam rejects that scenario. He must seek to fulfill his destiny without the guidance of his creator, and his solution is to turn to the "latest in scientific technology" and "state-of-the-art weaponry" that Walsh herself spoke so warmly of in "The I in Team." Adam, unlike Frankenstein's creature, becomes both creator and creation with this act of matricide. He (wrongly) believes that he understands his creator's will and seeks to implement a plan to destroy both the human and the demon worlds and create chaos.

Just as gender roles and expectations have been blurred, so the relationship between creature and creator in *Buffy* is more complicated and the boundaries are less clear. Adam, assembled with Initiative technology, has cutting-edge surveillance equipment and weaponry at his disposal: he is an improvement on the type created by Victor Frankenstein, and he quickly becomes malevolent creator as he sets about creating part-human, part-demon, part-machine beings like himself in a perverse interpretation of Walsh's plan.

Riley Finn is also, in a sense, a creature of Maggie Walsh. Walsh had a vision for Riley's future, and that future was closely tied to her cybercreation, Adam. It is Walsh who implanted the behavior modification chip in Riley, and Walsh who, as Adam says, "shaped" Riley ("Goodbye Iowa"). At first, Riley is helpless to resist Adam's summons, but then, at a critical moment, the power of his connection to Buffy allows him to regain his will and reject the dehumanization of technology. The connection between Riley and Adam is both implied and explicit. In "The I in Team," the episode in which Walsh tries to effect Buffy's death and is then killed herself by Adam, she says to Adam's as-yet-unanimated form,

"I know you'll make me proud." These words are repeated later when Walsh sends Riley on a mission to get him out of the way. As Riley leaves, not realizing that his mentor plans to eliminate Buffy, Walsh calls after him, "Make me proud." It soon becomes apparent that Riley has an implant that makes him susceptible to The Initiative's will. Riley, without his knowledge or consent, has been chemically and physically altered to be more like Adam. Thus, when Adam looks to Riley and tells him that "mother created you too," Riley protests, repelled by the suggestion. Adam dismisses Riley's "birth mother" in favor of Walsh, who has formed Riley in ways that even Riley does not realize.

Another important difference in this reworking of the Frankenstein myth is the role that the community has as a check on scientific experimentation. In his drive to successfully complete his experiment, Victor's end becomes all, and the means become irrelevant. Unfortunately for Victor and the entire Frankenstein family, he chooses to do his obsessive, "filthy" work furtively and in isolation. Had he shared his plans with a loved or trusted friend, he might have been made to see, before it was too late, the very real and dangerous consequences of his single-minded actions. In this, Shelley offers a clear critique of the selfish, albeit passionate, Victor Frankenstein. Victor's actions are irresponsible, as well as unnatural, and innocent people suffer. Shelley is critical of the solitary and secretive ethic of the Romantic hero embodied by Victor Frankenstein but cannot envision how his struggle could become less self-absorbed. She seems to have little patience for his selfishness, yet she harbors a respect for his noble intention. In *Frankenstein,* she implies that this idealistic solitude is both the strength and the curse of the hero, and his antisocial behavior, while it enables his passion and drive, also renders him unable to thwart the dark forces arrayed against him and within him; those forces have taken the very tangible form of the Creature. In refashioning the story, the creators of *Buffy* have suggested an alternative outcome.

Although the episode ("Primeval") in which events come to a climax is a violent one, ending in a Rambo-style, slow-motion bloodbath in The Initiative's headquarters, very few of the truly innocent die. Walsh, her assistant Angleman, the demons held in confinement cells, and the arrogant, mindless operatives of The Initiative can all be held accountable for the events precipitating this battle. In fact, the only blameless victim in this narrative line is the young boy whom Adam kills almost innocently, certainly dispassionately. In this sense, *Buffy*'s reshaping of the narrative can be said to end well. Conversely, in *Frankenstein,* all the creature's victims are innocent of any active part in the unfolding tragedy. The list of the dead include Victor's youngest brother, William; trusted servant and family friend, Justine Moritz; Henry Clerval; Victor's bride, Elizabeth; and Victor's benevolent father. None of these victims knew of Victor's unholy experiment and had no part in it, making it all the more painful and galling for Victor to bear witness to their deaths. Certainly Adam has fully as much malicious intent as does Frankenstein's creature. Given that all other variables are equal or even more heavily weighted on the side of disaster in the *Buffy* version, what allows this relatively happy ending? As the vampire Spike so insightfully observes in "The Yoko Factor," the "gang"—Buffy's friends and support system—is the variable.

This critical variable is demonstrated clearly in the scenes following the discovery of Walsh's body. Maggie Walsh understands, as Victor Frankenstein understood, that the kind of work she does is best done furtively and alone, ostensibly because it is so easily misunderstood, and Walsh decides that Buffy must die because she asks too many questions, gets too close to the truth. Yet, as Buffy uncovers Walsh's experiment, the "mad scientist" is not allowed to work in secret, and the community comes to notice her work; this is finally what sets the scene for Adam's defeat. After Walsh's attempt on Buffy's life, the Scooby Gang closes ranks and gathers together in Xander's basement apartment. They talk, watch cartoons, and argue as they discuss their next move. In *Buffy,* the family unit, represented by the Scooby Gang and Riley, is preserved, while in Shelley's tale Victor's family is completely destroyed by the creature. In a sense, Victor's loved ones are all sacrificed to his Romantic ideals, but Buffy's loved ones are saved; they become a part of the process.

The only thing standing between "life as we know it" and chaos is the Scooby Gang. Adam is too strong for even Buffy's slayer strength, so friends Willow, Xander, and Giles perform a conjoining spell to enhance and transform Buffy's strength with their individual strengths. The implication is that the isolated Romantic hero must fail in the face of a technological society if he or she remains isolated. Shelley asked whether, in a pursuit of knowledge, we risk our humanity. The answer in *Buffy* is a resounding yes. When our relationship with the intuitive, creative forces in the universe is cut off, what remains is mechanistic, antisocial, and chaotic. When our relationship with our creator is usurped by technological accomplishment, we lose our way.

When Mary Shelley wrote *Frankenstein,* she looked ahead to a world in which science and technology compromised our human nature. A curiosity and desire to know more and to move knowledge forward were noble impulses, but Shelley also perceived that the lone, rebellious, fiercely individual Romantic hero was stunting something important in himself by rejecting the community. Buffy Summers, in realizing that she simply cannot defeat Adam on her own, exhibits a strength even greater than her prodigious physical slayer strength. She understands that the most effective weapon to retain humanity and encourage creativity is the force of community. This postfeminist model of the world does not rely on a patriarchal or matriarchal construct, nor is it based in physical strength, although that certainly has a place. Without the combined efforts of the full community, it is impossible to defeat demons, both those made manifest and those that lie within.

In the end, Frankenstein's creature is not dead; he leaves Walton's ship after Victor's death to wander in the desolate reaches of the Arctic Circle. In much the same way, the dangers represented by The Initiative—the dangers of uncontrolled power and ungovernable knowledge—are not eradicated. They are quelled for the moment, and The Initiative's underground headquarters is encased in concrete, but the pride and the hunger for control that drove Maggie Walsh continue to drive our industrial culture. Buffy, unlike Victor, understands that a solitary quest to defeat evil of such magnitude is doomed to failure. The message of *Buffy* is essentially a hopeful one, as is the underlying ethic of Romanticism itself. Romantic ideology suggests that answers lie within the self. We must reach inside, listen, and learn what our "true" nature is. Victor Frankenstein perverted the natural order, and he paid a dear price. Evil—demons—are a part of that order, but, as Buffy and the Scooby Gang demonstrate, the combined power of the community can defeat them. The process is constant, however, and a machine- and technology-driven society presents a threat that the solitary hero cannot defeat. At the dawn of the twenty-first century, the importance of values like community, cooperation, and openness is ever more vital and urgent.

NOTES

1. There is at least one Web site (<http://home.4w.com/pages/btvs/index.html>) devoted to a discussion of "all things philosophical" on *Buffy* and its spin-off, *Angel*.

2. For an examination of the political and philosophical underpinnings of English Romanticism, see Abrams.

3. Interestingly, such heroes had to assert their masculinity in the face of all this sensitivity, and the brooding, "mad, bad, and dangerous to know" Romantic persona was perfected. To cite a particularly apt current example, the vampire Angel (David Boreanaz) is a very nearly perfect Romantic hero. He is a darkly good-looking loner who harbors a terrible and terrifying secret that necessitates his isolation from love and companionship. His stoicism masks a barely contained, deadly other self, and he suffers handsomely. As Riley says, somewhat jealously, in "The Yoko Factor" (4021), Angel is "all billowy coat, King of Pain, and girls really [go for that]." Angel is a man that the authors of *Wuthering Heights* and *Jane Eyre*, as well as *Frankenstein*, could easily recognize.

12

Sex and the Single Vampire
The Evolution of the Vampire Lothario and Its Representation in Buffy

Diane DeKelb-Rittenhouse

They do not speak with Eastern European accents, they have traded the clichéd formal evening capes for wickedly cool leather dusters, and far from bearing ancient, noble titles, one is the profligate son of a prosperous merchant, while the other is an effeminate, upper-class "bloody awful" poet who posthumously reinvents himself as a North London street tough. Yet, though they flout the stereotypical image of the vampire popularized in the twentieth century, Angel and Spike, the two most visible of the undead on *Buffy the Vampire Slayer,* are in fact the logical evolution of the Vampire Lothario, a literary creature[1] rooted in Eastern European folklore[2] that has been fascinating the public ever since Lord Ruthven slunk onto the pages of John Polidori's "The Vampyre" in 1819.

The folkloric tradition came to the attention of the West when, beginning in 1672, several vampire "plagues" swept through Eastern Europe (Barber 5; Frayling 19–23). Within sixty years, sensational accounts of official investigations into the more notorious cases found their way from the European press to newspapers in England, introducing the word "vampire" into the English language (Barber 5; Frayling 22, 27). As eighteenth-century scholars debated the scientific "proofs" that revenants existed, Western writers began depicting them in poetry and prose.

Folkloric vampires were simple creatures, driven to prolong their own unnatural lives by draining the lives of others, tormenting their families and neighbors with a variety of mischief, until their nocturnal adventurings were halted by the destruction of their corpses in the traditional manner: staking, decapitation, and burning. One sort of mischief they were known for involved disporting themselves with their widows. This sexual element of vampire mythos is prominent in the folklore (Barber 9), particularly among the gypsies, or, as they refer to themselves, the Rom. The Rom believed that a vampire's wife, subjected to her late husband's carnal as well as sanguinary appetites, could give birth to a *dhampire*. In some traditions, *dhampires* were exclusively male and fought vampires. Typically handsome, black-haired, and dark-eyed, they could see vampires in their invisible state and locate those graves that harbored revenants (Bunson 68–69).

Handsome, dark-haired, dark-eyed Angel bears more than a passing resemblance to the *dhampire*. Possessed of a soul—and with it, a conscience, ethics, and morals—Angel is, like the *dhampire,* inimical to the undead. In the *Buffy* pilot episode, "Welcome to the Hellmouth" (1001), Angel tells Buffy what he wants: "To kill them. To kill them all." He shows up periodically to give Buffy timely warnings, cryptic advice, and, when he thinks she looks cold, his black leather jacket. After rescuing Buffy from three "particularly virile" vampires in "Angel" (1007), he tells Buffy he fights them because "somebody has to." A few scenes later, his own vampirism is revealed. What is evident from his actions is that he is not evil, unlike all others of his kind. Though supernatural himself, he is set apart from other vampires, much as a *dhampire* is. Angel's ability to sense vampires when normal humans cannot, coupled with his knowledge of their underworld hangouts and habits, gives him powers comparable to the *dhampire*'s abilities to see the undead in their invisible state and to detect them in their graves.

In his role as a supernaturally empowered force for good, Angel's vampire "parents" might be said to be Darla, who turned him, and his own evil alter ego, Angelus. In "Angel" Giles's research reveals that Angelus was "a vicious, violent animal" who wrought "havoc in Europe for several decades." Angel admits to Buffy that he killed not only his own family but also "their friends, and their friend's children. For a hundred years I offered ugly death to everyone I met [. . .]." His career of violence ended when he fed on a gypsy girl, whose tribe took vengeance by restoring his soul. Ensouled, Angel became remorseful for the deeds he committed as Angelus and ceased preying on humans.

As a gypsy elder explains in "Surprise" (2014), Angel's curse is intended to make him "suffer, not to live as human." Angelus returns when Angel's one moment of happiness with Buffy in "Innocence" (2013) costs him his soul. The writers take great pains to make a distinction between ensouled Angel and soulless Angelus. In "Surprise," Jenny Calendar refers to the potential for Angel to lose his soul as the danger of Angelus returning. When his soul seems to have disappeared in "Eternity" (*Angel,* 1017), Angel snarls to Cordelia and Wesley, "Name's 'Angelus.'" While evil Angelus sometimes answers to the name "Angel," good Angel uses "Angelus" only for a set purpose: to convince others that he is evil (as he tries to do with

Spike in "School Hard," 2003, or as he does with Faith in "Enemies," 3017) or to invoke his reputation for ruthlessness in the vampire community (as he does in "War Zone" [*Angel,* 1020]). The importance of the distinction between Angel and Angelus is that Angel's remorse for the deeds committed by the demon within him is one of his prime motivations for fighting against evil.

While Angelus could be said to be "father to the man"—that is, the ensouled Angel—*Buffy* vampires do not follow the original folklore so closely that they are capable of engendering children normally, as Angel reveals to Buffy in "Bad Eggs" (2012). At the same time, they are not at the other end of the literary spectrum, incapable of normative sex and deriving gratification solely from the veins of their victims and paramours. Instead, they occupy a middle ground, taking sensual pleasure in both activities. In this much, at least, they have returned to the innate sexuality of the vampire myth, which is present in folklore and can be seen in the early literary works.

When the folkloric creature first made its transition to literature, its normative sexuality was very much part of the package. Male or female, vampires of the early stories possess a decidedly sexual, magnetic allure that enthralls and seduces victims. Brunhilda, of Johann Ludwig Tieck's "Wake Not the Dead!" so bewitches her husband that he is oblivious to her predations on his kingdom until his own children have sated her hunger. Polidori's Lord Ruthven is profligate enough when living. Dead, "who could resist his power?" (23). Certainly not the hero's sister, who marries him, only to be found dead in the last line of the story. Azzo, the Knight of "The Mysterious Stranger," fascinates Franziska, though others find him rude and ill-favored. Carmilla is said to fall in love with her victims, and the location of her grave is hidden by a former lover who hopes to shield her from damnation.

While greatly sublimated, the sexual element remains in that most influential of all vampire novels, Bram Stoker's *Dracula.* In *Dracula,* vampirism imparts beauty and sensuality to those it transforms. Dying, the innocent Lucy Westenra briefly becomes a voluptuary, demanding a final kiss from Arthur, her betrothed. Van Helsing intervenes, for which, herself again, she thanks him (175–76). Death restores her beauty, amazing Dr. Seward and making Arthur question whether she is truly dead (184). He gets his answer when, resurrected as the "Bloofer Lady," Lucy becomes far more seductive in her attempts to bring him into her arms. Knowing what she is, Arthur must yet be prevented by Van Helsing from going into her fatal embrace (232). This combination of dread and longing is seen throughout the narrative. When Jonathan Harker first encounters the three brides, though he loves Mina, he still feels "a wicked, burning desire that they would kiss me" (41). A similar ambivalence fills

Lucy. Describing her first sleepwalking episode, which is in fact the first time Dracula drinks from her, she speaks of "something very sweet and very bitter all around me at once" (108). One of Lucy's own young victims expresses the desire to leave the hospital so that he can "play with the 'bloofer lady'" (215). When Dracula turns his attentions to Mina Harker, who knows what befell Lucy, she does not wish to prevent his drinking from her (316).

This ambivalence is present in the earlier work "Carmilla." Not only does the heroine remember her tormentor with "ambiguous alterations— sometimes the playful, languid, beautiful girl; sometimes the writhing fiend" (Le Fanu 137)—she often thinks she hears "the light step of Carmilla at the drawing-room door" (Le Fanu 137). It is in this subtle revelation of longing, in the last lines of "Carmilla," that the story's true horror may lie.[3]

Clearly, then, vampires in this literary tradition use sexuality as a lure to draw in new victims. So do vampires in the *Buffy* universe, especially Spike and Angelus. While most vampires are shown in "game face"—that is, the demonic, almost deformed visage with ridged brow, distended fangs, and yellow, catlike eyes—we often see Spike and Angelus in human guise. We also see them use that guise to snare victims. In "School Hard" (2003), as Buffy's delinquent classmate Sheila leaves a bar with two scruffy young men, Spike disposes of them. When Sheila turns to speak to her companions, she encounters Spike, who soothes her momentary concern about the "two losers" by assuring her that "they got sleepy. And you just got something a whole lot better."

Angelus uses his charm to turn one of Buffy's classmates in "Phases" (2015). In "Passion" (2017), we are presented with an extremely provocative image that may be said to sum up the Vampire Lothario. Angelus, watching Buffy from the shadows, delivers the following narration over scenes of her dancing at The Bronze: "Passion. It lies in all of us. Sleeping, waiting, and though unwanted, unbidden it will stir: open its jaws, and howl." Leaving The Bronze, Buffy and her friends pass a couple apparently locked in a passionate kiss. Only after the young people walk on does Angelus drop the drained body of his partner, revealing the embrace for what it was: the counterfeit of love—a sensual, ecstatic rendering of death. This scene epitomizes the romance of the vampire and the appeal of the Vampire Lothario: the eroticization of death and the possibility of an eternity spent in sensual abandon.

Spike is a quintessential example of this eroticization. In a scene rife with sexual tension, he stalks Buffy as she dances with her friends at The Bronze in "School Hard" (2003). After she dusts one of his rivals, he reveals himself, addressing her with an endearment: "Nice work, love." In "Halloween" (2006), he again uses endearments when speaking of her: "Baby likes to play." Driven to ally himself with her to stop Angelus from having the world sucked into hell in "Becoming," part 2 (2022), he greets her with yet another endearment—"Hello, cutie"—and moments later calls her "pet."

Though very subtle in his early appearances, this sexual tension between Spike and his purported enemies, particularly Buffy and Willow, has since been explored more openly. In "Lovers Walk" (3008), a drunken Spike first cries on Willow's shoulder while lamenting Drusilla's desertion, then decides to seek a different sort of comfort: "I haven't had a woman in weeks." Willow avoids his embrace then but has another close call in "The Initiative" (4007). Here, having escaped from the mysterious military organization that, unbeknownst to him, implanted a chip in his skull, Spike attempts to bite Willow but is prevented by an excruciating pain in his head. Willow, already depressed because her boyfriend, the werewolf Oz, broke up with her, blames Spike's inability on her own lack of allure. Vampires think of her as a sister, she laments, not as someone to bite. Spike responds, "I'd bite you in a heartbeat," revealing that he considered biting her during their encounter in "Lovers Walk." Flattered, Willow suggests that they try again in half an hour, before coming to her senses, hitting him with a lamp, and escaping.

The sexual undercurrent between Spike and Buffy also receives humorous treatment. In "Something Blue" (4009), Willow, still depressed over Oz's departure, casts a spell that backfires, causing Buffy and Spike to get engaged. They kiss and cuddle throughout the episode, until the spell is broken—while they are in mid-lip-lock. They spring apart in horror, their exclamations of disgust more comic than convincing.

In "Who Are You?" (4016), we get a serious look at the subject. Buffy's spirit has been forcibly switched with that of her sister Slayer, and then-enemy, Faith. Her credo given as "Want. Take. Have" in "Bad Girls" (3014), Faith represents the darker side of Buffy herself: the power of the Slayer ungoverned by caution and unguided by morality. Faith tells Buffy (in "Consequences," 3015) that they are more similar than Buffy would like to admit: "You can't handle watching me living my own way, having a blast, because it tempts you. You know it could be you." Now, in "Who Are You?," Faith symbolizes Buffy's darker urges once more. Meeting Spike while in Buffy's body, she taunts him: "I could ride you at a gallop until your legs buckled and your eyes rolled up. I've got muscles you've never even dreamed of. I could squeeze you until you popped like warm champagne and you'd beg me to hurt you just a little bit more." Spike is infuriated but not uninterested, promising, "I get this chip out, you and me are gonna have a confrontation."

When the fabric of reality is distorted by a spell that one of the recurring characters, Jonathan, casts in order to make himself a hero, in "Superstar" (4017), Spike expresses his own desires. Confronted by Buffy and Jonathan, who are looking for information on a demon, Spike plays with Buffy's hair, then caresses her collarbone, saying, "Someday, sweet Slayer, I would love to take you on."

In these scenes, the distinction between sex and death is blurred: both are presented as erotic, desirable, and sensual outcomes for victim as well as vampire. This view of immortality as not a spiritual paradise but one that is decidedly earthly and fleshly has its own seduction for potential victims: Anne Rice's *Interview with the Vampire* ends with the young journalist, having failed to convince Louis to turn him, seeking out Lestat (307–10). In *Buffy*, Buffy's friend Ford is only one of a number of young people who have fallen in love with the romantic vampire image in "Lie to Me" (2007). As with the journalist in *Interview*, the members of the Sunset Club completely overlook the darker side of the romance: the pain and evil, the price for immortality.

In prior vampire fiction, the price is clear: forfeiture of one's immortal soul. Brunhilda's destruction will send her to perdition, Carmilla's to eternal suffering. The old myths held that a vampire could be reanimated either by the returned spirit of the dead or by a demon. In *Dracula*, a sort of fusion takes place. Stoker indicates that while vampires are hellish creatures and that Lucy is in danger of walking "in paths of flame" (225), there is a possibility of redemption for even such as they. Despite her career as "the Bloofer Lady," upon her staking Lucy is restored as "God's true dead, whose soul is with Him!" (238). Dracula himself, despite centuries of slaughter, is not beyond mercy. "I shall be glad as long as I live that even in that moment of final dissolution, there was in the face a look of peace," writes Mina Harker, describing Dracula's final death (416).

Buffy takes this fusion of the infernal with the merely human one step further. As we are told by Giles in "Angel," "A vampire isn't a person at all. It may have the movements, the memories, even the personality of the person that it took over, but it's still a demon at the core." Angel explains, "When you become a vampire the demon takes your body, but it doesn't get your soul. That's just gone. No conscience, no remorse. It's an easy way to live." We learn in "Passion" that once displaced from its body, the soul of the person who becomes a vampire floats in the ether.

In *Buffy*, then, the distinction between the human, evil or not, who existed and the vampire who took it over is very clear: the soul is removed entirely and is not involved in the crimes perpetrated by its demonically animated body. Despite this, Angel is not guiltless for the crimes Angelus committed. Unlike Dracula and Lucy, he cannot simply hope that the stake will restore him to a state of grace. "The balance sheet isn't exactly in your favor," as Doyle tells him in "City of . . ." (*Angel*, 1001). Angel must make a conscious effort to redeem himself. He must choose not only to abstain from evil but also to actively fight for good.

In this, Angel follows the latter-day tradition of the Vampire Lothario. While as early as *Varney the Vampire,* serialized in the middle of the nineteenth century, the undead creature exhibits remorse for his crimes—ultimately killing himself rather than continuing as he is—it is not until Anne Rice's works that we have our first truly sympathetic view of the vampire as a self-aware creature capable of choosing not to murder innocents. Following Rice, we have quite a number of beneficent bloodsuckers, including Fred Saberhagen's reinvention of Dracula in *The Dracula Tape,* Chelsea Quinn Yarbro's Comte Saint-Germain in *Hôtel Transylvania,* Tanya Huff's Henry Fitzroy in *Blood Price,* and the television prototype for Angel, Nick Knight.[4] During the romance novel heyday of the 1980s and 1990s, we even encounter a subgenre of such novels featuring vampire heroes and heroines, including a quartet by popular romance writer Linda Lael Miller.[5] In almost all these renderings, the vampire is no longer demonized and, even if a murderer, is no longer a creature of hell. Some, indeed, are capable of handling religious articles and do so with reverence and prayer. Such is not the case for Angel, who, no matter how selflessly he fights for the forces of "good," cannot endure sunlight, holy water, or the cross. So, while the vampiric state of many modern-day Vampire Lotharios is not seen as intrinsically evil, and they may make a conscious choice not to kill (or at least not to kill anyone who does not deserve it), Angel's demon is intrinsically evil. It is only when he is in possession of his soul that he is remorseful for his demon's actions, abstains from evil, and chooses to do good.

In many of the previously noted works, the subsuming of normal human sexuality into the vampiric act of draining blood, begun in *Dracula,* reaches its logical conclusion. The restraint that Stoker, writing during the Victorian era, used in describing sexual themes has been interpreted by later writers as an inability on the part of the mythic creature. Many Vampire Lotharios are thus presented as incapable of normative sex. The blood is the life, then, in more ways than one for our literary vampires. It is also the means by which they create more of their kind, and it serves as a sexual substitute by providing the vampire with the rapture usually associated with intercourse. In Fred Saberhagen's *Dracula* series and Anne Rice's popular Vampire Chronicles, blood drinking is presented as the primary erotic act, and the vampires are otherwise sexually impotent. In Chelsea Quinn Yarbro's works, this limitation is experienced by male vampires only. Both Olivia and Madelaine are capable of enjoying intercourse in the normal fashion. Saint-Germain himself is very considerate of his human partner's needs, which he manages to fulfill in other ways: "with lips and hands he worshipped her" (Yarbro 119).

This erotic element is present in *Buffy,* though not overtly depicted in every case. Once again, it is most strongly linked to Angel and Spike. In "School Hard," Drusilla cuts open Spike's cheek and licks off the resulting blood in a highly sensual exchange between the two. During "In the Dark" (*Angel*, 1003), Spike complains that Angel, interrupting Spike's feeding from an attractive young girl, is "a real buzz-killer."

Ensouled, Angel does not normally feed off humans, with one outstanding—and erotically charged—exception. In "Graduation Day," part 2 (3022), Angel is dying of a mystic poison, the only cure for which is the blood of a Slayer. Angel refuses to endanger Buffy's life by drinking from her, until she forces the issue. Physically attacking him until his demon emerges, Buffy bares her neck to her lover, who seizes her, carrying her to the floor. The sexuality of the scene is blatant. Buffy reaches to embrace her lover, raises her knee to stroke along his thigh, grips a pitcher until it crumbles in her hand, and, at the culmination of the act, kicks over a bench. In this scene we see that the erotic element of sharing blood can be experienced by victim as well as vampire.[6]

We have, then, two extremes of the Vampire Lothario presented in the *Buffy* universe. At one end of the moral spectrum, we have Spike and Angelus, motivated by their passions for destruction, violence, pain, and torture. They are openly sexual beings who use their sexuality to attract new victims: amoral, evil creatures concerned only with their own pleasure. At the other end of the spectrum, we have Angel, who is motivated by the desire to redeem himself. Angel must resist his own impulse toward sexuality not only because of the danger he poses to his partners but also because of the danger physical intimacy can pose to him: if it provides him with one moment of true happiness, it will cost him his soul.

But is the act of sex in and of itself enough to do this? Seemingly not. As Wesley tells Cordelia in "Eternity" (*Angel*, 1017), the real reason Angel lost his soul had less to do with having sex than with the person with whom he was having it: Angel's beloved Buffy. In "Epiphany" (*Angel*, 2016), Angel retains his soul after a night of passion with Darla gives him not happiness but "perfect despair." The obvious implication is that Angel can safely engage in normal sexual intercourse with another woman. The less obvious implication is that it is his relationship with Buffy itself that threatens his soul. As Angel says to her in "Amends" (3010), "I want to take comfort in you, and I know it'll cost me my soul, and a part of me doesn't care." To this point, the degree of comfort required to invoke the escape clause in the curse has been reached only when the two consummated their relationship. Subsequent sessions of passionate kissing did no damage. Still, there is the possibility that, over time, simply being with Buffy, the only woman he has ever loved in over 200 years (as he admits in "Earshot," 3018), might be enough to create that one moment of happiness that would recall Angelus and banish Angel to the ether once more.

Yet the very vehicle that can spell Angel's damnation, his love for Buffy and the sexual expression he gives that love, may also be the key to his salvation.

"Becoming," part 1 (2021), makes it very clear that Angel's motivation to redeem himself is inspired by seeing Buffy for the first time. His love for her is demonstrated throughout both series, most poignantly when he gives up his briefly restored humanity, in "I Will Remember You" (*Angel*, 1008), to ensure that Buffy will not die before her time. It is because of Buffy that Angel wants to make atonement for Angelus's deeds, to "become someone," as he tells Whistler in "Becoming," part 1. His love for her quite literally redeems him from hell itself in "Beauty and the Beasts" (3004), restoring his sanity after subjective centuries spent in the torments of the demon dimension.

Spike and Angelus, then, are the literary descendents of Ruthven and Dracula, the old myth updated, while Angel can claim kinship with Louis, Saint-Germain, and Nick Knight, the old myth reinvented. But they are also, separately and together, something more, another step in the evolution of the literary creation that first received expression some 200 years ago. For if Angelus is, as Angel, a creature capable of redemption through love, Spike himself, the gleefully evil "big bad" who seems to have no redeeming qualities, is not immune to the vulnerability imparted by this softer emotion. From the very first, we have seen Spike act selflessly with regard to one other creature, Drusilla. He strips off his coat to protect her from the cold in "School Hard." He gives up his hold on Buffy and a room full of captives to ensure Dru's safety at the end of "Lie to Me." And in "Surprise," an injured Spike interposes his wheelchair between an unsuspecting Dru and the Judge, a demon intent on destroying her as part of his mission to wipe out all vestiges of humanity on earth. The Judge observes that Spike and Dru "stink of humanity" because they "share affection and jealousy." In "Fool for Love" (5007), Spike's turn to vampirism is recounted. Rebuffed by the woman to whom he has just declared his love, Spike is vulnerable to as-yet-unknown Dru's enticement. His attraction to her, if not instant, is established within a few moments of their meeting, and he accepts her invitation as quickly and unknowingly as Angel, before him, accepted Darla's in "Becoming," part 1. Could it be that, in a mirror of Angel's situation, the one element that ensured Spike's damnation—his ability to love completely and selflessly—will ultimately pave the way for his redemption?

With a chip in his head and unable to harm humans, Spike has been forcibly drafted into the ranks of the good guys—reluctantly working with Buffy more often than against her. But he now has another motivation to help her. In "Out of My Mind" (5004), having failed to kill Buffy yet again, Spike literally wakes up to his true feelings for her. She comes to his crypt, confronts him, but cannot stake him. He pulls her into his arms, and they begin to kiss passionately. Spike declares his love, then sits up in bed, horrified by what we now see has been a dream.

Subsequently, to win Buffy's regard, Spike aids bleeding disaster victims without feeding on them in "Triangle" (5011) and protects Buffy's mother and sister in both "Checkpoint" (5012) and "Blood Ties" (5013). Instead of trying to kill Buffy, he saves her life in "Family" (5006) and "Listening to Fear" (5009) and helps her fight against the hell-goddess Glory in "Blood Ties." Spike may yet be dragged, undoubtedly protesting all the way, down the paths of virtue because of his all-too-human heart and all-too-active libido.

Spike and Angel/Angelus are new takes on an old topic: complex, multifaceted creatures who do more than suck blood and recruit new members. Until both series end and the ultimate disposition of the characters is known, it is not possible to say how far-reaching those differences will prove to be or how much influence they will have on future depictions of the Vampire Lothario. What is certain is this: Joss Whedon has shown himself a master storyteller, and the journey to whatever outcome he has planned is bound to be one heck of an—often erotic—ride.

NOTES

1. This chapter is concerned with the literary tradition as distinct from the cinematic treatment of vampires. While the latter certainly has an influence on the characterizations of Angel and Spike, it is a separate tradition with its own evolution.

2. Though since antiquity vampire lore has been found in cultures throughout the world, the vampires of Western literary tradition owe more to Eastern European folklore than to any other. To cite only a few examples involving some of the earliest, arguably most influential, works, the method used to make Brunhilda a vampire in "Wake Not the Dead!" is described in Romanian folklore, "German Ghost stories" allegedly inspired "The Vampyre," "Carmilla" has its *upirs,* and Bram Stoker conscientiously studied Transylvanian folklore and history while researching his background for *Dracula.*

3. Examples of this thematic ambiguity abound in vampire fiction, such as in the final lines of C. L. Moore's classic science fiction vampire tale "Shambleau," which have an effect similar to the last lines of "Carmilla."

4. The hero of *Forever Knight,* which ran for three discontinuous seasons between 1992 and 1996, Nick works the graveyard shift as a police detective, seeking to regain his humanity while trying to make amends for some 800 years of bloodletting.

5. Editors' note: On the ever-changing depiction of the vampire in contemporary fiction, see the essays by Abbott and Leon in *Slayage.*

6. Fearing that a battle sequence between graduating students and the demonic Mayor was too reminiscent of the school violence at Columbine High School, the network postponed the episode. Though unhappy with this decision, *Buffy* creator Joss Whedon expressed amusement that "all this fuss over the graduation scene means the scene at the end of act one just slipped right by 'em. La la la [. . .]" (joss says: [Thu May 27 08:26:10 1999]).

13

"Digging the Undead"
Death and Desire in Buffy

Elisabeth Krimmer and Shilpa Raval

Since its premiere in 1997, *Buffy the Vampire Slayer* has risen to cult status and has gained both critical and popular acclaim. With its clever puns and complex characters, the show has attracted an adult following as well as the expected teenage audience. While its appeal can certainly be attributed to the fact that it gives us an angelic hero who is to die for, the show's vampire lover is not the only site where the twin themes of death and desire converge. By replaying the master narrative of the star-crossed lovers whose passion ends in death, *Buffy* stages its own version of a "fatal attraction." This chapter explores how the series gives particular force to the intersection of death and desire through its innovative combination of genre conventions and narrative structures. The perpetuation of desire and the deferral of its fulfillment, inherent in the love-and-death (Liebestod) motif, are what keep Buffy hooked on Angel and the viewers hooked on *Buffy*.

"A MOMENT OF TRUE HAPPINESS"

For centuries, the obsession in Western culture with the conflation of death and desire has found expression in works of art ranging from *Romeo and Juliet* to *Tristan and Isolde* and, most recently, *The English Patient*. In these texts, death is both the origin and the necessary end of a passion that strives to overcome the pain of solitary existence. While works like *Tristan and Isolde* seem on the surface to celebrate the power of love, they are in fact driven by a desperate conviction of its impossibility. Far from striving to join the lovers, they expound on why the couple can never be together. The

153

tragic mishaps that keep the lovers apart are not the workings of a capricious destiny but symptoms of an ontological condition. By introducing obstacles that seem artificial at best, by spurning any solution that presents itself, these texts reveal their investment in the impossibility of love.

The failure to unite the couple is rooted in the romantic view of love to which these texts subscribe: inevitably, love is presented as the merging of two beings into one. But as life is always the life of an individual, this dream of oneness is thwarted by the realization that "love, while it is true that it has a relationship with the One, never makes anyone leave himself behind" (Lacan 47). Trapped in our bodies, we cannot achieve oneness without dissolving our very selves. Although love seems to fulfill our yearning for a state prior to individuation, only death can truly achieve "a fusion beyond any split" (Bronfen 66). Death is the only means to satisfy our longing for wholeness, for a "return to a symbiotic unity, to the peace before the difference and tension of life, to the protective enclosure before individuation and culturation" (Bronfen 65). The realization of a perfect love necessitates the annihilation of the lovers themselves.

Joss Whedon's horror-comedy plays with this rich tradition and exposes what is at stake in the association of love and death. Throughout the series, Buffy and Angel's desire for each other originates in, and is intensified by, the imminence of death. In the first season, the couple only meets when Angel needs to warn Buffy about the threat posed by the Vampire Master ("Welcome to the Hellmouth," 1001; "Harvest," 1002; "Teacher's Pet," 1004; and "Never Kill a Boy on the First Date," 1005). Buffy and Angel kiss for the first time after barely escaping the attack of the Three, warrior vampires sent by the Master ("Angel," 1007). The couple's second kiss follows the confrontation with Darla in which Angel saves Buffy's life by staking his sire and former lover. Given the omnipresence of death, it is not surprising that the cemetery is the locus not only of Buffy and Angel's first formal introduction ("Harvest") but also of many of their most passionate kissing sessions (e.g., "Bad Eggs," 2012).

In "Surprise" (2013), every kiss that the lovers share is precipitated by the threat of death. The episode opens as Buffy dreams of Angel's death at the hands of Drusilla, a vampire sired by Angel himself. Frightened by this premonition, she goes to Angel's apartment, where he reassures her with his kisses. Buffy's fears are justified the next day as they learn that Drusilla and her lover Spike are in the process of reassembling the Judge in order to "bring forth Armageddon." The lovers face the possibility of an indefinite separation as Angel proposes to transport the Judge's arm to a remote part of the world to prevent him from regaining his power. The couple's next kiss is preceded by Buffy's fear that their impending separation might be permanent: "Well, if you haven't noticed, someone pretty much always wants us dead." The notion of death as the impetus for passion, so predominant in this episode, reaches its climax when the Judge's attempt to kill Buffy and Angel functions as the catalyst for their sexual encounter.

The couple's urge to live fully and in the moment is rooted in the awareness of the transience of their existence. The notion of carpe diem is introduced at the beginning of the episode when a confused Buffy debates about whether she should "seize the day" and consummate her relationship with Angel. This theme is reiterated in her conversation with Angel when Buffy worries that they cannot know how long either one of them will survive. Angel responds by reminding her, "We can never be sure. No one can. That's just the deal." Buffy's acceptance of this remark later in the episode prompts Angel's declaration of love and leads to their sexual encounter.

The union of Buffy and Angel, while giving rise to "a moment of true happiness," is bought at the price of utter annihilation. For Buffy and Angel, the merging of two into one results in destruction. Though *Buffy* follows the tradition in that it reenacts the coupling of death and desire, the show also problematizes this nexus by taking it to the level of absurdity. While *Tristan and Isolde* limits itself solely to the death of the lovers, *Buffy* equates the lethal effects of an individual passion with the end of the world. Through its sympathetic representation of its protagonists, the series encourages its viewers' investment in Buffy and Angel's grand passion, but its ironical stance implicitly questions the concept of a romantic love that is based on failure and annihilation.

Buffy and Angel's "moment of true happiness" activates the curse placed on Angel and leads to the death of his soul. Because the curse was imposed by gypsy elders to torment Angel with memories of past crimes, his soul would be exiled again if he experienced even a second of true happiness. While the curse keeps Angel from killing by endowing him with a conscience, it also precludes sexual bliss and thus reinscribes the conflation of death and sexuality.

Consequently, the reintroduction of sexuality into Angel's life results in the return of death with a vengeance. As Angelus is reborn, he immediately feeds on a hooker. The sexual symbolism inherent in the act is made manifest as a newly invigorated Angelus blows steam out from his lips in a manner reminiscent of a postcoital smoke. In fact, one might even assume that in this scene, Angelus, who like all vampires has no breath, is releasing the smoke that the hooker inhaled when he took hold of her. For Angelus, the desire to love merges with the desire to kill. He himself gives expression to this twisted conflation when he tells Spike that "to kill this girl [Buffy], you have to love her" ("Innocence," 2014). The intensity of Angel's passion for Buffy survives in Angelus's obsession with tormenting her. Sending Buffy red roses in a black box with a death threat for Valentine's Day ("Bewitched, Bothered and Bewildered," 2016), Angelus reverts to his former habits of "wooing" women by threatening and killing their families and friends ("Phases," 2015, and "Passion," 2017). The turning point occurs when Angelus murders Jenny Calendar, a teacher at Sunnydale High and an intimate friend of Buffy's Watcher, Giles ("Passion").[1] This brutal act forces Buffy to acknowledge the destructive implications of her passion and strengthens her resolve to kill Angelus.

Buffy's determination is justified as Angelus progresses from individual kills to world destruction. In the season-finale episodes "Becoming," parts 1 and 2 (2021 and 2022), Angelus tries to awaken Acathla, an ancient demon whose breath has the power to pull everything on earth into hell. The mouth of hell momentarily opens as Angelus removes the sword from Acathla's breast, only to close again as Buffy runs him through with a sword and sends him to hell. The tragedy of the moment is heightened by the fact that Angel regains his soul just before Buffy stabs him. Knowing that only Angel's blood can prevent Acathla from awakening, Buffy is faced with a painful choice. Viewers witness her despair as she realizes that a union with her lover would entail the end of the world.

The connection between desire and cosmic dissolution is reiterated in a season 4 crossover episode. In "I Will Remember You" (*Angel*, 1008), Angel, after killing a demon whose blood has regenerative powers, is once again made human.[2] For a few brief hours, he and Buffy enjoy perfect happiness since the curse that excludes Angel from the realm of sexuality is no longer in effect. However, the couple's hopes for a permanent relationship are short-lived as Angel realizes that their union would set off the "End of Days." The only one who could prevent such an occurrence is the vampire Angel with his supernatural strength, while a human Angel would have no role in this cosmic fight. Angel's decision to save the world by becoming a vampire reinstates the curse, hence ending any prospect of a future with Buffy. The pattern of Buffy and Angel's entire relationship is aptly summarized by Cordelia when she remarks, "They suffer, they fight, that's business as usual; they get groiny with each other, the world as we know it falls apart" ("I Will Remember You," *Angel*, 1008).

"OVER *HIS* DEAD BODY"

While in many respects *Buffy* invokes the association of death and desire so prominent in Western culture, at the same time the show also subverts these conventions through a series of gender reversals. In fact, Joss Whedon describes the most obvious of these reversals as the raison d'être for the entire show. His motivation for creating the series was to respond to the genre of the slasher movie in which the beautiful blond girl is always the first to be killed (Lippert 25; Tracy 41). In *Buffy*, the cute blond cheerleader, far from being anyone's victim, is a powerful protector of the weak and "a supremely confident kicker of evil butt" (Katz 35).[3] The teaser of the pilot immediately establishes the show's investment in foiling audience expectations. The episode opens as two teens break into the dark and deserted school building. The boy (and the audience) thinks that he will be able to "take advantage" of his date, who seems intimidated by their daring adventure. The twist comes as the pretty blonde in the pleated skirt turns out to be the killer rather than the prospective victim.[4] The audience is shocked to see the Catholic schoolgirl transform into a vampire and feed on the boy.

This confounding of gender stereotypes is also evident in the manner in which the Buffy and Angel story unfolds. In her study *Over Her Dead Body*, Elisabeth Bronfen points out that the sacrifice of the female body often functions as the ground on which culture is built. From Roman foundation myths to eighteenth-century novels, the death of a woman is necessary for the establishment or the restoration of civil order. But in *Buffy,* this pattern is reversed, as it is the death of the male protagonist that guarantees the survival of civilization. As early as the first-season episode "Angel," Buffy's friends urge her to kill Angel because he is a vampire and thus poses a threat to the community at large. While these fears about Angel are not justified in the earlier episodes, they are realized in the second season, after Angel's transformation into Angelus. In "Innocence," Angelus works with the Judge to "bring forth Armageddon" and emerges as the major antagonist for the season. Although Buffy is not yet prepared to kill her former lover, it is apparent that only Angelus's death will put an end to his evil schemes. This is borne out in "Becoming," part 2, where viewers are informed repeatedly that only Angel's blood has the power to prevent the destruction of the world, once the demon Acathla has been awakened. Life goes on as Angel is sucked into hell. Within the framework of the series, the safety of Sunnydale and the world is dependent on *his* dead body.

In "I Only Have Eyes for You" (2019), Whedon again plays with the notion of the female corpse as the guarantor of cultural order. In this episode, various couples are possessed by spirits from the past and forced to reenact a murder-suicide. The possession dates back to 1955, when a female teacher had entered into a romantic relationship with a student and was killed by him as she attempted to terminate it. The cycle of death and revenge that this tragedy initiated is broken only when Buffy is compelled by the spirit of James to shoot Angelus, who himself is possessed by the ghost of Grace. Because bullets cannot kill a vampire, Angel/Grace survives and stops Buffy/James from committing suicide. The perpetuation of violence ends as James/Buffy is forgiven by Grace/Angel. "I Only Have Eyes for You" confounds gender stereotypes by presenting the death of the woman as the origin of chaos and not the beginning of a new order. Grace's death, rather than being the site of redemption, instigates further acts of violence, which in turn intensify James's feelings of guilt and thus ensure the continuation of a vicious circle. Once again, it is only Angel's "dead" body that allows for resolution and closure.

Furthermore, the possession plot calls into question the concatenation of death and sexuality so prominent in the series. In earlier episodes, Buffy repeatedly blames herself for Angel's transformation. In "Innocence," for example, in her final conversation with Giles, Buffy assumes full responsibility for Angelus's actions. She is tormented by the thought that she "destroyed the person that . . . [she] loved the most in a moment of blind passion" ("I Only Have Eyes for You"). While Angelus taunts her that she "made [him] the man [he is] today" ("Innocence"), "I Only Have Eyes for You" is quite explicit in stating that the forgiveness bestowed on James also frees Buffy from any guilt for the rebirth of Angelus. Even though the consummation of Buffy and Angel's relationship creates Angelus, Buffy's sexuality cannot be held accountable for the end of the world. In *Buffy*, traditional connotations of femininity are redefined since woman's death does not restore order, nor does her desire corrupt it.

A further variation on the theme of gender reversals is evident in the conflation of two different mythic strands in the season 1 finale, "Prophecy Girl" (1012). In this episode, Buffy has her final showdown with the Master, who attempts to open the Hellmouth. Although Buffy is killed by the Master, she is revived by Xander. Newly invigorated by her experience of death, she proceeds to do away with the Master. The initial encounter between Buffy and the Master is fraught with romantic imagery and thereby evokes the topos of Death and the Maiden: the white prom dress that she wears as she goes to meet the Master is eerily reminiscent of a bridal gown, the Master's underground cave is lit by hundreds of white candles, and with his mesmerizing gaze, the Master reduces Buffy to a passive object with no will of her own and then penetrates her neck with his teeth. The camera angles for the shots in the bite scene, with the close-up of Buffy's terrified face, her gasp, followed by the focus on the traces of blood on her white skin, make it clear that viewers are to read the Master's act as a form of sexual initiation.

Up to this point, the showdown between Buffy and the Master follows the mythic model that equates marriage and death and thus reads the wedding night as the symbolic demise of the virgin. However, the moment of Buffy's actual death initiates a deviation from this pattern.[5] Traditionally, the wedding night deprives the virago of her independence and strength and transforms her into an obedient wife. In "Prophecy Girl," the experience of a literal death endows Buffy with greater powers. The paradigm of Death and the Maiden is replaced by that of the hero who faces death and emerges stronger.[6] Buffy's second encounter with the Master replays her initial scene with him but reinscribes her as hero rather than passive object. When the Master tries again to hypnotize Buffy, she resists his gaze ("Save the hypnosis crap for the tourists") and kills him. While "Prophecy Girl" seems initially to reinstate traditional gender conventions, it ultimately subverts them from within through its juxtaposition of mythic models.

THE SERIAL LOVER

As our analysis of the show demonstrates, *Buffy,* through its deployment of the nexus of death and desire, insists that the relationship between Buffy and Angel is fundamentally impossible. While the presence of death in life gives rise to their yearning for a passionate and perfect union, actually achieving this union would represent stasis, foreclosing any further development and thus equaling death. Though the obstacles imposed upon the lovers seem to foreclose any hope for intimacy, they are, paradoxically, the very feature that sustains the couple's relationship. As Lacan points out, "Love, in its essence, is narcissistic, and [. . .] the substance of what is supposedly object-like [. . .] is in fact that which constitutes a remainder in desire, namely, its cause, and sustains desire through its lack of satisfaction (*insatisfaction*), and even its impossibility" (6).

The deferral of desire not only is at the heart of Buffy and Angel's relationship but is also the structural principle of the show itself. Erotic *insatisfaction* is replicated on the narrative level by the genre of television serials, a form predicated on repetition without closure. In her chapter on soap operas, the most exemplary form of television serials, Tanya Modleski notes that the narrative, "by placing ever more complex obstacles between desire and fulfillment, makes anticipation of an end an end in itself" (88). Closure, since it entails the end of the show, is to be avoided at all costs: "Tune in tomorrow, not in order to find out the answers, but to see what further complications will defer the resolutions and introduce new questions" (Modleski 88).

Although most viewers would not characterize *Buffy* as a soap opera, the show contains many of the features of a television serial. According to John Fiske, the television serial, as opposed to the television series, which consists of self-contained units, depicts a narrative progression whose climax is never reached. Unlike the series, which focuses on a limited number of protagonists, the serial employs multiple characters and plots. In the serial, the use of time parallels real time, and individual characters carry over their memories of events from one episode to another. Its portrayal of powerful female characters and sensitive men and its emphasis on relationships mark the television serial as a feminine genre (179–83).[7]

The serial's hallmarks—narrative deferral and a focus on romantic relationships—evoke Roland Barthes's analysis of "'erotic' books." Television serials, like "'erotic' books," "represent not so much the erotic scene as the expectation of it, the preparation for it, the ascent; that is what makes them 'exciting' and when the scene occurs, naturally there is disappointment, deflation" (*Pleasure* 58). It is this deflation that television serials need to avoid in order to keep viewers glued to the set. *Buffy* maintains audience interest by deploying a strategy of narrative deferral, evident both in the show as a whole and in individual episodes. Jane Espenson, a writer for the show, and Tim Minear, one of the writers and producers of the spin-off *Angel,* remark that the conception of every episode is influenced by the positioning of commercial breaks. Episodes are divided into individual segments or acts, and each act ends with a moment that must be "big and suspenseful." These crucial points, which Espenson calls the "tent poles that hold up the story" (<http://cityofangel.com/angel/series/summer/dragonCon7.html>, July 28, 2000), replay the cycle of expectation and deflation on the microlevel.

In addition to being motivated by the needs of the market, *Buffy*'s logic of deferral also illuminates an important feature of erotic discourse. In *The Pleasure of the Text,* Barthes draws our attention to a central contradiction between writing and erotic fulfillment, or, as Barthes calls it, 'bliss': "Bliss is unspeakable, inter-dicted [. . .] it cannot be spoken except between the lines. [. . .] Whoever speaks, by speaking denies bliss, or correlatively, whoever experiences bliss causes the letter—and all possible speech—to collapse in the absolute degree of the annihilation he is celebrating" (21). Language, as postmodern theory defines it, cannot speak the body, as it is predicated on the absence of the physical.[8] In the moment of bliss, there can be no writing; as soon as we write, we can no longer experience bliss.

Since bliss and representation are mutually exclusive, *Buffy* needs to portray continual ascent and avoid the "moment of true happiness" in order to guarantee its own survival. If Buffy and Angel were to find fulfillment, the show would be a short one. As Barthes explains, "A text on pleasure cannot be anything but *short* (as we say: *is that all? It's a bit short*); since pleasure can only be spoken through the indirection of demand [. . .] every text on pleasure will be nothing but dilatory; it will be an introduction to what will never be written" (*Pleasure* 18). Posting boards on the Internet (e.g., The Bronze and Watcher's Diary) testify to the fact that even the fans themselves are aware that any permanent union between the couple would necessarily entail the end of the series. Though many fans are firm in their belief that the series finale should reunite Buffy and Angel, they accept that deferral is the prerequisite for the continuation of the show.

The melancholy that pervades Buffy and Angel's relationship finds its uncanny double in the viewers' inability to achieve a fusion between the perfection of the series and the reality of their own lives. Because Angel is immortal, he cannot be a part of Buffy's life; because *Buffy* is a show, it can never be a part of our lives. Yet Angel's and *Buffy*'s unattainability can only heighten their allure. Like Buffy, who prefers the tragedy of a grand passion to a normal life, fans too place their hopes in an angelic savior who will take them away from their mundane existence.[9] Fixated on their respective objects of desire, both viewers and Buffy herself experience an emotional roller coaster of hope and disappointment. On the narrative level, we see this in the conclusion of episodes such as "I Only Have Eyes for You" and "Becoming," part 2 (2022), and in the season 4 crossover "I Will Remember You" (*Angel*, 1008), where Buffy enjoys a fleeting moment of happiness with Angel only to have her hopes immediately dashed. For the audience, the cycle of frustrated expectations is twofold. Not only do viewers share Buffy's despair over the loss of Angel, but they also lament the distance between the daily routine of their own lives and the glamour of the show.

Although fans will never be able to bridge the gap between representation and reality, there are mechanisms that provide at least the illusion of intimacy. One such vehicle is the Internet posting boards, where fans and stars can interact. While Buffy Web sites provide behind-the-scenes information, actors' biographies, and current gossip, chat rooms and posting boards, such as The Bronze, allow for actual exchange between fans and *Buffy* VIPs. On The Bronze, posts by VIPs are identified by their color coding, thus intensifying the fantasy of authentic communication. The illusion of contact is carried to an extreme by the posting board parties, where fans can meet up with "friends that they had made online" (<http://www.buffy.com>). Significantly, the description of the PBP (posting board parties) on The Bronze uses the term "friends" to designate both fans and crew members of the show alike, thus fostering a false sense of intimacy between viewers and stars.

Although the Internet facilitates direct communication, this mode of interaction is a very precarious one. Chat room visitors can never be sure of the identity of fellow participants. As Xander points out, "Sure he can say he's a high school student. I can [. . .] say I'm an elderly Dutchwoman. Get me? And who's to say that I not, if I'm in the Elderly Dutch Chat Room?" ("I Robot, You Jane," 1008). The lack of authenticity thus undermines the closeness that the informality of chat rooms seems to establish.

Moreover, the venue of electronic communication is itself implicated in the logic of deferral. The paradox inherent in e-mail and posting boards consists of the fact that they promise immediacy but deliver multiple layers of delay. Whether we are struggling to establish our Internet connection or waiting for a response on the posting board, instant gratification is never guaranteed. But even if we were granted an immediate reply, all we can expect are words. The Internet is predicated on absence and thus can never satisfy our true yearning for presence. After all, though the stars of *Buffy*— through the chat rooms and posting board parties—project an image of accessibility, they still partake of the cult of stardom, which is defined by unattainability.[10]

PLAY IT AGAIN, JOSS

If, as Elisabeth Bronfen argues, melancholy is an investment of desire in the dead, it is not only Buffy's love for the undead that is "rather poetic, re-ally—in a maudlin sort of way" ("Out of Mind, Out of Sight," 1011) but also that of the viewer, who is fascinated with a show that itself is an en-actment of life on dead celluloid. But if *Buffy* is bound to frustrate our ex-pectations, why do we engage in this cycle of hope and disappointment?

A postmodern reader might suggest that the allure of the series is not based on a maudlin enchantment with the dead (and undead) but lies in the moments in which the show deconstructs its own premises.[11] *Buffy's* use of excess and contradiction, its jokes, and its complex system of metaphors make it a "polysemic text" and allow for a multiplicity of readings.[12] *Buffy* gratifies the "split viewer," who simultaneously enjoys, through the text, the illusion of fulfillment and its collapse.[13] The grand passion of the Buffy and Angel love story satisfies our romantic cravings, while the show's wit and sense of irony appeal to our intellectual sophistication. Viewers are fas-cinated by Angel's dark charms and mysterious beauty but at the same time delight in the show's self-conscious deflation of its Byronic hero as Xander envisions a future in which Angel sits in front of the television "with a big blood belly and he's dreamin' of the glory days when Buffy still thought that this whole creature of the night routine was a big turn on" ("Surprise").

Buffy reenacts the master narrative of death and desire but does it so ex-cessively that it subverts the very paradigm that it establishes. The notion of excess is crucial to the manner in which the Buffy and Angel story un-folds. Whether they are fighting the Three, battling the Judge, or struggling to keep the Hellmouth from opening, the show emphasizes that the couple's desire both originates and ends in death. It is not just that Buffy and Angel kill and kiss or that they rendezvous in the cemetery but that they do so over and over again. Moreover, the persistent coupling of death and desire is not limited to the representation of Buffy and Angel's relationship but is reiterated in the show's ironic comments (such as Xander's "blood-belly" remark) and in its parodic subplots. While Buffy regularly meets Angel in the cemetery, her first date with Owen, a young man with a keen sense of necrophilia, ends in a funeral parlor ("Never Kill a Boy on the First Date"). From Owen's appreciation of the death motifs in Emily Dickinson's poetry to his fascination with Buffy's dangerous and exciting lifestyle, the theme of desire fueled by death is as omnipresent in this episode as in the larger Buffy-Angel narrative arc.

Whereas the Buffy-Angel story provides a critique of the conflation of the death and desire solely through repetition, "Never Kill a Boy" contains an explicit discussion of the model. At the end of the episode, Buffy expects Owen to be horrified at the unusual path that their date took but is astonished to realize that the mortal danger to which they were exposed has increased his interest in her. Although Buffy's passion for Angel is intensified by danger, her nascent relationship with Owen ends because of his obsession with death. In "Teacher's Pet," the nexus of death and sexuality is played out yet again when Xander develops a crush on the substitute biology teacher. Here the stereotype of the femme fatale is taken to the level of absurdity, as Ms. French turns out to be a praying mantis in disguise who decapitates her mates after intercourse. By producing inspired variations on the ever-same, the playful excess of the show deconstructs what it portrays, since "to repeat excessively is to enter into loss, into the zero of the signified" (Barthes, *Pleasure* 41). In the framework of the series, "excess allows for a subversive, or at least parodic, subtext to run counter to the main text and both 'texts' can be read and enjoyed simultaneously by the viewer, and his/her disunited subjectivity" (Fiske 91).

CONCLUSION: "A LOVER'S DISCOURSE"

One may well argue that the show achieves its success precisely because it creates a perfect blend between the imperatives of commercial television and the conventions of the erotic plot. As they watch the love affair between Buffy and Angel unfold, the audience itself is implicated in the discourse of desire. Seduced by *Buffy,* the viewer acts out the repertoire of the impassioned lover. "I forbid myself to leave the room, to go to the toilet, even to telephone. [. . .] I suffer torments if someone else telephones me. [. . .] I madden myself by the thought that at a certain (imminent) hour I shall have to leave, thereby running the risk of missing the healing [show]. [. . .] The being that I am waiting for is not real. Am I in love? Yes, since I'm waiting. The other never waits" (Barthes, *A Lover's Discourse* 38–39).

NOTES

1. As Kathleen Tracy observes, "Breaking the long-standing tradition of only killing off guest stars, having recurring characters regularly die will become a hallmark of the show" (146). The most dramatic instance of such terminations will be the death of Joyce Summers in "The Body" (5016).
2. The manner of Angel's transformation itself expresses the nexus of death and desire since his humanity, the prerequisite for a union with Buffy, is the result of inflicting death on another.
3. In *Buffy,* the figure of the (male) vampire expert, made famous by Bram Stoker's Van Helsing, is split into two characters: Buffy's Watcher, Giles, who is in charge of research and knowledge, and Buffy herself, who actually kills the vampire. On vampire experts, see Auerbach 62, 82–85.

4. With this scene, Whedon continues a tradition introduced by feminist directors, such as Kathryn Bigelow. In Bigelow's *Blue Steel,* a female police officer does not recognize that the petite blonde in the room is the one who will pull the gun on her. For further description of Bigelow's work, see Lane 99–123.

5. *Buffy* also deviates from established patterns in that it is not the "kiss of her prince" (i.e., Angel) that reawakens her but that of her buddy Xander.

6. This pattern is especially evident in classical epic heroes (e.g., Hercules, Odysseus, and Aeneas).

7. Significantly, horror as a genre was initially considered a female form. Compare Auerbach 3. For a description of the soap opera as a feminine genre, compare Livingstone 51–67.

8. Editors' note: For more detailed information on the relationship between language and body in postmodern theory, see Bronfen 195–97. See also chapter 6 in this volume.

9. For the vampire as "romantic redeemer," see Auerbach 165–69.

10. Fiske makes the point "that TV deals not with stars, but with personalities—stars have a glamour that sets them apart and above their fans: personalities have a familiarity that offers their fans a much more intimate, equal relationship" (150).

11. For a discussion of *Buffy* as a postmodern text, see Owen.

12. For a discussion of the features of a polysemic text, see Fiske 84–93. For a discussion of language and metaphor in the series, see Wilcox, "There."

13. Compare Barthes, *Pleasure* 21.

14

Spirit Guides
and Shadow Selves
From the Dream Life of Buffy (and Faith)

Donald Keller

Dreams are an important narrative element of *Buffy the Vampire Slayer*: an informal list reveals roughly thirty dreams over the course of the first four seasons (seventy-eight episodes). Our very introduction to Buffy, in the series premiere, "Welcome to the Hellmouth" (1001), finds her having a nightmare; the original film (1992) begins with a historical scene we later discover is, again, one of Buffy's nightmares. Dreams are, in fact, an identifying mark of the Slayer: Buffy is convinced, in the film, that her first Watcher, Merrick, is telling the truth that she is the Slayer because he knows the content of her nightmares; and Giles, her subsequent Watcher, transfixes Buffy (in "Welcome to the Hellmouth") with his ironic "It's not as though you're having the nightmares [. . .]." In both cases the corroboration leads Buffy to resign herself to her "sacred duty."

I do not propose to give a potted history of twentieth-century dream interpretation here; Stevens (35ff.) is a good short introduction. My interpretive approach will be Jungian, but with some cognizance taken of Freud as well: though Freud's own axiom was that "dreams are a product of the dreamer's own mind" (Freud, *On Dreams* 5), he did note that in the past people believed that "dreams had an important purpose [. . .] to foretell the future" (Freud, *Interpretation* 36). Since *Buffy* is a fantasy, there would be no hesitation in its making use of this function of dreams as a storytelling device.

Freudian dream interpretation concentrates on the past, on material the conscious mind has suppressed: childhood trauma, inappropriate feelings (almost always sexual), unacknowledged motivations (usually base). The *manifest* dream material (the symbols actually present in the dream) is less important than the *latent* material (the fixed meanings the symbols refer to). Jungian dream interpretation, in contrast, while it acknowledges the partial relevance of Freudian interpretation, concentrates on the present and the future and prefers to take the dream material (and its symbolic associations) at face value: Jung's view was that dreams tend to give a symbolic representation of the dreamer's current state and suggest what the dreamer needs to do next: not a prediction but a prescription. That is, it *prefigures* the path the psyche (including the unconscious) feels is appropriate to follow (Jung, *Dreams* 41). Buffy's dreams tend to be *broadly* prophetic, or rather oracular, in this sense: they differ from the ensuing events in specific detail but frequently give her information she could not have known otherwise.

As a "teaser" to a fuller study of dreams on *Buffy*, I have chosen two sets of three to explore here. The first set involves three occasions where Buffy has a dream about a "Second Slayer" (literally in the case of Faith, a fellow warrior in the cases of Angel and Riley), each of them Buffy's counterpart (or Jungian shadow), serving as her spirit guide to direct her to the unconscious where she can find out something she needs to know.[1] The second set, Faith's dream trilogy from "This Year's Girl" (4015), starts with a direct connection to one of Buffy's dreams and provides an especially rich challenge to interpretation.

"GRADUATION DAY": BUFFY'S DREAM OF FAITH

The battle between Buffy and Faith at the end of "Graduation Day," part 1 (3021), culminates in Buffy's stabbing Faith in the stomach and Faith's diving off the roof to escape her. Faith ends up in the hospital in a coma; Buffy, forced to cure the poisoned Angel with her own Slayer blood, ends up in the adjacent hospital room unconscious from blood loss. And Buffy has a dream.

On first viewing, it seemed instantly obvious that this was a dream, possibly because it was clearly too early in her hospital stay for Buffy to be up and around. The first sense one gets is that it is no nightmare: the mood is very serene, with all previous tensions and antagonisms seemingly vanished.

Two passages from Freud will prove useful here. The first, paraphrased by C. S. Lewis (126–27), gives "a few specimens" of Freud's specifying "constant meanings" behind dream symbols: "A *House* signifies the human body; [. . .] *Journeys*, death; *small animals* [. . .] one's brothers and sisters; *Fruit, Landscapes, Gardens, Blossoms*, the female body or various parts of it." In the same Freud passage that Lewis is summarizing (*Introductory* 188–92), one can find "sharp *weapons* of every kind, *knives, daggers*," and so on as phallic symbols. Frequently a whole group of dream symbols can have the same referent: Faith's apartment that Buffy walks through, with its smashed window, is Faith (house = human body); the cat is Faith (small animals = siblings; Buffy and Faith have each referred to the other as "sister"); and Faith of course is Faith as well. Buffy worries about someone taking care of the cat; Faith, like Buffy now (having fired Wesley), knows she can take care of herself; no Watchers, no Higher Powers are necessary. Buffy muses that there is something she is supposed to be doing; obviously this is her anxiety about stopping the Mayor (Faith's mentor and Buffy's major antagonist for the season), and the moment she wakes up from the dream, she's back in action.

Elsewhere Freud says, "There is often a passage in even the most thoroughly interpreted dream which has to be left obscure; this is because [. . .] at that point there is a tangle of dream-thoughts which cannot be unraveled. [. . .] This is the dream's navel, the spot where it reaches down into the unknown" (*Interpretation* 564). Faith says, "Miles to go. Little Miss Muffet counting down from seven-three-oh." Here, I think, we have Freud's "navel" of the dream. At the time, there was no way of knowing what this could mean; I had only two speculations: Little Miss Muffet in the nursery rhyme had to deal with a spider; the Box of Gavrok ("Choices," 3019) contained "spiders"; and spiders, like snakes, are creatures many people fear (the Mayor became a snake demon). And "counting down" might refer to the frequent countdown before setting off a bomb, as in "The Zeppo" (3013), or the explosives set off later in "Graduation Day" itself.

Jung attempted to demonstrate that numbers in dreams can result from quite complex unconscious calculation (*On Dreams* 13–20). "730" could have any number of meanings, the most likely of which is $730 = 365 \times 2$, or two years. (We have since learned from subsequent references in "This Year's Girl" [see the following discussion]; "Restless," 4022; and the events of the fifth season that the mysterious statement was oracular, referring to Buffy's "new" "sister" Dawn.) "Riddles," scoffs Buffy in reply. She also scorned Angel for "brain-teasers" in their argument in the street in "Graduation Day," part 1. Her quick, action-oriented mind is frustrated by obscurities.

"They're never gonna fix this," Faith says, referring to her broken window; but she means herself, as I mentioned (house = body). Then she says it is "getting towards that time"; she intends to leave behind all her belongings (perhaps her body as well? Note Freud's journey = death). This could merely express Buffy's feeling that she has killed Faith, though.

The knife fading in and out clearly symbolizes (how simply! how elegantly!) Buffy's realization that Faith's condition is *her* doing. It also prefigures the "solution" the dream is about to propose. The recent "official guide" *The Monster Book* (Golden, Bissette, and Sniegoski 368) suggests that Faith "gave Buffy some of her strength that she might carry on"; Faith is a goner, Buffy still needs to survive and keep fighting (an assertion rather contradicted by the fact that Faith later wakes up). However, I took Faith's "take what you need" to mean the knife (which is the solution I just mentioned: Buffy later uses it as a "carrot" to lure the Mayor to his destruction). Faith's "You ready?" means *she* is ready, and this is good-bye. (Or such is Buffy's dream thought.)

So far I have skipped over the two biggest dilemmas of the dream: Buffy's question to Faith, "your mind or mine?" and Faith's statement about the Mayor's "human weakness." They are in fact related. Whatever the actual case may be, which we cannot really decide on the evidence we are presented with, Buffy acts as though the dream was an actual communication with Faith: kissing her forehead in thanks and, later in the episode, reporting what Faith told her in the dream to the council of war in the library.

Apart from the dreams (sent by magic) explicitly shared with Angel in "Amends" (3010), a very special case, can we be sure that Buffy *communicates* with anyone else in her dreams? Do the series of dreams early in the third season ("Anne," 3001; "Dead Man's Party," 3002; and "Faith, Hope, and Trick," 3003) constitute *contact* between Angel and Buffy? Or were they merely easy-to-understand projections focused on her feelings about Angel? Or we can ask the question this way: has this sort of thing happened before?

It has.

"INNOCENCE": BUFFY'S DREAM OF ANGEL

In "Innocence" (2014), Buffy cries herself to sleep and dreams of her night of love with Angel; he says, "I love you," and the dream cuts to Angelus snarling at her; the dream cuts again, and a strangely calm Angel, standing in a daylit cemetery, says, "You have to know what to see." And Buffy turns to see Jenny Calendar—and immediately wakes up and storms off to school to interrogate said Ms. Calendar, in the process acquiring crucial information about the situation.

Compare these two cases. A former enemy stands serenely by. Angel: "You have to know what to see." Faith: "Human weakness. It never goes away. Even his." Is the parallelism an accident? I do not believe so. But where does that leave us?

One possible explanation is that the message in "Innocence" was from Angel's *soul,* which of course was no longer in residence in Angelus; and in "Graduation Day," Faith is in a coma, and it is plausible to suppose that her soul is on sabbatical as well and similarly met Buffy in her dream. This theory does fit the facts, but I remain doubtful, because as of "Innocence" we have no reason to think of shared dreams (a special case in "Amends," as I said); nor does Angelus have any motivation to help Buffy. At that particular moment, that dream did not seem like a communication, nor is "You have to know what to see" more than a vague wave in the right direction (Buffy turns and looks).

Is it possible, then, that the Faith dream is not a communication either? Can it be, as the Angel dream seems to be, simply a case of Buffy's unconscious appointing a spirit guide to help her solve a problem? In both cases she gets an oracular remark that she has to take action on herself. I lean strongly toward the opinion that in both these examples it is Buffy's dream only.

For the record, the official *Watcher's Guide 2* asserts that "even unconscious, Faith and Buffy share a bond. They communicate via dreams, and Faith tells Buffy how to defeat the mayor" (Holder 88; cf. also 189). And in Golden, Bissette, and Sniegoski (368), we find the idea that said dream constituted some kind of redemption for Faith. However, the fact that when Faith wakes up ("This Year's Girl," 4015) she gives no indication that she consciously knew there was a communication seems to contradict both of these statements. (We will have a look at Faith's dreams in that episode shortly.)

Buffy's later dream about Riley may provide some triangulation to help settle this puzzling interpretive problem.

"HUSH": BUFFY'S DREAM OF RILEY

"Hush" (4010) is the well-known episode for much of which the characters are magically deprived of voices.[2] As "Hush" begins, Buffy is listening to Professor Walsh (secretly head of The Initiative) give a psychology lecture and is called to the front of the class for a demonstration; this involves Riley (secretly part of The Initiative as well) kissing her. They find themselves in the college halls, where they hear a spirit girl chanting enigmatically about The Gentlemen; Riley puts his hand on Buffy's shoulder, and she turns to see him become a monster (a Gentleman, it later turns out). Buffy starts awake.

I am sometimes of the opinion that first-rate art can teach us how to "read" it. Consider the parallel between this opening dream in "Hush" and its counterpart in the teaser to "Beer Bad" (4005). In "Beer Bad," Buffy is daydreaming in class about Parker, her one-night stand, and Professor Walsh's psychology lecture is about the pleasure principle and the id. Afterward, Buffy reruns her daydream with only slight variation (but note that the daydream Parker's gratitude is broadly prophetic of the real Parker's gratitude at the end of the episode).

"Hush" shows a very similar structure, but its sandwich is inside out: "Beer Bad" has the lecture in the middle with daydream iterations on either side of it, while "Hush" has Professor Walsh's lecture at the beginning, the longer and more complex dream in the middle, and Willow's statement at the end (after Buffy wakes) that the lecture contained everything they needed to know for the final(e), which directly addresses the content of the dream and its importance for the rest of the episode. We can assume on the model we have been offered that Professor Walsh's initial statement does as well. Language and communication are not the same thing, she notes; much communication without spoken language happens later in the mostly silent episode. And her statement about inspiration connecting everything, and about experiences we have no words(!) for, seems to describe the nature of Buffy's significant dreaming.

But here's a wrinkle. Did Professor Walsh even deliver that lecture? One of the necessary decipherments in this scene is, when did Buffy fall asleep? Was she asleep when the episode opened? That seems the most likely interpretation: there is no obvious seam, no point before which she is surely awake and after which she is asleep. But *if* it is all a dream, is the opening lecture something Buffy's own mind came up with (as an explanation for its own functioning)? Or can we postulate that Buffy nodded off but was still awake enough to hear that part of the lecture?

I think we can safely assume that the demonstration never took place. But what does it mean in Buffy's dream language? It dramatizes Buffy's anxiety about, and wish for, her first kiss with Riley; but Riley's visible reluctance is puzzling. In the context of the dream, it may represent Buffy's own reluctance (since she moved too fast with Parker) projected onto Riley; does it also represent her fear of being manipulated against her will? And does the slightly adversarial relationship between Riley and Professor Walsh represent Buffy's conscious perception of their classroom interaction, or her unconscious perception of their clandestine interaction? That is, is it broadly prophetic of what she is to discover about them by the end of the episode?

Riley's statement "When I kiss you, it'll make the sun go down" is deeply resonant, reminiscent of the scene between Angel and Buffy in "Reptile Boy" (2005) where Angel says, "When I kiss you, you don't wake up from a deep sleep and live happily ever after." At first it seems to be the dream's Freudian "navel" (the equivalent of "Little Miss Muffet" in the Faith dream), but on second thought, in fundamental myth/dream symbology, sun/day = conscious and moon/night = unconscious, so Riley's pronouncement can be read as "Follow me to the unconscious." As in the two previously considered dreams, Buffy gets a message (again, she turns/goes around a corner to see a female figure—in this case, the chanting spirit-girl—who holds the key to the situation she is about to face).

The fact that Riley had not kissed Buffy yet in waking life (as they emphasize in the following scene after she awakes) is the reason that when he does so in the dream, it is a "signal" or "trigger" for "crossing a threshold" (major change of dream scenery). And notice that when he does so in waking life later in the episode, it precedes by only a short time another "crossing a threshold," that is, Buffy and Riley's discovering each other's "secret identities." This is followed by the moment when Buffy puts to use the knowledge she gained in the dream. The whole set of experiences thus collapses into a single symbolic equation (kiss = crossing threshold = gaining useful knowledge).

"Fortune favors the brave" (a quote from Vergil), which Buffy recites after the kiss when the scene changes, is less mysterious (but hardly less resonant); whatever its general applicability, it specifically refers to Buffy and Riley's apprehension about kissing. Note that Buffy forlornly echoes it when they fail to kiss at the end of the teaser. The kick-out from the dream, with Riley turning into a Gentleman (requiring bravery to face, indeed), is also a motif we have seen before: in Buffy's eerie dream in "When She Was Bad" (2001) where Giles starts choking her and turns into the Master, which also scares her awake.

And this brings up a provocative parallel. By "Innocence," Angel, Buffy's former comrade-in-arms, has turned evil; by "Graduation Day," Faith, Buffy's former comrade-in-arms, has turned evil. By "Hush," however, Riley was not yet Buffy's comrade-in-arms (or her lover either), and as far as we could tell, he was as good a guy as could be. Could we expect, nonetheless, that the parallel might follow through?

Consider Adam's exposition in "Goodbye Iowa" (4014) about how he and Riley are "brothers" in some then-unexplained way (which turned out to be that they were both "created" by Maggie Walsh, Riley in the sense that she fiddled with his metabolism). Consider also the scene in "Restless" where Buffy has a very uneasy dream encounter with (a more human) Adam and Riley; note that Riley calls her "Killer," treats her rather coldly, and walks away: much as he did more recently in "Into the Woods" (5010), when their relationship breaks up—not quite the same as turning evil but broadly similar as a conflict leading to a break.

Incidentally, the fact that dream Riley in "Hush" is clearly not the same as the real Riley (note his postdream conversation with Buffy where he clearly knows nothing that happened in the dream) further supports my contention that dream Faith in "Graduation Day" and dream Angel in "Innocence" are not the same as the real Faith and Angel.

To be fair, however, my sense of the strong parallels between the three dreams in this set is a little weakened by the fact that one can argue that they are three different cases: Faith is a true Slayer, a supernatural being herself with her own oracular dreams (as we will see shortly); Angel is a vampire with a soul who had a very close emotional connection to Buffy; and Riley is an ordinary human being whose connection to Buffy had yet to be forged. Still, symbolically the three figures are all Buffy's shadows, and the three dreams are structurally similar, and so I find the similarities more convincing than the differences.

All three of the dreams start with very realistic scenes—Buffy remembering her night with Angel, a visit to Faith's apartment (window still broken), a typical psychology class—and then there comes a signal from the spirit guide that Buffy needs to pay attention because a message is on the way: "You have to know what to see" (and Buffy looks), "You wanna know the deal?" (and Buffy remembers), "When I kiss you [. . .]" (and Buffy responds).

Buffy's three dreams, then, consider the role of the *positive* double, the helpful counterpart; Faith's dream trilogy, to which we will now turn, considers in contrast the role of the *negative* double, the antagonist counterpart. And, as we will see, for Faith that figure is Buffy.

"THIS YEAR'S GIRL": FAITH'S DREAMS OF BUFFY

Faith's First Dream

Our first glimpse of Faith after Buffy takes leave of her in "Graduation Day," part 2 (3022), is the dream that opens the fourth-season episode "This Year's Girl." It seems clear that it is the sequel, or rather the Faith alternative, to Buffy's dream with which this chapter began: it starts with the same serene mood (the same incidental music!), the same sense that both Slayers feel a deep bond to each other. In Buffy's dream, she is visiting Faith's (shattered) room, while in Faith's dream she is visiting Buffy's (very tidy) room. The bed-making routine appears to represent Faith's fundamental desire to be a part of Buffy's cozy (as Faith sees it) domestic situation and to work with Buffy. But it is not part of her experience ("I wouldn't know," she says), and Buffy's reply "I forgot" takes on an extra dimension with Faith's comment "I noticed"; this sounds the theme Faith picks up later in the episode, about being forgotten off in the hospital. There is an undercurrent of resentment (in the midst of the surface serenity) of Buffy's privilege and of Buffy's taking it for granted. Then there is the further disturbing element of Buffy's feeling she has to leave, that even this idyll is being taken away from Faith.

Faith's line about "little sis coming" seemed at the time a reference to Faith herself; Buffy refers to Faith as her "little sister" when Faith first appears in "Faith, Hope, and Trick," and Faith describes Buffy (in "Graduation Day") as "dressed up in big sister's clothes." Taken this way, it is the first hint that Faith is due to arrive, to wake up, to be a part of Buffy's life again. (But we know now that "little sister" was oracular—Faith and Buffy both being Slayers—prefiguring Buffy's younger sister Dawn's sudden arrival in the fifth season; compare also "Restless," 4022, where a significant section of Buffy's dream echoes this first dream of Faith's, just as it echoes Buffy's "Graduation Day" dream.)

Suddenly the dream tumbles into horror: the dripping blood on the sheet; the knife in Faith's side; Buffy, coldly menacing, shoving the knife further in. The knell of treachery is sounded: Faith feels not only condescended to, and snubbed, but betrayed.

Contrast this with *roughly* the same elements in Buffy's dream: the sisterly visit, the bond feeling, the sharing ("take what you need"), Buffy's sense of something she needs to do, the knife—but with what a different attitude! Buffy in her dream is acutely aware of how terrible a thing it was she did to Faith, her sister Slayer, and regrets it deeply. She clearly feels sympathy and compassion for Faith, which contrasts strongly with Faith's feeling, throughout *her* dreams, that Buffy is a cold and methodical killer and that Faith is helpless to oppose her (the reverse of our usual assessment of the two). Thus, dream-Buffy is as much a projection of dreaming Faith's as dream-Faith was of dreaming Buffy's.

If, then, I claim that Buffy and Faith had the "same" dream, why am I so sure they were not *sharing* it? First, it is not *quite* the same dream. It features many of the same elements but is arranged and colored in two entirely different ways. Second, the dreams, as far as we can tell, happen eight months apart; and if Buffy had shared this later dream with Faith, she would have known (or at least suspected) that Faith was about to wake up.

At the end of this first dream, mysteriously, we hear thunder and see lightning from the hospital room, not in the dream. But it is not rainy in the rest of the scenes in waking time. The thunder, lightning, and rain are more clearly *within* the subsequent two dreams.

Faith's Second Dream

The image of Faith lying in her hospital bed is gradually replaced by the images of her second dream. Thunder sounds in .he distance as Faith and the Mayor have a picnic in the park; Faith's first words are to wonder if it is about to rain.

On the surface, the cliché "rain at the picnic" suggests itself. There is also a good deal of biblical imagery, most particularly its Garden of Eden scenario: the Mayor and Faith enjoying another idyll. (Note the typical mythological blurring of father/daughter/lovers: remember that Eve was born of Adam's rib.) On that purely biblical level, the snake crawling onto their picnic blanket that the Mayor sends on its way represents the rejection of the temptation that would expel them from the Garden ("nothing's going to spoil our time together," avers the Mayor), but of course the snake is more than that: it represents the Mayor himself in his demon transmogrification (and his dismissing the snake is just putting off the transformation for a time).

But the snake *also* represents Buffy, the disturber of the peace as well as the Avenging Angel (who with his fiery sword expelled Adam and Eve from Eden); and it is a plausible piece of dream logic that the snake actually *turned into* Buffy. (The snake, as well as the knife, as mentioned earlier, are phallic symbols in Freudian terms; we will return to this point.) On the closer-to-waking-world level, Buffy's killing the Mayor represents just that (and note the knife in his gut, which matches her wounding of Faith), both a sign of Faith's anxiety that Buffy would find a way to kill the Mayor and a "message from beyond" that it had actually happened.

So in these first two parts we see Faith's longing for a stable, idyllic situation (one with Buffy and the other with the Mayor) twice frustrated, both destroyed by Buffy.

Faith's Third Dream

Here we have the recapitulation and coda to the previous two parts (it is really one long dream in three sections) and of the waking-world events they reflect: Buffy, knife in hand (and let's remember that the knife was a gift to Faith from the Mayor and was later appropriated by Buffy), inexorably pursues the fleeing Faith. Faith falls into a grave, which on the surface level is (like Freud's cigar) simply a grave: Buffy took her life, as Faith says later. But on a deeper level it represents unconsciousness (Faith's) and the unconscious, and we see Buffy pursuing Faith even into the grave.

Now there is an odd twist of dream logic: Faith falls into the grave, Buffy deliberately jumps into the grave, but only Faith emerges. This is possibly an anticipation of the subsequent episode, "Who Are You?" (4016), where Buffy "turns into" Faith and vice versa, and also plausibly the realization that they are "the same" in important ways. (We should also remember that there was only ever supposed to be one Slayer: note that in "Who Are You?" Faith in Buffy's body refers to herself as "the one and only" Slayer.)

Faith's rising from the grave (with echoes of vampires and Lazarus and Jesus) clearly presages her imminent return to consciousness; the rain culminates the thunder and lightning in the first dream and the threat of rain in the second dream, which means in retrospect we can see that even as of the first dream, she knows it is starting to be time to wake up.

From a Freudian point of view, Faith's dream trilogy is quite clear: she wanted to be a part of Buffy's life, Buffy rejected her, tried to kill her, and Faith wants to kill her in return (leave her behind in the grave) and take over as *the* Slayer. That is a perfectly legitimate interpretation (and is the interpretation Faith prefers, as her subsequent actions prove), but it is only partial; there is more to it than that.

The dreams constitute a kind of "wake-up call," a sense of urgency, like Buffy's in "Graduation Day," that Faith has something to do (which turns out to be the first steps toward her redemption); and note how, just like Buffy's dreams, they contain references to things she could not possibly have had real-world knowledge of that happened after she went into the coma: Buffy's killing the Mayor, particularly. This reference contradicts the "official" statement (Golden, Bissette, and Sniegoski 364) that "Faith has not revealed any prophetic dreams as of yet."

I have left one particular cluster of imagery in this dream trilogy to the end since it invites a more thorough analysis.

THUNDER, LIGHTNING, AND RAIN

Joseph Campbell (*Masks* 283), speaking of James Joyce's *Finnegans Wake,* points out that "exactly in the middle of the book, that thunder-clap resounds and a change begins." Campbell goes on to point out a similar case in T. S. Eliot's *The Waste Land* where "the same thunder and promise of renewed life sounds in the last section: Part V, 'What the Thunder Said.'"

Jung (*Psychology and Alchemy* 221) points out that the Hopi Indians believed snakes to be "flashes of lightning auguring rain." Jung (*Archetypes* 295) also states that "Lightning signifies a sudden, unexpected psychic change." Thor in Norse mythology and Indra in Hindu mythology are both not only warrior gods but storm gods, with weapons related to thunderbolts (cf. Zeus); I have argued elsewhere (Keller) that these warrior gods are the mythological underliers of the Slayers. So I will suggest a symbolic equivalence of snake = thunderbolt = stake = knife that applies to Faith's second dream. (Freud, as mentioned previously, would of course say these are phallic symbols, appropriate for warriors of any gender.)

As for rain, it generally means renewal, crops growing, and so on; Stevens (124) says that "the fertilizing principle becomes active, pouring from the (paternal) heaven to (maternal) earth, from (masculine) consciousness to the (feminine = anima) unconscious. Water pouring from the heavens is purifying and healing as well as generative. It helps to wipe out the past, and the guilty traces, and inaugurates a new fertile period of life."

Faith's third dream has an alchemical feel to it: two Slayers, light and dark, in the grave together, and only one emerges, revived by the rain. The alchemical *coniunctio* of opposites is too large a subject to be properly dealt with here (see Jung, *Alchemical, Psychology and Alchemy, Mysterium,* and *Psychology of the Transference*); but briefly, there is a point in that mystical/symbolic process where the united opposites (male/female, Sol/Luna, etc.) have conjoined into a single creature that dies and subsequently is revived by dew that falls from heaven. Campbell (*Masks* 294) quotes Jung: "The falling dew is the portent of the divine birth now at hand. [. . .] The black or unconscious state that resulted from the union of opposites reaches the nadir and a change sets in. The falling dew signals resuscitation and a new light: the ever deeper descent into the unconscious suddenly becomes illumination from above" (also in *Psychology of the Transference* 111, 119) And much more succinctly, Jung says that "dew wakens the dead" (*Mysterium* 492n).

In short: thunder signals the imminence of change, lightning the moment of change, and rain the renewal of life.

And Faith wakes up.

CONCLUSION, WITH ONE MORE DREAM

So far we have explored how dreams work in themselves as symbolic mini-narratives and how they relate to one another; the particular way they function within the episode in which they occur remains to be considered.

Umberto Eco (144–45) describes the concept of "paratext": "the whole series of messages that accompany and help explain a given text—; messages such as advertisements, jacket copy, title, subtitles, introduction, reviews, and so on." In a television program such as *Buffy*, paratext would include the intoned "In every generation [. . .]" that appeared before early episodes, "Previously on [. . .]" reminders of past episodes, commercials with previews of future episodes, and so on—that is, accompanying information *outside* the narrative frame. Structurally and formally, these paratexts resemble dreams: compact, disjunct, and highly referential.

Dreams in this sense are *internal* paratext: within the narrative frame, yet separate, nonrealistic; and their function, similarly, is to comment on the "text," that is, the events presented as "real." This commentary tends to address the past, present, *and the future:*

1. Summary (in brief) of past events
2. Highlighting of present anxieties
3. Hinting at (but not predicting) future possibilities

Consider, for example, the brief dream that opens "Consequences" (3015): Buffy underwater struggling upward, pulled down by the hand of Allan Finch (the Mayor's assistant accidentally killed by Faith in "Bad Girls," 3014), and, when she breaks the surface, pushed under again by the hand of Faith.

1. It sums up the events of "Bad Girls": Allan Finch killed and then dumped in the harbor by Faith, and Faith's antagonistic attitude toward Buffy

and the problem of the murder. The drowning motif refers not only to Buffy's faking drowning that previous episode but also to her temporary death by drowning in "Prophecy Girl" (1012), the first-season finale, which created the extra Slayer and thus eventually Faith.

2. It dramatizes Buffy's feelings of anxiety, caught between her external problem (the Mayor and his dead assistant) and her internal problem (fellow Slayer Faith).

3. It oracularly suggests the future, representing Faith as equivalent to Finch (the Mayor's once and future assistants).

In its almost iconic simplicity, then, it basically encapsulates the entire episode it introduces: the problem of the murder, the conflict between the Slayers, and Faith's final defection to the Mayor's side. It is essentially a single charged image; amazing how much freight it bears.

So this is the function of the dream in *Buffy:* dramatizing internal attitudes, symbolically representing crucial interrelationships, summing up episodes or longer narrative arcs (even the entire series to date; cf. "Restless") and oracularly hinting at events to come; in short, it is a crucial and unique narrative tool for presenting a maximum of information in the briefest and most resonant manner.

NOTES

This chapter was greatly enhanced by the receptivity, commentary, and material research help of the members of the "still point" e-mail list (and the GEnie bulletin board topic that preceded it), particularly Meredith Tarr, Jennifer Stevenson, David Bratman, Gayle Highpine, Bob Stacy, Susan Kroupa, and others I will regret not mentioning. I have also benefited from conversations with Jean Elizabeth Krevor and my daughter, Deirdre Faith Keller.

1. Editors' note: For a discussion of Faith and Buffy's history, see chapter 1 in this volume.

2. Editors' note: For a discussion of "Hush," see chapter 16 in this volume.

15

Hubble-Bubble, Herbs, and Grimoires

Magic, Manichaeanism, and Witchcraft in Buffy

Tanya Krzywinska

Giles: Yes, it's terribly simple: the good guys are always stalwart and true, and the bad guys are easily distinguished by their pointy horns or black hats. We always defeat them and save the day. No one ever dies and everyone lives happily ever after.
Buffy: Liar.

—"Lie to Me" (2007)

It is common for the horror film to present the practice of magic as floridly evil, often entailing a pact with the devil. But magic and the occult are not the sole preserve of the horror genre. Witches and magic have also featured in comedies, sitcoms, and fantasy texts for children and adults. In the occult sitcom *Bewitched* (1964–72), the location of the magic in contemporary suburban America tended to underplay its representation in horror as a threat to the soul, morality, and human values. *Buffy the Vampire Slayer* and *Angel* look both ways: they use horror film conventions, yet these are combined with an increasingly less polarized approach to the occult. What factors influence the configuration of witchcraft and magic in the shows? Does the serial format of the shows aid in the evolution of a complex vocabulary of the occult?

Both *Buffy* and *Angel* are part of a current trend that takes a relatively benign model of magic, informed by so-called new-age culture. The television series *Charmed* (1998–present) and the films *Practical Magic* (1998) and *The Craft* (1998) also do this, each addition fueling the emergence of the cycle and helping to consolidate a more general "magical revival." Against this new-age backdrop, I argue that *Buffy* and *Angel* create a self-conscious mixture of sitcom, fantasy, and horror that allows them to negotiate a ground between absolute categories of good/evil and a more relativistic approach. Their dramatic situations often rely on a familiar good-against-evil format, but this is often juxtaposed with a more contemporary, sometimes irreverent, view of magic that often provides the source of comedy, as when the gravity of the Mayor's ceremony to become a demon is undermined by his comment "We don't knock during dark rituals?" ("Graduation Day," part 1, 3021). Although Buffy is made in the superhero mold, protecting the innocent from the big bad ugly ones, she is also just an ordinary teenager with whom we can empathize. As the series have developed, a progressively more relativistic approach to the morality of magic has evolved, often endearingly endangering Buffy and the Scooby Gang's heroic status. This approach connects with the shows' address of an audience who are media literate and apt to question the ideological basis of morality and dominant values, including traditional approaches to magic, witchcraft, and the supernatural.

In a number of recent American-made "fantasy" television series (e.g., *Xena* and *Sabrina*), magic has a direct relationship with the acquisition of power and its ethics. The fantasy genre, which tends to be reliant on special effects, has an intrinsic relationship with the transformational powers of magic. As its name suggests, the genre offers an escape from the banality of everyday life, and part of the attraction of *Buffy* and *Angel* is the magical reenchantment of urban and city life. Both shows bring together and use oppositions to create suspense, enchantment, and a resonant array of intertextual references that are regularly played off against one another to comic effect. Bringing the trappings of the Gothic into the Californian sunlight is typical of the transformational capacity of the fantasy genre. Love spells, invocations, warping temporal or spatial dimensions, tapping into alternative realities: each helps transform everyday scenarios into the enchanted guise of a fairy tale. But like fairy tales, the appeal of *Buffy* and *Angel* is more than simply an escapism. Fantasy scenarios involving magic and the supernatural are offered up as a means of articulating and symbolizing the stresses and strains, as well as the consequences of actions, particular to the experience of contemporary everyday life. Trafficking in the forces of the occult is traditionally framed as a transgressive practice, and the series certainly make use of this to lend a certain dark attraction. So how do the shows balance images and concepts derived from dangerous and subversive occult territory with prime-time televisual values?

CONJURING MAGICS: MYTH, MORALITY, AND THE MANICHAEAN

The basic myth that underlies the narrative logic of both *Buffy* and *Angel* can be described as Manichaean. The term refers to a model of the universe formulated by a third- to fifth-century sect, the Manichees, for whom the cosmos is a site of an endless dualistic battle between good and evil. Human beings are simply the reflection of this struggle: the body and the material world are evil and must be destroyed if the divine soul is to be released. The Manichaean view was taken by various medieval sects and was regarded as heretical by dominant Christian groups; some historians believe it was the Christian struggle against Manichaeans that generated the persecution of witches as devil worshipers (Thomas 439). Historical precedents and nuances aside, the adversarial nature of the Manichaean view makes it an attractive proposition for fantasy/horror screenwriters, partly because it means that humans become tools or avatars in the fight between the forces of good and evil. The disadvantage is that humans are merely pawns in a larger game, so, in order to break the bonds of fate, a hero is introduced. But unlike most Hollywood heroes, Buffy and Angel are only partially free from the constraints of fate. This allows the shows to make a link between the Manichaean struggle and predetermination: Buffy is "chosen," and Angel's redemption depends on help from the "powers that be." Their paths are largely written for them, providing points of identification for viewers, as, like most of us, their actions and choices are constrained by extrinsic factors. This bucks the trend of aggressive individualism present in many Hollywood films where heroic protagonists often transcend the limitations of determination (social, psychological, or otherwise) and are able to control life rather than life controlling them.

Within the field of film studies, the term "Manichaean" has often been used by critics to refer to movies that simply divide the world into camps, good and bad people, or, as Xander puts it in "Doppelgängland" (3016), the "White Hats" versus the "Black Hats," providing an example of one of the show's characteristic self-referential comments. A dual structure has, of course, underpinned many stories and myths, including early melodramas. It is frequently linked to the restoration of the status quo, often connected with dominant moral values, and sits neatly with the most basic and fundamental shape of a story: equilibrium-disequilibrium-equilibrium. Many action movies take the same basic adversarial format, as do the majority of horror and science fiction films. To call this opposition Manichaean risks reducing the meaning of the term, however. Critics often use the term as shorthand for describing the moral polarity of texts and the way such texts invite audiences to identify with the "good" characters. Apart from the difficulty of determining how people *actually* identify with texts, something that film academics continue to wrangle over, one of the problems with this is that the subtle and fuller resonances of the dualism implied by the term get forgotten. My argument here is that *Buffy* and *Angel* do not blindly adopt the moral polarization of magic, as occurs in many horror, fantasy, and action/adventure genres; instead, they take up and play with the ramifications of the Manichaean mythological model. As a result, a vital distinction is made between the Manichaeanism of many "melodramas" and that of these shows. Importantly, this enables conventional categories of good and evil to be questioned and made relative.

For the Manichees, God and the devil were part of the same system, co-present throughout space and time; they do battle, yet neither exists without the other. As Giles explains in "Harvest" (1002), "The world is older than you know; demons preceded us" and these "old ones" seek to return to the world through the Hellmouth. Vampires also fit into this system, as they are humans whose souls are possessed by that of a demon. All those who display nonhuman and nonhumane characteristics (the two are often synonymous in the earlier seasons) are either demons or possessed by a demon. Possessions, often originating from other dimensions, are often utilized as plot devices to enable regular "good" characters to turn "bad." Angel is an obvious example, depending on whether or not he has his soul. He is a something of a Manichaean microcosm: a demon and his own soul reside in him, one of which is dominant at a given time. Other characters also have good and evil versions: Xander ("The Pack," 1006, and "Nightmares," 1010), Willow ("Nightmares" and "Doppelgängland"), Oz through his monthly werewolf transformations, and Buffy ("Living Conditions," 4002); even the venerable Giles reverts to his teenage bad-boy self, uncannily reminiscent of Spike, in "Band Candy" (3006). As with many Hollywood genre films, the shows use very direct means to underline the current nature of a split character. For example, "bad" Willow's black lipstick and leather or Angel's smoking and cruel laughter indicate their changed personas. Such polarized splitting adds surprise and diversity to the shows, often inviting viewers to choose whether they like a character in good or bad guise. The split character strategy may also provide an important resonance and meaning for audiences, as it offers a way of symbolizing one's own experience of conflicting character traits. This is perhaps most obviously articulated as a metaphor for the changes of adolescence by the werewolf and Dr. Jekyll transformations in "Phases" (2015), "Beauty and the Beasts" (3004), and "Wild at Heart" (4006).

Applied to the frequent splitting of characters, the Manichaean myth can be interpreted as allegory: a way of articulating the disjunctions between who we think we are and what we *in fact* do. As Joss Whedon has said, "Basically *Angel* is similar to *Buffy* in that it deals with monsters that are metaphors for life" (qtd. in Jamieson 78). Such readings may demand a fairly sophisticated level of engagement with the shows. This is actively encouraged through the use of a range of subtle inflections and textual strategies, such as intertextual references, hints of forthcoming events, and loaded exchanges between characters.[1] This technique is exemplified in "Doppelgängland" when Angel intimates that nothing can be done in another dimension or, as vampire, that is not already "in them." What Angel suggests here is that good and bad are not so far apart and that "bad" is not simply the domain of the "othered" bad guys but is, instead, the "other" within—and he should know. A further challenge to conventional polarization of self and other is also evident when Oz finds out that the wolf is "with him all the time" in "Wild at Heart." Similarly, in "Band Candy," Giles and Joyce revert to their "bad" teenage selves and even the turning-demon Mayor retains his interest in golf, manners, and positive attitudes.

Buffy and *Angel* open up the potential of the Manichaean myth to mean more than simply "White Hats" versus "Black Hats" by self-consciously referencing horror films that actively invite a "psychological" interpretation (werewolf, vampire, and possession films in particular). These films often work with the idea that the "demon" is not simply an externalized other but originates from within the self. This concept leans heavily on psychoanalytic thought, which claims that antisocial behaviors, ideas, and fantasies are repressed through the process of socialization. These repressed ideas nevertheless press hard to return from the realm of the unconscious. In accordance with the psychoanalytic understanding of the "other" within, the split characters are often drawn from the core "good guys" camp and demonstrate the idea that identity is ultimately fragile, unknowable, and liable to throw some surprises. Magic and supernatural power, in Oz's case meditation, is likely to be a method by which some control or power is sought over the "beast within" as well as the "beast without."

Spike is also something of a challenge to the conventional definition of the Manichaean. He certainly aspires to evil but rarely achieves it; he shows signs of humanity and is not simply "appetite on legs" like many of the vampires in the series. Spike loves Dru (and later Buffy), and there are signs of affection for the Scooby Gang. The Judge, in "Becoming," part 2 (2022), can smell love on him. Circumstances conspire to put Spike in need of help from the Scooby Gang—teaming up with them to destroy Angelus in "Becoming," part 2, soliciting a love spell from Willow in "Lovers Walk" (3008), and helping him cope with effects of the "antievil" chip in season 4. Spike's case is not so cut-and-dried as Angel's, and the appeal of the character lies partly in his ambiguous status, as well as wry comments that often inadvertently spotlight that which has been overlooked by the good guys ("Lovers Walk" and "Pangs," 4008). As the series has progressed, Spike is understood less in terms of occult evil or traditional magic and more as a breath of punk cheek and iconoclasm. "I don't go in much for tradition" ("Lie to Me," 2007), he says to the "anointed one," renamed the "annoying one." In the prologue of "In the Dark" (*Angel*, 1003), he wickedly parodies Angel. Hidden from view, Spike looks down on Angel as he rescues a damsel in distress. The scene effectively sends up Angel's "dark knight" persona yet also displays Spike's own feelings of frustration and aggression:

Spike [mimicking a girl's high voice]: How can I thank you, you mysterious black clad hunk of a knight thing. [mimicking a deep male voice, in parody of stereotyped Hollywood heroes] No need little lady, your tears of gratitude are enough for me. You see I was once a bad-ass vampire, but love and a pesky curse defanged me. And now I'm just a big fluffy puppy with bad teeth. [. . .] [male voice, as the girl reaches out to Angel] No, not the hair, never the hair. [girl's high voice] But there must be some way I can show my appreciation? [deep voice, getting more sarcastic] No, helping those in need's my job and working up a load of sexual tension and prancing around like a magnificent poof is truly thanks enough. [. . .] Evil's still afoot and I'm almost out of that nancy boy hair gel I like so much, quickly to the Angelmobile, away. [spoken as Angel and the girl walk to the car]

The scene culminates in a death threat, yet the monologue's mixture of frustration, humor, and truth encapsulates the fact that Spike has it both ways. He retains his outsider bad-boy appeal yet is unlikely to be staked by Buffy: indeed, his strong sense of irony and self-awareness adds to the generally self-reflexive mood of the show.

In the fourth season of *Buffy* and the first season of *Angel,* there has been an increasing move toward a more relativistic and nontraditional approach to the constituency and meaning of villainy. In *Angel,* it emerges that there are many races of demons, and some are persecuted for their demon or hybrid status, graphically illustrated in "Hero" (1009) when "Nazi" demons hunt down and kill hybrid demon families for corrupting "pure blood." *Angel* clearly steps away from the idea prevalent in *Buffy* that all demons are Buffy fodder, using sidekick Doyle's half-demon status and those of the persecuted demons to make a clear comment on racism and other forms of prejudice. This addition also extends the myth that underpins both shows, meaning that characters do not always neatly align as good or bad, and both demons and humans are potential avatars of evil. Doyle is the prime example of a (half-) demon operating on the side of good, to the extent of sacrificing his life to save the human/demon hybrids from racist demons. It is even suggested in the dream time of "Restless" (4022) that Buffy herself may be a demon: Adam says to her, "Aggression is a natural human tendency. But you and me come by it another way"; she replies, "We are not demons," to which he responds, "Is that a fact?" Buffy's dream sequence in the episode is geared around her attempt to keep her identity as human in fact, but the signs of her links to the primal force, embodied in the first slayer, are present. At the end of the episode, Buffy is told, "You think you know what's to come, what you are. You haven't even begun." While it might be claimed that these suggestions of demon status are in the fantasy space of dream time, there is also a far more obvious sense that the status of being Slayer, with its superhuman powers, means that Buffy is not simply human. However, the "darker" aspects of the Scooby Gang are often counterbalanced by their role as protectors of the innocent. Rather than the white hats' holier-than-thou Christian male patriarchs, as they often are in occult horror films like *The Devil Rides Out* (1968, U.K.), here it is witch Willow, sorcerer-librarian Giles, a vampire turned knight in shining armor, and a diminutive teenaged girl with supernatural strength, who replace the usual guardians of order and morality. This provides a further departure from the Manichaean vocabulary used in many Hollywood films.

A good example of the negotiation with the relativism of contemporary culture occurs in "Pangs." It is Thanksgiving Day, and Willow does not approve of the celebration because it marks a victory over indigenous peoples. While Willow and Buffy debate the meaning of Thanksgiving, a Native American spirit who has been released from a buried mission seeks vengeance on the race who killed his people. Willow is adamant that the spirit is justified, and the argument persists as the Native American and his warriors lay siege to Giles's apartment. Willow's protest places the Scooby Gang's moral assuredness under political scrutiny and thereby challenges the simple Manichaean basis on which the all-out massacre of supernatural threats is conducted. Spike has the last candid word on the dispute, saying that the frontiersmen had "better weapons" and that "you just can't say sorry" to a vengeful spirit. Faced with death and a moral conundrum with no easy answer, Willow begins to fight, not because what she is doing is "good" and "right" but because she must in order to survive. While this represents some kind of resolution to the moral dilemma, the dust raised by the argument never quite settles at the end of the show. "Pangs" is representative of the tensions that arise from the copresence of relativism and the Manichaean in its most simple Hollywoodized form.

While there are some direct incursions on the polarized adversarial order, the shows are often indirectly engaged in debates about what defines good and evil. This helps extend the meaning of the Manichaean beyond that which occurs in many popular texts. At the same time, concepts like redemption are important to the show, perhaps less in traditional spiritual terms but more in terms of morality, so that characters such as Angel, Faith ("Five by Five," *Angel,* 1018, and "Sanctuary," *Angel,* 1019), and Lindsey McDonald ("Blind Date," *Angel,* 1021) seek redemption from their previous cruel deeds. The shows are therefore juggling, often with critical intent born of its address to a contemporary "youth" audience, with the assumptions about good and evil made by popular culture. The result is that the two series have taken an ever more relativistic and multiculturally sensitive approach to the occult and moral values. Perhaps this shift has occurred because the producers and creators of the shows take notice of their fan base and recognize the audience's embrace of the more challenging aspects of the shows. Self-consciousness is a prime means of facilitating a more complex moral take. Before going on to explore this further, it is important to address the contribution made by serial form to the shows' engagement with the Manichaean.

FORMATTING MAGIC AND THE MEANINGS OF WITCHCRAFT

Requisite for the difference between *Buffy* and *Angel* and the standard portrayal of magic and the occult as evil in the horror film is the scope afforded by the series format. A horror film often works with a ninety-minute duration. This has a profound effect on the shape of a story line. In a film, there is no need to entice an audience to switch on again the following week or to plan story arcs that can be taken up by a range of screenwriters and directors. Long-running serials allow characters to be drawn in more robust ways, evolving in ways that the format of the horror film cannot accommodate. The serial format has a considerable effect on the representation of magic and witchcraft, helping *Buffy* and *Angel* depart from the simplified moral polarity deployed in occult horror films such as *The Exorcist* (1973), *The Devil Rides Out*, or *End of Days* (1999). The multinarrative format is now a staple of television serials. This involves a major story in each episode but without foreclosing all aspects raised. A story arc is built around the central characters, offering a forum for ensemble playing, and therefore gives a show a depth that pays dividends to those who watch regularly. Many series use this format, including *The X-Files* (1993–present), *Xena*, *Buffy*, and *Angel*. To an extent, the "cult" status of these serials depends on their sustaining a regular audience who closely follow the nuanced trajectory of character and story developments. Because *Buffy* and *Angel* trade on such developments, magic and witchcraft are open to a broader and more diverse set of meanings than those portrayed in the traditional occult horror film and similar in format to multinovel cycles, such as those written by Anne Rice or J. K. Rowling.

Hollywood's use of the Manichaean often entails that evil is combated by good. Such a triumph occurs at the end of a film, creating an "all is right with world again" sense of closure. Numerous academics have pointed out how closure operates in alignment with specific dominant views of the world, often working as an ideological sedative by creating the illusion of security and safety through the resolution of problems. In *Buffy* and *Angel*, there is (as yet) no such complete closure. As with the Manichees, the battle between good and evil is perpetual, and evil is not "man-made" or defeatable. In *Buffy* and *Angel*, small battles are won, even apocalypses averted, but the format demands that there are always more of the big bad ones out there. Furthermore, *Buffy* does not live happily ever after; she does not get to keep her dark tortured prince (so far), and she will not cease to be the Slayer until her death. Quite often these types of resolutions become tantalizingly close, but like a desert mirage they recede so that the series can go another season. This dynamic of *nearly* attaining the object of desire—that then inevitably slips away—plays a significant role in the dualistic nature of the shows and provides a crucial link to the nuances of the Manichaean in its original guise. The rule is that everything turns into its opposite or is taken away, as in "I Will Remember You" (*Angel,* 1008), where Buffy is doomed to forget her night of passion with the temporarily human Angel. While Buffy's life might look like that of a fairy tale heroine, it is constantly in the process of change, and she has little hope of a conclusive happy ending. Angel, at least, does have the hope of spiritual redemption, but this is infinitely extendable and could be reversed if it is necessary for the creation of a new season. Ironically, these formal factors make the shows more properly Manichaean than many melodramas and action/adventures, precisely because there is no cessation or closure on the "big bad."

The twenty-two episodes of each season afford a great deal of latitude for exploring different meanings of magic. The screenwriters draw from a wide variety of texts and have become increasingly self-aware of the various implications of traditional and nontraditional representations. This diversity becomes evident if we examine how the meanings of witchcraft have evolved throughout the shows. For centuries, the witches of myth, fairy tale, and literature have seduced men, disrupted patrilinear dynasties, caused storms, danced under the moonlight with the devil, captured and baked small children, and summoned the spirits of the dead to see the future. And it is to witchcraft that honest, clever Willow has become apprenticed.

For the duration of season 1, Willow showed no real interest in witchcraft; research was her main task as well as offering Buffy a close friend to talk to. Willow's first encounter with witchcraft came in "Witch" (1003). Amy Madison's witch mother swaps bodies with her daughter. She is a classic bad witch, using magic to serve her own narcissistic desires. Working alone in the attic, with a spell book, black cat, bubbling cauldron, and Barbie-turned-juju dolls, she performs her craft like many a fairy tale witch. As I have argued elsewhere, Amy's ex-cheerleader mom is a "postmodern" version of the classic Snow White–style witch who realizes that youth and beauty can be used as routes to power (Krzywinska 142–44). In this episode, witchcraft is set up as evil—a means of persecuting the innocent; the witch is summarily destroyed by Buffy and consigned to spend eternity trapped in a cheerleading trophy. Here and elsewhere, witchcraft is not directly aligned to a pact with devil or cult, as it is in many horror films, from *Häxan* (1922, Denmark) to *Little Witches* (1996). However, from very early on in the series, witchcraft is set up as the domain of women and is frequently linked to the powers of beauty and love.

In "Bewitched, Bothered and Bewildered" (2016), it is apparent that Amy has inherited her mother's powers, and Xander gets Amy to perform a spell for him to gain Cordelia's love. Like many of her witch predecessors, Amy calls on the ancient goddess Diana to conduct her amour spell. It might seem rather odd that Diana, Roman virgin-goddess of the hunt and the moon, rather than Venus, goddess of love, is called on. It is, neverthe-less, Diana's connection to the hunt and the moon that links her with witch-craft, and, presumably, it is from her mother, a fully fledged dark witch, that Amy gleaned her spells. With this particular invocation to a virgin-witch-goddess, it is almost inevitable that the spell backfires. Only Cordelia, for whom the spell was meant, is immune from falling in love with him, but all the other women of Sunnydale go Bacchae-crazy for Xan-der, seeking first his kisses and then his blood. At the end of the day, with the spell reversed, the hard lesson is learned that love cannot be forced by magic. This event has a profound effect on the rest of the series. Love spells are subsequently regarded as dangerous and are used only inadvertently, as with Willow's "I will it" spell that causes Buffy and Spike to fall in love in "Something Blue" (4009). Although Amy's love spell went awry, it was not intended to do harm. Thus, the beginnings of a concept of magic that is not simply appended to the forces of good or evil takes root in the series. There is something of a challenge to moral polarization here, and it certainly dif-fers from the more conventional, if resonant, approach taken by "Witch."

It is with the introduction of Jenny Calendar that the more traditionalist modes of presenting witchcraft become most clearly laced with contempo-rary notions. Jenny tells Giles that she is a "techno-pagan" and is part of a coven that meets on-line. It is her group who helps remove a medieval de-mon, Moloch the Corrupter, from the Web after he was uploaded during a library scanning session ("I Robot, You Jane," 1008). Jenny's computer skills help update the concepts of magic used in the show. Giles represents old knowledge: he is learned "of the books" yet is snobbily suspicious of computers. By contrast, Jenny synthesizes old and new knowledge. Her knowledge of witchcraft is partly a legacy of her Romany family heritage and also partakes of new-age cyber-culture. This meeting of the ancient and the postmodern is illustrated by the fact that she writes a computer program to translate the ancient Romanian spell needed to reunite Angelus with his soul so that he can become Angel again ("Becoming," part 1, 2021).

When Angelus kills Jenny, it is Willow who steps into the role of witch. She takes over Jenny's computer class and reads her computer-stored spells. From this point on, Willow begins to cast spells on a regular basis. This de-velopment allows witchcraft and its powers to be explored through a cen-tral, familiar character. As both Willow and Jenny are set up as benevolent and more "ordinary" than the preternaturally strong Buffy, witchcraft gets partially freed from many of the traditional trappings of transgression and salaciousness, particularly as featured in sexploitation-style horror films. Witchcraft is not entirely without its danger but is more closely aligned to occult sitcom than to the naked devil worshiping witches of most occult-horror films. Although Giles occasionally halfheartedly warns Willow that what she is doing may be dangerous—this might be because of the ill effects of Giles's own youthful dabbling with the black arts—it is markedly the case that witchcraft is no longer presented in the show simply in terms of evil. Unlike the teen witches of *Little Witches* and *The Craft,* Willow does not use her magic to conjure self-gratifying wishes and is not in the thrall of a demonic masculine force. Her magic is a more benign combination of "recipe" witchcraft and mind-based concentration; nevertheless, it still makes her powerful. As such, Willow is no longer just the "someone to speak to and protect" sidekick, and her spells are part of the armory of the Scooby Gang, designed to help fight the forces that threaten them (as they do in "Primeval," 4021).

Certain qualifiers frame the sympathetic approach to the practice of witchcraft, however. Willow "uses" magic, but she is not part of a cult or religious group. She may call herself a "Wicca," but she is never seriously linked to a Wiccan group. The term "Wicca" is Anglo-Saxon for a male witch, "Wicce" for a female one, but is now generally used to describe a particular version of modern paganism that broadly follow the model pagan developed by Gerald Gardner, a British occultist, in the mid-twentieth century. When Willow visits the Wiccan group at college, she is dissatisfied that they just talk "Gaia" rather than do spells. In comparison to theirs, her witchcraft is practical and not linked to environmental issues or spiritual matters. This keeps magic neatly in the realm of fantasy rather than as an alternative religion. Underscoring the practical nature of her magic, Willow's spells rarely involve the supplication of deities. As with the film *Practical Magic,* there is reference to new-age magic and spiritual ideas: yet Willow's spells are "ingredient" spells—herbs, objects, and incantations—and are located within the economy of the "magic shop" rather than religious rites. She may aspire to being a "baad-ass wicca" yet describes witchcraft, prosaically, as "chemistry with newt" ("Bad Girls," 3014). Hence, Willow is not identified directly as specifically "pagan" (her family and upbringing are Jewish). In not directly claiming Willow for paganism, the series strategically takes magic out of the contentious arena of religion and mysticism. This strategy also has the effect of displacing the way in which witchcraft was represented in conventional polarized terms as evil in the first-season episode "Witch."

In contrast to "Witch," "Gingerbread" (3011) provides a novel take on witch persecutions and burnings throughout history and exemplifies the more complex take on witchcraft adopted by the series as it has evolved. A ritual murder of two children has occurred, and witches or satanists are suspected of perpetrating the deed. Willow, Amy, and Michael (a goth boy) are suspected by an action group, Mothers Opposed to the Occult, spearheaded by Buffy's and Willow's mothers. A battle between mothers and daughters ensues, resulting in Amy, Willow, and Buffy nearly being burned at the stake, the pyre fueled by banned occult books. It transpires that the mothers have been goaded by what they think are the ghosts of the murdered children. Giles traces these ghosts to the fairy story "Hansel and Gretel" and realizes that they have been provoking witch-hunts throughout history. In fact, there are no ghost children, only a very ugly goblin that takes their form and whose whispered words turn people into vigilantes prepared to burn their own kin at the stake. This "explanation" of vigilantism brings to bear an unexpected Manichaean take on witch-burning crazes. It is not the doings of evil witches possessed by the devil that elicits their persecution but a form of demonic possession on the part of the accusers. This is a neat reversal, one that has political resonance. The episode clearly refers to Arthur Miller's play *The Crucible* (1953), in which the witch-hunt functions as metaphor for the McCarthyite (or any other) ideological persecutions, and, more than this, it also comments on the frequent occult scares and their effects that American culture seems particularly prone to.

In a departure from the usual conflation made by horror film and fairy tales of witches and evil, *Buffy* opens up witchcraft to a wealth of meanings. The considerable space assigned to the impact of Willow's engagement with magic and her adoption of a witch identity brings the recent reevaluation of, and romance with, witchcraft to bear strongly on the show, providing one of its primary pleasures. In part, it is the series format that promotes a sympathetic and culturally aware view of witchcraft to be taken. Such an approach depends on allowing viewers to watch Willow grow into the mysteries of witchcraft and how it has progressively shaped her identity. The model of witchcraft here is not that of the titillating spectacle of lascivious monstrous witches often seen in horror films. Instead, Willow is an apprentice witch, learning her spells, sorting out her identity, and helping her friends defeat the big bad. Similar to Hermione from J. K. Rowling's Harry Potter books, Willow's appeal is given an added depth and dimension through her kooky humor, negotiation with the contradictory values of her culture, and the travails of her romantic associations with Oz, a werewolf, and Tara, another practicing witch.

CONNECTIONS AND REFLECTIONS

Self-referentiality and knowing intertextual references are key ingredients that contribute to the popularity and cult appeal of *Buffy* and *Angel* and are important to the representation of magic as well as their complex negotiation with the Manichaean. By making overt or covert references to other

texts, whether they are fairy tales, horror films, or popular culture, the series engage viewers' cultural or subcultural capital. In part, this reflects the
self-referential trend in so-called postmodern slasher films and, significantly, has the effect of making the characters as well as viewers into readers of texts. By placing characters and viewers in a similar cultural and in-
terpretational space, topical tastes, debates, and antagonisms drawn from
contemporary culture are introduced. The carefully forged illusion is that
the viewer is living in the same cultural space and time as the Scooby Gang.
In "Lie to Me," Angel visits a "goth" nightclub and says that none of the
vamp-worshiping goths know anything about vampires or what they wear;
as he speaks, a club member pushes past him wearing exactly the same
clothes as he does. Such jokes, as well as direct or indirect references to
other shows like *Xena* or the novels of Anne Rice, are part of a common
cultural vocabulary that connects characters to a broader "real" world culture. Such references lend the series a greater sense of meaningfulness, time-
liness, and textual richness, further encouraging discussion between viewers
and helping to interlace the Buffyverse with everyday life.

As with many horror films, ideas gleaned from psychoanalysis are commonly featured in the shows, particularly the notion that there is another
level of autonomous existence that lurks beneath the surface and that the
repressed returns. As Xander says, "You can't just bury stuff, Buffy, it will
come right back to get you" ("Dead Man's Party," 3002). As well as direct
references, there are many metaphors for the unconscious in the shows, for
example, the underground crypt in which the Master is held captive or the
underworld of The Initiative where demons are imprisoned. This underworld spews forth a glut of textual links, including *The X-Files*–style con-
spiracy, cyber-punk, and *Frankenstein,* all of which see the "Gothic" un-
derside of science and government.

As in psychoanalysis and the horror genre, the repressed is frequently
linked to the primal, providing a further set of intertexts. Xander's and Oz's
transformation into hyena and werewolf returns them to an instinctual
state; likewise, most of the vampire Buffy fodder are strongly feral. Atavism
(a return to primal states) also prevails in the story line of "Primeval,"
where the spirit of the first Slayer is summoned to lend Buffy greater power
to destroy cyber-demon Adam. The primal power of the first Slayer is more
"magical" than Buffy's and is able, *Matrix*-style, to stop bullets in midflight
and dodge Adam's lethal blows. Atavism in cult and horror films like *Altered States* (1980), *Cat People* (1942, 1982), and *Company of Wolves*
(1984, U.K.) often draws on animal transformation myths stretching back
at least to Greek mythology, and through to reworkings of the "Jekyll and
Hyde" story in which science provides the regressive catalyst. Often the primal is linked to the release of sexual desires, as it is in many vampire narratives: once bitten, never shy.

In *Buffy*, teen-with-teen sex is seen in the general sense as a part and parcel of life, but it brings with it a gamut of meanings and emotions: trauma, romance, elation, and difficulties. The sexual relationships in the series are also often given something of a "queer" flavor. Many of the teens in question are witches, ex-demons, werewolves, or vampires—most of whom appear to be teens yet are hundreds of years old. The nature of such relationships is pointed out by Spike, acting as chorus, in "In the Dark," where he wryly comments on Angel's "perverse" relationship with Buffy—he is an over-200-year-old vampire, and she is a teenager and a Slayer. Yet despite the fact that the sexual relationships are sodden with transgression and exotic otherness, the act of sex itself is not presented as sinful or something that should be directly punished. In "Where the Wild Things Are" (4018), for example, it is sexual repression enforced onto orphaned adolescents by a puritan adult and not sex per se that triggers the haunting of Riley's frat house.

Some viewers of the series will recognize that the links made between magic and evil with "perverse" sexuality in many occult films are differently handled in the two series. In *Buffy*, there is a trend for the "bad" couples to refer to bondage. This is done in a comic way, but there is no equation, subtextual or otherwise, between homosexuality and evil in the series, as there is in *White Zombie* (1932), *The Bride of Frankenstein* (1935) or, more tacitly, in *The Devil Rides Out* (Krzywinska 94). Importantly, the rejection of the usual horror film strategy of linking monstrosity, evil, or occult practice to sexual "perversity" (so called) allows Willow and Tara's blossoming lesbian romance and sexual relationship to be framed by love, even though they are both practicing witches. Their relationship is therefore presented in a rather different way than the lesbian vampires or lesbian witches in, for instance, *Vampire Lovers* (1970, U.K.), *The Hunger* (1983), or *Virgin Witch* (1970, U.K.), where horror and sexploitation cinema meet. There is no predatory lesbian or titillating nude scenes in the series. Tara and Willow's relationship is delicately handled. It is probably the case that because we have known Willow before she became a witch and followed her relationship through with Oz, the "straight" audience is helped to read her as a person first and lesbian (and witch) second. There is an acknowledgment that such a relationship would take some viewers by surprise, however. This is managed by Buffy's shocked response to Willow's dilemma when she is forced to choose between Oz and Tara. Buffy accepts and supports Willow's decision after she has got over the initial surprise. The series also manages the inevitable prurient interest from some male viewers by referring directly to such a response through Xander's dream in "Restless." Once again we have to look at the extended form of a long-running series, its target audience, and the constraints set by scheduling times to help account for the care and gentleness—or "politically correct" handling, depending on your view—with which this relationship is represented. These factors also assist with an explanation of the key difference between the series depiction of Willow and Tara and the way in which witch-lesbians are portrayed in most occult/sexploitation films.

As readers of the shows, viewers are often invited to pick up on subtle references, recognize source material, and look for clues building toward later events. Characters, too, have to interpret a variety of texts, including their own thoughts, actions, and relationships, along with more obvious written types. The role of books in *Buffy* has become a little less important as the series has progressed; but in season 1 to the end of season 3, the library and books were of central importance to narrative. The watchers' diaries, first mentioned in "Angel" (1007), provide accounts of the identities and profiles of most of the important older vampires. Other books provide forms of information or incantations, and many of Willow's spells come from a book simply titled "Witchcraft"; it appeared in her room in "Graduation Day," part 1. This book was originally part of Giles's collection held in the library, before Mothers Opposed to the Occult burnt some and some of the rest were destroyed by proceedings of the Mayor's ascension. Many of these books are grimoires, a term used to describe a manual of magic. Examples include the "codex" given to Giles by Angel and later stolen by one of Spike's crew; *Malleus Maleficarum,* a fifteenth-century German book on witchcraft mentioned by Giles in connection to the transformation of pupils into hyenas, and the books of Therion. Some viewers may know that this is a tacit reference to British arch-occultist Aleister Crowley, who provided Gerald Gardner with the key rituals vital to the foundation of modern Wicca. Under the name "The Master Therion," he penned *Magic in Theory and Practice* (1929) as a guide to his own brand of magick (with a "k" adopted in all the tie-in Buffy novels). This textual reference to the man dubbed by the British tabloid press as "The Wickedest Man in the World," a notoriety gained through his combined use of sex, magic, and drugs, brings a sulfurous whiff of sex magick to the venerable librarian's book collection.

The Sunnydale High School library is full of ancient and esoteric texts brought by Giles from the British Library, which provides "real" life and fictional connections. The British Library appears in the occult film *Night of the Demon* (1958, U.K.), and the retelling of Giles's past sorceries, leading to the summoning of a deadly demon in "The Dark Age" (2008), is strongly reminiscent of this film. This also constructs, for the interested viewer, a link between Crowley—who was the model for the magician Karswell in the film—and Giles's magical dark past. Such references, alongside the collection of occult books and the Internet, provide an important way of linking the diegetic world to other texts, to history, and to viewers' cultural knowledge. This is important to the series's project of making connections with viewers' lives: the aim of which is to build a cultural vocabulary gleaned from the "real" world that is common to both viewers and characters.

The series's founding myth resembles that imagined by the writer H. P. Lovecraft (1890–1937). In Lovecraft's fictional universe, ancient demonic beings of cosmic origin, termed the "Old Ones," attempt to break through the membrane that divides their realm from ours. In "The Dunwich Horror," Lovecraft writes, "Nor is it to be thought that man is either the oldest or the last of earth's masters, or that the common bulk of life and substances walk alone. The Old Ones were, the Old Ones are, the Old Ones shall be. Not in the spaces we know, but between them. They walk serene and primal, undimensioned and to us unseen" (Lovecraft 117). This has strong echoes in Giles's speech about the origins of demons and vampires in "The Harvest." Lovecraft created a coherent and extendable creation myth that underpins his stories that, like *Buffy* and *Angel,* marry the supernatural with the everyday. "All my stories," he once said, "unconnected as they may be, are based on the fundamental lore or legend that this world was inhabited at one time by another race who, in practicing black magic, lost their foothold and were expelled, yet live on outside ever ready to take possession of the earth again" (Lovecraft 9). Like Lovecraft's Cthuhlu mythos, the Buffyverse has attained mythological status and is no longer simply the product of one author. As Joss Whedon says, *Buffy* can easily continue without him. By no means everyone will make a connection between Lovecraft and the Buffyverse, and many might rightly point out that Anne Rice's work is also a significant influence and intertext (e.g., "Lie to Me" and "Somnambulist," *Angel,* 1011). Nevertheless, the shows work hard to make direct and indirect connections to a range of texts. Not all are esoteric occult works, and many are far more widely known, particularly the frequent references to fairy tale. Whether it is these, *Frankenstein,* cyber-punk, Gothic novels from Stoker to Rice; occult lore, comics, youth cultures now passed into the hallowed halls of nostalgia; or popular film and television, *Buffy* and *Angel* make use of such references to help connect the shows to "real" life and to pull us into the rewards of attentive viewing.

Both shows take up different traditions of representing magic, mainly, but not exclusively, drawn from the horror genre and occult comedies. This blend gives a fairly wide variety of meanings to witchcraft and magic, and some of them are contradictory. Magic may be couched in a battle between good and evil, as occurs in many popular fictions, yet *Buffy* and *Angel* deliberately play with the assumptions that underlie both the ancient dualistic model of the Manichaean and the more polarized Hollywood version. In placing polarized good and evil alongside relativism and skepticism, the series becomes imbued with a productive and time-specific tension. This makes the shows sensitive to contemporary moral debates and dilemmas, as well as restaging the dualist problems of the original Manichaean myth, lost by many popular films. The copresence of diverse approaches to magic and witchcraft further allows these shows to deal with issues arising from life in a contemporary multicultural society. This widened vocabulary of the occult enables them to echo and symbolize parallel concerns that hover around identity and its fragmentation: difference and prejudice, which are particularly relevant to a young audience in the process of defining its own identities. It is this, alongside the complex negotiations with magic and Manichaean facilitated by the series format, that makes *Buffy* and *Angel* innovative and engaging additions to the growing cycle of occult television.

NOTE

1. Fantasy and cult television shows often use such devices to encourage close attention to the text and keep viewers ritualistically hooked into a series.

16

Whose Side Are You on, Anyway?

Children, Adults, and the Use of Fairy Tales in Buffy

Sarah E. Skwire

The grown-ups don't believe you, right? Well, I do. We both know that there are real monsters, but there's also real heroes that fight monsters, and that's me.

—Buffy, in "Killed by Death" (2018)

The utility of fairy tales as didactic tools has been familiar to students of the genre since long before the first appearance of Bettelheim's now-classic work *The Uses of Enchantment*. From their very first appearances in print, and presumably long before, fairy tales have been a way to tell a great story and do a little teaching at the same time. As fairy tales became part of written as well as oral culture, that didacticism was carefully managed and increased. With increasing stringency in successive editions, Jakob and Wilhelm Grimm edited and expurgated their *Nursery and Household Tales* to present readers with clearer, less morally ambiguous messages. They removed, for example, the premarital sex and impregnation from the story of *Rapunzel*, and they inserted increasingly strong religious themes into each successive version of *The Girl without Hands* (Tatar 10, 18). Disney's alterations of traditional tales into more didactically "acceptable" formats are famous—infamous, perhaps, for fans of Andersen's original version of *The Little Mermaid*. Nearly every modern critical or educational work on fairy tales presents the genre as a "teaching opportunity." The modern-day Gothic fairy tale that is the television series *Buffy the Vampire Slayer* is no less didactic in its use of fairy tales. *Buffy*, however, as it does with nearly every other convention, turns the didactic nature of the fairy tale on its head. The instructors become the instructed. The fictionalized literalization of the figurative becomes a figure no longer but is instead the bloodily and terrifyingly real. Everything that we have formulated about fairy tales as a safe place to explore distressing psychic realities dissolves in an instant.

Close examinations of three *Buffy* episodes—season 2's "Killed by Death" (2018), season 3's "Gingerbread" (3011), and season 4's "Hush" (4010)—in which fairy tales form a prominent part of the plot will help demonstrate the way in which *Buffy* uses fairy tales. They become not only a way of instructing those characters and audience members who "read" the episodes either by experiencing or by watching the tales as they unfold but also a way of measuring and directing Buffy's maturity and gauging her relationship to the complex categories of "child" and "adult."

"Killed by Death" and "Gingerbread," from seasons 2 and 3, when Buffy is still in high school, serve to distinguish uncomprehending adults who are blind to, and foolishly trapped by, demonic dangers from wise children who see what adults cannot see and who understand the reality of these "imaginary" evils. This distinction is, of course, a brilliant inversion of the generally accepted dynamic of fairy tales both as tales and as pedagogical devices. The stereotypical method of delivery for a fairy tale is a top-down model. An adult, in other words, tells the tale to a child. The adult has the information, the wisdom, and passes it down to one who needs to learn and understand. The top-down model of tale-telling is often emphasized by envisioning the tale-teller as even older and wiser than a parent figure—a grandparent, an aged nurse, an "old wife," even Burgess's "Old Mother West Wind." As Maria Tatar has observed, many early frontispieces to fairy tale collections served to enforce this generational hierarchy of tale-telling by fueling the "false notion that in 'the olden days' fairy tales were told exclusively by elderly peasant women to children" (Tatar 111). This top-down delivery of fairy tales has been strongly supported by Bettelheim's presentation in *The Uses of Enchantment* of fairy tales as a way for children to find or to be led toward psychological truths.

In order to master the psychological problems of growing up—overcoming narcissistic disappointments, Oedipal dilemmas, and sibling rivalries; becoming able to relinquish childhood dependencies; gaining a feeling of selfhood and of self-worth and a sense of moral obligation—a child needs to understand what is going on within the conscious self in order to also cope with that which goes on in the unconscious. The child can achieve this understanding, and with it the ability to cope, not through rational comprehension of the nature and content of the unconscious but by becoming familiar with it through spinning out daydreams—ruminating, rearranging, and fantasizing about suitable story elements in response to unconscious pressures. By doing this, the child fits unconscious content into conscious fantasies that then make it possible to deal with that content. It is here that fairy tales have unequaled value because they offer new dimensions to the child's imagination that would be impossible to discover alone. Even more important, the form and structure of fairy tales suggest images to the child with which to structure daydreams and, with them, give better direction to his life (Bettelheim 6–7).

In Bettelheim's construction, the fictions of fairy tales serve as metaphors to aid a child in learning truths about the world "which would be impossible for him to discover" alone. They transmit knowledge and information that the otherwise innocent and unaware child would have no way of attaining. As Bettelheim notes earlier in the same work, "The most important and most difficult task in raising a child is helping him find meaning in life. [. . .] Regarding this task, nothing is more important that the impact of parents and others who take care of the child" (3–4). Bettelheim's construction of the value of fairy tales at assisting in such a task and the generally accepted importance of an adult mentor in a child's search for meaning seem to me to be undeniably correct; certainly, it is not the project of this brief chapter to attempt to critique Bettelheim's masterful work. But Bettelheim's understanding of the ways that fairy tales work and the popular acceptance of that understanding are correct only in the world as we know it. In the world of *Buffy*, such constructions and assumptions are at best inaccurate and at worst life-threatening.

The first fairy tale episode, "Killed by Death," finds a fevered, delirious, and tranquilizer-drugged Buffy in the hospital being treated for a severe case of the flu and a near-fatal attack by Angelus. We soon learn that Buffy has been afraid of hospitals for years, ever since she witnessed the mysterious hospital death of her cousin Celia. Shortly after we learn this detail about Buffy's past, we see, through her eyes, a black-coated, black-hatted demonic figure following a small boy. Inevitably, children start dying.

At this point in the episode, we seem in unsurprising and familiar territory. As the introduction to the Junior Great Books series suggests, there is no mystery here. We know how to read this demon and this fear. "It is the hallmark of folktales to condense and suggest meaning [. . .] they must be read symbolically rather than literally" (Junior Great Books). Any reader of Bettelheim, Sheldon Cashdan, Maria Tatar, or any number of other fairy tale scholars and psychologists would explain that the "demon" is a physicalized representation of Buffy's fears about hospitals and death. That other children can see the demon suggests only, within the figurative reading of a fairy tale, that they share those same fears. Indeed, Willow and Giles come close to replicating this critical and interpretive position when they suggest that Buffy and the children have seen not Death or a demon but a suspicious doctor who may be the very real, very human source of these children's deaths.

We are not, however, in Bettelheim's universe. We are not in a world where reading figuratively will help us. "Decoding" the demon as the representation of an amorphous fear of death or as a way of understanding a frightening and threatening adult is useless. We are in Buffy's world, and, as she reminds us, that means, "It's real, which means I get to fight it."

The reality of the Demon, soon discovered to be the "Kindestod," which translates roughly as "Child-death," is one crucial component in *Buffy*'s inversion of our typical understanding of how fairy tales work. The other and equally important aspect is the mystification of the adults in the series. Adults cannot see the Kindestod. Xander and Willow, teenagers on the edge of adulthood, are unable to see him, and Buffy is able to see him only when her defenses are down because she is delirious with fever. In order for Buffy to track him, fight him, and defeat him, she has to inject herself with more flu virus to regain her delirium. The injection, though, is just a vehicle. The action it performs is to free Buffy from adult restrictions and to return her to a more childlike, more "open" state. In this way she is able to see the Kindestod and kill it. In doing so she rescues the children, solves the mystery of her cousin's death—she was killed by the Kindestod—and saves herself from her own fear of hospitals.

More important for our purposes than Buffy's victory, satisfyingly violent though that victory is, is the way her victory and her means of achieving that victory toy with our understanding of how fairy tales work. While the traditional fairy tale literalizes the figurative so that the reader may have the cathartic experience of finding the figurative meaning of the tale and thereby understanding its true message, *Buffy* insists on the literal truth of the tale as it stands. Demons are demons. They may also stand for childhood fears or teenage angst or any number of other things, but they are first, foremost, and always demons. And it is not adults who possess the Rosetta Stone of understanding, as it is with fairy tales; it is children, and it is Buffy.

The motif of the "clueless adults" and "wise children" reaches its height in the fairy tale episode "Gingerbread." From the moment that Buffy's mother, Joyce, arrives uninvited to watch Buffy patrol, it is clear that the conflict between adults and children will be central to the episode. After seeing Buffy kill a vampire, Joyce wanders over to a playground to regain her composure. There she discovers the murdered bodies of two beautiful young children whose palms are inscribed with a mysterious symbol. Joyce, understandably, is horrified, and she turns to Buffy for answers:

> *Buffy:* I'm so sorry that you had to see this, but I promise everything's going to be okay.
> *Joyce:* How?
> *Buffy:* Because I'm going to find whatever did it.
> *Joyce:* I guess. It's just you can't. You can't make it right.
> *Buffy:* I know. I'm sorry, but I'll take care of everything, I promise. Just try and calm down.

The inversion of traditional parent/child roles is clear and sets the tone for the remainder of the episode. All of Joyce's actions and choices will be governed by her desire to respond to these murders in a responsible and adult way. All of her choices will be wrong.

Persuaded by the mysterious symbol drawn on the children's palms, Joyce and Buffy suspect that the murders have some connection to the occult. Buffy reproduces the symbol for Giles, who believes that it indicates that the murder was the responsibility of a human occult group rather than a demon. Meanwhile, Joyce plans a town meeting and vigil for the murdered children. As the crowd gathers for the vigil that night, Willow's mother reports that "there's a rumor going around about witches—about people calling themselves witches who are responsible for this crime." Willow, a witch, begins to look very nervous, and we in the audience experience another moment of separation between adult and child.

It is Joyce, however, who draws the battle lines, and she does it in terms of adults and children:

> Silence is this town's disease. For too long we've been plagued by unnatural evils. This isn't our town any more. It belongs to the monsters and the witches and the slayers. I say it's time for the grownups to take Sunnydale back.

That Joyce, subconsciously or not, places teenagers into the category of "unnatural evils" is clear to the audience from the moment that she equates slayers and witches—her daughter and her daughter's best friend—with monsters. Her further injunction that it is "time for the grownups" to reclaim Sunnydale serves to make the message accessible only to those in Sunnydale who do not know about Buffy's secret identity and Willow's Wiccan explorations. Joyce's speech succeeds in firing up Sunnydale's adults, and many of the children as well, and for the moment we in the audience feel quite confident about right and wrong. Joyce and the adults are clearly on the wrong track, and Buffy and her friends will be vindicated.

Nothing on *Buffy* is ever quite that simple though, and the next scene we see is of Willow and several other Sunnydale witches performing an unidentified occult ritual that involves skulls, black robes, and other disturbing paraphernalia. As the camera pulls back from the ritual, we discover that they are seated around a large reproduction of the symbol found on the children's palms. The effect is shocking. We are no longer quite sure what to think. Is it possible that the adults could be right?

Our confusion and distress only increase as we watch Principal Snyder and local law enforcement open and search the lockers of all Sunnydale's "suspicious" students, looking for "witch stuff." Buffy, and we, are horrified to discover that Willow has a reproduction of the symbol from the murdered children's palms drawn in her notebook. As Willow tries to explain that the symbol is part of a protection spell she was trying to cast for Buffy, she is dragged away to Snyder's office. Reassured of Willow's goodness and slightly chagrined by the suspicions we have entertained, we are free to return to our exploration of the inverted adult/child interactions that flavor this episode.

The inversion intensifies as Joyce, who has now founded the protest group MOO (Mothers Opposed to the Occult) begins to challenge Buffy's abilities as Slayer. Buffy, watching the adult reaction to the murders spiral out of control and into locker searches and book burnings, attempts to convince Joyce to calm MOO's response a little by reminding her that the Slayer can, and does, take care of this sort of thing all the time:

> *Buffy:* Mom, I hate that those people scared you so much, and I know that you're just trying to help, but you have to let me handle this. It's what I do.
> *Joyce:* But is it really? I mean you patrol; you slay; evil pops up, and you undo it, and that's great. But is Sunnydale getting any better? Are they running out of vampires?
> *Buffy:* I don't think that you run out.

Buffy is the responsible figure here. She wants to do her job, methodically, carefully, and effectively. Joyce is childish, demanding immediate response and a fairy tale happy ending, with no evil at all left in Sunnydale. The impetus for this childishness becomes clear when we discover that the murdered children have begun to appear to Joyce and instruct her in what to do. They focus with particular intensity on the need to hurt the "bad girls" in the same way that they were hurt.

When the murdered children reappear, experienced watchers of *Buffy* know that we are in demonic territory. Soon, Buffy and her friends have discerned this as well. Realizing that no one knows any details about the murdered children—names, addresses, parents—Buffy and her friends do some research. What they discover presents us, once again, with a stunning inversion of everything we know, or think we know, about fairy tales. The canonical viewpoint is presented by Maria Tatar:

> [Fairy tales] hardly aim at achieving verisimilitude and the characters are generally unlike any encountered in everyday life. As W. H. Auden wrote: "No fairy story ever claimed to be a description of the external world and no sane child ever believed that it was." The assumption that folktales faithfully record reality simply does not hold up under close scrutiny of the tales. (56)

Fairy tales, in other words, are figurative and not literal. In Buffy's world, however, as we discovered in "Killed by Death," this assumption about the figurative nature of fairy tales does not hold up. The murdered children are actually the disguise of a demon, who has appeared every fifty years since

1649 as the murdered Hans and Gerte Strauss. In the moment when the Scooby Gang discovers this, the laconic Oz succinctly provides us with the appropriate *Buffy* view of fairy tales:

> *Giles:* Now, wait a minute. There is a fringe theory held by a few folklorists that some regional stories have actual, very literal antecedents.
> *Buffy:* And in some language that's English?
> *Oz:* Fairy tales are real.

Fairy tales are real, and their reality and the crucial understanding of their demons and their magic forms, once again, is the dividing line between foolish and fooled adults and wise children. The adults who have sworn to "take Sunnydale back" are in the hands of demons. By the close of the show, the adults are preparing to burn Buffy, Willow, and their friend Amy at the stake, on a pyre fueled by occult texts. In classic ironic *Buffy* fashion, the Demon is revealed and vanquished by an occult incantation and potion. The very objects and ideas the adults have tried to eliminate have saved them.

Once again, it is the proper understanding of how to "read" a fairy tale that has delineated the difference between adults and children. Once again, it is the ability to read a fairy tale as truth, to see the very real demons that hide behind the guise of a figurative, "psychologizing" reading of a tale, that has distinguished the wise from the foolish.

As Buffy ages, however, her relationship to the categories of "child" and "adult" changes, and a fairy tale is used to signal that change as well. In the most recent of these three fairy tale episodes, "Hush," the fairy tale ceases to be a method for allying Buffy with children and opposing her to adults. After all, Buffy is on the brink of adulthood herself, no matter how ambivalent her feelings about that change may be. Therefore, the action of "Hush" centers on the virtually adult and child-free environment of a college dorm as Buffy attempts to save her peers, and the rest of Sunnydale, from The Gentlemen: fairy tale menaces who steal speech in order to keep their victims from screaming when The Gentlemen cut their hearts out.

"Hush" opens with a scene of Buffy in her psychology class, listening to a lecture on communication. The lecture quickly fades into a dream that also explores issues of communication as words are heard, half heard, overheard, and missed entirely. Awake again, Buffy returns to her daily struggles with communication. She and her new love interest, Riley, attempt to discern each other's plans for the weekend. Hampered by the fact that each of them has a secret identity that is, as yet, unknown to the other, they are unable to explain what keeps them so busy, and their conversation deteriorates into half-finished sentences and awkward pauses. Like children made awkward by their first experiences of attraction, Buffy and Riley are unable to talk to each other.

Buffy's difficulties with communication are echoed by Willow's experiences with the campus Wicca group. Despite her high expectations for the group, Willow discovers that they are a gathering of "wanna-blessed-be's" who are, as she puts it, "Talk, all talk. Blah blah Gaia. Blah blah moon." Clearly, too much talk can be as bad as not enough. The lesson is simple, of course. It is the quality and not the quantity of the communication that matters.

Buffy soon has larger communication problems to deal with, however. The Gentlemen have come to Sunnydale. As the horrified town discovers one morning, The Gentlemen steal voices. The town is paralyzed, petrified by their inability to communicate. Soon, people begin turning on one another out of frustration and fear. The price of erasable message boards skyrockets, and Sunnydale is turned upside down yet again. Not every effect of The Gentlemen is negative, however. Buffy and Riley, out trying to restore some type of order in the streets, bump into each other. Unable to dissolve into their usual incoherence, they embrace and kiss. The complete eradication of speech has permitted Buffy and Riley to find real communication. "Hush" is, however, no more a "very special *Buffy*" than any other episode of *Buffy*. We are not here merely to get a lesson about communication and to watch Buffy and Riley tentatively work out their relationship. For those viewers interested in that sort of thing, we have *Dawson's Creek*. For the rest of us, we know that nothing can be that simple and that sweet on *Buffy*. The Gentlemen are still stalking Sunnydale.

Giles's lover Olivia happens to catch sight of one of The Gentlemen as he floats past her window on the first night of The Gentlemen's killing spree. Using her sketch of the monster, Giles is able to determine what type of monster The Gentlemen are and what, exactly, they want. As he tells Buffy and her friends by scrawling on overhead transparencies,

> They are fairy tale monsters.
> What do they want?
> Hearts. [. . .]
> No sword can kill them, but the princess screamed once and they all died.

Fairy tales have entered Buffy's world again, with a vengeance. The Gentlemen come, Giles tells us, straight from a fairy tale, and we are immediately certain that Buffy is the princess who will have to save Sunnydale.

At least as important for our purposes as the fairy tale origin of The Gentlemen, however, is their appearance. The Gentlemen are elegant. Tall and slim, they wear natty, dark, three-piece suits. They glide instead of walking, hovering about six inches above the ground.[1] Their long, pale fingers make graceful gestures as they communicate silently. Their suits, their height, and their elegance all serve not only to accent the horror of their bloodthirstiness but also to contribute to the very sophisticated, adult appearance of

The Gentlemen. These monsters may be from a child's fairy tale, but they are very grown-up. Once again, the entrance of the fairy tale motif into *Buffy* has brought focus to the categories of adult and child.

Now that she is in college, however, Buffy cannot place herself as firmly in the "child" category, as she did in both "Killed by Death" and "Gingerbread." In these episodes Buffy is still in high school, and the divisions between adult and child are more precisely drawn. College, with its opportunities for living away from home, organizing one's own time, and running one's own social life, serves as a time to transition into adulthood. For Buffy, this transition is particularly complicated. As "Killed by Death" and "Gingerbread" show, many of Buffy's greatest triumphs have come as a result of her ability to ally herself with wise children and against foolish adults. Now that she is on the brink of adulthood, her positioning relative to these categories is uncertain.

Setting the action of "Hush" primarily on Buffy's college campus accents the liminality of Buffy's categorization. Though all the citizens of Sunnydale lose their voices as a result of The Gentlemen, it is the college students who are their primary prey in their search for hearts. Buffy's task, then, is not only to save Sunnydale as she has done so often before but also to save the group of people in Sunnydale who are, like her, neither children nor adults. In doing so, Buffy becomes her own category. She is neither child nor adult. She is "Slayer."

Buffy succeeds, of course, as she, Riley, Willow, and Tara (Willow's newfound fellow witch) fight off The Gentlemen. Riley breaks the box in which Sunnydale's voices have been stored, and Buffy releases a piercing shriek that makes The Gentlemen's heads explode. Sunnydale is free again. Not all the troubles are over, however. While Willow has found a like-minded Wiccan with whom she can discuss and practice magic, Buffy and Riley are still mired in their inability to communicate. Despite the revelation of each seeing the other fully armed with "Slayer" and "Initiative" gear, they have not yet had time to discuss their secrets or their feelings for each other. Even given the time and the opportunity—as they are at the end of the episode when Riley stops by Buffy's dorm room—they don't get much further:

Riley: Hi.
Buffy: Hi.
Riley: I guess we have to talk.
Buffy: I guess we do.
[long silence]
[blackout]

Having vanquished The Gentlemen and regained their voices, Buffy and Riley have, in fine television fashion, learned a very important lesson. They know that in order to transition to a more adult, more satisfying relationship, they are going to have to learn to communicate. They are going to have to find, through words, the kind of closeness and trust that led them to embrace and kiss when their voices were taken away.

However, they do not find it. Not now. Instead, the episode ends. Ending the episode here, with Buffy and Riley still mired in their inability to communicate but poised on the edge of breaking through that inability, serves to remind viewers that the transitions these characters are making are not easy. Moving from childhood to adulthood, moving from silence to communication, these are challenges as severe as any monster Buffy has had to face.

The very real monsters of *Buffy* are not the figurative creatures of fairy tales. They do not stand as symbols of things. They are things. While interactions with these monsters often aid in Buffy's growth and development, the monsters are not meant merely to "translate [. . .] psychic realities into concrete images, characters, and events" (Tatar xv). The didactic use that *Buffy* makes of fairy tales and of fairy tale materials is not, as this look at these three episodes has shown, a simple process of translation. Instead, *Buffy* inverts the traditional didactic dynamic of the fairy tale. The perceptive, reality-aware child replaces the all-knowing, storytelling adult. The gullible adult replaces the naive child in need of instruction. The monsters cannot be defanged and declawed by being called metaphors, symbols, nightmares, or childish misunderstandings of the adult world. They are real. And it is Buffy's understanding of their reality that allows her to navigate her world, to negotiate the complicated intersecting categories of "child" and "adult," and to begin her own transition into her own category of "Slayer."

NOTE

1. Editors' note: We are indebted to Derek Duke for pointing out the similarity of The Gentlemen and The Strangers in Alex Proyas's 1998 film *Dark City*.

III

Forces of Art and Imagination (Present)
Fan Relationships, Metaphoric and Real

17

Crossing the Final Taboo
Family, Sexuality, and Incest in Buffyverse Fan Fiction

Kristina Busse

One of the most fascinating and creative facets of the fan culture of *Buffy the Vampire Slayer* is fan fiction, the creative works of predominantly female fans who "poach" characters from television shows in order to tell stories that television cannot or will not tell, to explore subplots and subtexts, to expand minor characters, or simply to offer the avid fans *more* of their favorite show.[1] *Buffy* is a popular series for fan fiction writers because its suggestive subtext offers an especially apt source for the fictional creations of its fans. Generating their own version of the Buffyverse, these fans use fiction to emotionally respond to the show, comment on its plot and character development, and, most important, interpret and analyze the series, thereby teasing out its subtext. Many of the shorter fan pieces have the sole purpose of filling in the blanks, usually providing us with the characters' inner thoughts and emotions; many of the longer ones develop unconventional relationships that may be hinted at on the show but are never stated explicitly. Willow's relationship with Tara, for example, was long outed in dozens of stories before the show got bold enough to make its lesbian subtext visible. In fact, many of the insights found in fan fiction also apply to the show itself, as *Buffy*'s fan fiction writers are not only some of the series' most devoted fans but also some of its most careful readers.

At the same time, fan fiction points us toward those emotional aspects of the show that resonate most strongly with these viewers/writers, thus offering the viewer a creative outlet to contemplate the issues of the show that she responds to most emotionally. In so doing, fan fiction brings out some of the appeals of the series as it externalizes and openly displays the more repressed aspects of the show and the unconscious desires it evokes. Consequently, a discussion of fan fiction must look at the relationship between the show and the stories as well as at the meaning of the stories beyond the show. This chapter thus considers both the parts of fan fiction that explore the unconscious facets of the show and those that go beyond the show itself to reveal the unconscious desires of both readers and writers. Since fan fiction is concerned mostly with the emotional state of and the personal interaction between the characters, I have chosen to concentrate on the central but particularly volatile constellation of the family—both natural and surrogate. Particularly, I focus on the subgenre of fan fiction called "hurt-comfort," which is a particular type of story featuring a protagonist who is ill, injured, or tortured, only to be nursed back to health by one of the other characters. The intimacy achieved during the convalescence usually reveals romantic ties, often leading to sexual relations.

This chapter focuses first on the show by looking at the representation of family in order to illustrate how vampiric relations are set up as a substitute for the dysfunctional natural families. Within the Buffyverse, vampires are presented as infantilized yet highly sexualized beings whose incestuous desires suggest a pre-Oedipal existence with its lack of inhibitions and polymorphous sexuality. These incestuous concepts are most particularly manifested in vampiric hurt-comfort and its conjunction of sex and nurture with its emphasis on familial relations. Hurt-comfort addresses many of the issues that are already implicit in the show as the viewer is confronted with the characters' contradictory emotional responses to such issues as familial intimacy, sexual relations, and incestuous desires. In so doing, hurt-comfort tenuously balances the sexual and violent with the nurturing and maternal. Collapsing the role of parent and lover, the vampire explores the duality of both positions and challenges the most fundamental prohibition that defines culture at its very core: the incest taboo. Moreover, as it merges familial and sexual love, vampiric hurt-comfort epitomizes two competing and somehow incompatible moments in fan fiction in general: the maternal care that is usually ascribed to the structure of fanfic communities and the often extremely pornographic contents we find in its writings. Emphasizing the particular fantasy formations involved in hurt-comfort, the role of the vampire and the use of hurt-comfort are emblematic not only for this particular genre or mediaverse but for the contested role of women in general.

One of the main reasons fan fiction can pick up easily on incestuous familial relations is that throughout *Buffy* the family motif is extremely important. Traditional nuclear families in the Buffyverse are mostly corrupt, and among the humans the healthiest relations occur in substitute families. The three principal characters come from more or less dysfunctional homes. Buffy's parents are divorced with her father absent and uninterested; he ignores Buffy's birthday ("Helpless," 3012) and prefers a European vacation with his secretary to supporting his daughters during their mother's illness ("Family," 5006). Buffy's mother, while obviously concerned and caring, is utterly oblivious to her daughter's nocturnal activities; in fact, when she finally does learn of Buffy's secret, in "Becoming," part 2 (2022), she refuses to accept it and shortly thereafter throws her out of the house. Xander's home life is characterized by his parents' drinking and fighting and suggests neglect if not abuse ("Amends," 3010; "Restless," 4022; and "The Replacement," 5003). Willow's parents, on the other hand, simply take no interest in their daughter. During "Gingerbread" (3011), for example, Sheila Rosenberg is depicted as a detached intellectual who cannot be bothered to remember the names of Willow's friends, does not notice for almost half a year that Willow has cut her hair, and generally fails to interact with her daughter.

In its place, the teenagers create their own family structure with Buffy's watcher, Rupert Giles, as surrogate father. Throughout, Giles's loving care for the teenagers stands in glaring opposition to their biological parents' lack of concern; in fact, Buffy realizes this as she asks Giles to stand in for her father at her wedding because, she explains, "this day is about family—my real family—and I would like you to be the one to give me away" ("Something Blue," 4009). Likewise, when confronting Tara's violent and manipulative father, Buffy answers his "We are her blood kin! Who the hell are you?" with a simple "We're family" ("Family"). Moreover, we observe the group acting like a family not only with the celebration of holidays ("Pangs," 4008, and "The Body," 5016) but also in times of crisis: both during Joyce's surgery and after her death, it is Buffy's friends who are there to help and to mourn with her ("Listening to Fear," 5009, and "The Body"). *Buffy*'s spin-off *Angel* also emphasizes the value of friends as surrogate family as Cordelia, Wesley, and Angel slowly develop familial attachments. In "To Shanshu in L.A." (*Angel,* 1022), Cordelia, in fact, acknowledges this development as she reproaches Angel when he tries to hide his feeding: "Don't be embarrassed. We're family."

Similarly, *Buffy* emphasizes the alternative family structure of vampires.[2] In the first two seasons, for example, the word "family" appears more often in connection with vampiric relations than it does with human ones: both the Master and Darla repeatedly refer to their clan as family ("Welcome to the Hellmouth," 1001, and "Angel," 1007). In fact, with few exceptions, all the principal vampiric characters on both shows are descendants of the Master, a relationship further emphasized by the use of the term "siring" to describe the act of creating a vampire. Even though vampires are mostly amoral, murderous fiends, they do watch out for their own and are attached to their immediate relations. The one vampire we see at length before and after his change is Angel, and his sire is clearly put in direct opposition to his father—with his vampiric parent as caring and nurturing and his biological one as overly critical and spiteful ("The Prodigal," *Angel,* 1015). Family, the most basic human unit, is thus mimicked in the vampire clan. While the vampiric family is represented in much more intimate terms, as its family members can also be sexual partners, the relationship is still based on blood—just like in the biological family. Most vampires begin their unlife by killing their biological relations, thus severing their old ties in order to become part of their new vampiric family. This substitution is most clearly shown in "The Prodigal," where Darla approvingly watches Angelus murder his family.[3] As Darla observes her new offspring's first kills, she instantly takes over the role of the dominant parent. In fact, the lack of actual parents is overcompensated with the sire's eternal parental dominance, a dynamic also explored in "Somnambulist" (*Angel*, 1011), where Penn tells his sire, "You are my real father, Angelus." Since the vampire as a somewhat overgrown infant never outgrows his initial dependency, the internal relationships must remain regressive. The vampire can never grow up and leave the nest with an ultimate reversal of caregiving in old age as we see in human families. Instead, he is caught in an eternal, repetitive circle of sex, violence, and submission to his sire.

One of the pivotal scenes in the second season of *Buffy* occurs in "Innocence" (2014) when Angelus returns to Spike and Drusilla after having lost his soul. Drusilla, who has called her sire "Daddy" on previous occasions, excitedly exclaims, "We're family again. We'll feed. And we'll play." In turn, Angelus asserts his parental rights to both discipline and comfort as he aggressively growls at Spike, only to bend down and kiss the wheelchair-bound vampire immediately thereafter. What makes this scene so startling is the concurrency of sexuality, killing, and familial affection, pointedly exemplified in Drusilla's characterization of family as feeding and playing together. This particular scene not only reconfirms the notion of Angel as parent to both younger vampires but also intimates his sexual involvement with them. His intimate relation with Drusilla is explicitly addressed in "What's My Line?" part 2 (2010), where he offers to give Spike pointers on how to properly satisfy the female vampire, and suggested in Angelus's taunting of Spike in "Passion" (2017) and "I Only Have Eyes for You" (2019). Angel's relationship to Spike is less obvious yet remains open to interpretation, an opportunity taken up by fans who use the subtext of the show—the intense hatred, the sexual innuendoes, the history between the two vampires—in order to support their reading of Spike and Angel as involved emotionally and, most likely, physically.

Angelus's return to his family is an important moment for many Spike/Angel fanfics, that is, stories that feature a relationship between the two vampires. Other scenes that are particular favorites with writers who develop the relationship between Spike and Angel, so-called S/A shippers, are Spike's disappointment in "School Hard" (2003) on realizing that Angel is no longer a soulless demon—"You were my Sire, man. My Yoda!"—and Angel's rescue and defense of Spike when Buffy tries to stake the younger vampire in "Lovers Walk" (3008). Though these scenes seem most innocuous for the majority of *Buffy* viewers, the shippers use them to support a deep affection that supposedly underlies the apparent hostility between the two vampires. After all, in most cases the writers do not simply reinvent these characters to fit their own fantasy scenarios but rather exploit and foreground issues that are already implicit in the source text. Furthermore, while a relationship between Spike and Angel may seem unthinkable to many viewers, they are by far not the most unconventional couple in a genre in which any character has the potential to be coupled with any other.[4]

Considering that one of the most popular genres of fan fiction is the infamous slash, the romantic entanglement of two male protagonists, the choice of coupling Angel and Spike seems fitting. Slash has received more academic attention than any other aspect of fan fiction, probably both for its sexy contents as well as for its curious fascination with male couples and gay sexuality. There are a variety of theories explaining its appeal to female readers and writers. Not only do most television shows tend to invite the viewer to identify with the male heroes, often failing to provide female role models worthy of identification, but many of the relationships between the male protagonists are already presented within a homosocial environment and often with only thinly veiled homoerotic subtexts (Bacon-Smith 231–38; Jenkins 202–5).[5] A feminist approach shows how slash can depict a love between equals that does not fall prey to hierarchical notions and explores both male and female sides of the characters. In fact, most slash protagonists are depicted as straight yet inexplicably drawn to their partner-to-be, thus suggesting that the homosexual relationship actually signals a displaced idealized heterosexual one that valorizes inner compatibility, true love, and deep friendship over sexual object choices (Russ; Lamb and Veith). Finally, a psychoanalytic reading reveals the definite erotic appeal of two beautiful men making love. Moreover, this particular scenario allows an identification with and desire for both protagonists, as the female writer/reader can both *be* and *have* the attractive male and does not have to "share" with another female (Penley). Clearly, the vampiric world of *Buffy* is an especially inviting source text since vampires are not only considered hypersexual but also often regarded as bisexual and, at least in much of the fan fiction, will have sex with "anything that moves." Furthermore, the vampire has often been read as a thinly veiled symbol for homosexuality. Both are extremely dangerous to the seemingly natural order of things, especially the traditional family, as they are marked by their inability to procreate naturally and replace their biological family with an adopted one of the like-minded.[6]

Fan fiction thus easily extrapolates from Angelus's chaste kiss and threatening growl in "Innocence" and translates it into stories depicting openly sexual and violently sadomasochistic relations between the two males. In a typical story, clearly enacting hurt-comfort conventions, one of the vampires will torture the other and/or rape him, but, soon thereafter, they both realize their underlying love and affection for one another. While hurt-comfort in itself is fascinating and often quite unsettling, the particular *Buffy* version is even more so, differing from traditional hurt-comfort in its excessive use of violence and brutality. Moreover, in *Buffy* fanfic, hurt and comfort often are given out by the same character, which contradicts Bacon-Smith's observation that "hurt-comfort places the source of the injury outside of the dyad of sufferer and comforter" (255). This description, which demarcates hurt-comfort from "sadomasochistic fantasy material" (255), fails to cover the Buffyverse with its variety of fics resembling traditional sadomasochistic porn. These intensely erotic yet brutally violent stories constitute an understandable response to a show that prominently features vampires; after all, the vampire symbolically connects pleasure and pain. In fact, as the stories project the reader's and writer's sexual and sadomasochistic desires onto the male bodies of the vampires, they offer a dual displacement. It is the figure of the vampire that connects *Buffy* and hurt-comfort, as both allow readers a certain level of distance from their unconscious desires and enable them to bring into the open feelings and ideas that they cannot normally face. Twice removed, the vampiric fan fiction provides a fantasy space in which the reader can imagine her innermost wishes while projecting them onto the vampiric other.

As the figure of the vampire reveals our unconscious desires, it not only collapses sexuality and violence—eros and thanatos are rarely as closely associated as they are in vampire lore—but also alerts us to the proximity of the childlike and the sexual. The vampire is *both* a highly sexualized and a peculiarly infantlike figure, so that any relationship with and between vampires tends to collapse familial and sexual bounds. Much of the vampire's infantlike portrayal in *Buffy* fanfic comes from vampire lore in general, though it is noteworthy how the fan fiction emphasizes the familial aspects, usually asking the reader to sympathize and identify with its protagonists. Obviously, the vampire exists outside any symbolic universe that would control and regulate his behavior. As pure id, he follows his every drive and desire, not thinking—or having to think—about potential consequences. The vampire collapses the oral-cannibalistic and the anal-sadistic stage: not only does his only sustenance come from sucking as he "eats" his victims, but he also is usually portrayed as cruel, uncaring, not concerned about his environment, and unable to control his urges. His sexuality is polymorphous and not restricted to sexual organs; in fact, the neck becomes one of the primary sources of pleasure, as most vampire accounts emphasize the enjoyment derived from sucking and being sucked. Other connections are less obvious but nevertheless there: Freud describes in "The Uncanny" that most people's worst fear is to be buried alive because it is the (un)familiar reminder of the womb (244). The vampire's immortality also resonates with the timelessness ascribed to the infant's state before self-consciousness: vampires—just like babies—exist outside temporal dimensions.

Finally, the connection among vampires as well as between vampire and victim is often described in nonverbal terms, which corresponds to the prelinguistic aspects that dominate early childhood. In a particularly poignant scene in one fanfic, the writer describes feeding as an "exchange of selves" and then continues, "As he felt her essence [. . .] sing from her life's blood, he experienced her life. And could feel him giving himself to her as well" (Drexel).[7] This connection is established and increases via feeding, similar to early childhood theories that posit a link between nursing and the immediate nonverbal connection between mother and child. In a Spike/Xander fic, for example, Spike fails to establish meaningful dialogue with his lover because "vampires did a lot of their communicating non-verbally. They could detect the smallest changes in expression, pick up the subtlest changes in body scent—indicating arousal, desire, need" (Esmeralda). This extralinguistic connection is often enhanced if the blood exchange occurs during sex: in the middle of this rape-turned-seduction of Buffy by Angelus, for example, we learn that the vampire can taste his lover's every emotion as Buffy "quickly reached another peak, and he savored the difference that made in her blood" (Le Faye).

Accordingly, the vampire's feeding is often connected to sexual intercourse; in many fanfic stories, the vampire cannot climax without taking blood, and in most the bloodletting enhances the sexual experience for both: "She had known that vampires experienced pleasure in the feed. It had shocked her to learn that there could be equal pleasure for the victims. [. . .] As he began to draw on her, every nerve in her body became alive, sensitive" (Le Faye). This connection between sexuality and feeding is intimated in the episode "Graduation Day," part 2 (3022), when Buffy forces Angel to drink from her and the viewer witnesses Buffy's thinly veiled orgasmic reaction; it is made explicit in Angelus and Darla's ferocious sexual blood play in "Untouched" (*Angel*, 2004). As *Buffy* itself suggests, the deep connection between those who have shared blood often extends into their everyday lives. Buffy and Angel can sense one another ("Pangs," and "I Will Remember You," *Angel*, 1008); Drusilla knows instinctively when Angel has lost his soul ("Innocence"); Angel shares dreams with Penn, one of the vampires he sired ("Somnambulist," *Angel*, 1011); and Darla describes how she feels Angel's presence and "always could" ("Judgment," *Angel*, 2001). This permanent mental, emotional, and psychic link is invoked in numerous fan fictions, demonstrating how the lovers are irrevocably bound to one another. In Esmeralda's story, Xander laments Spike's inability to communicate, only to discover that they can circumvent talking altogether: "I can sense you [. . .] I can feel where you are, even when I can't hear or see you." This link, it turns out, is based on both blood and sex as Spike explains, "'By sharing blood, especially during sex, [vampires] tie their chosen one to them, creating a kind of bond.'"

The most intense bond, of course, is the one created during the siring process and—at least in the fan fiction—usually cemented in sex and blood.

As a result, the maternal and familial imagery, the comfort and caring, is in many stories displayed in direct conjunction and correlation to very explicit sexuality.[8] What we find here is the superimposition and often direct inter-dependence between vampiric sexuality and nurture. The connection be-tween sucking blood and suckling on the breast is recurrent throughout vampire fiction from Count Dracula's forcing Lucy to drink from his breast to Anne Rice's Louis, who compares the experience of being turned to the pleasures of sucking as an infant (Stoker 210–11; Rice 19).[9] In *Buffy*, Darla turns Angel by slicing open her chest and forcing his mouth toward the open wound ("Becoming," part 1, 2021), a gesture that Drusilla repeats when re-turning her former "grandmother" Darla in "The Trial" (*Angel*, 2009).

Fan fiction repeatedly uses the image of the vampire suckling on the breast, both as nurture and as sexual pleasure. This motif is particularly compelling in Saber Shadowkitten's "Master of Puppets," in which Buffy and Spike have a relationship that Angel has accepted but Drusilla has not. Jealous, she uses her mental powers to drive Spike insane. Buffy finds An-gel and Spike together in bed with the older vampire protectively holding the younger. Watching the two, Buffy is reminded of "a mother comforting her child." The collapse of the parental and the sexual becomes even more obvious when Buffy joins the two. Buffy and Angel are facing each other, protecting Spike, who lies between them when "Spike [. . .] began suckling her tit like a babe, quickly slicing the tender skin around her nipple so her blood flowed like a mother's milk. [. . .] He never stopped suckling her breast as he slowly pushed into her core until he was fully sheathed within her heat." Spike, who is "sandwiched" between Buffy and Angel, his sire and her former lover, resembles a nursing child lying between his parents, a familial idyll that is, of course, disrupted by the fact that in this story line all of them have been lovers at one point or another. Throughout much of the fan fiction, familial aspects are immersed in sexual ones. In another story, Willow and Buffy encounter their respective vampire lovers together, mating violently. Willow explains to Buffy and the reader the role of sex in vampiric relations as "a vampire way of reassurance and sort-of caring" and compares it to "your Mom or Dad giving you a hug" (Shadowkitten, "Elaisias"). Accordingly, sex takes the place of other comforting gestures and is used as an expression of love—whether between partners or within families. The parent/child metaphor is further underlined in the particular terminology fanfic writers employ. Though many different vampire con-texts describe the parent-vampire as *sire*, *Buffy* fanfic is singular in describ-ing the offspring as *childe*.[10]

While fan fiction unveils the more hidden meanings of the show, it is also important to look at the particular subtexts fanfic writers have chosen to ex-plore. After all, as these writers are rereading, interpreting, and amending the original text, as they are exploring and exploding the show's subtext, they are also confronting and working through the specific topics in the show that are most important to them. Consequently, fan fiction tells us something not only about the show but also about the readers and writers of the multitude of stories inhabiting and creating the Buffyverse. As these stories conflate the maternal and the sexual by sketching the supposedly nonsexual parental relations onto the highly sexualized body of the vampire, they invoke the ambiguous emotional demands of motherhood with its contradictory roles of mother and caregiver as well as partner and lover. For the mother, the dual role of the female body as both sexual object and childbearing vessel is mirrored in the psychological dual demand of maintaining intimacy with a partner while attaining an ever more immediate intimacy with the child. This schizophrenia of the body and the mind, the competing natures of physical and psychological intimacy toward partner and child, gets played out in the various incestuous relationships that the vampire can create. As the vampires enact sexual and parental relationships, they question culture's clear separation of parent and lover, most explicitly expressed in the incest prohibition. Breaking the incest taboo, society's most fundamental and founding principle, immediately marks the vampire as excluded by culture and thus, by his very existence, disrupting and questioning its rules.[11]

Thus, the coexistence of the pre-Oedipal *and* the mature sexuality is most crucial in hurt-comfort. While we constantly attempt to separate the sexual and the parental, hurt-comfort brings these issues together and forces us to admit to the sexual aspects of mothering and the parental aspects of sexuality. Accordingly, these vampiric hurt-comfort stories explore the problems that most women face when trying to negotiate the various roles they are asked to perform simultaneously by collapsing the two opposites into one, allowing their characters to be *both* nurturing and sexual. The metaphor of the vampire is singularly well fitted to address these issues, as this figure is simultaneously hypersexual yet infantlike and therefore in need of care. Similarly, hurt-comfort as a genre enacts the dual need of parental care and adult sexuality. This ambiguity is not restricted to the mutually exclusive roles of mother and lover but must be generalized to include other contradictory roles that women in general are asked to occupy. Considering the central role of the Virgin Mother in Western culture, we can easily generalize the sexual/nonsexual opposition to include both the virgin and the mother on the side of the nonsexual.[12] As a result, hurt-comfort plays out women's desire both to be sexually aggressive and to maintain their feminine and maternal qualities. This allows us to explain the appeal of hurt-comfort to a wide variety of women, not only mothers, as my discussion might suggest.[13] As vampiric hurt-comfort collapses motherhood and sexuality—intimately connected yet one of the most primal oppositions—it suggests the attempt to disintegrate categories that are imposed onto women in order to label and, ultimately, control them.

Moreover, in its collapse of the opposing ideals of the sexualized lover and the maternally caring yet virginally innocent figure, hurt-comfort epitomizes two competing and somehow incompatible moments in fan fiction in general. Within feminist criticism, fan fiction is usually seen as subversive. Confronted with writings that simultaneously explore the pre-Oedipal as well as mature sexuality, it is important to look at its feminist implications. These contradictory movements correspond with two alternative interpretations of the underlying motivations of fan fiction. On the one hand, there is the more traditional feminist approach that disregards pornography and violent sexuality in favor of a pre-Oedipal communality. Camille Bacon-Smith's ethnographic study of fan fiction, for example, is less interested in the libidinous investment that fanfic writers have in their products than she is in the community that fan fiction creates. Though she describes the cathartic element of writing, the principal psychological motivations for her are the friendships forged around fan fiction and the care and concern for one another that its members display.[14] On the other hand, an analysis such as Constance Penley's rejects the standard feminist readings of popular culture that celebrate the pre-Oedipal as the only truly feminine space. Focusing on the exclusively male scenario of slash, she shows how women identify in fan fiction with any number of characters in a variety of ways. Emphasizing the role of fantasy in these identifications, Penley reveals the various means—both consciously and unconsciously—by which women use fan fiction to derive pleasure.

Of course, as this discussion of its exemplary subgenre hurt-comfort has shown, fan fiction is always both: it constructs fantasies as a means of identification at the same time that it provides communal comfort. The connection between the parental and the sexual indicates a tension played out not only in many hurt-comfort stories but also in the very structure of fan fiction itself. In its form and contents, adult fan fiction simulates the opposites of the maternal and the sexual: the structure of fanfic communities and the relationship between the writers is extremely supportive and nurturing, while the products of this nurture are often texts with no little resemblance to hard-core porn. Reading hurt-comfort allows the negotiation of two feminist approaches to fan fiction since it is the competing roles that women are asked to perform that is one of the crucial psychological motivations and achievements of fan fiction. As a result, fanfic writers are neither a feminist version of scribbling ladies nor wanton pornographers but women who attempt to negotiate different roles and demands in their lives—both *within* the fiction and in the process of its production.

NOTES

For Saber, without whom I would have never gotten addicted to Buffy fanfic, and Nymue, my guide to the intricacies of fandom and fanfic writing.

1. For discussions on fan fiction culture, see Jenkins, Bacon-Smith, and Penley. Even though it is restricted to *Xena: Warrior Princess,* Boese's dissertation is singular in its treatment of the on-line phenomenon of fan fiction. For *Buffy* fan fiction, see *Slayer's Fanfic Archive,* the largest archive for non–NC-17 stories, as well as *Sonja Marie's Buffy Fanfiction Links.*

2. As Wood and others have pointed out, the vampire mythology changes dramatically with Anne Rice. Whereas earlier vampire fiction focused on the humans, with the vampire as dangerous outsider, Rice shifts our identification onto the vampires, who have become tragic creatures, troubled and self-doubting. For an excellent discussion of the family motif in Rice's Vampire Trilogy, see Doane and Hodges. In general, beginning with the 1980s, vampire film and fiction have been distinguished by their strong emphasis on family and family values. For a discussion, see Auerbach and Nixon.

3. I follow fandom terminology in referring to Angel with a soul as Angel, without one as Angelus, even though the shows themselves do not always distinguish that clearly.

4. For an impressive sampling of nonconventional relationships, see *UCSL.*

5. For a discussion of the pervasive role of "male homosocial desire" in the American and British novel, respectively, see Fiedler and Sedgwick. For an adaptation of Fiedler's theories to fan fiction, see Selley.

6. For the seminal article on using the vampire as a figure for queerness, see Case.

7. Even though my selections cannot be comprehensive and may reveal my own preferences, they are representative of certain motifs I have encountered repeatedly.

8. Among the crucial essays on vampires and sexuality are those by Astle, Roth, and Stevenson. For an analysis of sexuality in more recent vampire fiction and its relationship to S/M, see Bosky. For a discussion of the incest motif in vampire fiction, see Twitchell.

9. For a connection between vampires and breastfeeding, see Gordon.

10. The term apparently originated with the role-playing game *Vampires: The Masquerade,* which spawned the short-lived Spelling series *Kindred: The Embraced* (1996).

11. Beyond its cultural role, the incest taboo constitutes one of the primary fantasies in psychoanalysis and is thereby integral to the construction of our fantasy space. For an introduction to the relation of fantasy and sexuality, see Laplanche and Pontalis.

12. For an excellent account of the role of the Virgin Mother in Western culture that thematizes as well as performs the semiotic/symbolic split, see Kristeva.

13. In my reading, however, I noticed that the authors of NC-17 fics and hurt-comfort seemed to be, on the whole, slightly older than some of the other writers.

14. In the on-line culture, examples of this include the help that writers give one another as so-called beta readers, the writing of fanfics as presents or to cheer up another member of the community, as well as the deep emotional friendships many writers create on and off lists.

18

"My Boyfriend's in the Band!"
Buffy *and the Rhetoric of Music*

S. Renee Dechert

Excuse me. Who gave *you* permission to exist?

—Cordelia, to Willow in "Welcome to the Hellmouth" (1001)

In "Welcome to the Hellmouth" (1001), Joss Whedon lays the foundation for *Buffy the Vampire Slayer* in terms of characters, monsters, mythology, and themes. A consistent "monster" that Buffy and the rest of the Scooby Gang[1] encounter is the same one faced everywhere by high school students (past, present, and future): alienation. Cordelia's comment to Willow sums up the power structure at Sunnydale High—clearly, Willow and those like her are on the outside. In the course of *Buffy,* the Scoobies learn that they do not need Cordelia to grant them existence, that they can find a place for themselves in the margins and do more there—for others and for themselves—than they ever could in the center. It is a liberating discovery as they realize that together they are, indeed, quite powerful, even though they are marginalized.

One factor that ties the Gang together is a shared love of popular music, and in this, the Scoobies are no different than typical teens. As Andrew Ross writes, "The level of attention and meaning invested in music by youth is still unmatched by almost any other organized activity in society, including religion. As a daily companion, social bible, commercial guide and spiritual source, youth music is still *the* place of faith, hope, and refuge" (3). Music is almost omnipresent on *Buffy,* appearing either in the background to enhance a scene, such as the song "No Heroes" when Joyce drops Buffy off at school on her first day, or as an essential component of the plot, like the Flamingos' "I Only Have Eyes for You" (2019) in an episode named for the song. One of the Gang's favorite hangouts is The Bronze, with its parade of (generally) unknown bands—and nothing makes Willow feel more socially validated than her relationship with Dingoes Ate My Baby guitarist Oz; then, she's able to beam confidently, "My boyfriend's in the band!" ("Bewitched, Bothered and Bewildered," 2016).

Simply put, music is at the heart of the Scooby Gang and *Buffy*. Indeed, it functions as a form of rhetorical discourse every bit as important as the lines characters speak. M. Jimmie Killingsworth and Michael K. Gilbertson have defined discourse as "the means by which communities develop and advance their agendas of action, build solidarity, patrol and extend their boundaries, and perpetuate themselves in the life of a general culture" (162). Clearly, the music on *Buffy* meets this definition because it provides a common "language" for characters and fans. John King, music supervisor for *Buffy* and *Angel*, describes how he selects the shows' music: "I get a script and think, what would this character listen to in this particular instance? I figure out the subtext" (Ostrow H01). That is, as Joanne Ostrow explains, King "listens for what is 'musically or lyrically significant,' but usually picks songs based on the vibe, not the literal meaning" (H01).

Buffy uses popular music in three primary ways—and the first two are fairly common to television, though *Buffy* always manages to give the show's music a uniquely Whedonesque spin. First, popular music contributes to the mood of various scenes, providing a thematic backdrop. Second, music is used to establish the identities of characters as well as to chart their growth. Finally, music works to reinforce the communal identity between the program, *Buffy*, and its fans, all of whom exist on the fringe of mainstream network television. (As the 2000 and 2001 Emmy nominations revealed, with the exception of Whedon's 2000 nomination for writing, *Buffy* was once again overlooked in favor of more traditional fare such as *The Practice* and *ER*.) In this chapter, I'll briefly discuss the first two topics before turning to the third, for *Buffy*'s use of music as a rhetorical tool in forging a relationship between the program and its fans is a unique one. (This point is reinforced with the 1999 release of *Buffy the Vampire Slayer: The Album*, a disc featuring the music of artists who had appeared on the show—and all sixteen tracks were handpicked by Joss Whedon.)

"IF YOU'D LISTEN": MUSIC AS A THEMATIC BACKDROP

In "Go Fish" (2020), "If You'd Listen," by Nero's Rome, plays in the background as Buffy keeps an eye on monster-in-training Gage. This is good advice to viewers because careful listening reveals that, like any program, *Buffy* employs music to establish and reinforce the mood of scenes, sometimes ironically, sometimes seriously. Consider "Bewitched, Bothered and Bewildered," as Xander enters the school to the Average White Band's "Got the Message" in a clear parody of John Travolta's famous strut in *Saturday Night Fever.* Or there's the ironic use of Patsy Cline's "I Fall to Pieces" as Xander moons over Buffy in "Prophecy Girl" (1012). (As Xander says after his rejection by the Slayer, "I'm just going to go home, lie down, and listen to country music, the music of pain.") The tone is not always ironic, however. For instance, at the end of season 2, there's the haunting "Full of Grace," by Sarah McLachlan, that plays as an older, wiser Buffy leaves Sunnydale. The Dashboard Prophets' "Ballad for Dear Friends" creates the background atmosphere in "The Harvest" (1002) as a group of vampires dramatically descends on The Bronze. And in "When She Was Bad" (2001), Allison Krauss and Union Station's "It Doesn't Matter" is not only aesthetically appropriate but also historically fitting given the band's bluegrass "High Lonesome" sound, which reinforces the episode's theme: the importance of community, that it *does* indeed matter.

At times, *Buffy*'s use of music as a thematic device is more overt. For example, in the previously mentioned "I Only Have Eyes for You," the Flamingos' song dominates the program, driving the plot and reinforcing the complexity of Buffy and Angel's relationship. Similarly, Cibo Matto's "Sugar Water" plays as Buffy teases Xander with her dancing—an act designed to hurt Angel—in "When She Was Bad." In each case, the music's role as a motivational force is front and center.

In stark contrast is "The Body" (5016) from season 5, an episode without music (with the exception of the theme song) as the Gang copes with Joyce's death. Suddenly common sounds—wind chimes, street traffic—are magnified, and the story becomes more real. There is no score to tell the audience how to feel; in the same way, Buffy and her friends struggle to understand.

Music also, literally, provides a visual backdrop for *Buffy.* When bands appear at The Bronze, there is generally a sign in the background giving their name. And as any close watcher of the show knows, the settings of Sunnydale High and Sunnydale University consistently display, along with Sunnydale High Razorback murals and placards for pep rallies, book clubs, and assemblies, posters of relatively unknown bands, even though the bands' music may not make an appearance on the program. For instance, posters for Widespread Panic, the Backsliders, Whiskeytown, and Greg Ginn have cropped up on *Buffy.* Such an action, again, reinforces how inherent music is to the identity of these characters, just as Ross has noted—it shows that music is as important to their lives as the other activities traditionally associated with growing up. Moreover, it also suggests a bit of humor—and musical taste—on the part of the set design crews.

"I'LL REMEMBER YOU": MUSIC AS A CHARACTER ELEMENT

In the closing moments of "Angel" (1007), the inclusion of Sophie Zelmani's "I'll Remember You" foreshadows a key element of Buffy and Angel's relationship: their enduring love despite the obstacles they will face—that they will remember each other. Similarly, linking music to characters helps the viewer "remember," indeed see, characters more clearly. *Buffy* has always used music to establish characters. Early in the series, for example, "Teacher's Pet" (1004) opens with Xander's rock-and-roll fantasy. As Xander dusts a troublesome vamp at The Bronze, an enraptured Buffy watches. After the fight, she exclaims, "You hurt your hand! Will you still be able to . . . ?" "Finish my solo, and kiss you like you've never been kissed before?" concludes Xander with the confidence reserved for rock stars, professional athletes, and Cordelia. Then he jumps onstage and whips out a Hendrixesque guitar solo while an awed Buffy looks up at him. (The camera angle further empowers Xander here, shooting up at him as he stands above the crowd, the light outlining his phallic guitar and empowered—and fashionably dressed—body.)

But given the nature of Xander's life, the moment has to end, and so it does as Buffy awakens Xander in class to tell him that he is drooling. Later, as Xander makes his way to the stage of The Bronze, the lead singer of Superfine looks down at him and grimaces. This is Xander's reality. His guitar fantasy also provides a contrast with Oz, a real guitarist who is far removed from the stereotypical "Guitar God" of Xander's dream. Additionally, the laconic Oz, always clad in a bowling shirt or a T-shirt that practically defines cool, refuses to use his status as lead guitarist when it comes to meeting women. But his association with music helps define his character.

Another good example appears later in the series. When Buffy first meets her demonic college roommate Kathy Newman, we know instantly, as she hangs up her Celine Dion poster while perkily predicting the year will be "Superfun!" that this is no typical coed. And our worst fears are confirmed in the next episode, "Living Conditions" (4002), when Kathy plays Cher's "Do You Believe in Love" repeatedly. Who but a monster could endure that? As Willow moves into Buffy's room at the end of the program, she brings with her a poster for the much cooler Dingoes Ate My Baby. The Dingoes may be unknown, but they sure beat a battery of primped and padded VH1 divas. That is, we know that Buffy is back with friends, and one illustration of this is their shared love of music.

Perhaps no character is more clearly defined (and developed) via music than Giles. Initially, one way in which *Buffy* highlights the generational difference between the Scoobies and Giles is through music. Consider Giles's comments in "The Dark Age" (2008) as Buffy works out to some electronica: "I know music. Music has notes. This is noise." When Buffy replies, "I'm aerobicizing. I *must* have the beat," Giles answers, "Wonderful. You work on your muscle tone while my brain dribbles out of my ears." At this point, the characters seem to have a fairly typical generation gap, a point reinforced by their varied musical tastes.

But Giles is soon revealed to be more than the stereotypical stodgy librarian addicted to Mozart; rather, he is a former British punk with a sizable collection of classic rock vinyl. Ironically, later in "The Dark Age," we see a picture of a leather-clad Giles/Ripper playing bass in a band. (Anthony Stewart Head revealed on *Fully Booked* that the photo is the actor's head superimposed on the body of legendary bad boy/Sex Pistol Sid Vicious [qtd. in Topping 99]. Such an action again calls attention to *Buffy*'s careful—and parodic—use of music.) Similarly, in "Band Candy" (3006), the awakened punk—clad in jeans, T-shirt, and Doc Martens (gone is the tweed)—lies on the floor of his apartment, smoking and listening to Cream's "Tales of Brave Ulysses." "This is the best bit," he tells Joyce as Eric Clapton's solo starts. "Man, I've *got* to get a band together!" Joyce is revealed to be considerably more square, asking an annoyed Ripper if he likes Seals & Crofts. (It is worth noting that these memories echo into season 5's "Forever," 5017, as we watch the Scoobies after Joyce's funeral. The scene opens with a close-up of a turntable, then the camera pulls back to reveal that Giles has just put on some music. Pensively, he walks to a chair while drinking and watching the record spin, and it becomes clear that the song playing is "Brave Ulysses." That is, Giles mourns Joyce by listening to music that he links with their shared past—and the viewer is encouraged to make the same connection. It is another way in which music creates communities on *Buffy*.)

In season 4, these elements of Giles's character coalesce as we are treated to his moving acoustic performances at a local coffeehouse—in one case of Lynyrd Skynyrd's much-maligned southern rock aria "Free Bird" ("Where the Wild Things Are," 4018). Clearly, Joss Whedon never loses his sense of irony.[2]

These strategies, while integral to the tone and theme of *Buffy* and Whedon's vision, are not unique to television. However, the way in which music solidifies the *Buffy* community bears further examination.

"BRING ME ON": MUSIC AS A UNIFYING DEVICE FOR THE *BUFFY* COMMUNITY

While Act of Faith's "Bring Me On" may be reduced to background music as Xander is hazed at a frat party in "Reptile Boy" (2005), *Buffy*'s inclusion of music is front and center, effectively bringing fans in to the Scooby Gang. But before considering how *Buffy* uses music to solidify its community of viewers, it is important to understand how the WB network has utilized popular music in all its dramas—and how *Buffy* strayed from its WB siblings, especially *Dawson's Creek, Felicity,* and *Roswell.*

At the end of most WB dramas (*Buffy* and *Angel* are exceptions) appears what the industry refers to as a "card," a five-second promotional spot consisting of a brief sample of the song incorporated into the program as well as a shot of the album's cover. While *Buffy* is credited with employing the first card, at the start of the second season (1997) with an ad for Cibo

Matto (more on this in a moment), the idea took off with the January 1998 premiere of *Dawson's Creek* and its use of Paula Cole's "I Don't Want to Wait." The relationship between the program and the singer was mutually beneficial. As Manuel Mendoza reports, playing Cole's song "helped generate advance buzz, including radio DJs referring to the song as *Dawson's* theme" (C13). Meanwhile, sales of Cole's album jumped by two-thirds (C13). Similarly, Madonna's "Power of Good-Bye," used on *Felicity,* became a hit, and *Felicity*'s and *Dawson's Creek*'s inclusion of two Heather Nova songs during a one-week period in October 1998 led to an almost 600 percent increase in sales of an album that before had been relatively unknown (Chetwynd 3D).

Clearly, the relationship between television and popular music is a lucrative one, especially given that WB programs are encouraged to utilize music recorded on WB-related labels, blurring the relationship between art and commercialism. All programs are quick to point out, however, that a band's label is never a determining factor when it comes to deciding whether a song will be included on a program. Lewis Goldstein, copresident of the WB's marketing department, has said of the process, "It was synergistic in that it was members of our company. [. . .] It wasn't meant to be just Warner Bros. We knew it would be easier to get things to happen quickly in the family than if we went out-of-house. But in no way was it ever intended to keep it in the family" (qtd. in Ostrow H01). (It is worth noting that when programs use WB-related music, they save $3,000 to $10,000 per song on licensing fees.) Furthermore, as J. J. Abrams, screenwriter and an executive producer of *Felicity,* notes, "If you're feeling annoyed by [the use of cards], I would remind you that if that little card is actually something that helps the show get made, I wouldn't resent that any more than a commercial between the acts of the show. [. . .] We can't make the show for free. We need sponsors" (qtd. in Mendoza C13).

Buffy uses popular music a bit differently. Even though *Buffy* employed the first card, the program, generally speaking, eschews them. In all five seasons, *Buffy* has used cards five times: for the previously mentioned Cibo Matto (interestingly, Cibo Matto is the only band to get "name checked," mentioned several times by Xander and Willow in "When She Was Bad"); Sisters of Mercy's "Never Land" in "Lie to Me" (2007)[3]; Third Eye Blind's "The Background" in "Faith, Hope and Trick" (3003); Lori Carson's "Fell into the Loneliness" in "Homecoming" (3005); and a fall 1999 promotional spot for the *Buffy* sound track. According to Joanne Ostrow, Joss Whedon "has abandoned the practice, saying it takes time out and hurts the dramatic impact and integrity of the show" (H01).

In fact, because of this, it can be difficult to find information on bands featured on *Buffy.* If you want a comprehensive listing of the bands that have provided *Buffy* music, you will have to do your homework. Rather than visit the official *Buffy* Web site or WB pages, fans are best served by going to the outstanding fan site *Buffy: The Music Pages* (<http://www.geocities.com/Hollywood/Lot/8864/music.htm>). In doing this, the clear message is that *Buffy,* unlike other WB shows, is an independent program with the same ethos as an independent record label, more interested in art than advertising. Unlike, say, *Dawson's Creek, Buffy* is not selling out. It suggests that *Buffy* viewers are smarter than the "*Creek*ers," people who must be told what they have just seen in an overt promotional strategy.

Moreover, *Buffy* tends to favor lesser-known bands. While known artists like Sarah McLachlan, Garbage, Lou Reed, David Bowie, and others have provided material, the show prides itself on working primarily with relatively unknown artists. John King explains, "We established early on, because we were a nobody show and we were usually denied [music] licenses, that we would go to the local music scene and use unsigned artists" (qtd. in Ostrow H01). That is, the very selection of artists who provide music for the program is in keeping with the thematic center of *Buffy.* An obvious case in point is Nerf Herder, the group that performs "Buffy's Theme." Similarly, Four Star Mary, the band that provides the music for "Dingoes Ate My Baby," is fairly anonymous, and when is the last time you heard Mad Cow on the radio, saw Bif Naked on MTV, or ran across Darling Violetta on the cover of *Rolling Stone*? Joss Whedon has noted that he likes giving unknown bands attention: "I like hiring unsigned bands because they're cheap. [. . .] No, not really. A lot of great bands just don't get enough exposure. And for some reason, all these bands sent in tapes of music for us to use" (qtd. in Tracy 155). Indeed, some of these artists receive overt exposure because of their appearances at The Bronze; furthermore, some were included on the *Buffy* sound track. All this suggests a very indie attitude: supporting those in the margins.

This relatively unknown music works on a number of levels. First, selecting unfamiliar musicians enhances the program's sense of community, a concept directly tied to the show's strong Internet presence. As Keith Topping has observed, "*Buffy the Vampire Slayer* is TV's first *true* child of the Internet age. [. . .] *Buffy* not only saw its fans embrace the new technology to (articulately) spread the gospel, but the Net itself became a part of the series' iconography. Within weeks of *Buffy*'s beginning, a flourishing Net-fan community had spawned newsgroups, posting boards and websites" (268). In fact, Joss Whedon regularly uses the official *Buffy* chat room—fittingly called The Bronze—to communicate with fans, and the *Buffy* community took the radical and very community-oriented action of forming an "Internet blackout" in the spring of 2000, a strike protesting the WB's lack of support for individual fan pages.

The music helps bring together the cyber-community of *Buffy* fans: it is another shared basis for communication. As Ostrow notes, "Now *Buffy* fans expect to discover new music via the shows each week" (H01). Come Wednesday morning, a common question on the *Buffy* message boards will ask if anyone knows the name of an artist who performed on the previous night's show. Moreover, music packs an emotional punch that transcends language; it enhances the experience at another level. All these elements are part of the *Buffy* discourse. What this means is that fans of this music belong to a smaller, more hip community—the fan base of Four Star Mary is certainly smaller and more intimate than that of 'N Sync. This lack of overt band promotion provides *Buffy* viewers with something else to talk about, something to learn about, something to bring them closer together as an "outsider" community. It becomes, "Well, we know who 12-Volt Sex is— they were on *Buffy* last night. Most people don't know this because they only listen to popular bands—like Matchbox TWENTY."

Second, *Buffy* encourages artists to submit their own music for possible inclusion on the show. According to *The Watcher's Guide,* "The post-production department has a policy of listening to every demo sent to them. They are particularly delighted when they find songs from up-and-coming groups to help them get exposure" (Golden and Holder 296). Such a populist approach further contributes to the formation of *Buffy's* community. That is, you do not have to be Stone Temple Pilots or Macy Gray to have your band on *Buffy*. Additionally, the fact that, according to the WB, the *Buffy* music crew listens to all tapes it receives adds to the audience's sense of empowerment and belonging; after all, that could be *your* band on the stage of The Bronze, hanging out with the Scooby Gang.

Significantly, this rhetoric ties in with the dominant theme of *Buffy,* a program that has always been about those who are different, who do not "fit." Like the characters, these unknown bands do not "fit" either—at least not yet. The music is a way of solidifying the community of *Buffy* watchers, all fans of a show that cannot seem to garner mainstream acceptance. Keith Topping has written, "The characters in *Buffy* are characters that we empathize with, because we were all once like them. Outsiders" (262).

"MY WAY": THE *REAL* SCOOBY GANG

One of *Buffy's* great musical moments takes place at the end of "Lovers Walk" (3007), as a rejuvenated Spike drives out of Sunnydale, enthusiastically singing along with Sid Vicious's cover of "My Way."[4] Of course, the joke of Vicious's cover has always been his appropriation of a song generally considered the territory of mainstream icon Frank Sinatra. Vicious's wonderfully parodic version is perfect for Spike, the stereotypical British punk with his Billy Idol look, tough talk, and love of violence, who has always

done things his way—and also for *Buffy,* a show that continues to defy the
"rules" of network television, to do things "her way."

While Spike is, generally, a loner, he too understands the occasional need
for community; his first alliance with Buffy, albeit a brief one, bears examining. In "Becoming," part 2 (2022), a desperate Buffy, with her new friend
Spike, frantically searches to find an excuse that will explain her behavior
to her mother. Fittingly enough, she falls back on every teen's fantasy:

> *Joyce:* Buffy, terrible things have happened. What were you doing?
> *Spike:* What? Your mom doesn't know?
> *Joyce:* Know what?
> *Buffy:* That I'm [quick pause] in a band, a rock band with Spike here.
> *Spike:* Right. She plays the . . . the triangle. . . .
> *Buffy:* —Drums!
> *Spike:* Uh, drums, yeah. She's hell on the old skins.
> *Joyce:* And what do you do?
> *Spike:* Well, I sing.

While they are working together for a larger common goal, a point reinforced by their ability to collaborate on an impromptu narrative, music
provides a cover for their being together. That Spike sings, by the way, is
appropriate. After all, he is never shy about saying what he thinks. And
Buffy fans have never been a silent crew either. They're a wonderfully active community, engaged in a vibrant, dynamic dialogue. This conversation between *Buffy* and its fans takes place to a sound track of (largely)
unknown bands also on the outside. Like Willow, the viewer gets a sense
of belonging, of being "in the band."

NOTES

1. Significantly, like Buffy and her friends, the original Scooby Gang was also a
marginalized community, always snooping around where the police did not want
them to—and then outsmarting the police by solving the case—so the Buffy team
builds on a great tradition.

2. In the fall of 2001, look for Anthony Stewart Head to release his first CD—
with contributions from some of the *Buffy* cast. At another level, then, music connects fans with *Buffy.*

3. This song appeared on the program's first transmission. Then, because of
copyright problems, it was removed and replaced with "Blood of a Stranger," by
Shawn Clement and Sean Murray.

4. Actually, it is Gary Oldman's *Sid and Nancy* cover of Sid's version. Certainly,
the *Buffy* writers' comments about Spike and Drusilla are relevant here. Marti
Noxon observes, "We always said the inspiration was Sid [Vicious] and Nancy
[Spungen]" (qtd. in Golden, Bissette, and Sniegoski 108).

19

Buffy's Mary Sue Is Jonathan
Buffy *Acknowledges the Fans*

Justine Larbalestier

Several episodes of *Buffy the Vampire Slayer* acknowledge active fans of the show, their on-line discussions, and the fan fiction that they write. These episodes acknowledge the complex relationship between fan and professionally produced *Buffy* texts. The five such episodes I will examine are "The Wish" (3009), "Doppelgängland" (3016), "Something Blue" (4009), "Superstar" (4017), and "Restless" (4022). The relationship between the producers of the authorized *Buffy* texts and the fans is mixed; while most of these episodes play with fannish engagement, "Superstar" is more ambiguous and can be read as a parody of a particular set of fan rewritings of the show.

Joss Whedon and others involved with the creation of *Buffy* follow fan discussion and interaction with the show. They have a presence on-line, having participated in discussion on The Bronze—the official fan posting board (<http://www.buffy.com/slow/index_bronzepb.html>): "Thanks for listening and watching and caring. What you say on the board does affect the cast and crew of Buffy land" (Amber Benson, The Bronze, February 27, 2001). Whedon has hinted at The Bronze about what is to come on the show. For example, Whedon responded to fan speculation about the relationship between Willow and Tara:

> Willow and Tara's relationship is definitely romantic. [. . .] Thorny subject; the writers and I have had long [talks] about how to deal with the subject responsibly, without writing a story that sounds like people spent a long time discussing how to deal with it responsibly. To me it feels just right. All the relationships on the show are sort of romantic (hence the [Bring Your Own] subtext principle) and this feels like the natural next step for [Willow]. [. . .] We're not going to do an *Ally* [*McBeal*] or *Party of Five* in which we promote

the hell out of a same-sex relationship for exploitation value that we take back by the end of the [episode] [. . .] I just know there's a sweet story there, that would become very complicated if Oz were to show up again. (Golden, Bissette, and Sniegoski 172)

Whedon discusses not only future events (yes, Oz does return) and how they are handled but also the ways in which fans are responding to the show when he says, "hence the [Bring Your Own] subtext principle" (Golden, Bissette, and Sniegoski 172). *Buffy* is a show that runs on subtext so that it frequently becomes text. This makes the kind of "poaching" activities that Henry Jenkins discusses even more complex. How do you poach a show that poaches itself, i.e., that has stand-alone episodes that appear to ignore the general arc of the show and play on the "what if" scenarios beloved of fan fiction?

READING *BUFFY*

In a sense, every episode of *Buffy* after the pilot[1] actively acknowledges the fans and invites a specialized reading. This extends beyond the repertoire of knowledge of events and characters that every serial, from *The Brady Bunch* to *Days of Our Lives* or *The Sopranos,* requires. Like *The Simpsons,* *Buffy* has developed its own visual and linguistic style, a language that the fans become fluent in, as I have found when trying to introduce other people to *Buffy.* Initially, I would show them the current episode. The response would often be bewilderment. They would say things like "They talk funny" and "Why are you laughing?" This last question would involve explanations such as "Well the rat is actually Amy" or "They used that exact same shot in an earlier episode" or "They always unpack metaphors to the nth degree." My friends would look at me oddly. One said, "So you're saying that if you haven't watched every single episode since the year dot, this show makes no sense at all?" I can't be saying that because the show garners new fans all the time, and I have successfully introduced some friends to it. What they all say is that the more they see of the show, the more pleasure they find in it. Typically those who have gotten the bug borrow and beg what earlier episodes they can and read the on-line guides to increase their reading repertoire.[2] The more they know of the back stories and the debates around them, the more pleasurable the show becomes.

MESSING WITH THE SHOW: BAD WILLOW

Some ways of reading the show are dependent not only on familiarity with previous episodes but also on participation in *Buffy* fandom. This can range from speculating about the show with your friends to being part of an on-line discussion group to reading and writing fanfic: fan-authored stories that take place within the *Buffy* universe, or Buffyverse. The scope for speculation within the Buffyverse is much greater than that of nonfantastic serials because, of course, almost anything is possible. In this way, *Buffy* fandom has a great deal in common with *Xena* fandom[3] and with the very first media fandom, *Star Trek*. "The Wish," "Doppelgängland," and "Something Blue" provide responses to fan speculative scenarios: what if vampires ruled Sunnydale and Willow and Xander were vamps? What if the Vamp Willow and the good Willow were to meet? What if Buffy and Spike were engaged? These episodes acknowledge the fun that fans have playing in the *Buffy* universe by putting seemingly impossible scenarios on the screen while at the same time reasserting control by making those scenarios part of the official *Buffy* universe.

"The Wish" takes place after Cordelia and Xander's breakup. Everyone knows that Xander has cheated on Cordelia with Willow; Cordelia is not only hurt but humiliated. A vengeance demon (or, as Cordelia sees her, "a good fairy. A scary, veiny, good fairy"), Anya/Anyanka, grants Cordelia's wish that "Buffy Summers had never come to Sunnydale." The minute the wish is granted, Cordelia finds herself in Sunnydale, where the students dress in subdued colors, there is a curfew, and the Master, arch-villain of season 1, rules the town. Willow and Xander are leather-clad vampires—much cooler than they ever were as humans; there is no Scooby Gang, just a small, desperate group, including Oz and Giles, fighting a rearguard action. Throughout the episode, all the cast regulars, except Giles, are killed; each death plays on the various characters' relations in the "normal" world of Sunnydale. Cordelia, who seems at first to be the episode's focus, is killed about halfway through in an erotic triptych by the two who recently betrayed her, Willow and Xander, while Giles watches helplessly from within the book cage. The rest of the deaths happen during the climactic confrontation between the resistors and the Master and his minions: Xander, always uneasy around Angel, kills him; Buffy then kills Xander; Oz kills his girlfriend Willow, and the Master kills Buffy—for the second time—by snapping her neck, echoing Angelus's murder of Jenny Calendar.

At first the episode works as a knowingly jokey take on the normal *Buffy* world—what fun: Xander and Willow dressed in Goth gear, looking cool. This playfulness disappears, however, and "The Wish" becomes one of the darkest of *Buffy* episodes. The moment Vamp Xander and Vamp Willow kill Cordelia—without remorse and with visible pleasure—the tone of the episode shifts, climaxing in the scene where the cast regulars are killed in slow motion with haunting music underneath. I did not expect (as someone who avoids spoilers) to see everyone die. I have seen this episode many times, and each time I am affected; tears form in my eyes. The slide from comic and wry to serious is typical: "For all that these matchups are often played for comic effect, they are at least as often played, as Whedon notes, in almost embarrassingly deadly earnest. Most often it's both" (Udovitch 66).

There is a vicarious pain/pleasure in "The Wish." On the one hand, there is the play of seeing such erotically charged and assured versions of the normally uncool Willow and Xander.[4] On the other hand, they are monsters, killers who take pleasure in torture, both psychological (killing Cordelia in front of Giles's eyes) and physical (Willow's treatment of her "puppy" Angel). The result of a world in which Vamp Willow and Vamp Xander exist is the death of Cordelia, Willow, Xander, Angel, and Buffy.

Vamp Willow returns in "Doppelgängland." *The Monster Book* claims that fan reaction to Vamp Willow played some part in that return: "It didn't hurt that fans loved the sexy, evil vampire Willow, and wanted to see her again" (Golden, Bissette, and Sniegoski 137). Where "The Wish" was searing, "Doppelgängland" is playing with "The Wish" and fan expectation in less painful ways though the episode begins with a discussion of Faith between Willow and Buffy: Willow assures Buffy that "some people just don't have that in them"—that is, that Buffy could never be the cold-blooded killer that Faith has become. In the alternate reality of "The Wish" however, that is exactly what Buffy had become—her modus operandi is to kill first and ask questions later. Like Faith.

When Vamp Willow arrives in the normal continuum of the Buffyverse, she is as confused and disconcerted by the new world as Cordelia was when thrust into the alternate reality of a Sunnydale without its Slayer. The two are directly paralleled: in "The Wish," Cordelia, increasingly anxious, walks along the dark main street of Sunnydale emptied of humans by the curfew; in "Doppelgängland," Vamp Willow takes the same stroll, the street is full of color and humans, and Vamp Willow's confusion is as marked as Cordelia's. She makes her way to The Bronze: the contrast in her demeanor as she walks around The Bronze to that of Willow is marked. Vamp Willow regards everyone she sees in an overtly sexual way; she is assured and powerful.

Later, Vamp Willow is locked into the book cage in another parallel to "The Wish"—only this time it is the vampire who is tortured by Cordelia with her one-sided discussion of "the ethics of boyfriend stealing":

> *Cordelia:* Okay, it wasn't even like I was that attracted to Xander, it was more just that we kept being in these life or death situations and that's always sexy and stuff. I mean I more or less knew he was a loser but that doesn't make it okay for you to come round and—what? Do I have something on my neck?
>
> *Vamp Willow:* Not yet.

This brings to mind just what was on Cordelia's neck in "The Wish" when Vamp Willow was on the other side of the cage. This time there is little pathos as Cordelia examines her neck looking for a zit.

In "Doppelgängland," too, the Scooby Gang are given a glimpse of the alternate reality that was erased by the smashing of Anya/Anyanka's ring.

Willow is allowed to see how she would be were she bad:

> *Willow:* It's horrible! That's me as a vampire? I'm so evil and . . . skanky. And I think I'm kinda gay.
> *Buffy:* Willow, just remember, a vampire's personality has nothing to do with the person it was.
> *Angel:* Well, actually [looking like he's going to contradict Buffy then changing his mind] . . . That's a good point.

And with the introduction of Tara in "Hush" (4010), there is further evidence that Angel is right—there is a connection between a vampire's personality and the person he or she once was—for Willow, it turns out, *is* "kinda gay."

"SOMETHING BLUE"—BUFFY/SPIKE

In "Something Blue," *Buffy* plays on the genre of fan fiction known as slash fiction. Slash fiction—so called because of the slash between the two characters linked—is fanfic in which two characters not explicitly romantically or sexually linked in a show are brought together. Originally a *Star Trek* phenomenon, the first slashed pair was Kirk/Spock (Bacon-Smith; Russ). The earliest examples of the genre were all same-sex couples and were a means of opening up the universe of the show—*Star Trek* was a heterosexual universe; slashing highlighted the unspoken possibilities that existed between Kirk and Spock, turning homosocial love into homosexual desire. This has long since extended to any pairing not directly posited by a show. Fans are forever romantically pairing cast members, and the show is forever playing with these expectations.[5] Slashing *Buffy* presents a challenge. After all, this is the show that opened the possibility of not only a same-sex pairing but a same-person pairing—that is, Willow/Vamp Willow in "Doppelgängland"[6]—and gave us a same-sex pairing that is a long-term relationship involving one of the main characters, Willow. Again, as Joss Whedon observes, "All the relationships on the show are sort of romantic (hence the [Bring Your Own] subtext principle") (Golden, Bissette, and Sniegoski 172). Every relationship in the show, therefore, invites slashing, but if the relationship is explicit, not implicit, on the show, like Willow and Tara's, it can no longer be slashed.

In "Something Blue," *Buffy* takes up the slashing tradition by taking two characters who are, within the context of the show, unlikely to be a pair: Buffy and Spike (the arch-villain, along with Drusilla and Angelus, of season 2). Spike/Buffy have been slashed frequently in *Buffy* fan fiction (as have Spike/Willow; see, e.g., <http://www.geocities.com/sabershadowkat/BtVS2.html>). Bringing Spike and Buffy together combines two halves of two different though equally fraught love relationships: Buffy and Angel's tragic relationship is traced through the first three seasons of the show, and Spike's love for Drusilla is played out and referred to through seasons 2 to 5.

Spike and Drusilla are the punk/goth vampires who love each other—the first time romantic love between two vampires has been shown in the Buffy-verse.[7] Writer/producer Marti Noxon notes, "We always said the inspiration [for Spike and Drusilla] was Sid [Vicious] and Nancy [Spungen]" (Golden, Bissette, and Sniegoski 108).[8] Spike's love for Drusilla, though often played for comedy, particularly after she leaves him, is represented as genuine. Spike rescues Drusilla from certain death in Prague, making sacrifices and risking death to restore her to health. Spike is the first vampire other than Angel to be shown as more than a demon bent on human destruction. His love for Dru complicates him, making him more than a mere villain such as the Master. His love and suffering also make him perceptive about other people's love as in the famous "Love's bitch" speech from "Lovers Walk" (3008).[9] In "Something Blue," Spike is the only one aware of how much Willow is suffering following Oz's departure. After Giles and Buffy have exchanged comments on how much better Willow's doing, Spike interjects, "What are you people, blind? She's hanging on by a thread. Any ninny can see that."

Bringing Spike and Buffy together could have been (and often is in fanfic) a tragedy. Instead, the episode is played for laughs, poking fun not just at the fanfic versions of Buffy/Spike but also at the whole slash genre. Instead of the tragedy of mismatched lovers—age-old vampire and vampire slayer in love—this love is ludicrous.

Buffy and Spike do not fall in love but are magicked into wanting to marry each other by a spell of Willow's that goes awry. The romance is centered on arrangements for the wedding ceremony, the details of which neither Buffy nor Spike can agree about:

> *Buffy:* Ceremony, guests, reception. There's so much to decide.
> *Spike:* Well, first thing, I'd say we're *not* having a church wedding.
>   [Spike crosses an item off the list as Buffy runs her fingers through his hair.]
> *Buffy:* How about a daytime ceremony in the park?
> *Spike:* Fabulous. Enjoy your honeymoon with the big pile of dust.
> *Buffy [getting impatient]:* Under the trees. Indirect sunlight only.
> *Spike:* A warm spring breeze tosses the leaves aside and, again, you're registering as Mr. and Mrs. Big Pile of Dust.
> *Buffy:* Okay, stop it! This is our wedding, and you're treating it like a huge joke!

The additional pleasures for the active fan of *Buffy* in this episode are the acknowledgment of the slash genre and of the ways in which some fans have slashed *Buffy*. This functions as a kind of sly wink that says almost any possible way of poaching the show can be done legitimately as part of the show itself. Season 5 has turned "Something Blue" into a perverse glimpse of the future as Spike falls in love with the Slayer.

BUFFY'S MARY SUE IS JONATHAN

In "Superstar," Jonathan Levenson uses an augmentation spell to make everyone believe he is perfect. The spell causes an alternate world where all that is changed is people's perception of Jonathan: instead of being the minor character he has been previously, he is the show's center.[10] This is the wish fulfillment fantasy of every fan who has ever watched a show and longed to be part of it. Within fanfic there is a tradition of writing oneself into a show in just this way. These stories are called "Mary Sues"; like slashing, the phenomenon emerges from *Star Trek* fandom.

While the episodes I have discussed acknowledge fan engagement with the show in playful ways, "Superstar" can be read as doing exactly the opposite, commenting on the fan/object of desire relationship, on the Mary Sue phenomenon. Mary Sue is defined in "Dr. Merlin's Guide to Fan Fiction" by Dr. Merlin (alias Melissa Wilson):

You already know Mary Sue. Mary Sue is the perky, bright, helpful sixteen-year-old ensign who beams about the ship. Everyone on the ship likes Mary Sue, because Mary Sue is good at everything. Mary Sue is an engineer, a doctor in training, a good leader, an excellent cook, and is usually a beautiful singer. Mary Sue often has mental powers that may manifest themselves as telepathy, precognition, or magic. If Mary Sue is very young, she is often the offspring of one or two already established characters. If she's a little older, she will probably end up sleeping with the author's favorite character. Her name is often the author's name, be it a net.name, a favored nickname, or the author's middle name (this is seen in the most famous Mary Sue of all time, Wesley Crusher, who was named after Trek creator Eugene Wesley Roddenberry). By the end of the story, Mary Sue will be in bed with the desired character, will have beamed away amid cheers from all the regulars, or will be dead, usually accompanied by heavy mourning from the cast. The reader, on the other hand, will be celebrating. (<http://www.missy.reimer.com/library/guide.html>)

A Mary Sue par excellence, "Superstar" functions on two levels. One is the desire to interpolate into a text—Jonathan literally inserts himself in Buffy's place; she becomes his sidekick, and he becomes everyone's hero. Of course, Superstar Jonathan is an overblown version of slayer Buffy; not only can he deal with demons and vampires, but he has coached the U.S. women's soccer team to the World Cup, starred in *The Matrix*, written books, and has his own comic book series. There is nothing he cannot do. (There is, of course, a good deal Buffy cannot do, like driving.) The other level is the basic desire most of us have to belong, to be part of a community—in this case Buffy's community of colleagues and friends, the Scooby Gang.[11]

"Superstar" addresses what it is like to not be part of the cool crowd and yearn for it, as Jonathan so clearly does. He wants to be a Scooby; as he says at the end of the episode, all he really wants is to have some friends. There are a number of ironies here; first, Xander and Willow and even, at times, Buffy were not cool when still attending Sunnydale High. Willow was too smart and wore the clothes her mother chose for her. Xander was not wealthy, good enough at sports, or any of the other things that would have made him cool. Instead, he tried to achieve acceptance by playing at being the class clown.[12] Banding around Buffy, they create their own community, becoming absorbed in the fight against evil and less concerned about whether they fit in at high school.

Although within the show the characters of Willow, Xander, and Buffy were constituted as losers, none of the actors looks like the kind of kid who did not fit in at high school. Jonathan, however, really does look like a loser—short, not conventionally attractive, a bad dresser—he is even singled out as the epitome of a loser at the beginning of "The Wish" when Harmony offers him to Cordelia as the ideal recovery guy. One of the discomforts of "Superstar" is seeing the Scooby Gang bowing to someone not nearly as cool, capable, or worthy as they are: someone ordinary, without magic, Slayer powers, strength, or bravery. Does it imply that all fans are wanna-be's—that their engagement with a show like *Buffy* is caught up in their/our desires to be a better Slayer than Buffy, more knowledgeable than Giles, and so on?

It is also a commentary on the Mary Sue because *Buffy*'s Mary Sue, Jonathan, is unable to control his text—literalized as the monster version of himself. By the end of the episode, Jonathan must return to being uncool and must endure the pain of his grandiose desires becoming public knowledge. Not only is he pathetic, but everyone knows that he is pathetic. The object of desire, the show and its actual central character, Buffy, is punishing the one who desires it: the fan. Based on newsgroup, mailing list, and other discussions with fellow fans, the response to "Superstar" is polarized. Those fans I have spoken to who liked it refer to it as an episode for the fans. Almost all those who enjoyed it a great deal are familiar with the Mary Sue phenomenon and enjoy the way "Superstar" comments on and mocks Mary Sues. They enjoy all the little in-jokes about Jonathan's involvement with the show. (For example, in "Superstar" it is Jonathan who receives the Class Protector Award, whereas in "The Prom," 3020, it was Jonathan who presented it to Buffy.) Those who dislike the episode and find it uncomfortable to watch are also responding to the episode's Mary Sueness. Jonathan's desires to be a Buffylike superhero and to be publicly acknowledged as such (an acknowledgment that Buffy, with the exception of "The Prom," does not receive) are embarrassing and come dangerously close to caricaturing the relationship of fans to the show.

"RESTLESS": FEEDING THE FLAMES OF FAN SPECULATION

"Restless" is more than a sly acknowledgment of the fans like the scene in "Phases" (2015) in which Oz notices the trophy in which the witch Catherine Madison is trapped: "The cheerleader trophy," he says. "It's like its eyes follow you where ever you go. I like it." New viewers of the show will not get the reference; fans will. "Restless" is more in the tradition of the "war games" between writer Dorothy Dunnett and her fans, in which the books in her historical series become more and more dependent on prior knowledge on the part of the fan, frequently using that fan knowledge to plant false clues and be deliberately obscure, leaving the fans to speculate and argue among themselves—as indeed they have in the aftermath of the fourth series finale. Joss Whedon has a much bigger problem than Dorothy Dunnett: when there's a whole team of writers, producers, cast, and crew, it becomes nearly impossible to stop spoilers from getting out. As Joss acknowledged on The Bronze posting board,

> I've also seen other things that disturbed me a bit—information about upcoming eps and such that is painfully detailed. Some of it well-protected by spoilers, some of it not, but none of it the sort of thing that should be leaked. Some of you may know the value I place on surprise, an element that seems nearly impossible to maintain these days. A casting memo, a huge audio clip, a complete rundown of "Restless" [. . .] yikes. It saddens me a bit. (May 21, 2000)

"Restless" is an episode that is almost meaningless for the uninitiated. Even some regular fans have said that they found the episode plotless and dull. The episode is divided into four acts with each act being the dream of one of the four central characters: Willow, Xander, Giles, and Buffy herself. "Restless" does far more than simply acknowledge fan engagement with the show; it makes it absolutely central to making sense of the episode—the more knowledge you have of the show, the more meaning you can make. This is the opposite of a stand-alone episode like "Hush," nominated for an Emmy for Outstanding Writing in a Drama Series. It would be impossible for an episode like "Restless," brilliant though it is, to get such a nomination because it is so dependent on fan knowledge of the show.

"Restless" transforms the viewing process into a hunt for clues—what is the writing on Tara's back? A search on the Web and a question to a *Buffy* discussion list revealed it to be Greek—a poem by Sappho. Why is Tara the spirit guide? The question of Tara's identity had been opened up in "Goodbye Iowa" (4014), where she ruined a demon-seeking spell. That opened up speculation about whether she was a demon or, as some fans argue, the goddess Thespia (or perhaps her daughter) who was invoked in the ruined spell.[13] What did the man with the cheese who appeared in all four dreams signify? Nothing, as Joss Whedon has claimed on-line, or is that just a smoke screen?

Another of the pleasures of "Restless" is the way it violates the formula the series has built up for itself. It is not a traditional *Buffy* finale, where the season's villain is defeated, as had happened in each of the previous finales: "Prophecy Girl" (1012); "Becoming," parts 1 and 2 (2021 and 2022); and "Graduation Day," parts 1 and 2 (3021 and 3022). The previous week's episode, "Primeval" (4021), served that function with the defeat of Adam and the end of The Initiative. The episode's underlying narrative of the First Slayer hunting them in their dreams and Buffy having to fight her only very gradually emerges. Like the season 3 episode "The Zeppo" (3013),[14] "Restless" is a direct comment on and defiance of the show's structure. It also sets up many of the themes of season 5—the strengthening of the bonds between the Scoobies, the need for Buffy to come to terms with her slayer heritage; and it hints at the introduction of Buffy's younger "sister," Dawn.

"Restless" comments on the development of the characters, not just over series 4 but over all four seasons—complete with Willow wearing her outfit from the very first episode—still living with the fear of not being cool enough. It refers back to the dream sequences in the third-season finale, "Graduation Day," and in "This Year's Girl" (4015), where Faith and Buffy are shown making Buffy's bed. In "Restless," Buffy looks at that same bed and remarks that she and Faith had just made it. There are myriad other references to previous episodes, including to Principal Snyder being eaten by the Mayor in "Graduation Day" and Willow's fear of being made to perform in *Madame Butterfly* ("Nightmares," 1010). The theater sequences in Willow's dreams have echoes of the talent show in "The Puppet Show" (1009), and there are many other references, sly and otherwise.

"Restless" speculates about the relationship between the four characters: in the first three dreams, those of Willow, Giles, and Xander, all four are present. In Buffy's dream, she seeks her friends, catching only a glimpse of Xander before losing him. Willow and Giles appear only briefly at the very end, when Buffy dreams that she is back in her house in front of the television. The drifting apart of the Scooby Gang had been a major part of season 4 and of the transition from high school to college. Her separateness from the others because she is the Slayer is underlined; in a sense, Buffy's search for friends has been perhaps the central issue of the show since the first episode. Friends are what makes Buffy different from all other Slayers.[15] She says to the first Slayer, "Give me back my friends!" "No friends," the First Slayer replies.

In her article about *Buffy*'s feminism, A. Susan Owen argues that "Buffy's strength and confidence are not learned from the vast experiences of past generations of women; rather, they are her mystical birthright as a Slayer" (31). I dispute this—each season has shown Buffy growing and learning and increasing in both strength and confidence— but "Restless" itself opens up the possibility of Buffy coming from a long line of Slayers, "past generations of women." What she does and who she is has a history: as she says, "The first Slayer. I never really thought about it. It was intense."

CONCLUSION

The five episodes I have discussed acknowledge fans and their discussions and writings about the show. Not only do they acknowledge those practices but they interact with them as well—they are responses to slashing and Mary Sues as well as to the practice of some fans of finding out as many spoilers as they can. "Restless" is an episode that is very difficult to "spoil" even if you know ahead of time that the force hunting the Scooby Gang is the First Slayer: there are so many visual references and so much stylistic play—so much generally going on—that seeing a script ahead of time cannot possibly prepare you for the experience of watching the episode and speculating endlessly about what it means.

All these episodes of *Buffy* take place in an altered universe away from the usual arc of the show, from the extremes of that "weird Hell place" and the nightmare/dream landscape of "Restless" to the slightly altered world of "Something Blue." These episodes mess with the usual arc of the show— Willow as a vampire? Spike and Buffy? Jonathan a superhero? None of these things are "real" in terms of the show's overall arc, yet at the same time all these episodes *are* part of that fabric: "The Wish" introduces Anya, who becomes a recurring character and sets up "Doppelgängland"; "Doppelgängland" introduces the idea that Willow might be bisexual, setting up her relationship with Tara in season 4; "Something Blue" is part of the setup of Spike as a disruptive factor in the Scooby Gang's dynamic as well as introducing the possibility of Spike's love for Buffy, which has become a major subplot of season 5; "Superstar" builds on the idea of alternative universes while also showing the shifts in power and loyalties within the Scoobies; and "Restless," taking place in a dreamscape version of Sunnydale, is also squarely within the series 4 arc—it is, after all, the season finale— exploring the development of the main characters to one another and the ways they have changed since the beginning of *Buffy*.

NOTES

For Mimi Panitch.

Thank you to Ginjer Buchanan, Keith DeCandido, Jennifer Ford, Karen Fowler, Pamela Freeman, Kelly Link, Irene Leung, Joe Monti, Mimi Panitch, and Liz Wickersham for allowing this televisionless *Buffy* addict to get to see the show and for their wonderful and endless *Buffy* discussions. I would like to thank Kelly Link for her comments on this article; any remaining problems are mine.

1. Even the first episodes, "Welcome to the Hellmouth" (1001) and "The Harvest" (1002), can be read in different ways by those familiar with the 1992 eponymous film.

2. An excellent on-line guide is <http//:www.buffyguide.com>.

3. There is even a fan-authored text in which the two universes, that of *Buffy* and *Xena/Hercules,* are combined. The remarkably good "When Hellmouths Collide," by Kimberley Rector and Martha Wells Wilson, can be found at <http://www.rtis. com/nat/user/chimera>.

4. At the beginning of the episode, Cordelia is taunted because she is now "Xander Harris's cast-off," not even good enough for a dork like Xander.

5. In *The Watcher's Guide,* there is a section, "Sunnydale Love Connections," on the romantic liaisons of the characters (Golden and Holder 164–94).

6. Willow, after Vamp Willow has licked her face, observes, "This just can't get more disturbing."

7. Vamp Willow and Vamp Xander from "Doppelgängland" are another such vampire love match.

8. The inspiration is so clear that in an article about *Buffy,* A. Susan Owen consistently refers to Spike as "Sid" (27–28).

9. Spike lectures Angel and Buffy: "You're not friends. You'll never be friends. You'll be in love till it kills you both. You'll fight, you'll shag, you'll hate each other till it makes you quiver, but you'll never be friends. Real love isn't brains, children, it's blood, it's blood screaming inside you to work its will. I may be love's bitch, but at least I'm man enough to admit it."

10. Jonathan has been a minor recurring character on the show for several seasons, making his first appearance in the season 2 episode "Inca Mummy Girl" (2004). He reappeared at the end of "Reptile Boy" (2005) and continued to make brief appearances until "Earshot" (3018), where he got much more screen time as Buffy prevented him from committing suicide or possibly murdering some of his fellow students. Before "Superstar," he was last seen presenting Buffy with her Class Protector award in season 3's "The Prom" (3020) (Holder 185).

11. Indeed, *Buffy*'s community, the Scooby Gang, and their relations with each other is the central focus of every season, especially season 4, where the Scooby Gang seemed to be drifting apart.

12. A crown cruelly denied him in the third-season episode "The Prom" (3020).

13. We learn in the season 5 episode "Family" (5006) that Tara is not a demon, and given that the season 5 villain, Glory, is a god, it seems unlikely that Tara is one too.

14. In "The Zeppo," the main threat of an attempt to open the Hellmouth, which normally would be the primary story arc, becomes the secondary one to Xander's attempts to make himself useful when he is so clearly without the special skills of the rest of the Scooby Gang. Glimpses of Buffy and the others battling to prevent the end of the world are caught in the background as Xander wages his own, less important battle.

15. Certainly Kendra and Faith were without friends, and early on Giles cautions her to secrecy and warns her that she should not be letting others know what she is. At the beginning of "The Wish," Buffy tells Xander and Willow that what got her through the bad times with Angel was her friends. In a season 5 episode, "Fool for Love" (5007), Spike remarks that it is Buffy's friendships and family that have kept her death wish at bay thus far.

20

www.buffy.com
Cliques, Boundaries, and Hierarchies in an Internet Community

Amanda Zweerink and Sarah N. Gatson

Giles: Uh, when I've examined it, you can, uh, uh, skim it.

Ms. Calendar: Scan it, Rupert. That's scan it.

Giles: Of course.

Ms. Calendar: Oh, I know, our ways are strange to you, but soon you will join us in the twentieth century. With three whole years to spare!

Giles: Ms. Calendar, I'm sure your computer science class is fascinating, but I happen to believe that one can survive in modern society without being a slave to the, um, idiot box.

Ms. Calendar: That's TV. The idiot box is TV. This [indicates a computer] is the *good* box!

Giles: I still prefer a good book.

Fritz: The printed page is obsolete. Information isn't bound up anymore. It's an entity. The only reality is virtual. If you're not jacked in, you're not alive.

Ms. Calendar: Thank you, Fritz, for making us all sound like crazy people.

—"I Robot, You Jane" (1008)

Many of us are familiar with the idea of communication on the Internet. Aside from our own forays into the arenas of e-mail, on-line research, and other information-gathering activities, we are fast reaching (have reached?) the saturation point of media interpretations of the cyber-world. In this chapter, we delve into some of the nonvirtual realities of some people's use of Internet technology and the mass media product *Buffy the Vampire Slayer* to form a community based in a textually mediated format, that exists simultaneously on- and off-line, namely, the devotees of the linear posting board of the official *Buffy* Web site, otherwise known as The Bronze and Bronzers.[1]

In essence, there are many ways in which themes, episodes, and quotations from *Buffy* speak to Bronzers in particular as an on-line community. Buffy's commentary to Willow about the meaning of Halloween has been particularly resonant with members of this community: "You're missing the whole point. [. . .] It's come as you aren't night" ("Halloween," 2006). The question of the presumption of Internet anonymity and its meaning for community building has been the core question of our project; for example, do Bronzers "come as they aren't," or do they present the rest of us with authentic, real-world information about themselves? *Buffy*'s portrayal of the various uses and abuses of the Internet (particularly that of the episode "I Robot, You Jane," Ms. Calendar's character in general, and Willow's hacking ability) has also resonated with our ongoing research questions.

"I Robot, You Jane" fits into the traditional "Internet as dangerous and deceptive tool" of one side of the technology debate we discussed previously. We have to wonder whether there are any of the people on the other end of these connections like Malcolm/Moloch—not technically demons but persons using a presumably faceless and anonymous medium for nefarious purposes (see, e.g., Katovich). Ms. Calendar and Willow tended to represent the opposite side of that cultural debate, using the Internet to identify the demon Moloch behind Malcolm as well as, in general, using Internet technology in the aid of Buffy's fight for good over evil. Finally, both Ms. Calendar's successful merging of the techno with the pagan as well as her use of the Internet for specifically community purposes (e.g., keeping up with her fellow techno-pagans enough to form the necessary magic circle on command) were the most reflective of The Bronze's use of a new tool to do what is arguably the most traditional of human work: building community (see Clerc 51).

THE INTERNET AND TELEVISION: A FRUITFUL MERGER?

One of the reasons that concerns over the Internet as a communications technology have surfaced is its potential for influencing the development of human communities. In the site we have been studying for the last thirty-six months, people have adapted the advertising purpose of the site itself and colonized it as a point of entry for face-to-face socializing, networking, and other community-building activities.[2]

"TV James" intentionally created the continuous, multitopic, or linear posting board because he did not like threaded bulletin boards or chat rooms and wanted to create a more open and less frenzied forum. At the same time, Joss Whedon asked for and got "color codes" so that he and others directly involved in the production of *Buffy* could participate in the budding community and not as "undercover" or anonymous posters (although they can do that as well). It has even been suggested by some in the posting board community that Whedon intended for a kind of author-audience interface to develop: "I think it was his intent to foster this kind of community, but it's gone way beyond his dream. He has instantaneous feedback and interacts directly with his audience" (Closet Buffyholic, field notes, August 7, 1999; see also Tulloch and Jenkins [13] for a discussion of how the fans of another producer/writer—Gene Roddenberry—have interpreted him as subversive of the network's desires; Reeves, Rogers, and Epstein 28).

In one sense, then, the Internet merely accelerated a process that took the original highly public fan-based community—the fans of the original *Star Trek*—decades to achieve (Reeves, Rogers, and Epstein 26). The technology made it easier to find like-minded people on at least one issue: *Buffy*. In addition, the already existing base for gathering together series and/or genre fans—*Trek*-like and sci-fi conventions and "comic-cons"—has been put to good use by the members of The Bronze. Kellner might say that this is all an instrumental process, especially for the corporate end of the production team. The WB network gets free publicity generated by the most loyal fans. However, as we will show in this chapter, it is not always the kind of passive word of mouth that it might, according to Kellner, prefer.

BUFFY CREATES A COMMUNITY

Buffy is a television show that has always prided itself on the realistic way in which the angst of growing up is portrayed. Joss Whedon, the show's creator, has said the show is his version of high school—and now college—as hell, literally. Living within these Dante-like layers of Whedon's brainchild are the social groups inherent in such situations: elite cheerleaders and jocks, members of the drama and science clubs, and kids who band together because no one else will accept them. And then there's the threesome comprised of the show's main character, Buffy, and her friends Willow and Xander. Each of them brings to the table something that, individually, would put them in one of these stereotyped groups. Buffy is a former cheerleader, Willow is a brainiac, and Xander has never fit in anywhere else.

Such a hodgepodge of characters is able to relate to an equally diverse audience. For every pom-pom girl, though, there are five viewers who identify with the show because for once they have been given underdogs who actually win on occasion:

> We, at The Bronze, have a way of relating Buffy's issues with our own (real) issues. It makes sense to us and becomes an even better show for that reason. [. . .] It may not have been the prettiest [of] times, or even the nicest [of] times, but it's our life. And now we can reflect on it and see how we reacted to everything that was dealt to us. (Sara)

Each character has significantly evolved in the show's four seasons. The shy Willow has come into her own as a powerful witch as well as recently exploring a new sexual identity. The misfit Xander still struggles to find direction but comes through time and again with fierce loyalty. Even Buffy herself has overcome the stereotypical "dumb blond" label to become one of the most effective and innovative slayers in history. Somewhere, in some universe, the outcasts are having their revenge.

This becomes less of an interesting observation about an enjoyable pop culture phenomenon and more a comment on human nature when we look at The Bronze. Fully 50 percent of respondents to our on-line survey of The Bronze membership admitted to seeking out a forum as a way to talk about a show their peers could not, or refused to, understand. What hooked them was the community that sprang up around the site. With that community, however, came the very class structure Whedon sought to satirize (and he did so admirably enough to draw in said viewers).

"The posting board began by bringing people together [because] of their interest in the show. However, over time, friendships, relationships, engagements, and marriages have come from the board. There is a genuine sense of sincere caring for one another," said Blade the Vampire Hunter, who began posting the very first week of the site. Blade himself helped shape the community that spawned all these feelings of goodwill and also founded the event that would create some of the biggest conflicts and jealousies in The Bronze and in Buffy fandom in general.

In February 1998, the very first Posting Board Party (PBP) was held in Los Angeles. This party was suggested by Blade and open to regular posters from The Bronze who had by this time gotten to know one another virtually through the site. Designed to give Bronzers as a group a chance to meet each other face to face, it also created an opportunity for the cast and crew of the show to mingle with some of their most avid fans. Unlike many other events of this kind, the VIPs were not under contractual obligation to attend, nor was there a larger media or corporate presence that would make attending desirable. Instead, invitations were issued to Whedon, the actors, and the crew, just as they were to interested members of The Bronze. What made this party so special to The Bronze is that many of the VIPs accepted the invitation and attended as normal guests.

The Bronze would never be the same. A small group had now met the actors and had the photographs and signatures to prove it. They achieved an elevated status that seemed impossible to match (for accounts of how the early fan base of *Star Trek* also cultivated a more personal interaction with Roddenberry and thus gained prestige within the larger fan community, see Tulloch and Jenkins 13).

In many cases, the attendants of the first PBP were the same people who had been the most outgoing on the board in the first place. Therefore, they had already been recognized as some of the most creative and outspoken members of The Bronze. These posters were already speaking to one another on the board because they were drawn to one another's bold, "talkative" personalities. Their brush with fame at the PBP merely solidified their positions in a quickly dividing community—before PBP and after.

"Unfortunately, there is a tendency for 'cliques' to form. (See, we're not that far from real life!) People who have met each other sometimes get lost in their own little world of inside jokes. After the first PBP, there was a feeling of alienation of those who had not gone from those who had," said Queen Jenna. While the first cliques were, in fact, formed in this manner, one particularly noticeable group grew in size following another posting board fan gathering in Chicago just two months after the first PBP. These fifteen or so people (the group has always evolved in size and members) began speaking more to one another and less to the board at large. "One of the things I dislike most about the board is the cliquiness [*sic*]," said Jan. "There are cliques that only talk to certain other posters and ignore you if you try to ask them a question or get into their conversation. It's annoying, but real life is like that as well." Jan is not the only Bronzer who complained about these new group boundaries.

A continual debate within The Bronze has always been "off topic," or non-*Buffy*-related, posts. Since almost all the earlier inhabitants sought out the board to talk about the show (now the community is also a significant draw), it was disappointing to some when conversation turned to real-life issues or silly space fillers, such as rousing rounds of "anywhere but here." Unsurprisingly, the number of off-topic posts grows significantly when people have just returned from a gathering and can share their face-to-face experiences of getting to know one another and draw that aspect into the computer-mediated community where it all began:

> We all first went to the PB because of Buffy, but I think most everyone stays because of the people and the discussions (on- and off-topic). There are groups of people that have become friends in real life, as well as others who've never met in (real life) but would call themselves friends. We care about each other's (real) happenings. There are groups of people who generally talk to each other more than to other posters, just like would happen at a large (real) gathering. (I don't see this as exclusionary or "clique-ish" the way some do; and that's a whole different topic entirely.) (Nancy E.)

Indeed, many people do see this facet of The Bronze as exclusionary. When it came time to plan for the next PBP, this became especially clear. The planners of the second party made a couple of decisions that would further divide the board. First, it was decided that the event would be used to raise money for a charity in the name of the show and its fans. This idea in and of itself was not so objectionable, but the price of tickets would have to increase significantly, making the trip for many people too expensive. Second, the planning committee legally formed a board of directors, making the PBP a nonprofit organization with the mission of raising money each year through the party. It also, of course, gave the board members unquestionable decision-making power over any and all PBP proceedings. Finally, because of the now widespread interest in the event, only a set number of people would be able to attend.

The most common concern about the board revolved around this last item. If there were a limit on the number of people who could attend, how would the guest list be decided? The board designed an official site and conducted the sign-ups electronically. It was simple: the first 150 people to sign up were allowed to attend with a guest. Everyone else would be put on a waiting list, and if someone in the first group did not pay for his or her tickets in time, that spot would go to someone on that list.

When sign-ups were done and it became clear who on the posting board had made it and who had not (through cheers of joy and grumbles of displeasure, mostly), it looked as if the attendees were mostly members of the "popular" cliques, or at least friends of them. Accusations of favoritism spread throughout the posting board. A rule that only "regular" posters could attend the party sparked even more debate, as, apparently, the official PBP board was the final word in how the term "regular" was actually defined. While members of the community generally agreed that this rule was necessary, it went against the nature of the posters to have things defined for them given that the posting board had usually behaved as a democracy.

Regular interaction with members of the show's cast and crew is another of the ways The Bronze is differentiated from many other fan- or even corporate-driven Web sites. This willingness to interact with fans extends to the PBP, as was seen by the voluntary presence of VIPs at the first party. As we have noted, Whedon himself is a semiregular fixture in The Bronze, and many members of the *Buffy* cast have made appearances. The writers are the most often "seen" visitors, as they tend to show up after a new episode airs to answer questions and defend plot decisions.

With the creation of a nonprofit fund-raising organization, the PBP became a public relations vehicle as well. The WB network was more than willing to step in and help members of the PBP board organize the party and contact the VIPs. In return, the party would have official tie-ins with the *Buffy* fan club and magazine, the WB, and *Buffy*'s production company, Fox. The party was gradually becoming a corporate venture rather than an "organized by Bronzers, for Bronzers" party.

Naturally, with an increase in size and popularity, the question arose of VIP security. While it was still the intent of the board and its separate planning committee for Bronzers to have unrestricted access to VIPs, it was clear through conversations with the networks and a handful of VIPs that there had to be someplace for the VIP guests to escape the crowds.

Thus, a VIP room was created and guarded by hired private security personnel.

The only members of The Bronze allowed into the VIP area were members of the PBP board and planning committee. As this group had already been labeled as elitist, this all-access pass to the VIPs made them seem even more so, regardless of any operational reasons that may have made sense. Moreover, certain members of the general posting board community had formed friendships with writers, stunt personnel, and producers and somehow made their way into the VIP area. Once there, they were able to invite other Bronzers in to join them. To attendees who were left standing at the door, only to catch glimpses of the VIPs, this looked like the board and the committee were once again playing favorites.

While there are always trickles of newbies coming by to ask the ubiquitous questions of "When does so and so from the show post?" and "When is the party, and how do I get to go?" all during the year, intense PBP discussion usually starts around November and continues well into spring. People begin to get angst-ridden about knowing when the sign-ups will occur; if they will really be on a first-come, first-served basis; and, most troubling in terms of community, who should really be eligible to go. In other words, just who counts as a real Bronzer? This last issue is the part of the debate that the community carries on the longest, and it is one of the most prolific ongoing discussions on the posting board. Jennie says,

> Last year I was lurking at around this time, and I was a newbie. I was terrified of everyone on here. The party sounded like a great laugh, but 1: I didn't have the money and 2: As a newbie I felt it was not my place to go to the party until I had made better friendships with the people going. Of course I love meeting other Buffy fans and always have, but I hadn't struck up any real friendships. I noticed that a lot of other newbies came to the board while I was lurking, and I personally got quite annoyed with the way they did it. I thought it was inconsiderate to think they had the right above regulars. I've now been on the board almost a year, and have made many friends and spoken to many people; okay granted I haven't got my siggy together yet any more than my shout out list, but I'm sure people know who I am! I have made friends I would love to meet as I have with my fellow UK posters! We clicked straight away and I've never known a nicer bunch of people. Therefore, this year I would consider myself to have the right to attend the party. (October 14, 1999)

Lovely Poet says,

> taking a deep breath and wading in. [. . .] My PBP Thoughts [. . .] I wasn't present in LA for the first PBP because at the time I was a newly de-lurked newbie. I did watch the goings on from my computer though and I heard many of the stories eventually from Nick's Xander dance to the hotel from hell with the leaky roof (let's face it, bronzers have bad hotel karma) but what really struck

me is that I had managed to happen across one amazing group of people and I wanted to meet some of them. This is why I attended the second and third PBPs. I didn't go to see the VIPs (even if I did hyperventilate when I realized they were there). I went to see my friends. Because of this, I would have been happy no matter where the party was held. I didn't go for a snazzy location or a band or anything else. I went to see my friends. (April 21, 2000)

The responses of the PBP board and its committee have continued to be rather piecemeal. In the second instance of the PBP board offering a survey to gauge the opinion of the PBP attendees, the on-line survey was finished and made available to the community (through the PBP Web site) only in May 2000 after a very heated and long debate over the nature of the posting board, the PBP, and the PBP board and committees. On July 27, 2000, the committee released the survey results and issued a call for a "Bronzer Liaison" position, with written submissions to be available for all to read and vote on. Complaints began almost immediately, focusing mainly on the perception that the offering of the liaison position emphasized merely that the committee members were not as involved in the day-to-day activities of the community and thus needed a go-between. At the same time, this position and the manner in which it was filled was an attempt to respond to complaints of undemocratic behavior in the past.

The PBP exists as the representative crux of all the issues regarding the class structure held up to such ridicule both by Whedon's take on high school social structure and by many members of The Bronze community. As it brings together fans and the talent from the show in a rarefied atmosphere where the uniqueness of the community and its relationships are emphasized, the beliefs and feelings of being "in the know" and connected to the backstage goings-on are also emphasized. The firing of the show's stunt coordinator (also one of the most active VIP Bronzers), which happened to occur in the midst of all the most recent bitter discussions about the PBP and the community, highlighted these feelings and demonstrated the limits of that connectivity. The Bronzers took sides, with many newbies and trolls joining in. Thus, a change occurred that many saw as cataclysmic to the show and that seemed as if it might be cataclysmic for The Bronze as well. However, the community was somewhat vindicated in their belief in its construction of its collective self when Whedon finally entered the fray:

I see people having a hard time knowing how to behave, veering from flaming rage to desperately cautious oversensitivity. All of these things are connected simply by the fact that the internet (and particularly the Bronze) are new societies, still forming, and the rules, the boundaries, are still unclear. Feels a bit like the end of the STAND, when the police are asking to be armed and they wonder if the new society will be any better—or any DIFFERENT—from the old. Well, this one will be different. Privacy and propriety are going to become very tricky issues here. I don't really have any brilliant conclusion [. . .], and I'm certainly not here to say "Don't do the following!," or "Behave this way!" I just want to say that it's hard. [. . .] It used to be simpler, but now this community has grown to the point where laws start to be made. Personally, I feel like we have way too many and not nearly enough, depending on the day of the week. But it's a good community—a lot of you have posted things that I love—and I'm not referring to the PRAISE, love the PRAISE, but that's not what I mean here—things that made me think, reassess, laugh, plot the untimely death of Fury, all kinds of stuff. And I know it's a blast for the writers and others to talk to you guys and get the PRAISE and joke around—none of us could have had that contact without this, and we treasure it. It's just that there is a dark side to it, and it showed up with a vengeance. (May 21, 2000)

Whedon's observations and interactions with The Bronze—along with much of the writing and production staff—do seem to have placed this community and fan site at the top of the hierarchy of *Buffy* fan sites on the Web. At the same time, this aspect of the community has also been one of the main things that could be its downfall. All communities shift, grow, form subgroups, and even splinter. However, as a *chosen* community (the "chosen one"?) and as one that has no stable, traditionally understood *physical* space, the ease with which disgruntled members can leave is a danger to its stability. The frequency with which its high-intensity production-fan interface both attracts and repels membership may influence the turnover rate of this community. Whether the site gets sucked into the Internet version of the Hellmouth remains to be seen.

The Bronze community exists because of *Buffy* and Joss Whedon in particular. Members and nonmembers understand it as "his baby" and ultimately as his space. It is the only site on the Web where he participates—to the extent that he does not participate even in the threaded board at the buffy.com site (the threaded board format reportedly confuses him) or the threaded board at the WB's site. It is now commonly understood on the Internet as the place to go if you want a special kind of interaction with the show *and* other fans. In some ways, it can be understood as similar to Willow's excitement in telling everyone, "My boyfriend's in the band" (see also chapter 18 in this volume). However, there has been a new development that is demonstrating the further move away from the content of the show and toward the community ties and political interpretations of who should hold power in The Bronze.

CONCLUSION: COMMUNITY OF FANS, OR A FANDOM COMMUNITY?

Bronzers as a community exist at a nexus of innovative uses of particular technologies whose dominant cultural images have tended to embody presumptions of danger, mindlessness, and fragmentation. While The Bronze itself as a "space" on the Internet is the official home for *Buffy* and is thus primarily part of an advertising site, there exists a somewhat subversive core of community builders. These people are indeed fans of *Buffy*, and they came to this site specifically as fans first. However, more and more of their conversation is about themselves as a community per se, not as a community of *Buffy* fans—that aspect is almost taken for granted at this point. Newbies (and not only newbies by any stretch), in fact, have become frustrated with these expressions about community and the ongoing battles, discussions, and formations that are now the everyday explicit and accepted tasks of the core.

When members of other *Buffy* fan forums, or just lurkers and drive-bys in general (or indeed some disgruntled Bronzers), have commented on the overseriousness with which Bronzers take their community boundaries (e.g., "It's *just* a TV show! Why are you getting so bent out of shape?"), there has been a strong response that it is *not* the show they are vehemently protecting but the atmosphere and community rules and ties developed over a three-year-plus period. On-topic versus off-topic debate continues to rage on The Bronze, and newbies as well as some long-established Bronzers feel that at the *official Buffy* site Buffy-talk should dominate. However, this site is home for much more than fan deconstruction and analysis. A community has formed with explicitly political discussions of boundaries, rights, participation, and decision making occurring on the site and with an increasing number of other on-line and off-line settings. While it seems that at least a segment of it will likely go on past any future demise of *Buffy/Angel*, at present that segment is also fiercely defensive of its stake in the official world of *Buffy* fandom.[3]

While a community of fans, we question whether "fans of Buffy" is actually this group's primary identity. They are not a representation of the "single-issue groups" discussed by Reeves, Rodgers, and Epstein (24), nor are they a fanfic community as described by Bacon-Smith. By this we do not mean to deny their foundations and participations in the larger world of either *Buffy* fandom or media fandom more generally; they (we) are consummate cultural consumers. However, the volume of critique from other fans and fan communities about both the hierarchical place of The Bronze and its lack of "enough" on-topic posting and discussion suggests that maintaining a link and loyalty to *Buffy* as a product is declining in significance in holding together this community. That none of us use the official title of the site as a whole (www.buffy.com) but rather hold tenaciously to an identity as Bronzers instead makes us wonder whether once the "fan of" identity is formed (or indeed any initial community identity is marked), a space for broader and more diverse communal ties may open up.[4]

NOTES

1. While the participants in the threaded board hosted at this same Web site also refer to their space/place as "The Bronze" and themselves as "Bronzers," our work focuses on the linear (continuous, multitopic) board, and they have tended to make a more forceful and publicly accepted claim to these identities.

2. We prefer the term "face to face" rather than the term "real life," or "RL," to refer to in-person meetings and activities. In the literature, "virtual" is often compared to "real." While The Bronze is indeed a virtual space, the community itself and the activities and interactions it produces are grounded in the collective material experiences of its membership. The communal feelings produced are real, as are the communications in which members engage. See Turkle 10, 23, 66; Couch and Chen; McLuhan and Powers. See also Dorothy Smith's discussion of the importance of both the face-to-face and the textual in community building.

3. Bacon-Smith's discussion of the size beyond which communities begin to fragment and her discussion of fission, interlocking, and core circles are particularly germane to the ways in which The Bronze community is evolving (24–25; 29–31). It is in its Internet manifestation that these insights become even more interesting, in that there is a simultaneity to the interactions among and between circles, as members have several windows open: onto The Bronze, in AIM, in e-mail, and in other *Buffy* and non-*Buffy* posting communities. This aspect of the community plays out in interesting ways when all this interactive knowledge is carried into the off-line meetings of Bronzers, as we discuss extensively elsewhere (Gatson and Zweerink, "Choosing," "Ethnography").

4. Editors' note: With *Buffy*'s shift from WB to UPN, The Bronze ended in July 2001. It remains to be seen whether the community will, like *Buffy*, be reborn at the new UPN site.

Afterword
The Genius of Joss Whedon
David Lavery

You could never hope to grasp the source of our power.

> —*Über*-Buffy to Adam in "Primeval" (4021)

But Joss just keeps saying, "Don't worry. I have it right here."

> —Sarah Michelle Gellar on the filming of "Restless" (4022)

You think you know . . . what's to come . . . what you are. You haven't even begun.

> —Tara (channeling for the First Slayer), to Buffy in "Restless" and
> Dracula to Buffy in "Buffy vs. Dracula" (5001)

As Robert C. Allen has observed, "Because of the technological complexity of the medium and as a result of the application to most commercial television production of the principles of modern industrial organization [. . .], it is very difficult to locate the 'author' of a television program—if by that we mean the single individual who provides the unifying vision behind the program" (9). Long considered a producer's medium (see Newcomb and Alley), television's attentive viewers may well know of producers like Grant Tinker, Norman Lear, Steven Bochco, Joshua Brand and John Falsey, Dick Wolf, Ed Zwick and Marshall Herskovitz, and John Wells, though it is doubtful they can name a single writer or director of, respectively, *The Mary Tyler Moore Show*, *All in the Family*, *NYPD Blue*, *Northern Exposure*, *Law and Order*, *thirtysomething*, or *ER*. In the first decade of a new century, it is entirely possible to be a regular watcher of *Boston Public*, *The Practice*, and *Ally MacBeal* and know nothing of David E. Kelley, to be a devout *West Winger* and have never heard of Aaron Sorkin, or to be a *Sopranos* regular and be oblivious to David Chase.

It is not at all difficult, however, to locate the author of *Buffy the Vampire Slayer*. As its creator, executive producer, writer/cowriter of twenty-two episodes, and director of eighteen, Joss Whedon is, beyond question, the "mad genius" (Gellar, "An Interview") of *Buffy*.[1]

When Mim Udovitch visited the set of *Buffy* while writing a cover story on the show for *Rolling Stone,* she learned that the final episode of season 4, then only days away from production,[2] was not yet written. "Like, in a couple of days we start shooting the last episode of the season," Sarah Michelle Gellar would observe, "and no one has any idea what happens. But Joss just keeps saying, 'Don't worry. I have it right here'" (62). Whedon, we learn later in the article, had an emergency appendectomy earlier in the week, delaying his completion of the script for the season finale.

A few days later, Whedon had evidently completed the script for "Restless" (4022),[3] and he would also direct, for the fourth consecutive year, the season's final episode, which would air on May 23. Confirming his injunction to his star not to worry, "Restless" turned out to be a truly extraordinary hour of television, a kind of television 8½,[4] a postmodern, self-referential, diegesis-bending[5] hour that would succeed in summing up *Buffy*'s first four seasons and pointing to its future.

Fans of *Buffy* (myself included) had been surprised to find that "Primeval" (4021), 1999–2000's penultimate episode, had seemingly brought closure to the year's story arcs. Adam had been vanquished, The Initiative was no more, and the Scooby Gang had ceased their backbiting, overcoming the "Yoko Factor" and working together more powerfully than ever before to defeat a potent enemy.

But hadn't the narrative peaked too soon? To what purpose would Whedon dedicate his anticlimactic season finale? As Larbalestier notes in chapter 19 in this volume, "Restless" "is not a traditional *Buffy* finale where the season's villain is defeated as had happened in each of the previous finales." After all, the Master had not killed Buffy, opened the Hellmouth, and then been staked by a reborn Slayer in the next-to-last episode of season 1 but, rather, in the last episode, "Prophecy Girl" (1012; written and directed by Whedon). Angelus's resurrection of Acathla and Buffy's world-saving dispatching of her lover to hell had not transpired in episode 21 of season 2 but, rather, in "Becoming," part 2 (2022; written and directed by Whedon). And the Mayor's Ascension and then immolation in the inferno of Sunnydale High did not take place in "Graduation Day," part 1 (3021) but, rather, in part 2 (3022; written and directed by Whedon). But beyond the sense of high expectation that having the Whedon stamp on it naturally inspired, neither I nor anyone else in *Buffy*'s audience knew what we were in for beyond an Internet rumor, correct as it turned out, that it would be a dream sequence. Whedon himself had disclosed that much:

> The last episode is all dreams, and it's just about as strange as it needs to be. It was a very fun and beautiful way to sort of sum up everything everyone had gone through, what it meant to them and where they are. It's divided into four acts that are four dreams: Giles, Willow, Xander and Buffy. (Interview with Fanforum)

We did not know, however, that each of these dreams would in fact be equal in style and strangeness and oneiric suggestiveness to the famous "dancing dwarf" dream of Dale Cooper in the third episode of *Twin Peaks,* a series Whedon has often cited as among his all-time favorites.

Exhausted from their final battle with Adam and from the enjoining spell that made their victory possible, the Gang gathers at Buffy's house to unwind and watch videos. Before they have finished even the coming attractions on the first tape, they are, however, all sound asleep. Their dreams, however, are anything but sweet, as we learn by entering the "mindscreen" (as Bruce Kawin calls it) of first Willow, then Xander, Giles, and Buffy. Each of the four is stalked in turn by the spirit of the First Slayer.

As the Scooby Gang wanders through their respective dream worlds—as Willow struggles with her stage freight, fear of opera, and doubts about her evolution beyond nerd status during a surreal performance of *Death of a Salesman,* worrying all along that her secret will be discovered; as Xander dreams of assignations with not only Willow and Tara but Buffy's mother and worries about his future while finding himself in the midst of an *Apocalypse Now* redux (Principal Snyder as Kurtz); as Giles becomes Buffy's father and frets about the clash between Watcher duties and his "own gig," merging the two as he bursts into song at The Bronze (which has merged with his own living room); and as Buffy finds herself perplexed by a pure-bureaucratic Riley and a human Adam who accuses her of being a demon, before her own final struggle with, and vanquishing of, the First Slayer—the dream diegesis merges with the real set of the Santa Monica studio where *Buffy* is filmed.

In one captivating tracking shot, a fleeing Xander runs from the First Slayer; the camera, in one continuous steady-cam take, follows him into Giles's apartment, through a hallway, and out into Buffy's dorm, into Buffy and Willow's room, and through a closet into his own dank basement apartment, where his father/the First Slayer plucks out his heart. The textual geography of the shot makes perfect dream sense—for in dreams, after all, are not all places and times contiguous? But the dream contiguity of the diegesis of "Restless" is in reality the equally surreal contiguity of the extradiegetic actual television shooting set. Whedon has simultaneously taken us inside the unconscious minds of the Scooby Gang and behind the scenes of a television show's production.

In Xander's "Restless" dream, Buffy and Giles express their disappointment with *Apocalypse Now,* and Xander finds himself defending it. Then a
popcorn-chomping Giles reverses his critical opinion, announcing his sudden realization: "I'm beginning to understand this now. It's all about the
journey, isn't it?" Giles's "this," we may say, refers not to Coppola's film
but to Whedon's creation. The line is not the only one in "Restless" that
takes on self-referential meaning.[6] Even the line twice repeated (first by
Tara, then in the last shot of "Restless" in Buffy's own mind)—"You think
you know . . . what's to come . . . what you are. You haven't even begun"[7]—seems to speak to the destiny not only of Buffy the Vampire Slayer
but also of *Buffy the Vampire Slayer.*

Whedon has often hinted that Tony Head's prediction (that the movies
will steal him away from television) will prove correct: "Ultimately you
want to move on from [television]," Whedon tells the authors of *The
Watcher's Guide 2:*

> You just want to say, "Okay, now I want to do something where I have the time
> to create everything that's in the frame. Everything." And that's sort of where I'm
> starting to be. I'm getting to the point now where I'm like, "Okay, I've told a lot
> of stories. I've churned it out." I just feel like I want to step back and do some-
> thing where I can't use the excuse of "I only had a week." (Holder 323)

In the same volume, we find Marti Noxon—one of Whedon's principal pro-
tégées, writer of (as of midway through season 5) fifteen episodes, and the
only woman so far to both write and direct an episode of *Buffy* ("Into the
Woods," 5010)—admitting,

> I don't think Joss is gonna stay with the show forever. I have very mixed feel-
> ings about what that means for the rest of us. Part of me thinks, "How can we
> ever do this without him? How could it ever be what it is, because it is so much
> his vision." (Holder 326)

Yet, in February 2001, Whedon signed a four-year production deal—reported
to be worth $20,000,000—to create and produce new programs for 20th
Century–Fox, so it would appear that the genius of Whedon will make television its playground for the foreseeable future.

Whedon once called *Buffy* "a show by losers for losers" (qtd. at <http:
//wwwcrosswinds.net/~tlbin/cast/joss.html>), and we understand what this
self-described nerd who conjured a surprising series about outsiders who
routinely save the world meant.[8] *Buffy,* Joyce Millman has observed, "is an
ode to misfits, a healing vision of the weird, the different and the marginalized finding their place in the world and, ultimately, saving it." But Whedon certainly did not mean that the series itself is not about success. "As far
as I am concerned," he admitted to *Entertainment Weekly,* "the first
episode of *Buffy* was the beginning of my career. It was the first time I told

a story from start to finish the way I wanted." But who knew that *Buffy* would continue to evolve to become the special creation it is today? When Whedon previewed the "what's to come" of season 5 to his central cast and crew, Marti Noxon was stunned: "I think what's going to happen is going to astound people. I was astounded when Joss told me. I went 'That is unbelievable!'" (Holder 326).[9] Now (I write these words with only six episodes to go in season 5, one episode after one of the entire series' finest episodes, "The Body," 5016, written and directed by Whedon) that we know much more about what Noxon heard—I, for one, believe her. I, for one, will continue to root for *Buffy the Vampire Slayer* and in so doing sustain my faith in the creative potential of television.

POSTSCRIPT

The preceding was written prior to the end of *Buffy*'s fifth season; I write these words just prior to the first episode of season 6 and the beginning of the UPN era (and *Buffy*'s rebirth in syndication on FX). Now we know what dumbfounded Noxon—that Buffy would die in the 100th episode of the series. We have seen the gravestone:

> BUFFY ANNE SUMMERS
> 1981–2001
> BELOVED SISTER
> DEVOTED FRIEND
> SHE SAVED THE WORLD
> A LOT

Buffy will, of course, return somehow, just as Angel did after he died in the final episode of season 2. But Joss Whedon will not—not in the same way as before. *Entertainment Weekly* reports that Whedon's daily helming is over. As Whedon devotes himself to development of two new series (an animated *Buffy* and a BBC spin-off featuring Giles) and, significantly, directing his first feature film, Marti Noxon will become *Buffy*'s executive producer (Jensen 65).

The UPN era may be the post-Joss era as well.

NOTES

1. In his ET Online interview, Whedon offers the following account of his obsessive involvement in the creation of *Buffy*:

> I have control over all the shows. I'm responsible for all the shows. That means that I break the stories. I often come up with the ideas and I certainly break the stories with

the writers so that we all know what's going to happen. [. . .] The good thing is that I'm surrounded by people who are much smarter than I am. So gradually I have been able to let certain things take care of themselves, because my crew, my writers, my post-production crew, everybody is so competent, that I don't have to run around quite as much as I used to.

2. Udovitch's piece was published in the May 11, 2000, issue of the magazine, but we know from several references (she refers in the article to Gellar's on-set visible scar, acquired in Buffy's flight from Adam in "The Yoko Factor" [4021]; she watches the filming of a scene in which Buffy regrets having studied French instead of Sumerian) that her visit took place during the filming of "Primeval" (4021), the next-to-last episode of season 4.

3. We should not find such rapid production in the world of television that surprising. In an interview with ET Online, Whedon had confessed, "When we fall behind, which tends to happen, I've been known to write a 'Buffy,' start to finish, in three days," and the incredibly prolific David E. Kelley, who at one point in the 1999–2000 season was writing scripts for *Ally McBeal, The Practice,* and *Snoops,* has been known to write more than one per week.

4. During the filming of Fellini's masterpiece, the Italian director had also deflected the concerns of everyone from his producer to his star, Marcello Mastroianni, as to whether "the maestro" actually knew what *8½* was about. Fellini would, of course, incorporate these doubts into the film itself, making it in large part a movie about the inability of Guido Anselmi (Mastroianni, Fellini's alter ego) to make a movie.

5. Gerald Prince defines "diegesis"—a term now common to the critical approach usually known as narratology—as "the [fictional] world in which the situations and events narrated occur" (20).

6. Another example: in the scene at The Bronze in Giles's dream, we find the following exchange:

Willow: Something is trying to kill us. It's like some primal . . . some animal force.
Giles: That used to be us.
Xander: Don't get linear on me now, man.

Of course, there seems little danger of "Restless" itself becoming linear, even in straight-arrow Giles's dream segment.

7. In the first episode of season 5, "Buffy vs. Dracula" (5001), written by Marti Noxon, Dracula, seeking to convince Buffy that her power is very near his own, intones the same line to her.

8. "I was a pathetic loser in high school and Sunnydale is based largely on my experience and the experience of other writers who work on the show. I attended a school in New York for several years [Riverdale] where I underwent many humiliations and much anxiety and that finds its way into the series."

9. Interviewed while filming season 5's finale, Sarah Michelle Gellar also spoke of "an ending I think nobody will ever expect—and nobody will believe. Even I couldn't believe it when I read it" ("The Slayer Speaks").

Episode Guide for Seasons 1 to 5

SEASON 1

Air Date | Number | Title | Writer | Director

03/10/97 | 1001 | Welcome to the Hellmouth | Joss Whedon | Charles Martin Smith

03/10/97 | 1002 | The Harvest | Joss Whedon | John T. Kretchmer

03/17/97 | 1003 | The Witch | Dana Reston | Stephen Cragg

03/25/97 | 1004 | Teacher's Pet | David Greenwalt | Bruce Seth Green

03/31/97 | 1005 | Never Kill a Boy on the First Date | Rob Des Hotel and Dean Batali | David Semel

04/07/97 | 1006 | The Pack | Matt Kiene and Joe Reinkemeyer | Bruce Seth Green

04/14/97 | 1007 | Angel | David Greenwalt | Scott Brazil

04/28/97 | 1008 | I Robot, You Jane | Ashley Gable and Thomas A. Swyden | Stephen Posey

05/05/97 | 1009 | The Puppet Show | Rob Des Hotel and Dean Batali | Ellen S. Pressman

05/12/97 | 1010 | Nightmares | Joss Whedon and David Greenwalt | Bruce Seth Green

05/19/97 | 1011 | Out of Mind, Out of Sight | Joss Whedon, Ashley Gable, Thomas A. Swyden | Reza Badiyi

06/02/97 | 1012 | Prophecy Girl | Joss Whedon | Joss Whedon

SEASON 2

Air Date | Number | Title | Writer | Director
09/15/97 | 2001 | When She Was Bad | Joss Whedon | Joss Whedon
09/22/97 | 2002 | Some Assembly Required | Ty King | Bruce Seth Green
09/29/97 | 2003 | School Hard | David Greenwalt and Joss Whedon | John T. Kretchmer
10/06/97 | 2004 | Inca Mummy Girl | Matt Kiene and Joe Reinkemeyer | Ellen S. Pressman
10/13/97 | 2005 | Reptile Boy | David Greenwalt | David Greenwalt
10/27/97 | 2006 | Halloween | Carl Ellsworth | Bruce Seth Green
11/03/97 | 2007 | Lie to Me | Joss Whedon | Joss Whedon
11/10/97 | 2008 | The Dark Age | Rob Des Hotel and Dean Batali | Bruce Seth Green
11/17/97 | 2009 | What's My Line? (part 1) | Howard Gordon and Marti Noxon | David Solomon
11/24/97 | 2010 | What's My Line? (part 2) | Marti Noxon | David Semel
12/08/97 | 2011 | Ted | David Greenwalt and Joss Whedon | Bruce Seth Green
01/12/98 | 2012 | Bad Eggs | Marti Noxon | David Greenwalt
01/19/98 | 2013 | Surprise (part 1 of 2) | Marti Noxon | Michael Lange
01/20/98 | 2014 | Innocence (part 2 of 2) | Joss Whedon | Joss Whedon
01/27/98 | 2015 | Phases | Rob Des Hotel and Dean Batali | Bruce Seth Green
02/10/98 | 2016 | Bewitched, Bothered and Bewildered | Marti Noxon | James A. Contner
02/24/98 | 2017 | Passion | Ty King | Michael E. Gershman
03/03/98 | 2018 | Killed By Death | Rob Des Hotel and Dean Batali | Deran Serafian
04/28/98 | 2019 | I Only Have Eyes for You | Marti Noxon | James Whitmore Jr.
05/05/98 | 2020 | Go Fish | David Fury and Elin Hampton | David Semel
05/12/98 | 2021 | Becoming (part 1) | Joss Whedon | Joss Whedon
05/19/98 | 2022 | Becoming (part 2) | Joss Whedon | Joss Whedon

SEASON 3

Air Date | Number | Title | Writer | Director
09/29/98 | 3001 | Anne | Joss Whedon | Joss Whedon
10/06/98 | 3002 | Dead Man's Party | Marti Noxon | James Whitmore Jr.
10/13/98 | 3003 | Faith, Hope and Trick | David Greenwalt | James A. Contner

10/20/98 | 3004 | Beauty and the Beasts | Marti Noxon | James Whitmore Jr.
11/03/98 | 3005 | Homecoming | David Greenwalt | David Greenwalt
11/10/98 | 3006 | Band Candy | Jane Espenson | Michael Lange
11/17/98 | 3007 | Revelations | Douglas Petrie | James A. Contner
11/24/98 | 3008 | Lovers Walk | Dan Vebber | David Semel
12/08/98 | 3009 | The Wish | Marti Noxon | David Greenwalt
12/15/98 | 3010 | Amends | Joss Whedon | Joss Whedon
01/12/99 | 3011 | Gingerbread | Jane Espenson | James Whitmore Jr.
01/19/99 | 3012 | Helpless | David Fury | James A. Contner
01/26/99 | 3013 | The Zeppo | Dan Vebber | James Whitmore Jr.
02/09/99 | 3014 | Bad Girls | Douglas Petrie | Michael Lange
02/16/99 | 3015 | Consequences | Marti Noxon | Michael Gershman
02/23/99 | 3016 | Doppelgängland | Joss Whedon | Joss Whedon
03/16/99 | 3017 | Enemies | Douglas Petrie | David Grossman
04/21/99 | 3018 | Earshot | Jane Espenson | Regis Kimble
05/04/99 | 3019 | Choices | David Fury | James A. Contner
05/11/99 | 3020 | The Prom | Marti Noxon | David Solomon
05/18/99 | 3021 | Graduation Day (part 1) | Joss Whedon | Joss Whedon
07/13/99 | 3022 | Graduation Day (part 2) | Joss Whedon | Joss Whedon

SEASON 4

Air Date | Number | Title | Writer | Director
10/05/99 | 4001 | The Freshman | Joss Whedon | Joss Whedon
10/12/99 | 4002 | Living Conditions | Marti Noxon | David Grossman
10/19/99 | 4003 | The Harsh Light of Day | Jane Espenson | James A. Contner
10/26/99 | 4004 | Fear, Itself | David Fury | Tucker Gates
11/02/99 | 4005 | Beer Bad | Tracey Forbes | David Solomon
11/09/99 | 4006 | Wild at Heart | Marti Noxon | David Grossman
11/16/99 | 4007 | The Initiative | Douglas Petrie | James A. Contner
11/23/99 | 4008 | Pangs | Jane Espenson | Michael Lange
11/30/99 | 4009 | Something Blue | Tracey Forbes | Nick Mark
12/14/99 | 4010 | Hush | Joss Whedon | Joss Whedon
01/18/00 | 4011 | Doomed | Marti Noxon, David Fury, Jane Espenson | James A. Contner
01/25/00 | 4012 | A New Man | Jane Espenson | Michael Gershman
02/08/00 | 4013 | The I in Team | David Fury | James A. Contner
02/15/00 | 4014 | Goodbye Iowa | Marti Noxon | David Solomon
02/22/00 | 4015 | This Year's Girl (part 1 of 2) | Douglas Petrie | Michael Gershman
02/29/00 | 4016 | Who Are You? (part 2 of 2) | Joss Whedon | Joss Whedon
04/04/00 | 4017 | Superstar | Jane Espenson | David Grossman

04/25/00 | 4018 | Where the Wild Things Are | Tracey Forbes | David Solomon
05/02/00 | 4019 | New Moon Rising | Marti Noxon | James A. Contner
05/09/00 | 4020 | The Yoko Factor | Douglas Petrie | David Grossman
05/16/00 | 4021 | Primeval | David Fury | James A. Contner
05/23/00 | 4022 | Restless | Joss Whedon | Joss Whedon

SEASON 5

Air Date | Number | Title | Writer | Director
09/26/00 | 5001 | Buffy vs. Dracula | Marti Noxon | David Solomon
10/03/00 | 5002 | Real Me | David Fury | David Grossman
10/10/00 | 5003 | The Replacement | Jane Espenson | James A. Contner
10/17/00 | 5004 | Out of My Mind | Rebecca Rand Kirshner | David Grossman
10/24/00 | 5005 | No Place Like Home | Doug Petrie | David Solomon
11/07/00 | 5006 | Family | Joss Whedon | Joss Whedon
11/14/00 | 5007 | Fool for Love | Douglas Petrie | Nick Mark
11/21/00 | 5008 | Shadow | David Fury | Daniel Attias
11/28/00 | 5009 | Listening to Fear | Rebecca Rand Kirshner | David Solomon
12/19/00 | 5010 | Into the Woods | Marti Noxon | Marti Noxon
01/09/01 | 5011 | Triangle | Jane Espenson | Christopher Hibler
01/23/01 | 5012 | Checkpoint | Jane Espenson and Douglas Petrie | Nick Marck
02/06/01 | 5013 | Blood Ties | Steven DeKnight | Michael Gershman
02/13/01 | 5014 | Crush | David Fury | Daniel Attias
02/20/01 | 5015 | I Was Made to Love You | Jane Espenson | James A. Contner
02/27/01 | 5016 | The Body | Joss Whedon | Joss Whedon
04/17/01 | 5017 | Forever | Marti Noxon | Marti Noxon
04/24/01 | 5018 | Intervention | Jane Espenson | Michael Gershman
05/01/01 | 5019 | Tough Love | Rebecca Rand Kirshner | David Grossman
05/08/01 | 5020 | Spiral | Steven DeKnight | James A. Contner
05/14/01 | 5021 | The Weight of the World | Douglas Petrie | David Solomon
05/21/01 | 5022 | The Gift | Joss Whedon | Joss Whedon

Bibliography

Abbott, Stacey. "A Little Less Ritual and a Little More Fun: The Modern Vampire in *Buffy the Vampire Slayer.*" *Slayage: The Online International Journal of Buffy Studies* Number 3 (June 2001) <http://www.middleenglish.org/slayage/essays/slayage3/abbott.htm>.

Abrams, M. H. *Natural Supernaturalism: Tradition and Revolution in Romantic Literature.* New York: Norton, 1971.

Adams, Michael. "Slayer Slang (Parts I and II)." *Verbatim: The Language Quarterly* 24.3–4 (Summer/Autumn 1999): 1–4, 1–7.

Aldiss, Brian. "Vampires—the Ancient Fear." Gordon and Hollinger ix–xi.

Allen, John L., Jr. "Teens on Screen: How Teenagers Are Portrayed." *National Catholic Reporter* 35.2 (26 Mar. 1999): 17.

Allen, Robert C. "Introduction to the Second Edition: More Talk about TV." *Channels of Discourse, Reassembled.* Ed. Robert C. Allen. Chapel Hill: U of North Carolina P, 1992. 1–30.

Anderson, Lisa M. *Mammies No More: The Changing Image of Black Women on Stage and Screen.* New York: Rowman & Littlefield, 1997.

Astle, Richard. "Dracula as Totemic Monster: Lacan, Freud, Oedipus and History." *Sub-Stance* 25 (1980): 98–105.

Auerbach, Nina. *Our Vampires, Ourselves.* Chicago: U of Chicago P, 1995.

Augustine. *The Confessions of St. Augustine.* Trans. Rex Warner. New York: Penguin, 1963.

Bacon-Smith, Camille. *Enterprising Women: Television Fandom and the Creation of Popular Myth.* Philadelphia: U of Pennsylvania P, 1992.

Barber, Paul. *Vampires, Burial and Death: Folklore and Reality.* New Haven: Yale UP, 1988.

Barlow, John Perry. "Declaration of Independence for Cyberspace" <http://www.clas.ufl.edu/users/seeker1/cyberanthro/decl-indep.html>.

Barreca, Regina. *They Used to Call Me Snow White . . . but I Drifted: Women's Strategic Use of Humor.* New York: Viking, 1991.

Barthes, Roland. *A Lover's Discourse.* Trans. Richard Howard. New York: Hill and Wang, 1978.

———. "Myth Today." *A Barthes Reader.* Ed. Susan Sontag. New York: Hill and Wang, 1982. 93–149.

———. *The Pleasure of the Text.* Trans. Richard Miller. New York: Hill and Wang, 1975.

Belensky, Mary Field, Blythe McVicker Clinchy, Nancy Rule Goldberger, and Jill Mattuck Tarule. *Women's Ways of Knowing: The Development of Self, Voice, and Mind.* New York: Basic, 1986.

Bellafante, Ginia. "Bewitching Teen Heroines: They're All Over the Dial, Speaking Out, Cracking Wise and Casting Spells." *Time* 5 May 1997: 82–84.

Bettelheim, Bruno. *The Uses of Enchantment: The Meaning and Importance of Fairy Tales.* New York: Vintage, 1989.

Bloom, Harold. *The American Religion: The Emergence of the Post-Christian Nation.* New York: Simon and Schuster, 1992.

Boese, Christine. "The Ballad of the Internet Nutball: Chaining Rhetorical Visions from the Margins of the Margins to the Mainstream in the Xenaverse." 25 June 2000 <http://www.nutball.com>.

Bogle, Donald. *Blacks in American Films and Television.* New York: Simon and Schuster, 1988.

———. *Toms, Coons, Mulattoes, Mammies and Bucks: An Interpretive History of Blacks in American Films.* 3rd ed. New York: Continuum, 1996.

Bosky, Bernadette Lynn. "Making the Implicit, Explicit: Vampire Erotica and Pornography." Heldreth and Pharr 217–66.

Bowers, Cynthia. "Generation Lapse: The Problematic Parenting of Joyce Summers and Rupert Giles." *Slayage: The Online International Journal of Buffy Studies* Number 2 (Mar. 2001) <http://www.middleenglish.org/slayage/essays/slayage2/bowers.htm>.

Braun, Beth. "Buffy Meets Freud: A Psychoanalytic Look at Television's Vampire Slayer." Augusta: Popular Culture Association in the South Conference, 8–10 Oct. 1998.

Breton, Rob, and Lindsey McMaster. "Dissing the Age of Moo: Initiatives, Alternatives, and Rationality in *Buffy the Vampire Slayer.*" *Slayage: The Online International Journal of Buffy Studies* Number 2 (Mar. 2001) <http://www.middleenglish.org/slayage/essays/slayage2/bretonmcmaster.htm>.

Bronfen, Elisabeth. *Over Her Dead Body: Death, Femininity and the Aesthetic.* New York: Routledge, 1992.

Brown, Lyn Mikel. *Raising Their Voices: The Politics of Girls' Anger.* Cambridge: Harvard UP, 1998.

Brown, Mary Ellen, ed. *Television and Women's Culture: The Politics of the Popular.* London: Sage, 1990.

Bunson, Matthew. *The Vampire Encyclopedia.* New York: Crown, 1993.

Burke, Kenneth. *A Grammar of Motives.* Los Angeles: U of California P, 1969.

———. *Language as Symbolic Action.* Los Angeles: U of California P, 1966.

———. *A Rhetoric of Motives.* Los Angeles: U of California P, 1969.

Callandar, Michelle. "Bram Stoker's Buffy: Traditional Gothic and Contemporary Culture." *Slayage: The Online International Journal of Buffy Studies* Number 3 (June 2001) <http://www.middleenglish.org/slayage/essays/slayage3/callandar.htm>.

Campbell, Bebe Moore. *Your Blues Ain't Like Mine*. New York: Ballantine, 1992.

Campbell, Joseph. *The Hero with a Thousand Faces*. 2nd ed. Princeton: Princeton UP, 1968.

———. *The Masks of God: Creative Mythology*. New York: Penguin, 1968.

Campbell, Richard, and Caitlin Campbell. "Demons, Aliens, Teens and Television." *Television Quarterly* 31.4 (2001): 56–64. Republished in *Slayage: The Online International Journal of Buffy Studies* Number 2 (Mar. 2001) <http://www.middleenglish.org/slayage/essays/slayage2/campbell.htm>.

Caputo, John, and Michael Scanlon. *God, the Gift, and Postmodernism*. Bloomington: Indiana UP, 1999.

Carby, Hazel. *Reconstructing Womanhood: The Emergence of the Afro-American Woman Novelist*. New York: Oxford UP, 1987.

Carson, Tom. "So-Called Vampires: Buffy Battles Teendom's Demons." *Village Voice* 10 June 1997: 51.

Case, Sue Ellen. "Tracking the Vampire." *Differences* 3.2 (1991): 1–20.

Cashdan, Sheldon. *The Witch Must Die: The Hidden Meaning of Fairy Tales*. New York: Basic, 2000.

Chetwynd, Josh. "Networks Promote Musicians for a Song." *USA Today* 28 Oct. 1998: 3D.

Chodorow, Nancy. *The Reproduction of Mothering: Psychoanalysis and the Sociology of Gender*. Berkeley: U of California P, 1978.

Christian, Barbara. *Black Women Novelists: The Development of a Tradition, 1892–1976*. Westport: Greenwood, 1980.

Clark, John. "Women Can Be Empowered by Anger, Study Says." *Context on-line* (Sept. 1997) <www.utenn.edu/uwa/vpps/ur/context/Sept97Context/features/anger.html> (22 Apr. 1999).

Clerc, Susan. "DDEB, GATB, MPPB, and Ratboy: The *X-Files*' Media Fandom, Online and Off." Lavery, Hague, and Cartwright 36–51.

Collins, Patricia Hill. *Black Feminist Thought: Knowledge, Consciousness and the Politics of Empowerment*. New York: Routledge, 1991.

Conkin, Paul K. *American Originals: Homemade Varieties of Christianity*. Chapel Hill: U of North Carolina P, 1997.

Connell, Ian, and Adam Mills. "Text, Discourse and Mass Communication." *Discourse and Communication: New Approaches to the Analyses of Mass Media Discourse and Communication*. Ed. Teun A. van Dijk. Berlin: Walter de Gruyter, 1985. 26–43.

Contemporary Ethnography. Publications of the American Folklore Society. New series. Philadelphia: University of Pennsylvania.

Couch, Carl J., and Shing-Ling Chen. "Orality, Literacy and Social Structure." *Communication and Social Structure*. Ed. David R. Maines and Carl J. Couch. Springfield, IL: Charles C. Thomas, 1988. 155–71.

Creed, Barbara, "Lesbian Bodies: Tribades, Tomboys and Tarts." *Sexy Bodies: The Strange Carnalities of Feminism*. Ed. Elizabeth Grosz and Elspeth Proby. London: New York: Routledge, 1995.

Crowley, Aleister. *Magick in Theory and Practice.* Privately published 1929. New York: Castle Books, n.d.

Cunningham, Scott. *Living Wicca: A Further Guide for the Solitary Practitioner.* St. Paul: Llewellyn, 1993.

Curtis, Pavel. "Mudding: Social Phenomena in Text-Based Virtual Realities." *Reinventing Technology, Rediscovering Community: Critical Explorations of Computing as a Social Practice.* Ed. Phillip E. Agre and Douglas Schuler. Greenwich: Ablex, 1997. 143–63.

Dery, Mark. *The Pyrotechnic Insanitarium: American Culture on the Brink.* New York: Grove, 1999.

Doane, Janice, and Devon Hodges. "Undoing Feminism: From the Preoedipal to Postfeminism in Anne Rice's Vampire Chronicles." *American Literary History* 2 (Fall 1990): 422–42.

Dolan, Marc. "The Peaks and Valleys of Serial Creativity: What Happened to/on *Twin Peaks.*" *Full of Secrets: Critical Approaches to Twin Peaks.* Ed David Lavery. Contemporary Film and Television Ser. Detroit: Wayne State UP, 1994. 30–50.

Dollimore, Jonathan. *Sexual Dissidence: Augustine to Wilde, Freud to Foucault.* Oxford: Clarendon, 1991.

Douglas, Susan J. *Where the Girls Are: Growing Up Female with the Mass Media.* New York: Times Books, 1995.

Drexel, Lisa. "Serendipity or Immortality's a Bitch." 25 June 2000 <http://www.crosswinds.net/~lisay/serendipity-2.htm>.

Dundes, Alan, ed. *The Vampire: A Casebook.* Madison: U of Wisconsin P, 1998.

Eco, Umberto. *Six Walks in the Fictional Woods.* Cambridge: Harvard UP, 1994.

Epstein, Edmund. Private conversation with Gregory Erickson. May 2000.

Esmeralda. "The Situation." 25 June 2000 <http://adult.dencity.com/Lady_Sunshine/Situation.htm>.

Espenson, Jane, and Tim Minear. Interview. 28 July 2000 <http://cityofangel.com/angel/series/summer/dragonCon7.html>.

Faderman, Lillian. *To Believe in Women: What Lesbians Have Done for America—a History.* Boston: Houghton-Mifflin, 2000.

Farrington, Carl, and Evelyn Pine. "Community Memory: A Case Study in Community Communication. *Reinventing Technology, Rediscovering Community: Critical Explorations of Computing as a Social Practice.* Ed. Phillip E. Agre and Douglas Schuler. Greenwich: Ablex, 1997. 219–27.

Fiedler, Leslie. *Love and Death in the American Novel.* New York: Anchor, 1960.

Fillion, Kate. *Lip Service: The Myth of Female Virtue in Love, Sex and Friendship.* London: HarperCollins, 1996.

Findlen, Barbara, ed. *Listen Up: Voices from the Next Feminist Generation.* Seattle: Seal Press, 1995.

Fiske, John. *Television Culture.* New York: Routledge, 1987.

Frayling, Christopher. *Vampyres: Lord Byron to Count Dracula.* London: Faber and Faber, 1992.

Freud, Sigmund. *The Interpretation of Dreams.* Trans. and ed. James Strachey. New York: Discus/Avon, 1965.

———. *Introductory Lectures on Psycho-Analysis.* Trans. and ed. James Strachey, biographical introduction by Peter Gay (Standard Edition). New York: Norton, 1966.

——. *Jokes and Their Relation to the Unconscious.* Trans. James Strachey. New York: Norton, 1960.

——. *On Dreams.* Trans. and ed. James Strachey; biographical introduction by Peter Gay (Standard Edition). New York: Norton, 1952.

——. "The Uncanny." 1919. *The Standard Edition of the Complete Psychological Works of Sigmund Freud.* Trans. James Strachey. Vol. 17. London: Hogarth, 1974. 217–52.

Fudge, Rachel. "The Buffy Effect: or, A Tale of Cleavage and Marketing." *Bitch: Feminist Response to Pop Culture* 10 (1999):18.

Gatson, Sarah N., and Amanda Zweerink. "Choosing Community: Rejecting Anonymity in Cyberspace." *Research in Community Sociology* 10 (August 2000): 105–37.

——. "Ethnography Online: Practicing Community in an 'Anonymous' World." Typescript, 2000.

Geertz, Clifford. *The Interpretation of Cultures.* New York: Basic, 1973.

Gellar, Sarah Michelle. "An Interview with Sarah Michelle Gellar." *Spectrum: The Magazine of Television, Film, and Comics!* December 1999: 2–9.

——. "Sarah Smiles." Interview. By Michael Logan. *TV Guide* 19–25 Feb. 2000: 19–29.

——. "The Slayer Speaks: Buffy on Soul Mates, Spinoffs, Strong Women and Her New Scooby Gang" <http://www.eonline.com/Features/Features/Buffy/TheSlayerSpeaks/index.html>.

Gilbert, Sandra M., and Susan Gubar. *The Madwoman in the Attic: The Woman Writer and the Nineteenth-Century Literary Imagination.* New Haven: Yale UP, 1979.

Gilligan, Carol. *In a Different Voice: Psychological Theory and Women's Development.* Cambridge: Harvard UP, 1982.

Gitlin, Todd. *Inside Prime Time.* Berkeley: U of California P, 1999.

——. "Prime Time Ideology: The Hegemonic Process in Television Entertainment." *Social Problems* 26 (1979). Rpt. in *Television: The Critical View.* 3rd ed. Ed. Horace Newcomb. New York: Oxford UP, 1982. 426–54.

Golden, Christopher, Stephen R. Bissette, and Thomas E. Sniegoski. *Buffy the Vampire Slayer: The Monster Book.* New York: Pocket, 2000.

Golden, Christopher, and Nancy Holder. *Buffy the Vampire Slayer: The Watcher's Guide.* Vol. 1. New York: Pocket, 1998.

Gordon, Joan. "Sharper Than a Serpent's Tooth: The Vampire in Search of Its Mother." Gordon and Hollinger 45–55.

——, and Veronica Hollinger. "Introduction: The Shape of Vampires." Gordon and Hollinger 1–7.

——, eds. *Blood Read: The Vampire as Metaphor in Contemporary Culture.* Philadelphia: U of Pennsylvania P, 1997.

Grant, Kenneth. *Aleister Crowley and the Hidden God.* London: Skoob, 1992.

Greenberg, Harvey R. "In Search of Spock: A Psychoanalytic Inquiry." *Journal of Popular Film and Television* 12.2 (1984): 52–65.

Halberstam, Judith. *Skin Shows: Gothic Horror and the Technology of Monsters.* Durham: Duke UP, 1995.

Hart, Roderick. *Modern Rhetorical Criticism.* 2nd ed. Boston: Allyn and Bacon, 1997.

Hawthorne, Nathaniel. "Young Goodman Brown." 1835. *Mosses from an Old Manse. The Complete Works of Hawthorne.* New York: Thomas Y. Crowell, 1902. 66–80.

Hegel, George Wilhelm Friedrich. *Lectures on the Philosophy of Religion.* Ed. P. Hodgson. Berkeley: U of California P, 1984.

Heldreth, Leonard G., and Mary Pharr, eds. *The Blood Is the Life: Vampires in Literature.* Bowling Green: Bowling Green State U Popular P, 1999.

Helford, Elyce. "Feminism, Queer Studies and the Sexual Politics of *Xena: Warrior Princess.*" Helford, *Fantasy Girls* 135–62.

———, ed. *Fantasy Girls: Gender and the New Universe of Science Fiction and Fantasy Television.* Lanham: Rowman & Littlefield, 2000.

Hill, Carl. *The Soul of Wit: Joke Theory from Grimm to Freud.* Lincoln: U of Nebraska P, 1993.

Holder, Nancy. *Buffy the Vampire Slayer: The Watcher's Guide.* Vol. 2. New York: Pocket, 2000.

hooks, bell. *Black Looks: Race and Representation.* Boston: South End, 1992.

"Hot Summers." *Xposé* Sept. 1998: 28–33.

Howe, Neil, and William Strauss. *Millenials Rising.* New York: Vintage, 2000.

Huff, Tanya. *Blood Price.* New York: DAW, 1991.

Hurston, Zora Neale. *Their Eyes Were Watching God.* New York: Harper and Row, 1937.

Jamieson, Stewart. "University Challenge." Interview with Joss Whedon. *SFX* Oct. 1999: 76–79.

Jaynes, Gerald David, and Robin M. Williams Jr., eds. *A Common Destiny: Blacks and American Society.* Washington: National Academy Press, 1989.

Jenkins, Henry. *Textual Poachers: Television Fans and Participatory Culture.* New York: Routledge, 1992.

Jensen, Jeff. "*Buffy the Vampire Slayer.*" *Entertainment Weekly* 7 Sept. 2001: 60–61, 64–65.

Jesus Christ: Who Is He? N.p.: Watch Tower Bible and Tract Society of Pennsylvania, 1999.

Jewell, K. Sue. *From Mammy to Miss America and Beyond: Cultural Images and the Shaping of US Social Policy.* New York: Routledge, 1993.

Jewett, Robert, and John Shelton Lawrence. *The American Monomyth.* Garden City: Anchor/Doubleday, 1977.

Jung, C. G. *Alchemical Studies.* Trans. R. F. C. Hull. Bollingen Ser. 20: The Collected Works of C. G. Jung, Vol. 13. Princeton: Princeton UP, 1967.

———. *The Archetypes and the Collective Unconscious.* Trans. R. F. C. Hull. 2nd ed. Bollingen Ser. 20: The Collected Works of C. G. Jung, Vol. 9, Part 1. Princeton: Princeton UP, 1969.

———. *Dreams.* Trans. R. F. C. Hull. Bollingen Ser. 20: The Collected Works of C. G. Jung, from Vols. 4, 8, 12, 16. Princeton: Princeton UP, 1974.

———. *Mysterium Coniunctionis.* Trans. R. F. C. Hull. 2nd ed. Bollingen Ser. 20: The Collected Works of C. G. Jung, Vol. 14. Princeton: Princeton UP, 1970.

———. *Psychology and Alchemy.* Trans. R. F. C. Hull. 2nd ed. Bollingen Ser. 20: The Collected Works of C. G. Jung, Vol. 12. Princeton: Princeton UP, 1968.

———. *The Psychology of the Transference.* Trans. R. F. C. Hull. Bollingen Ser.20: The Collected Works of C. G. Jung, from Vol. 16. Princeton: Princeton UP, 1966.

"Junior Great Books: The Value of Folktales" 19 July 2000 <http://www.greatbooks.org/junior/philosophy/folktales.html>.

Katovich, Michael A. "Inauthentic Identities, Suspicion, and Honor." *Communication and Social Structure*. Ed. David R. Maines and Carl J. Couch. Springfield: Charles C. Thomas, 1988. 113–29.

Katz, Alyssa. "Buffy the Vampire Slayer," *Nation* 6 Apr. 1998: 35–36.

Kaveney, Roz. *Reading the Vampire Slayer: An Unofficial Critical Companion to Buffy and Angel*. New York: St. Martin's Press, in press.

Kawin, Bruce F. *Mindscreen: Bergman, Godard, and First-Person Film*. Princeton: Princeton UP, 1978.

Keller, Donald G. "The Dharma of Buffy." Paper presented at the Philcon Science Fiction Convention, Philadelphia, PA, 13–15 November 1998.

Kellner, Douglas. "Advertising and Consumer Culture." *Questioning the Media: A Critical Introduction*. Ed. John Downing, Ali Mohammadi, and Annabelle Sreberny-Mohammadi. Thousand Oaks: Sage, 1995. 329–44.

Killingsworth, M. Jimmie, and Michael K. Gilbertson. *Signs, Genres, and Communities in Technical Communication*. Amityville: Baywood, 1992.

Kindler, Damian. Personal interview with Camille Bacon-Smith. Toronto, 1995.

Kristeva, Julia. "Stabat Mater." *Tales of Love*. Trans. Leon S. Roudiez. New York: Columbia UP, 1987. 234–63.

Krzywinska, Tanya. *A Skin for Dancing In: Witchcraft, Possession and Voodoo in Film*. Trowbridge: Flicks Books, 2000.

Lacan, Jacques. *On Feminine Sexuality: The Limits of Love and Knowledge, 1972–1973*. Ed. Jacques Alain Miller. Trans. Bruce Fink. New York: Norton, 1975.

Lamb, Lynette. "Media Criticism: The Sad State of Teen Television." *New Moon Network: For Adults Who Care about Girls* 7.2 (1999): 14.

Lamb, Patricia Frazer, and Diana L. Veith. "Romantic Myth, Transcendence, and *Star Trek* Zines." *Erotic Universe: Sexuality and Fantastic Literature*. Ed. Donald Palumbo. New York: Greenwood, 1986. 235–55.

Lane, Christina. *Feminist Hollywood: From* Born in Flames *to* Point Break. Detroit: Wayne State UP, 2000.

Laplanche, Jean, and Jean-Bertrand Pontalis. "Fantasy and the Origins of Sexuality." *Formations of Fantasy*. Ed. Victor Burgin, James Donald, and Cora Kaplan. New York: Routledge, 1989. 5–34.

Larson, Bob. "Immortal Combat: The World of Angels and Demons." *Christian Single* October 1999, 17–25.

Lavery, David, Angela Hague, and Marla Cartwright, eds. *Deny All Knowledge: Reading* The X-Files. Syracuse: Syracuse UP, 1996.

Le Fanu, J. Sheridan. "Carmilla." 1872. Ryan 71–137.

Le Faye, Margot. "The Silken Cage Series: Capture." 25 June 2000 <http://pages.prodigy.net/leighschneider/capture2.htm>.

Lee, Patrick. "Joss Whedon Q&A from *Science Fiction Weekly*." Posted at the Buffy Cross & Stake Spoiler Board <http://www.insidetheweb.com/messageboard/mbs.cgi>.

Leeming, David Adams. *Mythology: The Voyage of the Hero*. 3rd ed. Oxford: Oxford UP, 1998.

Leibman, Nina C. *Living Room Lectures: The Fifties Family in Film and Television*. Austin: U of Texas P, 1995.

Leon, Hilary M. "Why We Love the Monsters: How Anita Blake, Vampire Hunter, and Buffy the Vampire Slayer Wound Up Dating the Enemy." *Slayage: The Online International Journal of Buffy Studies* Number 1 (January 2001) <http://www.middleenglish.org/slayage/essays/slayage1/leon.htm>.

Lerner, Harriet Goldhor. *The Dance of Anger: A Woman's Guide to Changing the Patterns of Intimate Relationships.* New York: Harper and Row, 1985.

Lesage, Julia. "Women's Rage." *Marxism and the Interpretation of Culture.* Ed. Cary Nelson and Lawrence Grossberg. Chicago: U of Illinois P, 1988. 419–28.

Lévi-Strauss, Claude. *The Raw and the Cooked.* New York: Harper and Row, 1969.

Lewis, C. S. *They Asked for a Paper: Papers and Letters.* London: Geoffrey Bles, 1962.

Lippert, Barbara. "Hey There, Warrior Grrrl." *New York* 15 Dec. 1997: 24–25.

Livingstone, Sonia. *Making Sense of Television: The Psychology of Audience Interpretation.* London: Routledge, 1990.

Lorde, Audre. "The Uses of Anger: Women Responding to Racism." *Sister Outsider: Essays and Speeches.* Freedom: Crossing Press, 1984. 124–33.

Lovecraft, H. P. *The Haunter of the Dark and Other Tales.* London: HarperCollins, 1994.

McLuhan, Marshall, and Bruce R. Powers. *The Global Village: Transformations in World Life and Media in the 21st Century.* New York: Oxford UP, 1989.

Mellor, Anne K. *Romanticism and Gender.* New York: Routledge, 1993.

——, ed. *Romanticism and Feminism.* Bloomington: Indiana UP, 1988.

Mendlesohn, Jennifer. "The Sexiest Vampire Slayer Alive: TV's 'Buffy' Leads a New Wave of Intelligent Chills." *USA Today Weekend* 23–25 Oct. 1998: 10.

Mendoza, Manuel. "Pop Go Teen TV Shows." *Ottawa Citizen* 25 Nov. 1998: C13.

Miller, Linda Lael. *Forever and the Night.* New York: Berkley, 1993.

Millman, Joyce. "The Death of Buffy's Mom." 12 Mar. 2001 <http://www.salon.com/ent/col/mill/2001/03/12/buffy_mom/index.html>.

Modleski, Tania. *Loving with a Vengeance: Mass-Produced Fantasies for Women.* Hamden: Archon, 1982.

Moore, C. L. "Shambleau." 1933. Ryan 255–81.

Morreale, Joanne. "*Xena: Warrior Princess* as Feminist Camp." *Journal of Popular Culture* 32.2 (Fall 1998): 79–86.

Moss, Gabrielle. "From the Valley to the Hellmouth: *Buffy*'s Transition from Film to Television." *Slayage: The Online International Journal of Buffy Studies* Number 2 (Mar. 2001) <http://www.middleenglish.org/slayage/essays/slayage2/moss.htm>.

"The Mysterious Stranger." 1860. Ryan 36–70.

Newcomb, Horace, and Robert S. Alley. *The Producer's Medium: Conversations with Creators of American TV.* New York: Oxford UP, 1983.

Nixon, Nicola. "When Hollywood Sucks, or, Hungry Girls, Lost Boys, and Vampirism in the Age of Reagan." Gordon and Hollinger 115–28.

Ono, Kent A. "To Be a Vampire on *Buffy the Vampire Slayer:* Race and ("Other") Socially Marginalizing Positions on Horror TV." Helford, *Fantasy Girls* 163–86.

Ostow, Micol. "Why I Love Buffy." *Sojourner: The Women's Forum* 24.3 (1998): 20.

Ostrow, Joanne. "WB Shows an Entree for Unsung Musicians." *Denver Post* 13 Feb. 2000: H01.

Owen, A. Susan. "Vampires, Postmodernity, and Postfeminism: *Buffy the Vampire Slayer.*" *Journal of Popular Film and Television* 27.2 (Summer 1999): 24–31.

Penley, Constance. "Feminism, Psychoanalysis, and the Study of Popular Culture." *Cultural Studies*. Ed. Lawrence Grossberg, Cary Nelson, and Paula A. Treichler. New York: Routledge, 1992. 479–500.

Polidori, John. *Lord Ruthven*. London, 1819.

———. "The Vampyre." 1819. Ryan 7–24.

Pozner, Jennifer L. "Thwack! Pow! Yikes! Not Your Mother's Heroines." *Sojourner: The Women's Forum* 23.2 (1997): 12–13.

Prince, Gerald. *A Dictionary of Narratology*. Lincoln: U of Nebraska P, 1987.

Rector, Kimberley, and Martha Wells Wilson. "When Hellmouths Collide." 27 Jan. 1999 to present (in progress) <http://www.rtis.com/nat/user/chimera/>.

Reeves, Jimmie L., Mark C. Rogers, and Michael Epstein. "Rewriting Popularity: The Cult *Files*." Lavery, Hague, and Cartwright 22–35.

Reynolds, David. *Faith in Fiction: The Emergence of Religious Literature in America*. Cambridge: Harvard UP, 1981.

Rheingold, Howard. *The Virtual Community: Homesteading on the Electronic Frontier*. Reading: Addison-Wesley, 1993.

Rice, Anne. *Interview with the Vampire: A Novel*. The Vampire Chronicles 1. New York: Knopf, 1976.

———. *The Vampire Lestat*. St. Ives: Futura, 1985.

Rickels, Laurence A. *The Vampire Lectures*. Minneapolis: U of Minnesota P, 1999.

Robertson, Pamela. *Guilty Pleasures: Feminist Camp from Mae West to Madonna*. Durham: Duke UP, 1996.

Rochlin, Margy. "Slay Belle." *TV Guide* 2 Aug. 1997:17–21.

Ross, Andrew. Introduction. *Microphone Fiends: Youth Music and Youth Culture*. Ed. Andrew Ross and Tricia Rose. New York: Routledge, 1994. 1–13.

Roth, Phyllis. "Suddenly Sexual Women in Bram Stoker's *Dracula*." *Literature and Psychology* 27 (1977): 113–21.

Rowe, Kathleen. *The Unruly Woman: Gender and the Genres of Laughter*. Austin: U of Texas P, 1995.

Russ, Joanna. *Magic Mommas, Trembling Sisters, Puritans & Perverts: Feminist Essays*. Crossing Press Feminist Ser. Trumansburg: Crossing Press, 1985.

Ryan, Alan, ed. *Vampires: Two Centuries of Great Vampire Stories*. Garden City: Doubleday, 1987.

Rybacki, Donald Jay, and Karyn Charles Rybacki. *Advocacy and Opposition: An Introduction to Argumentation*. New York: Allyn and Bacon, 1999.

Rymer, James Malcolm. *Varney the Vampire: or, The Feast of Blood* [London, 1845–47]. 8 Oct. 1998–27 July 2000 <http://www.comclin.net/humphrey/varney/varney.htm>.

Saberhagen, Fred. *The Dracula Tape*. New York: Warner, 1975.

Samanta, Anamika, and Erin Franzman. "Women in Action." *HUES: Hear Us Emerging Sisters* 4.3 (1998): 28.

Searle, John R. *Expression and Meaning: Studies in the Theory of Speech Acts*. Cambridge: Cambridge UP, 1979.

———. *Speech Acts: An Essay in the Philosophy of Language*. Cambridge: Cambridge UP, 1970.

Sedgwick, Eva Kosofsky. *Between Men: English Literature and Male Homosocial Desire*. New York: Columbia University Press, 1985.

Selley, April. "'I Have Been, and Ever Shall Be, Your Friend': *Star Trek, The Deerslayer,* and the American Romance." *Journal of Popular Culture* 20.1 (1986): 89–104.

Shadowkitten, Saber. "Elaisias." 25 June 2000 <http://www.geocities.com/Area51/Hollow/5214/elaisias5.html>.

———. "Master of Puppets." 25 June 2000 <http://www.geocities.com/Area51/Hollow/5214/game7a.html>.

Shelley, Mary. *Frankenstein, or, the Modern Prometheus.* Case Studies in Contemporary Criticism. Ed. Johanna M. Smith. Boston: Bedford, 1992.

Showalter, Elaine. *Sexual Anarchy: Gender and Culture at the Fin de Siècle.* New York: Penguin, 1991.

Slayer's Fanfic Archive. Ed. Anya and Biohaz. 25 June 2000 <http://www.slayerfanfic.com>.

Sloan, Michael. Personal interview with Camille Bacon-Smith. Toronto, 1995.

Smith, Dorothy. "Textually Mediated Social Organizations." *International Social Science Journal* (1984): 59–74.

Sonja Marie's Buffy Fanfiction Links. Ed. Sonja Marie. 20 June 2000–25 June 2000 <http://orbital.planetx.com/buffy/sonja/BtVSurls/fic.html>.

Sontag, Susan. "Notes on Camp." *Against Interpretation.* New York: Farrar and Strauss, 1996. 275–92.

Stafford, Nikki. *Bite Me! Sarah Michelle Gellar and* Buffy the Vampire Slayer. Toronto: ECW, 1998.

Stam, Robert. *Film Theory: An Introduction.* Malden: Blackwell, 2000.

Steinberg, Neil. "'Millennial' Generation a Return to Duty, Values." *Chicago Sun-Times* 12 July 2000: 3.

Stevens, Anthony. *Private Myths: Dreams and Dreaming.* Cambridge: Harvard UP 1995.

Stevenson, John Allen. "A Vampire in the Mirror: The Sexuality of *Dracula.*" *PMLA* 103 (Feb. 1988): 139–49.

Stoker, Bram. *Dracula.* 1897. Oxford: Oxford UP, 1983.

Stoller, Debbie. "Brave New Girls: These TV Heroines Know What Girl Power Really Is." *On the Issues* Fall 1998: 42–45.

———. "The 20 Most Fascinating Women in Politics: Fresh Blood." *George* Sept. 1998: 110–13.

Strangelove, Michael. "Cyberspace and the Changing Landscape of the Self." N.d. <http://www.clas.ufl.edu/users/seeker1/cyberanthro/cybgeog.html>.

Tashiro, C. J. *Pretty Pictures: Production Design and the History Film.* Austin: U of Texas P, 1998.

Tatar, Maria. *The Hard Facts of the Grimms' Fairy Tales.* Princeton: Princeton UP, 1987.

Taylor, Charles. "The WB's Big Daddy Condescension." 26 May 1999 <http://www.salon.com/ent/log/1999/05/26/buffy_rant/index.html>.

Taylor, Mark C. "Betting on Las Vegas." Caputo and Scanlon 229–42.

———. *Nots.* Chicago: U of Chicago P, 1993.

Thomas, Keith. *Religion and the Decline of Magic.* London: Weidenfeld & Nicolson, 1971.

Thompson, Robert J. *Television's Second Golden Age: From* Hill Street Blues *to* ER. New York: Continuum, 1996.

Thompson, Sharon, "What Friends Are For: On Girls' Misogyny and Romantic Fiction." *Sexual Cultures and the Construction of Adolescent Identities.* Ed. Janice M. Irvine. Philadelphia: Temple UP, 1994. 228–85.

Tieck, Johann Ludwig. "Wake Not the Dead!" [1823?] 6 June 2000 <http://www.sff.net/people/doylemacdonald/l_wakeno.htm>.

Topping, Keith. *Slayer: The Totally Cool Unofficial Guide to* Buffy. London: Virgin, 2000.

Tracy, Kathleen. *The Girl's Got Bite: The Unofficial Guide to* Buffy's *World.* Los Angeles: Renaissance, 1998.

Tucker, Hannah. "High School Confidential." *Entertainment Weekly* 1 Oct. 1999: 23.

Tucker, Ken. "High Stakes Poker." *Entertainment Weekly* 1 Oct. 1999: 20–23.

Tulloch, John, and Henry Jenkins. *Science Fiction Audiences: Watching Doctor Who and Star Trek.* London: Routledge, 1995.

Turkle, Sherry. *Life on the Screen: Identity in the Age of the Internet.* New York: Simon and Schuster, 1995.

Twitchell, James. *The Living Dead: The Vampire in Romantic Literature.* Durham: Duke UP, 1981.

UCSL: Unconventional Relationshippers' List. Ed. Kate Bolin. 25 June 2000 <http://www.dymphna.net/ucsl>.

Udovitch, Mim. "What Makes Buffy Slay?" *Rolling Stone* 11 May 2000: 60–62, 64, 66.

"The Ultimate Guide to *Buffy the Vampire Slayer.*" *Entertainment Weekly* 1 Oct. 1999: 20–49.

Ventura, Michael. "Warrior Women: The Popularity among Teenagers of TV Shows Like *La Femme Nikita, Xena: Warrior Princess* and *Buffy the Vampire Slayer.*" *Psychology Today* 31.6 (Nov.–Dec. 1998): 58–61.

Vowell, Sarah. "Please Sir May I Have a Mother?" 2 Feb. 2000 <http://www.salon.com/ent/col/vowe/2000/02/02/vowell_wb/index.html>.

Wagner, C. Peter. *Warfare Prayer: How to Seek God's Power and Protection in the Battle to Build His Kingdom.* Ventura: Regal, 1992.

Walker, Nancy. *A Very Serious Thing: Women's Humor and American Culture.* Minneapolis: U of Minnesota P, 1988.

Whedon, Joss. "The Creator Speaks: Joss Whedon on Sex, Death, Gaping Holes and Horrible Things Ahead." N.d. <http://www.eonline.com/Features/Features/Buffy/TheCreatorSpeaks/index.html>.

——. Interview. "Angel + The Puppet Show." Videocassette. 20th Century Fox, 1998.

——. Interview. "Welcome to the Hellmouth/The Harvest." Videocassette. 20th Century Fox, 1998.

——. Interview with BBC Online. N.d. <http://www.bbc.co.uk/buffy/reallife/jossinterview.shtml>.

——. Interview with David Bianculli. *Fresh Air.* 9 May 2000. Available on-line at <http://whyy.org/cgi-bin/FAshowretrieve.cgi?2876>.

——. Interview with ET Online. N.d. <http://www.theslayershow.com/chat8.html>.

——. Interview with Fanforum. N.d. <http://www.fanforum.com/buffy/news/786.shtml>.

———. Interview with Fraxis. N.d. <http://websites.cable.ntl.com/~fraxis/the_ww/features/whedon.html>.

———. Interview with The Watcher's Web. N.d. <http://websites.cable.ntl.com/~fraxis/the_ww/features/epk/joss.html>.

———. "joss says: (Thu May 27 08:26:10 1999)." On-line posting. 27 May 1999. The Bronze VIP Posting Board Archives. 25 July 2000 <http://www-pub.cise.ufl.edu/cgiwrap/hsiao/buffy/get-archive?date=1990527>.

Wilcox, Rhonda V. "Dating Data: Miscegenation in *Star Trek: The Next Generation.*" *Enterprise Zones: Critical Positions on Star Trek.* Ed. Taylor Harrison et al. Boulder: Westview, 1996. 69–92.

———. "Lois's Locks: Trust and Representation in Lois and Clark: *The New Adventures of Superman.*" Helford, *Fantasy Girls* 91–112.

———. "'There Will Never Be a "Very Special" *Buffy*': *Buffy* and the Monsters of Teen Life." *Journal of Popular Film and Television* 27.2 (1999): 16–23. Republished in *Slayage: The Online International Journal of Buffy Studies* Number 2 (Mar. 2001) <http://www.middleenglish.org/slayage/essays/slayage2/wilcox.htm>.

Williams, J. P. "All's Fair in Love and Journalism: Female Rivalry in *Superman.*" *Journal of Popular Culture* 24 (1990): 103–12.

Williams, Peter. *Popular Religion in America: Symbolic Change and the Modernization Process in Historical Perspective.* Englewood Cliffs: Prentice Hall, 1980.

Wood, Martin. "New Life for an Old Tradition: Anne Rice and Vampire Literature." Heldreth and Pharr 59–78.

Yarbro, Chelsea Quinn. *Hôtel Transylvania: A Novel of Forbidden Love.* New York: St. Martin's, 1978.

Zanger, Jules. "Metaphor into Metonymy: The Vampire Next Door." Gordon and Hollinger 17–26.

Index

working class. *See* class
Wuthering Heights, 142n3

Xena, Warrior Princess, xxiv, 3, 36, 37,
  45, 46, 179, 185, 190, 217n1, 229,
  238n3
The X-Files, xxiii, 9, 109, 185, 190
X-Men, xxi

Yarbro, Chelsea Quinn, 149
Yeoh, Michelle, 36
"Young Goodman Brown," 15

Zelmani, Sophie, 220
Zweerink, Amanda, xxvii, 239,
  249n3
Zwick, Edward, 251

About the Contributors

Camille Bacon-Smith is a folklorist and novelist, author of *Enterprising Women, Science Fiction Culture,* and novels such as *The Face of Time* and *Eye of the Daemon.*

Kristina Busse is a doctoral candidate at Tulane University. She teaches at the University of South Alabama.

S. Renee Dechert is an assistant professor of English at Northwest College in Wyoming. She writes primarily about country music and is cocreator of the *Country Music Moment* syndicated radio program.

Diane DeKelb-Rittenhouse is a writer in the horror, murder, and science fiction genres whose short fiction includes the vampire story "To Die For" in *Night Bites: Vampire Stories by Women* (edited by Victoria A. Brownworth, Seal Press, 1996).

Lynne Edwards received her Ph.D. at the University of Pennsylvania. She teaches at Ursinus College.

Gregory Erickson teaches English at Medgar Evers College and music at the Brooklyn Conservatory of Music. He has degrees in both English and music and is currently a Ph.D. candidate in English at the Graduate Center in New York City.

Sarah N. Gatson earned her Ph.D. at Northwestern University and is an assistant professor of sociology at Texas A&M University, where her current interests include the subfields of inequality, race, ethnicity, law, gender, culture, and qualitative methods. She is the author of "Labor Policy and the Social Meaning of Parenthood" (1997, *Law and Social Inquiry*) and is coauthor, with Amanda Zweerink, of "Choosing Community: Rejecting Anonymity in Cyberspace" (*Research in Community Sociology*, Volume X, August 2000).

Elyce Rae Helford is associate professor of English and director of women's studies at Middle Tennessee State University. She is the coeditor of *Enterprise Zones: Critical Positions on Star Trek* (Westview Press, 1996) and editor of *Fantasy Girls: Gender in the New Universe of Science Fiction and Fantasy Television* (Rowman & Littlefield, 2000).

Donald Keller has been writing criticism and publishing fanzines about science fiction and fantasy for the last quarter century. He has been publisher and editor of the small press Serconia Press, putting out critical works by Brian Aldiss, Samuel R. Delany, and John Clute over the last decade. He was managing editor and frequent contributor to the *New York Review of Science Fiction* from 1990 to 1995. He coedited (with Ellen Kushner and Delia Sherman) *The Horns of Elfland* (Roc, 1997), an anthology of fantasy stories about music. He contributed a number of entries to *The Encyclopedia of Fantasy* (1997). His e-mail list *the still point* discusses contemporary music and *Buffy the Vampire Slayer*. He is a proofreader by profession.

Elisabeth Krimmer is assistant professor of German literature at Mount Holyoke College. She received her Ph.D. at the University of Massachusetts at Amherst with a dissertation on women's cross-dressing in the seventeenth and eighteenth centuries. Most of her recent publications deal with eighteenth-century women's literature.

Tanya Krzywinska is a professor of film studies at Brunel University in London. She is the author of *A Skin for Dancing In: Possession, Witchcraft and Voodoo in Film* (Flicks Books, 2000) and coauthor (with Geoff King) of *Science Fiction Cinema: From Outerspace to Cyberspace* (Wallflower Press, 2000) and *ScreenPlay: Cinema/Videogames/Interfaces* (Wallflower Press, 2001).

Justine Larbalestier is a research fellow at the University of Sydney. Her book on the battle of the sexes in science fiction film is forthcoming from Wesleyan University Press. She is currently writing a book about the history of science fiction in New York City from 1938 to 1960.

David Lavery is professor of English at Middle Tennessee State University. The author of over forty essays in journals ranging from *Parabola* to *Georgia Review,* he is the author/editor-coeditor *of Late for the Sky: The Mentality of the Space Age* (Southern Illinois UP, 1992), *Full of Secrets: Critical Approaches to* Twin Peaks (Wayne State UP, 1994), *"Deny All Knowledge": Reading* The X-Files (Syracuse UP, 1996), Twin Peaks *in the Rearview Mirror: Appraisals and Reappraisals of the Show That Was Supposed to Change TV* (forthcoming from Wayne State UP), *Teleparody: Predicting/Preventing the TV Discourse of Tomorrow* (forthcoming from Wallflower Press), and *This Thing of Ours: Investigating* The Sopranos (forthcoming from Wallflower Press/Columbia UP). The coeditor (with Rhonda V. Wilcox) of *Slayage: An Online International Journal of Buffy Studies,* he is on the board of *Studies in Popular Culture* and *Intensities: The Journal of Cult Media.*

Farah Mendlesohn is features editor for the British science fiction journal *Foundation.*

Mary Alice Money is professor of English at Gordon College and chair of the Science Fiction and Fantasy Discussion Circle of SAMLA (the South Atlantic Modern Language Association).

Karen Eileen Overbey is a doctoral candidate at the Institute of Fine Arts at New York University; her dissertation focuses on the objects and ritual practices of the cult of the saints in medieval Ireland. Like Lahney Preston-Matto, she is a member of GRIAN, an interdisciplinary Irish studies organization, and an editor of *Foilsiu,* GRIAN's journal. An authority on haircuts and Japanese fashion, Karen (not so) secretly desires to be the Willow of her social circle.

Patricia Pender is a doctoral student in the English Department at Stanford University and a graduate dissertation fellow at the Stanford Institute for Research on Women and Gender. She is writing a dissertation on early modern women's writing and contemporary feminist theory.

Lahney Preston-Matto teaches in the English department at Montclair State University in New Jersey. She received her doctorate from New York University's English department in May 2000. Her area of specialization is medieval and twentieth-century Irish literature. Although her friends think that she watches *Buffy the Vampire Slayer* for the fashion and language play, she has been secretly carrying a torch for that tweedy Englishman, Rupert Giles, since the inception of the show.

Shilpa Raval is assistant professor of classical studies at Yale University. She received her Ph.D. from Brown University and has published articles on the intersection of gender, language, and sexuality in Latin epic. She is currently working on an article on cross-dressing and gender identity and a monograph on the representation of rape in various texts from first-century Rome.

Anita Rose received her Ph.D. at the University of North Carolina at Greensboro, where her dissertation was on nineteenth-century socialist utopias. Formerly a teacher at Concord College, West Virginia, she now teaches English at Converse College.

Catherine Siemann earned the J.D. at New York University School of Law and is a doctoral candidate in English at Columbia University. She is currently teaching at Columbia University and Iona College.

Sarah E. Skwire received her Ph.D. in English from the University of Chicago. She has published a composition textbook, an article on chronically ill seventeenth-century poets, a variety of book reviews, several poems, and an on-line humor column. She now works for The Liberty Fund.

Rhonda V. Wilcox is professor of English at Gordon College in Barnesville, Georgia. The author of numerous essays on popular culture, including "'There Will Never Be a "Very Special" *Buffy*': Buffy and the Monsters of Teen Life" in *The Journal of Popular Film and Television,* 1999), she wrote the chapter on television for the forthcoming *Handbook of American Popular Culture* (3rd ed.) and, with J. P. Williams, is the author of *Unreal TV* (forthcoming). The past president of the Popular Culture Association in the South, she is coeditor (with David Lavery) of the online journal *Slayage* and a member of the editorial boards of *Studies in Popular Culture* and *Intensities: The Journal of Cult Media.* She wrote her doctoral dissertation on Joss Whedon's favorite novelist, Charles Dickens.

J. P. Williams teaches at North Carolina State University. With Rhonda Wilcox, she is the author of *Unreal TV* (forthcoming).

Amanda Zweerink is a professional in the advertising industry, holding a B.A. in English literature. Studying The Bronze, to her, has always been about telling a story. With a journalism and public relations background, she is most interested in finding ways to portray the reality of the board to those who are not involved with it.